Physically-Based Modeling for Computer Graphics:
A Structured Approach

PHYSICALLY-BASED MODELING FOR COMPUTER GRAPHICS

A Structured Approach

Ronen Barzel

Computer Graphics Group
California Institute of Technology
Pasadena, California

ACADEMIC PRESS, INC.

Harcourt Brace Jovanovich, Publishers

Boston   San Diego   New York
London   Sydney   Tokyo   Toronto

ACADEMIC PRESS, INC.
1250 Sixth Avenue, San Diego, CA 92101-4311

United Kingdom Edition published by
ACADEMIC PRESS LIMITED
24–28 Oval Road, London NW1 7DX

ISBN 0-12-079880-8

PRINTED IN THE UNITED STATES OF AMERICA

92 93 94 95 96 97 EB   9 8 7 6 5 4 3 2 1

Schematic Overview

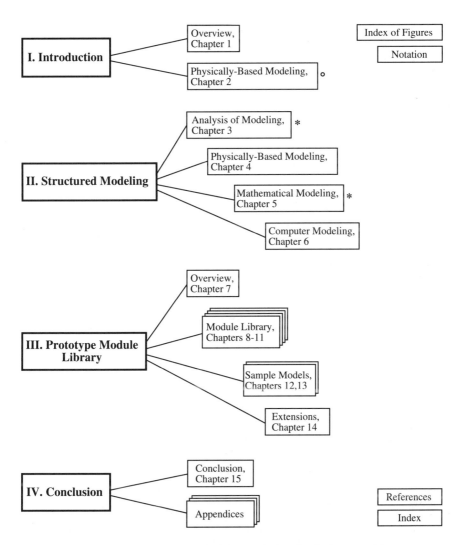

The chapter marked ○ provides background but is not required reading for later material.

The chapters marked ∗ do not depend strongly on previous material.

Otherwise, the material in each chapter depends on the previous chapters.

Contents

Foreword

Newtonian physics has been one of the grand success stories in science. The set of physical principles that underlies the mechanics of everyday objects has proven to be startlingly robust and has not changed significantly since Isaac Newton published his three laws of motion (in his *Principia*) in 1687. The Newtonian paradigm has maintained its utility despite the stunning conceptual advances developed by Einstein and others for relativistic and quantum physics.

The study of Newtonian dynamics is no longer an active field of research within physics itself. Researchers vigorously pursued classical dynamics studies during the next few centuries after Newton; Euler provided a more convenient formulation of Newton's laws, followed by the mathematical advances of Lagrange, Cauchy, and Hamilton. By the twentieth century, however, research efforts branched and created new fields with different goals. Some of the new fields were applied mathematics, engineering mechanics, and more recently, robotics.

The branching of research efforts into new fields is happening again, this time into the field of computer graphics. The driving force of the change is the goal to model heterogeneous systems of physical objects with computers. In 1987, I organized a tutorial in "physically-based modeling" for the computer graphics community.[1] The purpose of the tutorial was not to compress all of freshman physics into a one-day lecture; instead, the purpose was to integrate Newtonian physics and constraints into the conceptual foundations of computer graphics objects.

Physically-based modeling is a new field with a particular emphasis on realization and computation. It has different ends than its parent fields, physics and applied mathematics, and is somewhat different from its sibling fields, such as computational physics and classical computer graphics. Its long-term goal is to develop methods enabling people to specify, design, control and build computational models of heterogeneous physical systems of objects. The results need to be suitable for making computer graphics images and animations of the models.

Several research questions arise. What computational methods allow us to

---

[1] Coincidentally, it was the the tricentennial anniversary of the publication of Newton's laws of motion.

handle models that are orders of magnitude more complex as well as more accurate than those we can handle at present? What research progress is needed in representing models and in determining the mathematics of the models? How will we perform the computations? How would we implement the methods to achieve these ends? And to what extent will the physically-based paradigms and solutions created for computer graphics be useful for the modeling efforts of other fields?

The principles and methods developed in this book are an effort toward the preceding research goals and questions. The book's purpose is to develop robust structures for making physical models in a modular and reusable fashion. People should read this book if they are interested in the philosophy and practice needed for modular modeling of heterogeneous systems of objects. It provides an explicit and self-consistent approach for the modeling efforts.

The book also describes mathematical and computational "glue" for modeling Newtonian systems. The results are developed from years of experience and are likely to help implementors avoid modeling pitfalls that we have encountered. It develops many of the principles useful for future architectures and structures, and suggests principles that could prove useful for future computer languages, algorithms, and hardware for physically-based modeling.

Alan H. Barr
California Institute of Technology
Pasadena, California
April 1992

Preface

The ideas in this book developed gradually during the course of several years' work in Al Barr's computer graphics group at Caltech. In studying techniques for "physically-based modeling," we gradually came to recognize various stumbling blocks that would recur, such as a model being overly sensitive to numerical parameters, a technique that seemed to perpetually almost-but-not-quite work, and a new model being unable to reuse components from a previous model because they weren't set up quite right. We[1] began to develop an overall style and approach toward modeling which tried to steer clear of these pitfalls.

Eventually, our focus shifted from studying specific techniques to studying the emerging strategy for modeling. This shift in focus continued further, carrying us to the realm of abstract questions such as, "What is a model?" We found that exploration of these issues was not merely of academic interest, but was also of practical benefit: Our improved understanding of the underlying concepts led to a greater facility for creating, analyzing, discussing, and implementing models.

This book charts the reverse path: from the abstract back to the applied. We start by discussing the philosophical questions, then derive a strategy for modeling, finally reaching details of computer program design. A large portion of the book then describes a simple, general-purpose "library" for physically-based modeling.

The intent of this book is to convey an approach that can help researchers and practitioners to be more productive and effective in doing physically-based modeling. We create a structure that tries to protect us from the all-too-frequent pitfalls that we originally encountered—by avoiding them before they become problems. The importance of the structure is not in the details of its construction, but in its overall ethic of eschewing ad hoc methods, focusing on goals, and emphasizing reusability of models.

---

[1] Readers will likely be quick to notice an overenthusiastic use of the "author's *we*" in this book. This is partly due, I must admit, to my fondness for the pedantic tone it lends to the work. Much more significant, however, is that I often intend "we" to mean "Al Barr and I." In his role as colleague and graduate advisor, Al has been closely involved in this work from its conception, to the point that in many cases it's impossible to say that an idea is "mine" versus "his." (But as for the overenthusiastic use of footnotes in this book, I have been unable to come up with a way of blaming Al.)

We have tried to make this book be self-contained. Nevertheless, some familiarity with computer graphics, mathematics, physics, and computer science will
prove helpful to the reader, and we have attempted to provide sufficient references
to background and related material.

Many thanks are due to Al Barr, for research collaboration, for creating a
research environment without which this work would not have taken place, and
for his role as editor and critic of this text. My fellow students in the graphics
group have been a source of ideas, discussion, and friendship during my career at
Caltech: Bena Curin, Kurt Fleischer, Jeff Goldsmith, Devendra Kalra, Dave Kirk,
David Laidlaw, John Platt, John Snyder, Brian Von Herzen, Adam Woodbury.
Thanks in particular to Adam Woodbury for enthusiastically using and extending
the prototype model library and code. Thanks also to Dave Kirk, David Laidlaw,
Mark Montague, Jeannette Tyerman and Adam Woodbury for reading drafts and
suggesting many valuable improvements. Thanks to John Hughes for several
mathematical discussions, and to Mark Montague for discussions of early philosophy. Thanks to my doctoral examining committee, Jim Kajiya, Carver Mead,
Mani Chandy, and Joel Burdick, for their suggestions and guidance. Thanks to
Carolyn Collins for her warm care during my first few years at Caltech. Thanks
to Sandra Reyna for dealing with things, and to Dian De Sha for invaluable help
with the manuscript. Thanks also to John Snyder for help with typesetting. Special thanks to my parents for long-distance encouragement and support during the
writing of this book. I am also grateful to the AT&T Foundation for providing me
with scholarship support. Apple Computers, Hewlett Packard, and the National
Science Foundation (STC for Computer Graphics and Scientific Visualization)
have been sponsors of the Caltech graphics lab, thus making this work possible.

Physically-based modeling is by its nature a cross-disciplinary field, including elements of applied mathematics, numerical analysis, computational physics,
computer graphics, software engineering, and so on. I am certainly not an expert
in all these and have written this book from my own, occasionally idiosyncratic,
perspective. There are many issues that have doubtless been given less attention
than they deserve. Thus this book is intended not as any sort of "final answer,"
but as an exploration of ideas, and perhaps a reference point for future work.

Ronen Barzel
California Institute of Technology
Pasadena, California
April 1992

Index of Figures

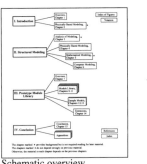
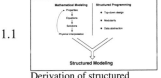
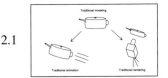
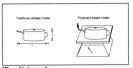

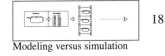
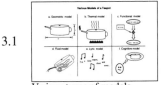
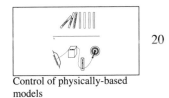

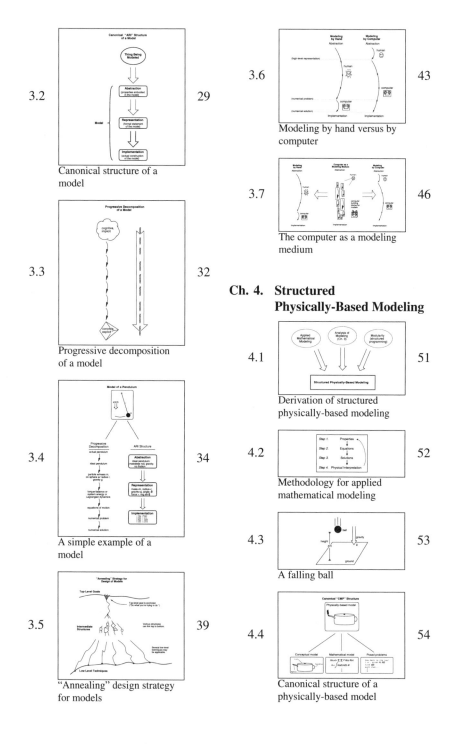

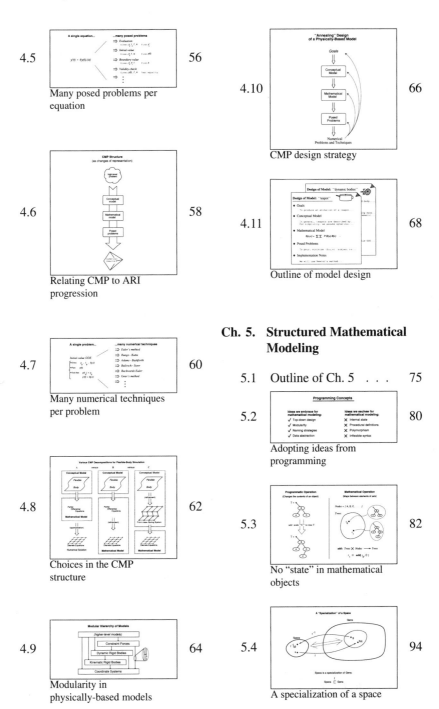

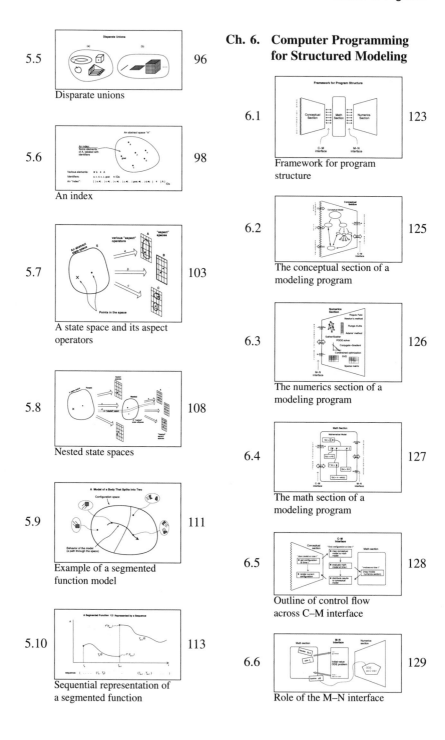

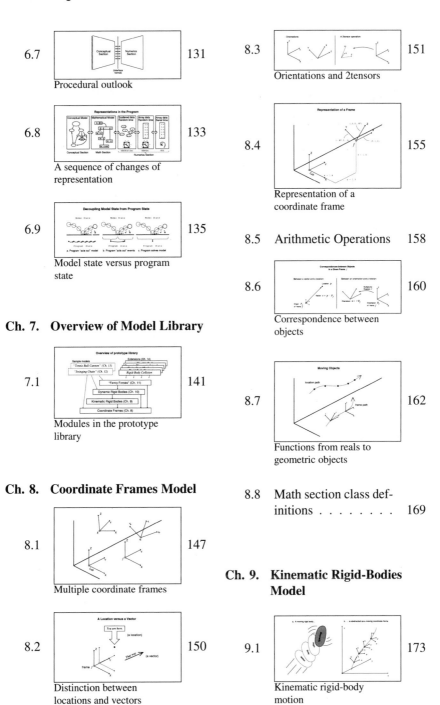

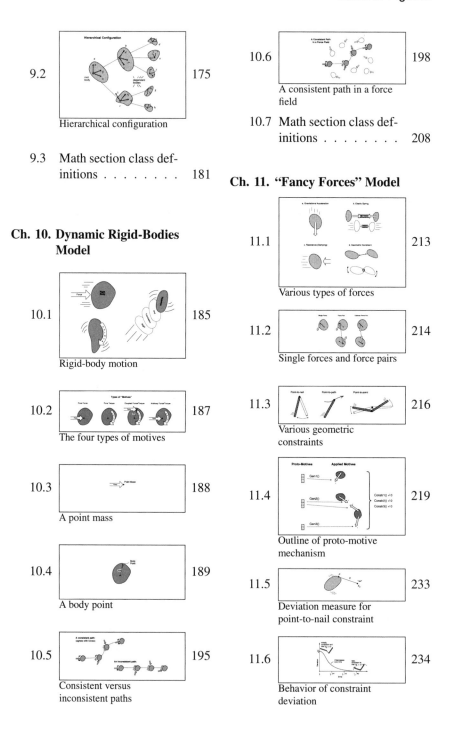

Ch. 12. Swinging Chain Model

Swinging chain model

A cylindrical link

Joint between links

Ch. 13. "Tennis Ball Cannon"

Sample segmented model

Detail of cannon

Detail of a ball bouncing

Ch. 14. Extensions to the Prototype Library

Rigid-body collision

Rigid-body contact

Finite-state machine

Interchanging dynamic and
kinematic motion

Mixed static and dynamic
parts

Flexible body

App. A. Miscellaneous Mathematical Constructs

A forest of trees

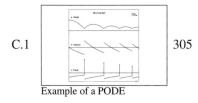
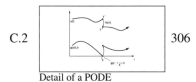

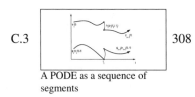

Notation

New Notation

Standard Notation

$f\colon A \to B$ "function named f, which maps from space A to space B"

                        f The function as a whole

                        $f(x)$ The value of the function acting on $x \in A$

iff   If and only if

$\Re$ The real numbers

                        $\Re^n$ 1-d real arrays having dimension n

                        $\Re^{m \times n}$ 2-d real arrays (matrices) w/ dimensions m and n

$\emptyset$ The empty set

$\left\{ x \mid condition \right\}$ The set of all x such that *condition* holds

v^* Antisymmetric dual $\begin{bmatrix} 0 & -z & y \\ z & 0 & -x \\ -y & x & 0 \end{bmatrix}$ of a 3D vector $v = \begin{bmatrix} x \\ y \\ z \end{bmatrix}$

$\times$ Cartesian product, when used with spaces, e.g., $f\colon A \times B \to C$

$\times$ Cross product, when used with 3D vectors, e.g., $v = \omega \times r$

PART I

INTRODUCTION

Background concepts and motivation.

- ## Ch. 1. Overview
  The basics of what "Structured Modeling" is about: what kinds of models and what kinds of structure; attitudes and philosophy; notes for readers with different backgrounds.

- ## Ch. 2. Overview of Physically-Based Modeling
  "Physically-Based Modeling" is the field of computer graphics that this work addresses. Gives our definitions of the field and slant on the issues, to help motivate the remainder of the work.

Chapter 1

Overview

As the computer graphics field matures, there is an increasing demand for complex, physically-based models. However, little attention has yet been focused on design methodologies for such models. Hence, models have often been ad hoc, special purpose, abstruse, and/or hard to extend.

In this work, we describe a strategy for designing and managing the complexity of physically-based computer graphics models in order to increase understanding, generality, reusability, and communication of the models, i.e., to make us better at developing and using such models. The strategy spans the entire activity of model creation, from specifying an initial concept down through computer programming details. Because the strategy takes advantage of known principles and methodologies of structured programming and mathematical modeling (see Fig. 1.1), we call it *structured modeling*.

This chapter sets the stage for structured modeling, to explain the overall world-view of the work. It includes motivation, goals, attitude, philosophy, and so forth. It also contains a guide for readers, explaining the organization of the later chapters and including notes for readers with various backgrounds.

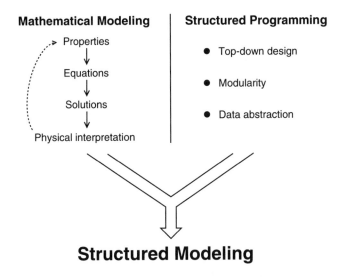

Mathematical Modeling

Properties
↓
Equations
↓
Solutions
↓
Physical interpretation

Structured Programming

- Top-down design

- Modularity

- Data abstraction

Structured Modeling

Figure 1.1: Structured modeling draws from principles of mathematical modeling and structured programming to derive a design methodology for physically-based computer graphics modeling. □

1.1   What Kind of Modeling?

"Modeling" and "model" are words with a remarkably broad collection of meanings. Model rockets. Model United Nations. Molecular models. Scale models. A model student.

A document about modeling must define which type of modeling is to be discussed and what "modeling" means in the context of interest.[1] Considering only scientific and computer modeling, there is still a wide variety: climate modeling, economic modeling, performance modeling, cognitive modeling, to name only a few.

We are, of course, interested in computer graphics modeling. But even here, there are many types of modeling: solid modeling, 3D modeling, etc. Our particular focus is on *physically-based modeling*, in which the behavior of objects is determined via simulations of physical laws. (Chapter 2 gives an overview of physically-based modeling.)

In this work we develop a foundation through an analysis of modeling in general, and then we embed physically-based computer graphics modeling within that context. Additionally, because physically-based modeling is inherently mathe-

---

[1]Even after choosing a type of modeling, we are left with a bit of a muddle: The word "model" can be a noun, adjective, or transitive or intransitive verb. It is possible *to* model, or to create *a* model. One could *use* a modeler to do so; one would then *be* a modeler. In this work, we shall try to provide sufficient context so that the meaning is always clear.

matical, this work devotes considerable attention to techniques for *mathematical modeling*. Again, we first develop fairly general techniques, then apply them to physically-based modeling.

1.2   What Kinds of Structure?

In order to manage the complexity of models, we try to identify or create "structure": that is, replace a vague or amorphous modeling problem with one that is well organized. Having a philosophy or premise that almost any structure is better than no structure at all, we will try to foster an overall "make it organized" attitude. Of course, we wish to seek out structures that are best suited to our purposes; this work presents various structures and structuring techniques that we have found valuable for physically-based modeling. Note that we don't wish to impose a single overall structure to all models or all of modeling, but rather offer and bring into play various structures and techniques when and where they are appropriate.

Some broad structuring techniques discussed in this work:

- Decomposition of a model into abstraction, representation, and implementation (Ch. 3)

- Partition of a physically-based model into conceptual model, mathematical model, and posed problems (Ch. 4)

- A modular, library-oriented approach to physically-based modeling (Ch. 4)

- Mathematical techniques to help structure complex mathematical models (Ch. 5)

- Programming techniques to help structure physically-based modeling programs (Ch. 6)

The model subdivisions draw from applied mathematical modeling techniques. The mathematical structuring techniques draw from structured programming, object-oriented programming, and software engineering.

Note that in this work we will generally use the term "structured programming" very loosely, to include software engineering and object-oriented programming as well as the traditional structured programming methodology. From our point of view, these are all approaches to organizing the problems of program design, hence they are all "structured"—albeit with different specific structures—and we will use principles and techniques from all three. This may contrast with other outlooks, especially in object-oriented design circles, where investigators often emphasize the distinctions between object-oriented and traditional structured techniques and question their compatibility (see [Booch91, p. 18] or [OOPSLA91]).

1.3 Why "Structured Modeling"?

At the current state of the art, creating new types of computer graphics models is to a large extent a programming task. In particular, creating physically-based models requires the translation of mathematical expressions of behavior into computer programs. Thus a practitioner of physically-based modeling typically creates a model by jotting down mathematical equations, then writing a program that embodies the model.

Because of the importance of programming in computer graphics modeling, shouldn't our efforts should focus on the program design, rather than on abstract issues of modeling or the structure of models? In our experience as practitioners of physically-based modeling, we of course try to write our programs well—i.e., pay attention to program structure and modularity, take advantage of object-oriented techniques and languages, and so forth—in order to make the programs and hence the models be robust. However, we have found that careful program design doesn't eliminate many types of stumbling blocks frequently encountered when modeling, especially as we attempt to create models of increasing complexity. For example:

- Even with a well-structured program it can be difficult to extend a model to have new mathematical functionality and behavior. Changing the equations often requires substantial rewriting of the program.

- It can be difficult to merge different models and programs, especially when written by different people. For example, in our own work we wanted to merge the rigid-body constraint mechanism of [Barzel,Barr88] with the flexible-body constraint mechanism of [Platt,Barr88]—but the independently designed programs didn't "mesh" directly.

- A program is only as robust as the model it embodies. That is, careful program design doesn't ensure that the underlying mathematical equations are robust. For example, a rigid-body program that uses the penalty method to meet constraints in dynamic models will not perform as well in general as one using analytic or inverse dynamics techniques (see [Baraff89]).

- Programming a model doesn't help us to understand the model. It can be hard to separate the fundamental principles of the behavior of a model from the details of program construction, and hard to distinguish minor tweaking and debugging of a program from major changes to the model.

- Similarly, programming a model doesn't help us to communicate the model. Research papers must often resort to describing the computer program that embodies a model rather than describing the model itself in some more direct manner. For example, see [Barzel,Barr88], [Bruderlin,Calvert89], [Chadwick *et al.*89], [Girard,Maciejewski85], or [Isaacs,Cohen87] (to list just a few)—to fully explain their models, each devotes a large portion to a discussion of computer program details.

We conclude from the above that it is important to study the design and structure of models at a more abstract level than that of computer programming. The structured modeling strategy in this book gives a methodology for designing models "on blackboards," before implementing them as computer programs.

1.4   Goals for Structured Modeling

The preceeding sections discussed our desire to have a strategy and methodology for designing physically-based computer graphics models. Here, we list several specific goals for the strategy:

- **To facilitate the understanding and communication of models.** We want to be able to create and describe complete, well defined models which are independent of the programs that implement them.

- **To facilitate the creation of models with high degrees of complexity.** A variety of factors contribute to the complexity of models: size, in terms of numbers of objects and possible interactions between them; the desire to model real-world phenomena with increasing accuracy; mathematical complexity; intricacy of numerical computational techniques; and so on. We are particularly interested in heterogeneous models, in that model elements may have behaviors that differ qualitatively from each other or over time.

- **To facilitate the reuse of models, techniques, and ideas.** We want new models to "stand upon the shoulders" of previous ones and we want to be able to merge models that are designed separately.

- **To facilitate the extension of models.** When new techniques and methods are developed, we want to be able to use them to enhance existing models and capabilities without having to start over with a new design.

- **To facilitate the creation of models that are "correct."** We want each model to achieve its particular goals. We want to avoid ad hoc techniques so that models will be useable (and reusable) in a wide variety of circumstances.

- **To facilitate the translation of models into programs.** Ultimately, we will implement models via computer programs. We want the program layout and structure to correspond as closely as possible with the blackboard design of a model.

To meet these goals, the structured modeling strategy emphasizes low-level methods intended for "hands-dirty" model makers. We will not attempt to define a high-level specification or environment for end-users of physically-based modeling programs. However, the low-level methods are intended to form a base upon which such high-level constructs can be built.

A fundamental part of the structured modeling strategy are the attitudes and philosophy that provide the first steps towards meeting the above goals. Section 1.2 has already discussed our emphasis on structure; the next two sections discuss our emphases on explicit mathematical modeling and on strongly goal-oriented modeling methods.

1.5   Mathematical Modeling Premise

Our approach to structuring physically-based models includes an emphasis on creating separate, complete mathematical models. This emphasis is both based on and leads to the following premise:

> *Premise:* If we want reliable simulations, we must first create well-defined mathematical models.

This premise expresses our feeling that it's unproductive to try and program simulations if we don't have a thorough understanding of the equations we're trying to solve. Without such an understanding, it can be hard (at best) or hopeless (at worst) to try and debug or explain unexpected simulation results, especially as the models get complicated.

Continuing from the above premise, we reason that if a mathematical model is well defined, we ought to be able to write it down. Thus we have the following goal:

> *Goal:* To be able to write down complete, explicit equations for complex physically-based models.

This perhaps innocuous-seeming goal is in fact quite a challenge, leading to an overall design philosophy and various mathematical techniques, developed in Ch. 5. The models in Part III have all been designed in keeping with this goal.

1.6   Theme: A Goal-Oriented Approach

"Do what you're trying to do"
"Solve the problem you're trying to solve"

The above slogans sound silly and obvious. The reader is probably thinking "of course, I always do that," and either agrees heartily with us or is annoyed at our seemingly patronizing attitude (and either way, probably intends to skip the rest of this section). However, we feel there is a real issue here.

Phrased more specifically: We advocate a strongly goal-oriented approach toward modeling. In addition, we feel that the process of modeling—especially physically-based modeling—harbors tendencies to subtly divert a model from its original goals. Examples of such diversions include

× Using methods that seem intuitive but aren't guaranteed to work (e.g., penalty methods for meeting constraints)

× Replacing a model with one that is more primitive or easier to compute (e.g., a mass-point-and-springs model for flexible bodies)

× Being driven by available tools that don't really solve the problem at hand (e.g., continuous ODE-solvers used across discontinuous events)

× Using ad hoc or expedient methods that work for special cases, but don't generalize

× Forgetting that an approximation isn't *the* correct answer, but is merely one in a space of solutions within the requested tolerance

The best ways that we have found to avoid these pitfalls are to be aware of them, to be vigilant, and to nurture a goal-oriented approach to modeling.

An important first step in designing a model is typically to ask oneself, "What am I trying to do?" We try to be as explicit as possible about goals, assumptions, problem statements, and so forth, in order to comply most directly and unambiguously with them. Thus we have a "purist" outlook on modeling.[2]

Admittedly, a perfect statement of goals, assumptions, and so forth is almost impossible in most cases (except in retrospect). Often, we're researching new problems, or trying out new ideas, or whatnot. But when things aren't working, when we seem to have hit a snag, we have found it helpful to step back and ask, "OK, what is it that I'm trying to do *here*?" and identify the problem statement (formally/mathematically when appropriate) and goals, etc. Surprisingly often

---

[2]Lest one think that a "purist" outlook is opposed to a "realist" outlook, we point out that the answer to "What am I trying to do?" is often "I am trying to get concrete results"—meaning that real-world constraints must be considered.

it turns out that the techniques we're using can't solve the problem at hand—a different technique is needed, or, if there's no practical way to solve the problem, we must choose a different problem. As we get more fluent in goal-oriented modeling, we try not to wait for snags to arise, but ask ourselves the same question at each juncture in the modeling process.

When it is infeasible to solve the originally stated problem, there is often a "nearby" problem that is feasible and suffices for one's basic goals (or we're willing to settle). In such a case, we advocate explicitly stating why the original problem is infeasible, and explicitly replacing it. We like to emphasize the shift in solution, so that we don't accidentally expect the new model to behave in accordance with the original problem statement, and so that we don't confuse colleagues by telling them we're solving one problem, but in fact solving another.

This outlook is geared toward accomplishing specific tasks, rather than amorphous exploring or learning or just playing. We do not deny the value of such experimentation—indeed, exploration is perhaps the best way to learn about a field or problem. However, when there is a specific task to be accomplished, a goal-oriented approach is valuable. Of course, for many tasks, one "learns on the job," i.e., learns about a problem in the course of trying to solve it; but as discussed above, the goal-oriented attitude is still practicable.

1.7   Wherein Computer Graphics?

Some readers might imagine that physically-based modeling, because of its emphasis on physics and simulation, isn't "really" computer graphics, but rather numerical simulation; or one might wonder if physically-based computer graphics modeling is different from other types of technical or scientific modeling. We feel that computer graphics modeling is indeed sufficiently different from simulation or scientific modeling to be worthy of study on its own: For computer graphics, issues such as reusability, heterogeneity, generic tools, and so on come to the forefront. These are discussed further in Section 2.4.

The converse question might arise: Since we go to some lengths to develop general methods for modeling, why apply those methods only to computer graphics? Here, too, the answer lies in the particular emphases of computer graphics. We have created general techniques to provide a firm foundation for the ideas that underlie our computer graphics work; but our ultimate goal has been the computer graphics, and the general techniques have not yet been tried nor proven in other contexts.

1.8   Reader's Guide

1.8.1   Organization

This work is presented in four parts (see overview, p. v):

- **Part I: Introduction.** This chapter and Ch. 2, an overview of physically-based modeling.

- **Part II: Structured Modeling.** The presentation of the structured modeling methodology. It is divided into several chapters: background concepts that define a common framework and terminology for modeling (Ch. 3), development of physically-based computer graphics models within this framework (Ch. 4), mathematical modeling methodology and techniques (Ch. 5), and program design methodology and techniques (Ch. 6).

- **Part III: Prototype Physically-Based Model Library.** The structured modeling methodology is illustrated via a small prototype library of "modules" that can be used to model the dynamics of rigid-body motion, and by a few models built using the library.

- **Part IV: Conclusion and Appendices.** Among other things, the appendices include functional specification of the software modules of our prototype modeling environment.

Additionally, for those trying to go back to something that caught their eye, the iconic index of figures (pp. xv–xxiii) may help.

1.8.2   Notes for the Computer Graphics Modeler

Those for whom "modeling" typically means 3D shape modeling (surface patches, etc.) should be reminded that here we address physically-based modeling, mostly applied to modeling the dynamic behavior of physical bodies, to produce animation. Chapter 2 gives an overview of what we mean by "physically-based modeling," what our emphases are, and how it fits into other types of modeling.

We place heavy emphasis on the mathematical modeling that lies behind physically-based modeling. Thus we expect readers to have a certain degree of mathematical sophistication and to be willing to define mathematical models in order to directly use our techniques. We are not targeted toward "end-users" of prebuilt physically-based modeling programs (though the ideas herein can be used in creating such programs).

The library of model "modules" defined in Part III is intended not only to illustrate structured modeling, but also to be a first step toward a general purpose, dynamic rigid-body modeling environment.

1.8.3 Notes for the Computer Graphics Programmer

Programmers may notice that it is not until Ch. 6 that we focus on computer programming techniques. We have made a deliberate effort to separate model design issues from programming issues. The programming principles and techniques in Ch. 6 derive from the analysis and development in the earlier chapters; we do not recommend reading it on its own.

Within Ch. 6 we give a framework and strategy for physically-based modeling programs. The approach is built around a modular, extensible design: The intent is not so much to build a specific program or programs, but rather to support an environment of modules and techniques that can be assembled and extended as needed for future applications.

Part III defines a library of model "modules" that intend to be useful as examples both of structured modeling and of physically-based modeling of rigid-body systems. Program specifications are included with each module—each has been implemented—and an overview of the prototye environment as a whole is in Appendix B.

Programmers may also notice that the mathematical techniques in Ch. 5 contain many elements familiar from programming: data abstraction, modularity, name scoping, and others. These are *not* attempts to "mathify" programming constructs; rather, we are employing in the mathematical domain analogs of constructs that have proven useful for programming.

1.8.4 Notes for the Applied Mathematician

The notion of an explicit mathematical model of natural phenomena, separate from both its numerical solution and its physical interpretation, is well-known to applied mathematicians and is the basis for the modeling philosophy in Part II.

The mathematical design philosophy and techniques in Ch. 5 may be of interest; these consist mostly of definitions of constructs (e.g., types of sets) and notations that aid us in creating well-defined mathematical models for complex systems, in accordance with the "complete, explicit models" goal of Section 1.5. The techniques adopt notions, such as modularity and scoping, that are known to be effective in managing complexity of computer programs.

We attempt to maintain mathematical rigor; as discussed in Section 1.5, a basic assumption of structured modeling is that there is no point trying to numerically simulate a mathematical model if that model is not a priori well defined.

1.8.5   Notes for the Mechanical Engineer and the Numerical Analyst

Those with strong backgrounds in classical mechanics or numerical simulation should note that we are studying the *process* of modeling (as discussed in Section 2.4), rather than the underlying numerical techniques or physical principles. Or, phrased another way, this work does not emphasize new numerical techniques or physical principles, but rather studies ways in which to put together and take advantage of those that already exist. Our paradigms for decomposing models, which we discuss in Chs. 3 and 4, are similar to those in the field of engineering design.

Physics and engineering textbooks typically define what we refer to as "model fragments"—individual equations that embody physical principles—but leave implicit the "glue" needed to assemble them into complete models. This idea is discussed in Section 2.7 and provides a motivation for the effort made in Ch. 5 to define mathematical techniques allowing equations that embody entire complex models.

Related Work

[Brooks91] addresses the same question as we do: how to manage complexity of computer graphics models. Like us, he adapts ideas that are familiar to programmers; he addresses issues such as debugging, versioning, documentation, etc. Thus his focus is more macroscopic than ours: His effort might be called "model engineering" (from software engineering), as compared to our "structured modeling" (from structured programming). There is, of course, overlap between the two.

[Booch91] is similar in spirit to our work—design techniques to manage complexity—but in the domain of object-oriented programming rather than physically-based modeling. Our work does have some object-oriented elements however, in mathematical modeling approach and in program design.

Much of our work is based on structured programming and software engineering; when not directly in techniques, then in the ethic of abstraction and modularity as a basic principles of design. [Dahl *et al.*72] and [Dijkstra76] provide the foundations of structured programming. ([Booch91] contains an extensive bibliography on software engineering.)

Our "solve the problem you're trying to solve" arguments echo a similar diatribe for the field of computer vision: [Jain,Binford91] emphasizes a need to avoid being tool-driven, to avoid claiming to solve a problem when really only solving an approximation to it, and so forth.

A final note: In 1990, "managing complexity" and "modeling reality" were the topics of an ACM Conference on Critical Issues ([Frailey91]). Its focus was on computer control of complex systems (such as nuclear power plants) and on computer models of socioeconomic systems, thus it is not closely related to our work. We mention it because the names *seem* similar to our work—this highlights the need for care when using such broad terms as "modeling" or "complexity." □

Chapter 2

Overview of Physically-Based Modeling

Computer graphics is a wide-ranging field; at conferences, practitioners and researchers discuss issues such as computer-aided design (CAD), computer–human interaction, scientific visualization, real-time simulation, animation, modeling, rendering, medical imaging, image processing, display hardware, input hardware, computational hardware, numerical analysis, 2D, 3D, and so forth. Indeed, any application that has a computer produce some sort of visual output—i.e., just about any application—is fair game for computer graphics. Note, however, that rather than being interested in specific applications, the computer graphics community is interested in general techniques that can be used in many applications.

This chapter describes *physically-based modeling,* which is the focus of the structured modeling design techniques to be discussed in later chapters. We present this description not so much as a prerequisite for the later discussion, but rather to give our outlook on the field and where structured modeling fits into it. This chapter discusses such issues as goals for modeling, realism, control and animation, and the relationship of physically-based modeling to "teleological" and scientific modeling.

Traditional modeling

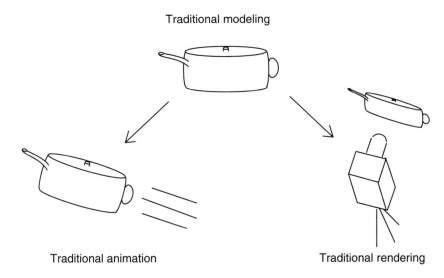

Traditional animation   Traditional rendering

Figure 2.1: Traditional computer graphics separation: First, a geometric model of the scene is defined. To animate, parameters of the model, such as positions and angles, are varied over time. To make an image, a rendering technique is used to compute an image of the model. Physically-based modeling techniques blur this separation, as dynamic behavior or light interaction becomes inherent in the model; see Fig. 2.2. □

2.1   Background: Traditional Computer Graphics Modeling

A large part of computer graphics can be termed *pretty-picture making,* in which the goal is to produce realistic images or movies of actual or hypothetical objects and scenes. Pretty-picture making is important for CAD, scientific visualization, and, of course, commercial and entertainment graphics.

Pretty-picture making is traditionally (if one may use the word in so young a field) separated into three parts (see Fig. 2.1):

- *modeling*—defining the geometry of the objects in the picture,

- *rendering*—computing the image of those objects, and

- *animation*—manipulating the objects over time.

The traditional computer graphics model is geometric, a description of shapes of objects. A large variety of geometric modeling techniques has been developed, such as parametric surface patches, constructive solid geometry, etc. To support animation, the models are parametrized, for example, into articulated hierarchies; animating the model is then a matter of varying the parameter values over time.

Traditional (shape) model   Physically-based model

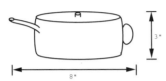

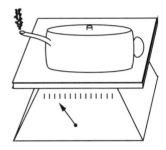

Figure 2.2: Traditional versus physically-based modeling: Traditional modeling is purely geometric. Physically-based modeling additionally incorporates physical characteristics, allowing computation of dynamic behavior or subtle interaction with light. Thus the traditional separation of modeling from animation and rendering can be blurred. □

2.2   Striving for Realism

A common goal in computer graphics is realism. Historically, the quest for realism has focused on "photorealism" ([Foley *et al.*90, Ch. 14]) — mostly a rendering problem. But in addition to realistic rendering techniques, there must be realistic models, and their motion must be realistic.

The traditional method for realism of model shape and motion is to provide a rich set of geometric techniques, allowing the user to directly specify whatever shape and motion are desired (e.g., keyframe animation of bodies and control points). This is powerful, but if the user completely controls motion manually, as by keyframe animation, the motion frequently looks unrealistic and puppetlike. Additionally, it puts a large burden on the human modeler or animator to adjust many parameters at a fine level of detail (*The Adventures of Andre and Wally B.* [Lucasfilm84], a landmark computer-graphics short film, had over 700 model parameters that were hand-animated via keyframe interpolation).

Recent modeling methods try to give direct computer support for models of increasing complexity and realism. This can be done by augmenting what we mean by the "model" to include not just geometric shape information, but other parameters that the computer can use to compute motion. In this way, the appropriate complexity and realism of behavior are inherent in the model, rather than needing to be imposed by the user.

2.3   Physically-Based Modeling

Physically-based modeling is modeling that incorporates physical characteristics into models, allowing numerical simulation of their behavior (see Fig. 2.2). It has become somewhat of a catchall term for a variety of techniques that all share the approach of defining physical principles of behavior for their models, then having the computer compute the details of the behavior. Physically-based modeling is a relatively new branch of computer graphics.[1] A brief survey of the field can be found in [Foley *et al.*90, Ch. 20].

Common elements in physically-based modeling are classical dynamics (motion based on forces, mass, inertia, etc.) with rigid or flexible bodies; interbody interaction; and constraint-based control. Physically-based models are founded on mathematical equations and often involve numerically intensive computation to simulate their behavior.

Physically-based models most often focus on how bodies move and change shape over time. But also, sophisticated rendering techniques can be tied in with descriptions of the models, since rendering can be viewed as simulating a model of the interaction of light with matter. Thus, in general, physically-based modeling blurs the traditional distinction between modeling, rendering, and animation.

2.4   Goals for Modeling

Physically-based modeling combines elements of applied mathematics, numerical analysis, physics, mechanical engineering, computational mechanics, etc. But is physically-based modeling different from just a smattering of ideas from those other fields? Are there special problems or issues from a computer graphics viewpoint?

We think that the answer to the above questions is "yes" (not surprising!). Some goals specifically for the computer-graphics aspect of physically-based modeling are

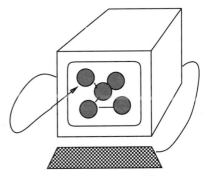

Figure 2.3: From a computer-graphics viewpoint, the emphasis of physically-based modeling is not so much on "physically-based," but rather on "modeling." Thus, we use techniques from fields such as numerical analysis and mechanical engineering, but the focus of computer-graphics research is on tools that facilitate the creation of models that incorporate those techniques. □

---

[1] The field was first named in a course in the 1987 ACM SIGGRAPH (the Association for Computing Machinery's Special Interest Group on Computer Graphics) conference, "Topics in Physically-Based Modeling" [Barr87].

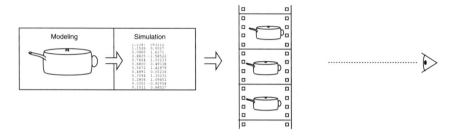

Figure 2.4: There are two phases to the overall process of physically-based modeling: *Modeling* defines the formal behavior and equations of the physical system. Given a definition of behavior, *simulation* is performed to solve the equations numerically. Since the output shown to the user is the immediate result of the simulation, the user may not see the behind-the-scenes modeling. □

Reusability. We don't want "one-shot" models; we are interested in generic, reusable techniques.

Extensibility. As we gain in knowledge and attempt to reach new heights in the capabilities of our models, we don't want to start over from scratch. Instead, we want to build upon and extend existing models.

Heterogeneous models. Users may want to combine different types of components and behaviors into a single model. A consistent framework is required to allow mixing and matching of different techniques and primitive elements, with proper interaction between them.

Modeling tools. We want easy-to-use tools to help users create models: modeling languages, interactive workstations, etc., and the underlying techniques that support them.

Control. We want the users to retain control over the models and their behavior. (This is discussed further in Section 2.5.)

Nonexpert users. Modelers and animators are not always physicists, but should still be able to use and benefit from physically-based models.

The bottom line is that for computer graphics, we address the task of modeling. Our emphasis is on general methods for modeling, rather than any specific physical models or techniques. Note in particular that we are not doing research in numerical analysis, mechanical engineering, etc.—rather, we are "customers" of those fields; we use their techniques as building blocks in our models (see Fig. 2.3).

Thus we make a distinction between *simulation,* which emphasizes computation of behavior given a model, and *modeling,* which focuses on the creation of the models. Note that since we ultimately simulate our models to determine their behavior and create images or animations, the simulation is what is most directly visible to an observer; the modeling work itself is often behind-the-scenes, a matter of defining *what* to simulate (see Fig. 2.4).[2]

Those with experience in simulation might comment, "I can write simulation programs without needing a fancy modeling mechanism." Our response is twofold:

- It is true that, in principle, any simulation that is put together using fancy modeling techniques could also be written directly. However, such a direct simulation is special-purpose; we are studying the creation of reusable models and tools.

- While, in principle, any simulation can be put together directly, in practice the complexity of simulations can grow to such an extent that doing so becomes infeasible. The programmer or modeler must focus attention on issues at increasingly high levels of abstraction and would get bogged down in details.[3]

For the remainder of this work, we will assume our distinction between the meanings of the words *modeling* and *simulation*.

2.5   Control of Physically-Based Models

An important issue that arises when one defines physically-based models is how to control them: If the model's behavior is inherent in the model, the model will behave in the way *it* wants, rather than the way *we* want it to. Mathematically, physically-based models often translate into differential equations, which are typically posed as initial-value problems; the user has little control other than setting up the initial configuration (see Fig. 2.5).

In exchange for the realism of physically-based models, we seem to have traded the control afforded by traditional techniques; thus we are plagued by an apparent dichotomy:

Realism The model behaves realistically, but we have little control.

Control The model does what we tell it, but it doesn't behave realistically.

---

[2]Since modeling and simulation are tied together closely—we can't perform a simulation unless we are given a model, and we can't examine the behavior of our model without simulating it—the boundary between modeling and simulation can be ambiguous. Although we make a distinction between them, exactly where to draw the line between them can be a matter of one's perspective.

[3]This argument parallels an old compiler-versus-assembler argument. It was once commonly argued that any program written in a high-level language could be written directly in assembler and would run faster, too, so why invest time and effort in high-level languages? See [Wexelblat81].

Control of physically-based models remains a research issue. A common and fertile approach is to use constraint-based techniques, which allow users to specify required values for various properties of the models. To name just a few: [Witkin, Kass88] describes a formation of animation as a constrained multipoint boundary-value problem, thus allowing the user to specify intermediate and final configurations as well as the initial; [Barzel,Barr88] describes how to constrain physical models to follow user-specified paths; [Isaacs, Cohen87] and [Schröder,Zeltzer90] combine constrained dynamics with kinematic control; [Platt,Barr88] uses constraint techniques for flexible bodies; and [Kalra90] discusses a framework to combine various constraint methods.

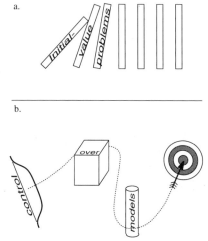

Figure 2.5: a. Physically-based models are often set up as initial-value problems; the user has control only over the initial conditions, and it is difficult to determine later behavior. b. Constraints and other control techniques are current research topics in physically-based modeling. □

2.6 Applications of Physically-Based Modeling

2.6.1 Animation Production

A significant area of application of computer graphics is for animation production (commercial or entertainment animation). At the current state of the art, most animation is done using traditional kinematic techniques.

Even animations that have featured dynamics, such as *Balloon Guy* ([Wedge87]), have thus far used only "passive" dynamics: The animator controls the central motion kinematically, and limbs are dragged along via dynamic simulation.

Some sources of difficulty in incorporating dynamics into animation are

- Physically-based modeling techniques have been special-purpose; they have not yet been widely integrated with traditional computer animation products.

- Lack of flexibility and animator control over models. Animators want "direct manipulation" over their models.

- Computational speed; animators want to create motion interactively.

We feel that these difficulties can be overcome: This work addresses the problem of models being special-purpose; the issue of control is being addressed as discussed in Section 2.5; and there is continuing research in faster numerical techniques.

2.6.2 Scientific Modeling

Scientists can make use of computer graphics as a tool to aid in their own research. *Scientific visualization*—making images of scientific data—is an area of active research in computer graphics (which we do not pursue here). Scientific data can arise as a result of measurements or of simulations of models. For scientific models, the physically-based modeling techniques described in this work may be appropriate.

Accuracy is an important issue for scientific models. Heretofore we have been saying we want models to *look* realistic; for scientific models, however, we want them to *be* realistic. Thus numerical and mathematical correctness is essential.

Scientists are interested in computer graphics as a means for their research, not as an end in itself; scientists who use computers in their work have been known to complain about time spent "doing computers" instead of "doing science." Scientists are technically sophisticated in their fields, but are not necessarily expert programmers or computer graphicists.

Tools for physically-based modeling should help make it easier for scientists to do graphics by building models at a higher level of abstraction, rather than being caught in the details of computer graphics. Although scientific models may be highly special-purpose, generic modeling tools can help manipulate those models or help to create a graphical model given an existing scientific model.

2.6.3 Teleological Modeling

For scientific modeling, the typical goal is to model existing things. Often, however, we make models of hypothetical things: We have something in mind that we want to create, and the computer provides tools to build it. This is the essential activity of computer-aided design and manufacturing (CAD/CAM). Even for scientific research, a model may be made to test a hypothesis; a model is built based upon a theory, and its simulation results are compared with real-world data.

Thus, rather than trying to mimic existing behavior and characteristics, we want to create models that meet our a priori purposes and conditions. With most modeling techniques, we must manually figure out how to put together a thing that will do what we want. Instead, we ideally want to be able to do modeling at a "goal" level: Operations would be of the form "create an object such that...."

Teleological modeling ([Barr91]) addresses the creation of models via specification of goals. When combined with physically-based modeling, teleological modeling is closely tied to the issue of constraints, as discussed in Section 2.5.

2.6.4   User Interaction

Physically realistic behavior does not have to be an "output-only" property of
models, but can be used in interactive model creation. Interactive modeling
programs that embrace familiar behaviors such as inertia and body–body contact
can help give better feel and power to interactive modeling. This can be true even
if the final model does not need to exhibit physical behavior ([Witkin *et al.*90]).

2.7   Notes on Physically-Based Computer Models

(or, "Physics Was Developed before Computers")

In approaching the problem of computer modeling of physical systems, it is worth
noticing that the principles and equations of classical physics were developed
hundreds of years before computers. In fact, the majority of mathematical notation
and techniques upon which physics (both classical and modern) is based was
developed hundreds of years before computers. Let us consider some of the
implications of this fact:

- **Common use of computers is as calculators.** Commonly, humans derive equations by hand, then write programs to crunch the numbers. Or,
  according to the terminology of Section 2.4, computers are used more for
  simulation than for modeling.

- **Equations are derived by/for pen and paper.** The aesthetic and metric
  as to what makes equations on paper "good" are not necessarily the same
  as those for equations in computers. On paper, concerns such as visual
  compactness and clarity are paramount, along with analytic solubility. In
  computers, other concerns, such as computability or numerical behavior,
  might be overriding; computers can handle long, tedious chains of terms
  without blanching.[4]

- **Classical formalism is a collection of equations.** Traditional physics is
  geared toward expressing general principles as equations. Each of these
  equations can be thought of as a "model fragment," but a complete model
  consists of representations of the state of the entire system, plus all the
  equations that describe the interaction and behavior of the components of
  the system. Lacking computers that could implement entire models, the
  classical formalisms did not develop "glue" to go between the fragments,
  i.e., techniques for creating complex models.

---

[4]Note that we still take the view that we want to be able to write down our equations by hand
(Section 1.5). However, we will be using equations whose solutions are intractable by hand. Since
without the use of computers such equations were fruitless, no compact way of writing them has been
developed. Chapter 5 addresses this goal.

2.8 Where Does Structured Modeling Fit In?

The preceding sections attempted to convey an overview of physically-based modeling as it appears from our vantage. We haven't yet mentioned how *structured modeling* fits into the landscape. Naturally, many of the landmarks we pointed out are those that are relevant to our work. But also, we can't, of course, cover *all* the ground in sight, so we focus on what we consider to be the basics and the features that relate to our overall goals discussed in Section 1.4.

Structured modeling addresses the goals for modeling in Section 2.4, particularly the first four: *reusability, extensibility, heterogeneous models,* and *modeling tools.* The distinction between *modeling* and *simulation* will be taken for granted. To be in accord with scientific modeling, Section 2.6.2, we will stress correctness via an emphasis on having well-defined mathematical models that underlie the physically-based models. In the spirit of teleological modeling, Section 2.6.3 (and our overall goal-oriented approach as per Section 1.6), structured modeling will emphasize identifying and meeting the goals that drive any particular model. Finally, in bringing computers into the modeling process, we will address the points in Section 2.7: how to use computers for more than just simulation, how to express equations that are more complex than was common before computers, and how to create well-defined models that include the "glue" between the classical equation fragments.

To put together all of the above, structured modeling will define philosophy, strategy, terminology, and techniques for creating robust, extensible, and reusable models, and ultimately implementing them on computers. The focus will be on fundamental organizational and structural concepts and frameworks—low-level tools and techniques—rather than on snazzy high-level effects.

2.9 Summary

This chapter presented *physically-based modeling,* in which physical characteristics are incorporated into models. The behavior of a model is determined automatically by simulation. Thus, in contrast with the traditional separation of "modeling" from "rendering" and "animation," the process of physically-based modeling also ties in closely with animation, and even with rendering.

For the study of physically-based modeling, we emphasize the modeling process, as opposed to the numerical techniques that are used for simulation at the bottom line. Thus this chapter made a distinction between *modeling* and *simulation.*

Finally, this chapter discussed the relationship of physically-based modeling to other types of computer graphics modeling, pointed out some issues that arise when we try to merge classical physical formalisms with computer modeling, and gave a brief overview of what structured modeling is about.

Related Work

We are not aware of other work that addresses physically-based modeling with the emphasis on modeling as a field. Most of the works in physically-based modeling are descriptions of techniques to implement various types of effects and behavior. Section 2.5 lists several works addressing constraint-based modeling. We mention here a smattering of some others: [Badler *et al.*91] gives techniques for modeling and simulating articulated figures (figures with limbs, such as people and animals); [Raibert, Hodgins91] discusses walking and running (this work has a scientific modeling perspective; in addition to making computer animation of locomotion, the authors build robots that implement their techniques); [Terzopoulos, Fleischer88] models inelastic flexible bodies; [Reynolds87] models flocking behavior of animals; [Fournier,Reeves86] models ocean waves.

[Zeleznik *et al.*91] presents an interactive modeling system that, although not specifically focused on physically-based modeling, similarly blurs the traditional modeling–rendering–animation distinction: "We wish to expand the definition of 'modeling' to include the realms of simulation, animation, rendering, and user interaction."

There is a large body of literature on simulation and numerical techniques; see, e.g., [Ralston,Rabinowitz78] for an introduction to numerical analysis, and [Press *et al.*86] for a collection of numerical subroutines. □

PART II

STRUCTURED MODELING

The development of our approach to physically-based modeling proceeds from a general analysis of modeling through to computer programming techniques.

- ## Ch. 3. A Structured Analysis of Modeling
  A general paradigm and terminology for modeling. Discussions of design strategies and of the role of computers in modeling.

- ## Ch. 4. Structured Physically-Based Modeling
  A paradigm specific to physically-based modeling. Discussion of a modular approach to physically-based modeling.

- ## Ch. 5. Structured Mathematical Modeling
  Techniques to allow definition of complete mathematical models of complex systems. This chapter may be read on its own.

- ## Ch. 6. Computer Programming for Structured Modeling
  Overall framework for programs that implement structured physically-based modeling, closely following the ideas in Chs. 4 and 5.

Chapter 3

A Structured Analysis of Modeling

W hat is a "model"? It is hard to give an absolute, all-encompassing definition; there are many related meanings, and hence many different types of
models. Ultimately, we will be interested in "physically-based computer graphics
models"—but even that covers a lot of ground, leaving us ample room for confusion
as to what is and isn't part of a model, how two models differ, and so on.

This chapter clarifies what we mean by "a model" and by "modeling." We define
a paradigm and terminology to be applied to modeling, based upon two canonical
ways of viewing models:

- *Abstraction–representation–implementation (ARI) structure* for extant models, and

- *Progressive decomposition* for the creation of models.

When we merge the two views, we refer to them jointly as an *ARI progression*.
These constructs provide framework for the discussion of issues such as design
methodologies, communication of models, and the use of computers as modeling
tools.

The ideas in this chapter are somewhat abstract, attempting to address modeling in
general; Ch. 4 will apply the ideas to physically-based modeling, and, ultimately,
Ch. 6 will apply them to computer program design.

Various Models of a Teapot

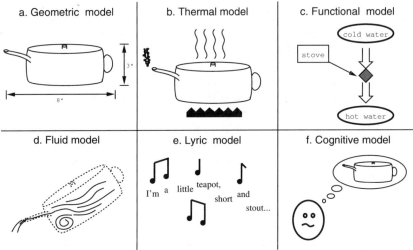

a. Geometric model	b. Thermal model	c. Functional model
d. Fluid model	e. Lyric model	f. Cognitive model

Figure 3.1: There are many ways of modeling things and many types of models. There is plenty of opportunity for confusion: What is and isn't part of a model? How are two models different? □

3.1 Canonical "ARI" Structure of a Model

Figure 3.1 illustrates that there may be many different types of models, even of a single object. There is no single "best" model—different models serve different purposes. There is, however, some commonality among models; in this section, we define (using admittedly broad strokes) a structure to be applied to any model. Canonically,

A model is an *implementation*
of a *representation*
of an *abstraction*
of a *thing*.

We call this decomposition the *abstraction–representation–implementation* structure, or *ARI* structure for short (see Fig. 3.2).[1]

---

[1] The ARI structure of a model follows a line of reasoning similar to those arising in other areas. For example, [Dahl *et al.*72, p. 83] defines abstraction–representation–manipulation–axiomatisation for abstract data types; [Traub,Woźniakowski91] discusses phenomenon–mathematical formulation–computation as a background to numerical complexity analysis; [Pahl,Beitz88] and [French85] separate engineering design into analysis–conceptual design–embodiment design–detail design. In particular, we have based the ARI structure on known mathematical modeling methodology, which we discuss in Section 4.2.

3.1.1   The Thing Being Modeled

Every model is a model *of* something; we cleverly call that something the *thing being modeled*, or just *thing* for short.[2] Note that there may be many different models of a single thing, e.g., all the models illustrated in Fig. 3.1 are models of the same teapot. Note also that the thing being modeled does not have to be an existing physical object: It is possible to make models of hypothetical things (e.g., a model of a space shuttle before the space shuttle is built), or of intangible things (e.g., a model of behavior), or of collections of things, etc.

The thing being modeled is not part of the model per se. It is useful to remember the distinction between the model and the thing itself. In some cases, particularly for intangible things, it may be easy to accidentally think that the model *is* the thing. However, as we shall discuss below, the model is typically a simplification of the thing, only capturing a subset of all the features that make up the thing.

3.1.2   The Abstraction ("A")

The most fundamental aspect of a model is the set of features and characteristics of the thing being modeled that the model embodies. We call this set the *abstraction*. Rarely, if ever, will a single abstraction capture all the aspects of a thing; instead, the abstraction is typically an idealization of the thing, focusing on those aspects of the thing that are relevant to one's purpose in creating the model, and excluding those that are irrelevant. For example, in Fig. 3.1, the color of the teapot probably wouldn't be part of the abstraction for the "Fluid" model, probably would be for the "Cognitive" model, and might or might not be part of the "Thermal" model, depending on whether or not one wished to include the effect of color-dependent radiative heat transfer.

Ultimately, a model's abstraction is the set of ideas that underlie the model; it can be considered in some sense to be the "axiomatic system" for the model. But it is not necessarily mathematically precise: In many cases, much of the abstraction is implied by the context or intended use of the model; and the concepts in the abstraction may be informal, vague, or abstract. Thus the abstraction is not necessarily a concrete, manipulable entity.

3.1.3   The Representation ("R")

A model can of course be described in some complete, well-defined, and (hopefully) compact manner. We call this description the *representation*. Unlike the

---

[2]Unfortunately, the English language does not seem to have a suitable word with the meaning we want. *Object* has too many meanings; *target, source, ensample* and similar words don't quite have the correct connotations; *quaesitum* might do, but is obscure. One might coin a word such as *modeland* (à la *operand*) or *modelee*, but we haven't found any that is sufficiently appealing. We have settled on *thing being modeled* as sufficiently clear, though a bit cumbersome.

**Canonical "ARI" Structure
of a Model**

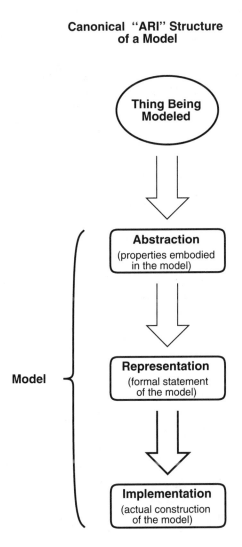

Figure 3.2: Canonically, a model can be decomposed into an abstraction, a representation of that abstraction, and an implementation of that representation. The decomposition is called the "ARI" structure. □

abstraction, the representation is concrete—it can be edited, copied, analyzed, and so forth. The representation contains sufficient information to actually "build" a model. For example, in Fig. 3.1, the "Geometric" model could be represented by blueprints, the "Functional" model by the diagram shown, the "Lyric" model by sheet music and performance notes, and the "Thermal" and "Fluid" models by mathematical equations.[3]

The representation is a formalization of the abstraction for the model. Note that for a given abstraction, many different representations may be possible. For example, the "Thermal" model may represent temperature as $°F$ or C or K, or may express the equations in terms of heat rather than temperature. Thus it is possible for two models to appear different by virtue of having different representations, but yet be essentially equivalent in that they share a single abstraction.

3.1.4   The Implementation ("I")

At the bottom line, the model is constructed or executed in all its grungy detail. We call this final construction the *implementation*. In the examples of Fig. 3.1, it might be a miniature plastic teapot for the "Geometric" model, a performance of the song and dance for the "Lyric" model, or numerical simulation program and data for the "Thermal" and "Fluid" models.

The implementation thus expands or carries out the representation in some medium. Note that it may be possible to have many different implementations of a single representation. The implementations would differ only in details that are artifacts of the implementation medium. Those details are in principle irrelevant to the representation and abstraction and do not correspond to properties of the thing being modeled. For example, the "Geometric" model of Fig. 3.1 might be implemented in plastic or wood or clay; and each performance of the "Lyric" model's song is a different implementation.

3.2   Discussion of the ARI Structure

The ARI structure of a model gives a succinct overview and encapsulation of the model. Identifying the abstraction, representation, and implementation of a model is an important aid in understanding the model's makeup and function. We use the decomposition when we try to understand other people's work (or even our own). When we examine a model, we ask ourselves:

- "What are they trying to do?" (abstraction)

- "What is their approach?" (representation)

- "What are the details?" (implementation)

If we have difficulty identifying and separating the three parts, that can be an indication that the model is muddled (or, at least, that we don't understand the

---

[3]The representation is only sufficient given the domain or context for the problem; one needs to know how to read a blueprint, for example.

model). For example, if items that are presented as implementation details actually affect high-level properties of the model, that can indicate a poorly designed model—the creator's results may not be repeatable by others.

For a designer of models, who focuses on creating and analyzing plans or techniques for models rather than on specific instances, a "model" might include only the abstraction and representation; implementation details might not be included as part of the model. Also, it may sometimes be hard to distinguish between an abstraction and a representation, or between a representation and an implementation: Merely stating the abstraction may be a suitable representation, or making a formal representation may be sufficient as an implementation. For example, a blueprint representation of the "Geometric" model of Fig. 3.1 is likely to be sufficient for people to analyze the model, without having to actually build one.

We mentioned earlier that multiple representations are possible for a given abstraction. The converse is also possible, i.e., a single representation may be shared by many abstractions: For example, chemical diffusion and heat conduction share the same mathematical equation.[4]

It is also possible to have multiple ARI models within the context of a single overall model or project. There may be separate models that focus on different properties, or a larger model may be subdivided into several smaller subparts. For example, a given teapot project might use both the "Geometric" and "Functional" models of Fig. 3.1, or the "Fluid" model of a teapot might include a "Geometric" model of the teapot as a subpart.

The ARI structure clearly isn't a surgically precise specification; we don't suggest that one must force-fit an exact ARI decomposition to every single model. However, we have found that the ARI structure serves as a useful guide when analyzing or contemplating models. In particular, the emphasis on separating the important ideas of a model from the details of its construction has proven helpful in our understanding of models.

3.3 Progressive Decomposition of a Model

The ARI structure described in the previous section is well suited to analysis of extant models. However, for the development of a model, we take a slightly different outlook.

A model starts out as some cognitive notion that is eventually developed into a concrete entity (see Fig. 3.3). The cognitive notion includes ideas and properties that are implicit; they depend on context and real-world experience in order to make sense. Gradually, a series of refinements is applied to the notion; these

---

[4]See, e.g., [Lin,Segel74]. The fact that one representation can be used for many abstractions is a source of the power of mathematical modeling: Techniques developed for canonical sets of equations can be applied to a wide variety of purposes. (Mathematical modeling is discussed in Section 4.2.)

**Progressive Decomposition
of a Model**

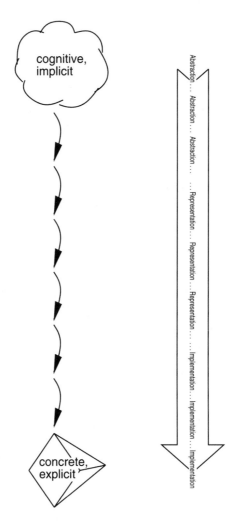

Figure 3.3: The development of a model can be thought of as a progression from a cognitive notion with implicit context to a concrete entity with all details spelled out explicitly. This progression is often as a series of steps or refinements and corresponds roughly with a gradual transition from the canonical "abstraction" through to the "implementation." □

refinements pin down the notion, transforming tacit properties into explicit ones and narrowing the scope to focus on elements that are relevant to the model's purpose.

For example, consider the development of the "Geometric" model in Fig. 3.1. We start with the notion of a "teapot"—something which is commonly understood, but not very precise. A series of refinements makes precise what we're interested in for the model: We consider only the geometric shape of the teapot; we decide what the components are (Does it have a bottom? Is the lid removable?); eventually we describe the shape, via blueprints or whatnot; ultimately we may build a physical miniature.

Often, the steps of a progression comprise a series of *changes of representation.* Each different representation might emphasize different aspects, cast the problem in a new light, or be more convenient to manipulate, etc. A change of representation might be informal, at a high level (e.g., an analogy), or might involve posing the problem in terms of other problems that are more familiar or simpler (e.g., "if we express the model as ... we see it is equivalent to...."). Executing a model may involve a series of changes in data representations and formats (e.g., converting spatial-domain data to frequency-domain via Fourier transform). Each change of representation typically marks the boundary between different functional subparts of a model.

The steps of a progression do not necessarily have a precise ordering: Various refinements may be independent of each other and thus may be performed in any order (or in parallel); or perhaps there may be two properties, either of which may be assumed, and the other one derived from it. The changes of representation may not always be refinements, but just alternate representations; thus from any given spot along the progression, it may be possible to go in many different directions. And it may be possible to reach a given spot from many different origins (as per the discussion in Section 3.2 of different abstractions sharing a common representation). However, although "locally" there may not be a single path toward the final product, there is generally a "flow" from the cognitive and implicit toward the concrete and explicit.

Finally, note that if a model is divided into submodels, the progressive decomposition view can apply recursively to each.

We feel that the progressive decomposition is a process that occurs in the development of most models, whether or not the designer engages in it explicitly. Identifying (or attempting to identify) the progressive decomposition—its refinements and changes of representation—can aid in understanding the workings of the model.

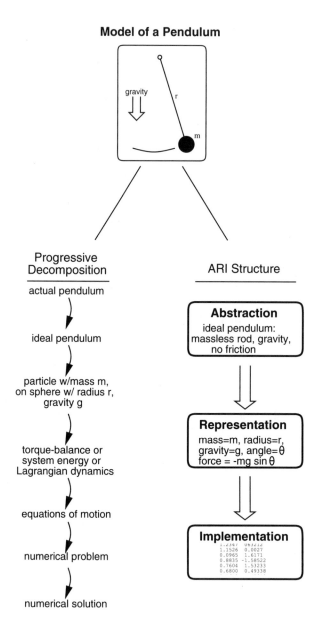

Figure 3.4: A simple example of a model. We illustrate a model of a pendulum, showing both a progressive decomposition used to create the model and the ARI structure that describes it. Section 3.7.1 uses this model as an example for discussion of the computer's role in the modeling process; Chapter 12 describes a model not just of a simple pendulum, but of a chain of linked segments. □

3.4   Relating ARI and Progressive Decomposition

The ARI structure in Section 3.1 describes extant models, while the progressive decomposition in Section 3.3 describes the development of models. Yet there is a rough correspondence between the two.

As we perform a progressive decomposition from a cognitive notion to an explicit entity, we are essentially performing a transition from abstraction through representation to implementation: A general abstraction is refined into a more specific one; a representation is transformed into a representation of a more immediately useful form; an implementation is built upon an existing, more primitive implementation (see Fig. 3.3).

Notice that in a progressive decomposition there is no well-defined boundary between the abstraction and the representation, or between the representation and the implementation. For example, any refinement step may limit the focus of the model, thus contributing an extra specification in the abstraction; such a step may be taken even after earlier steps have specified particulars of representation.[5]

Broadly, however, the early steps in the progression will be refinements of abstraction, the middle steps will be changes of representation, and the final steps will specify details of implementation (see Fig. 3.4). If lines were to be drawn between abstraction and representation or between representation and implementation, the precise location of those lines might depend on one's perspective.

We will often merge the progressive decomposition with the ARI structure, and refer simply to a series of steps from an abstraction to an implementation, or to an *ARI progression.*

3.5   Design Methodologies for Models

Thinking about design strategies for computer programs is familiar from software engineering. For designing models, the ARI progression similarly lends itself to discussion of strategies. To design a model, our task is to construct a series of steps from an abstraction to an implementation. Three basic approaches are to construct it from the top down, from the bottom up, or through a mixed "annealing" approach.

3.5.1   Top-Down Design

The top-down design method is a cornerstone of structured programming and software engineering. Stated simply: First compose a specification based on

---

[5]Thus, given a model constructed by progressive decomposition, we can create the canonical structure by "projecting upward" the limitations that affect the abstraction, "projecting downward" the choices that are implementation details, and "projecting inward" the specifications that comprise the representation.

functional goals, then implement as per the specification. Because of the emphasis on specifying the functionality up front, top-down design is philosophically akin to our slogan "solve the problem you're trying to solve" (Section 1.6). Thus we find top-down design to be very appealing.

In the realm of modeling, top-down design means to follow the ARI progression: First specify the abstraction, then the representation, then finally the implementation.[6] A full design sequence would thus include the following:

- **Specify overall goals.** At the top level of any project are the goals for the project, its purpose and reason for existence. In order to meet those goals, it is worthwhile to state them explicitly, as per Section 1.6.

- **Choose the properties for the abstraction.** List the expected results that follow from those properties. Also, mention properties that are explicitly being excluded and what behaviors are not to be expected. (Repeat if there's a series of refinements of abstraction.)

- **Define a representation.** Explain how the representation relates to the abstraction. (Repeat if there's series of changes of representation.)

- **Specify implementation details.** Make various technical decisions: specific materials or algorithms, etc. Note what artifacts may occur. (Repeat if there's a series of refinements.)

- **Build it.** Implement according to the specification. If there were a series of refinements that build on each other, they would be assembled bottom-up.

When doing this process, we like to be as explicit as possible—about everything, from the most basic goals ("we're doing this because the boss said so") down to implementation trivia ("use a tolerance of 10^{-6}"). In particular, we like to be explicit about what the model does *not* do ("we do not consider high-order effects of . . . ") in order to help understand and explain the model. In general, being explicit, combined with the stepwise refinement structure, helps make it easier to extend and reuse models later.

Unfortunately, despite its appeal, the top-down method is a theorist's approach, or an optimist's—pure top-down design is unlikely to work well in practice. It is an open-loop or "point and shoot" method, in that there's no feedback from later stages to help design the initial parts. Top-down design therefore presupposes that one has "perfect aim" in order to get a working implementation: Without perfect aim, one might specify an abstraction or representation that turns out to be infeasible to implement. In practice, the choice of a representation must often be

---

[6]We mentioned earlier that a given model does not always break down easily into a neat abstraction–representation–implementation decomposition. However, when designing a model *ab initio,* one can attempt to keep those parts separate.

based on or limited to that which can be implemented, and the choice of abstraction will in turn depend on what can thus be feasibly represented.

If one had complete understanding of the problem and implementation techniques, one could carry out a top-down design and make a working model in one pass. However, for problems that are sufficiently complex, or that we don't understand well enough,[7] another method will be needed.

3.5.2 Bottom-Up Design

At the other extreme from top-down design is bottom-up implementation. Actually, the two commonly go together; a structured programming motto is "design top-down, implement bottom-up." Thus the bottom-up approach is not typically considered a design strategy.

However, de facto, projects are often designed bottom-up. As an experienced practitioner in a field, one is typically aware of available implementation techniques and also aware of interesting or unsolved problems. It's not unreasonable that given the techniques, one might try to fit them together to solve some of those problems. This lends itself to the model being designed as it is built.

Bottom-up design allows us to explore and learn as we work on the model. It doesn't require full understanding up front. Furthermore, unlike top-down design, we never design something that is infeasible—when building bottom-up, everything can be made to function at each step.

However, bottom-up design doesn't guarantee that it will actually solve the top-level problem. Like top-down design, it's a "point and shoot" method, here relying on one's intuition and experience to predict that the techniques that are used will in fact yield a product that meets the goals.[8] Furthermore, bottom-up design encourages ad hoc techniques, doesn't encourage reusability or extensibility, and may get results that aren't easily repeatable by others—or no results at all.

It's easy to slip into bottom-up design and slide away from one's top-level goals, especially when extending an existing model to meet new goals. The allure of just making a small change to an existing design, rather than starting over from the top, is a powerful force toward bottom-up design. Unfortunately, achieving a new top-level goal may require new or different bottom-level techniques.

For example, suppose one has a rigid-body simulation system based on continuous numerical integration of forces, and that one wanted to ensure that bodies do not interpenetrate. It is natural to introduce penalty forces that push bodies apart (based upon how much they interpenetrate), since such forces are continuous and

---

[7] As researchers, our basic activity is to try to solve problems that we don't fully understand (if they were completely understood, there would be no research involved).

[8] Has this ever happened to you: You are really close to the final result you want—"just need to tweak a few parameters and it'll be perfect"—you spend hours, days, or weeks tweaking, spiraling around the goal but never reaching it, only to realize eventually that your technique (provably) *can't* solve the problem? It's happened to us!

fit into the existing system. However, the penalty method doesn't exactly solve the problem of noninterpenetration, but only provides an approximation, which may work well enough in simple test cases but may be insufficient under more stringent conditions.[9]

To avoid slipping away from one's goals when working bottom-up, one must religiously ask oneself, "Does this technique *really* solve the problem I'm trying to solve?" as per Section 1.6. Additionally, an emphasis on designing models so that they can be easily modified and extended in order to meet unforeseen goals can also help make the above "inadvertent" bottom-up design scenario work more robustly.

3.5.3 "Annealing" Design

To reconcile the "do what you're trying to do" attitude with a need for a pragmatic "learn as you go" method that supports difficult projects, we use an *annealing* approach: Given the extent of our understanding of the high and low ends of the problem, we initially design something coarse or informal that spans between them, and gradually firm and improve it, allowing it to change as it grows (see Fig. 3.5).

The first step is to make an explicit statement of our goals, as per a top-down design (Section 3.5.1). This "anchors" the design to help keep it from drifting. Next, we sketch out the rest of a top-down design, or we try to build up from the bottom, or we develop some intermediate structures, or we try to do it all at once—whatever seems best for the project at hand. As we build, experiment and learn, we make changes or adjustments as they are needed, at any level of the design.

What keeps annealing design from being merely a jumble is

- **Keeping the top-level goal fixed.** We must be vigilant so that it doesn't slip; as per Section 1.6.

- **Keeping in mind ARI structure.** As we work on and modify the design, we think about each modification and its side effects: Is it an implementation detail? An alternate representation? A shift in the basic abstraction?

- **Identifying changes of representation.** If two parts of the model use different representations, note each representation and how to convert between them.

Notice that having an explicit ARI structure can help debug difficulties by isolating sources of trouble. If our results are unsatisfactory, we can ask: Does the

---

[9]For a discussion of penalty versus discontinuous methods for noninterpenetration of rigid bodies, see [Baraff89]. Also, Appendix C describes a method for handling discontinuities in differential equations.

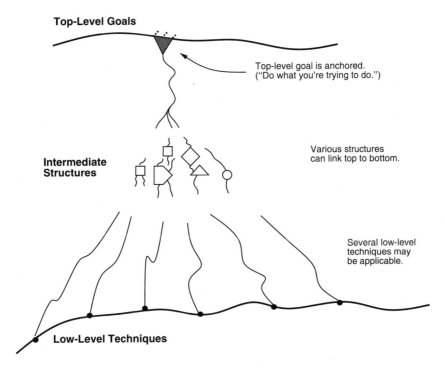

Figure 3.5: "Annealing" design strategy for models. A purely top-down strategy can be unrealistic: It may ignore what is feasible at a low level. A purely bottom-up strategy can be hit-or-miss: It may not achieve the desired goals. We take a mixed approach: We start with a top-level goal, which is fixed. Building upon our knowledge of low-level techniques that are available, we work trying to link the top and bottom, creating appropriate intermediate structures as needed. This design is adaptable: As we use the model and learn more, we may alter our choice of structures and techniques, but the top-level goal remains fixed. If we learn that our top-level goal is infeasible or undesirable, we may choose to "uproot it," i.e., pick a modified, more attainable goal instead—but if so, we consider that to be a new, different model. □

implementation follow the representation? Is the representation insufficient? Is the abstraction missing a property? Maintaining this framework helps ensure that we continue to understand the model as we evolve it.

Sometimes, we may even realize that the problem we're trying to solve isn't the one we *really* want to solve, i.e., we didn't fully understand our goals or requirements. Or sometimes, the problem we're trying to solve is intractable. In either of these cases, we must start over with a different goal. Hopefully, we'll be able to reuse some of the structure that has already been built, but essentially we are working on a different model—thus we like to state the new model explicitly, as per Section 1.6.

Changes of representation are often significant parts of a model. Rather than try to have a single representation that covers everything, we keep a watch for different representations and explicitly describe how to convert between them. This can provide "impedance matching" between various components of a model and can help minimize trivial errors; it will be emphasized for programming physically-based models in Ch. 6 (Figure 6.8 illustrates a sequence of changes of representation in a physically-based modeling program, between a high-level model and its underlying numerical differential equation).

As we work on a model, we can try to identify separable subproblems. Decomposing a problem into smaller subproblems is a very powerful method of managing the complexity of a model. Each subproblem can be designed "recursively," i.e., with its own top-level goal and so forth, using the annealing design method.

Overall, the annealing method is perhaps nothing more than designing in any way that is convenient, but with an extra emphasis on goals and structure (as per Section 1.6). Because of our emphasis on goals, we think of top-down design as the idealized strategy, and annealing design as the pragmatic. The more experience and understanding one has for a given project, or the simpler the project, the more a top-down approach will be viable; but as projects grow in complexity, an annealing design remains effective.

3.6   Communicating a Model to Other People

We often want to describe a model to others: in written form as a paper or article, spoken at a talk or seminar, or informally when chatting with colleagues. We would like our audience to understand us, and we would like to understand them when they ask questions, so that we can properly explain (or defend!) our models.

As discussed in Section 3.2, we find that identifying the ARI structure of a model helps us to understand it. As such, to communicate a model, we find that we can effectively streamline the communication by presenting the model directly in ARI form. When questions arise, it can be helpful to identify which domain the question belongs to, in the same manner as debugging during annealing design (Section 3.5.3). If somebody asks "How come ...?" an answer such as "That's an implementation detail (or artifact)," or "That's inherent in our choice of abstraction," or "That wasn't our goal in building the model," and so forth, can help minimize misunderstandings and circular arguments.

In general, for communication, we find a top-down approach to work the best: First introduce the work with a background or overview, then describe the goals, then the abstraction, then the representation, then the implementation, and end with a wrap-up. Some points that are often worthy of mention:

- Features of the thing being modeled that have been excluded, as well as those that are part of the abstraction

- Refinements that are due to low-level considerations ("For speed of computation, we will assume spherical teapots.")

- The reasons for a particular choice of representation, if many are possible

- The reasons for a particular choice of implementation, if many are possible

The three-part ARI structure can provide a good overview and encapsulation of the model, which is especially suited to a general audience. For an audience familiar with work in the field, who wishes to duplicate the results, it can be effective to follow the various steps of a progressive decomposition. This allows a modular presentation, decomposing the model into various components along the progression, and identifying the changes of representation between them.

3.7   The Role of Computers in Modeling

In the preceding sections, we have avoided mentioning computers, so as not to confuse modeling via computers with the general/intellectual act of modeling. Now, in this section, we discuss how computers fit into the modeling framework that we defined.

A computer model of a thing is, de facto, an implementation of a formal representation. However, there may be a series of changes of representation in the progressive decomposition leading to the computer program, and within the computer program itself a series of changes of representation may be performed until the bottom-level computation is performed.[10]

Based on how much of the progressive decomposition is actually done within the computer program, we define three broad categories of roles of computers: for low-level implementation, for high-level end-user tools, and as a medium for constructing models. The discussion uses numerical simulation as the bottom line (since that is our main interest), but the ideas are intended to be general.

---

[10][Blaauw,Brooks93] takes the view that all computations by computer inherently involve a series of changes of representation, with computation done at the lowest level, and the results transformed back up to the higher levels of representation.

3.7.1   Modeling by Hand

Computers are well known for their ability to do "number crunching," i.e., numerically solving mathematical equations: A scientist creates some formulas and then writes a program to do the number crunching.

Using the terminology of Section 2.4, we would say that the scientist does the "modeling," and the computer is used for "simulation." Using this chapter's terminology, the human performs various steps of abstraction and representation, and a computer program is written to execute the final step of implementation. Since the human does the bulk of the modeling manually, we refer to this as *modeling by hand* (see Fig. 3.6).

Example: A pendulum, modeled by hand

Consider modeling a planar ideal pendulum, as described in Fig. 3.4—this is a standard introductory physics problem. We follow the example in [Marion70, p. 159ff] to illustrate modeling by hand:

- Solution #1: Our intuition tells us that "the gravitational force acts, of course, in the downward direction, but the component of this force which influences the motion is that which is *perpendicular* to the support rod. This force component is ... $F(\theta) = -mg \sin\theta$. ... The equation of motion of the plane pendulum is most easily obtained by equating the torque about the support axis to the product of the angular acceleration and the moment of inertia about the same axis." This leads to the differential equation $\ddot{\theta} + \omega_0^2 \sin\theta = 0$; one can assume small angles and approximate the system with a simple harmonic oscillator.

- Solution #2: Alternatively, "if we wish to obtain the general result ... we can ... obtain a solution by considering the energy of the system rather than by solving the equation of motion." This eventually leads to the period of oscillation as an elliptic integral.

- Solution #3: A third approach is to derive the behavior using Lagrangian dynamics in generalized coordinates; this quickly leads to the same equations.

After obtaining equations of motion using one of the above approaches, a computer program can be written to solve the equations numerically.

The use of a computer as an implementation medium has good features: It can be relatively straightforward to write the simulation programs—many utilities such as numerical software packages exist to support such programs—and scientists can be skilled at doing the modeling. Thus this approach often follows the principle of "let the computer do what computers are good at, and let the humans do what humans are good at."

Modeling by hand, however, suffers from the difficulties that motivated the discussion in Section 2.4: It places a large burden on the human, and the results

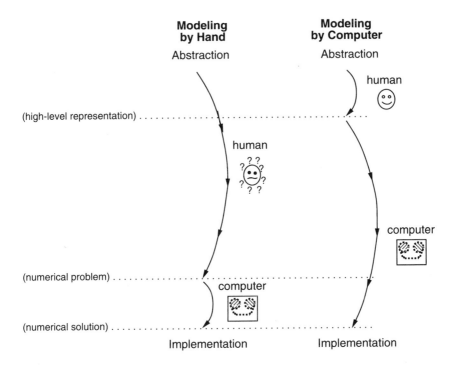

Figure 3.6: Modeling by hand versus by computer. The traditional use of a computer is as an implementation medium: The human performs all the modeling tasks up through posing a low-level problem—such as a numerical problem—and a computer program is written to solve that problem. For more complex models, the computer needs to take a larger share of the task: The human would specify the formal problem at a relatively high level, and the computer would perform various refinements of representation leading to posing and then solving the low-level problem. □

typically are not reusable or extensible. As the models get increasingly complex, it becomes harder for a human to carry out the modeling steps down to so low a level. In the above example, a great deal of effort and intuition goes into hand-derivation of equations even for simple physical systems. Deriving the equations of motion of more intricate systems will become yet harder; the complexity of the equations might grow quickly with the size of the model. If, instead of the simple pendulum above, we were to model a multiple-link compound pendulum, i.e., a chain, suspended from both ends, the equations would be unwieldy.[11] Additionally, once the equations are derived for any given model, the simulation program still remains to be written—and it will be specific to that model.

Thus, while modeling by hand may be suitable for simple models, we feel that for complex models, this method becomes untenable.

---

[11]We do in fact model a suspended, multiple-link chain, in Ch. 12—but not by hand.

3.7.2   Modeling by Computer

In the previous section, we said that modeling by hand puts too much of a burden on the human. At the other extreme, we want to let the computer do all the work. Ideally, we might want the human to start with the high-level abstraction and tell it to the computer with as little effort as possible. The computer would choose a representation and implementation and proceed directly to the simulation of the model. In the general case, this is as yet unfeasible. But considering the progressive decomposition of modeling into a series of steps, we can try to push the computer's role higher: have the human take fewer steps, and the computer more steps (see Fig. 3.6).

For a given domain, a generic representation of a high level of abstraction can be supported by a computer program. Given that high level, the computer can perform the various steps of change of representation and directly implement the result. We refer to this as *modeling by computer.*

This approach leads to tools such as CAD workstations, expert systems, and so forth. Our "Dynamic Constraints" work ([Barzel,Barr88], see also Ch. 11) supports modeling by computer for the domain of simple rigid-body systems; the following example follows the dynamic constraints method:

Example: A pendulum, modeled by computer

We again examine the pendulum of Fig. 3.4, this time modeling by computer. The user specifies the representation to the computer, at a fairly high level:

1. There is a particle of mass m.

2. It is constrained to move on a sphere of radius r.

3. It is influenced by gravity, no other external forces.

The computer takes over from there, assembling the appropriate equations, then numerically solving them to simulate the behavior of the model. Note the computer uses implicit knowledge of rigid-body mechanics. We have successfully used this approach to model and simulate a 10-link chain suspended from its two ends, as well as other constrained rigid-body models ([Caltech87]).

Modeling by computer has an assortment of good features:

√ The human doesn't have to be an expert about the thing being modeled. Notice in the above example that the human need only have knowledge of the concepts such as "particle," "constraint," etc., but need not have intimacy with the precise equations of motion, nor the intuition to choose the proper formulation (such as torque balance) or mathematical approach (such as Lagrangian dynamics).

√ Whether or not the human is knowledgeable about the thing being modeled, the human doesn't have to handle all the details. In particular, as the physical system being modeled becomes more complex, the human's task continues to be merely to describe the high-level model directly to the computer; the creation of the equations of motion, with their burgeoning complexity, is handled by the computer.

√ The computer can choose the representation based on conditions, or can keep multiple representations. Additionally, the computer can choose between different implementations based on conditions.

However, there are some drawbacks to high-level end-user modeling programs:

× Lack of flexibility. Such programs will typically have a limited domain of applicability; users may often want to create or control models in ways that are beyond the range of capabilities of the program. In particular, if the users *are* experts, they may know what they want better than the program.

× Hard to extend. The program may itself be complex enough that it's difficult to add new features.

× Who's going to write the program? And how will he or she do it? Although the user of the program need not be an expert about the problem domain, the author of the program often must be.[12]

A side note on high-level modeling tools: If the tool does the job well enough, one might argue that the human's task of specifying the formal representation to the computer is the "real" modeling—what the computer does is still just the implementation, just sophisticated simulation or number crunching. That's OK; as discussed in Section 3.4, the choice of what's what is often a matter of perspective. If the question becomes worthy of debate, we should take it as a good sign about the quality of computer tools for modeling.

---

[12] See **Danny Dunn and the Homework Machine** [Williams,Abrashkin58].

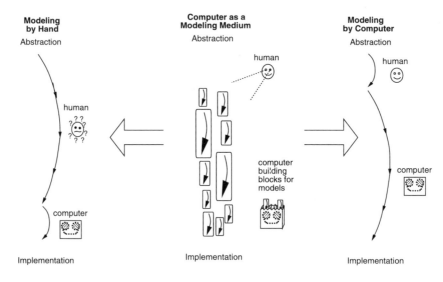

Figure 3.7: The computer as a modeling medium. Rather than interacting with a single program that supports only a specific class of models, the human can build models directly. A library of computer building blocks is used as the material from which the model is built. These building blocks perform various steps of the progressive refinement from abstraction to implementation. If only low-level tools are used this approach is similar to modeling by hand; while if high-enough-level tools are used the approach becomes similar to, and can be used to implement, modeling by computer. Part III and Appendix B describe a collection of building blocks for rigid-body modeling, that we put together modularly to construct a model of a multiple-link chain in Ch. 12; these building blocks start at a low level, but when they are all put together the model in Ch. 12 is specified at a fairly high level. □

3.7.3 The Computer as a Modeling Medium

Modeling by hand (with a low-level computer implementation, as per Section 3.7.1) and modeling by computer (Section 3.7.2) are commonly done today. Both have the problem of inflexibility: The human is limited to models that are supported by the computer program; to make different models one must rewrite the program, which is often a major task. An alternative use of the computer is as a medium for modeling—a human designs and builds a model manually, but does so using computer building blocks.

"The computer as a modeling medium" is an ornate way of describing software libraries and environments providing tools, such as modules and objects, that perform various steps of refinement of representation and implementation for various problem domains. The human builds models by piecing together such modules. Additionally, more complex modules can be built based on simpler ones and added to the environment.

Notice that this computer medium approach spans the ground between modeling by hand and by computer: If the tools used are low-level number-crunching tools, the modeling is being done by hand as per Section 3.7.1; but as the tools get increasingly sophisticated, the human's role gets increasingly high-level, as per Section 3.7.2.

This approach shares many advantages of the two extreme methods: The human's expertise in model creation is exploited; existing software (such as numerical libraries) can be exploited; the computer tools can handle the details of growth of complexity. The human can pick and choose the tools that are used, can have high-level support from the computer when needed, or can dive in and craft the details when appropriate.

An additional advantage of this approach is that the environment can be modular and extensible, allowing flexibility in the models that are built and reuse of components of models in future models.

A drawback of the computer medium approach is that to a certain extent it requires the humans to have expertise both in the problem domain and in manipulating the medium, i.e., be both scientists and programmers. (Or, perhaps, scientists and programmers could work together to create the models.)

And, of course, there's no escaping making the tools, which requires designing, debugging, and so forth. But here, the individual tools are presumably small, with well-defined functions, so they will be relatively easy to write and get working. As well, tools can be built modularly and hierarchically so that new tools can take advantage of existing ones.

In principle, one might design a modeling environment that is geared directly toward using the computer as a modeling medium for some problem domain. But for our purposes, we will assume a standard programming environment, in which we will define fundamental building blocks that programmers can use to build high-level tools (such as a modeling environment, or a "modeling by computer" workstation as per Section 3.7.2). Chapter 6 defines a framework for this approach, for the domain of physically-based computer graphics models.[13]

3.8   Summary

This chapter reflects the fundamental philosophy of structured modeling: encouraging a basic structuring of ideas. Just as structured programming attempts to eliminate "spaghetti code," we are trying to eliminate "spaghetti concepts."

We have provided two related ways of decomposing a model: into a canonical abstraction–representation–implementation form (Section 3.1), suited to describ-

---

[13]The modular, building-block approach to program design and implementation is essentially that of object-oriented programming. The framework discussed in Ch. 6 and the prototype environment discussed in Appendix B make extensive use of object-oriented tools and techniques. See [Goldberg,Robson89] for a discussion of Smalltalk, a seminal object-oriented programming language, and [Booch91] for discussion of basic concepts of object-oriented design and programming.

ing extant models; and into a progressive decomposition from cognitive notions to explicit entities (Section 3.3), suited to describing the development of models. These decompositions reflect structures that we believe are inherent in all models. By explicitly identifying these structures, we hope to be more effective at discussing and analyzing models and the modeling process, and thus ultimately to be more effective at creating models of increased complexity.

Section 3.5 presented a brief discussion of design strategies for models; that discussion is perhaps a primitive distillation of the vast field of software engineering. However, in the realm of modeling it is not currently common to think of designing models in terms analogous to designing software. We emphasized an "annealing" method as being an effective combination of our goal-oriented approach (as per Section 1.6) with a common need to learn-by-doing as we build complex models.

A discussion of the use of computers in the creation of models (Section 3.7) identified two extremes: modeling by hand, in which the model designer does the brunt of the work manually, and modeling by computer, in which monolithic programs try to automate the modeling process. We settled on an intermediate role, in which the computer would provide simple building blocks from which complex models could be built.

The ideas in this chapter are admittedly and intentionally somewhat abstract and vague. Our intention has not been to provide a "cookbook" or "magic bullet" for modeling, but rather to try to gain a basic understanding of what modeling is about. Thus, although we can't eliminate the work that is needed in order to create models, we can hope to streamline the process by providing a vocabulary and mental framework.

Chapter 4 refines the ideas in this chapter, and makes them more concrete, for the domain of physically-based modeling.

Related Work

[Brooks91], like us, talks about design of models from a software engineering viewpoint. [Boehm88] discusses a "spiral" model for software design, similar to our annealing method in its restart-from-the-top attitude, but it is based on risks rather than goals. Software engineering design methods are generally broad in scope, addressing management of huge software projects, as opposed to our focus on design in the small. [Booch91, Ch. 6] describes a "round-trip gestalt" method for object-oriented program design that is similar to our annealing method in its learn-as-you-go attitude, but it does not share our emphasis on goals and structure.

[Blaauw,Brooks93] has a view similar to ours of a computer performing a series of changes of representation.

[Crow87] contains a geometric model of a teapot, as well as a discussion of the history of the teapot in computer graphics. □

Chapter 4

Structured Physically-Based Modeling

The previous chapter describes a general-purpose framework and analysis of modeling—but we're specifically interested in physically-based modeling. We want a more concrete structure that will help us to design these models and, in particular, to design complex models in a reusable manner.

Thus this chapter echoes Ch. 3, but focuses on physically-based modeling. The ideas of the abstraction–representation–implementation (ARI) structure and progression are combined with a paradigm of mathematical modeling to yield a canonical structure for physically-based models. This structure is suited to a modular, hierarchical approach to the design of models, an approach that is familiar from structured programming.

The emphasis in this chapter is on the design or specification of physically-based models, as opposed to their implementation. Our approach is to develop and discuss a model on a blackboard, i.e., create a *blackboard model*, before implementing it in a computer program. The framework developed here, however, is carried over directly to the design of programs, in Ch. 6.

This chapter might seem somewhat theoretical; to see the methods "in use," the reader is encouraged to skim the models described in Part III. (Note however that the techniques and notation used for the mathematical subparts of the models in Part III are not defined until Ch. 5.)

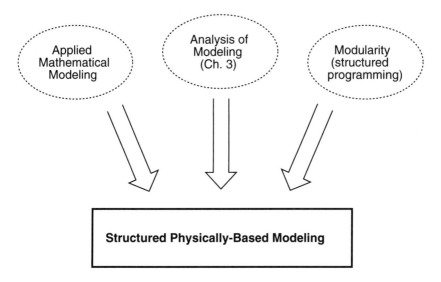

Figure 4.1: Structured physically-based modeling derives from merging applied mathematics' methodology for modeling with the structured analysis of modeling that was developed in Ch. 3. The result
is a structure tailored and specific to physically-based models. The structure is defined so as to allow
a modular, hierarchical design of models in a manner analogous to structured programming. □

4.1   Overview

A physically-based model includes physical characteristics of the thing being
modeled (Section 3.1.1) and specifies its behavior via mathematical equations.
Thus a large component of physically-based modeling is *mathematical modeling*.
As per Ch. 3, we want to organize models into well-defined canonical parts, but
here we include a mathematical modeling slant and an emphasis on modularity
(see Fig. 4.1).

The underlying structure of a physically-based model is independent of its
computer implementation. We will therefore talk mostly about the design of
blackboard models, i.e., models that are worked out on paper or on blackboards,[1]
without being tied to programming details. Thus we take the model-designer's
view of the ARI decomposition (Section 3.2):The "model" includes the high-level
plans, but we de-emphasize the implementation details.

We are ultimately interested in computer simulation of our models, so the
ideas developed here are intended to be practical and implementable—indeed, the
computer program design discussed in Ch. 6 follows directly from the structure
in this chapter. Moreover, Ch. 6 assumes that a blackboard design of a model

---

[1]We use the term *blackboard models* rather than *paper models* so that the models are not thought
of as paper tigers or origami.

has been worked out before the model is transferred to a computer; the models
described in Part III are designed in such a manner.[2]

Note that the discussion in this chapter does not make a heavy distinction
between a *model* (such as a teapot or space shuttle) and a *modeling technique*
(such as a particular constraint method). In particular, for the approach we will be
discussing, models will be assembled from building blocks, or "modules," which
can in turn be built from smaller modules. All the modules in this hierarchy will
be designed in the same basic style, be they low-level tools or the top-level model.

4.2   Background: Applied Mathematical Modeling

We present here a brief discussion of mathematical modeling as it
is done by applied mathematicians,
in order to provide background for
the physically-based modeling strategy of Section 4.3.   This discussion is distilled from the ideas in
[Boyce81].

Figure 4.2 shows the sequence
of steps that make up mathematical
modeling. To illustrate the steps, we
consider the following simple (triv-

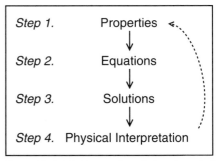

Figure 4.2: Methodology of applied mathematical
modeling. These steps are discussed in the text. □

ial) problem: "How long does it take for a falling ball to hit the ground?" We will
make a model of the physical system and use that model to predict an answer to
this question (see Fig. 4.3).

Step 1. Choose properties to include in the model.   Doing so typically involves
    making simplifying assumptions. For our example, we assume horizontal
    motion is irrelevant; gravity provides a constant downward acceleration g;
    friction is irrelevant; and the ball starts at rest. We will examine the height
    of the ball as a function of time $z(t)$.

Step 2. Create equations for the behavior.   These are the *mathematical model*. For
    our example, we have the differential equation:

$$\frac{d^2}{dt^2} z(t) + g = 0$$
$$\frac{d}{dt} z(t)\Big|_{t=0} = 0$$

---

[2]Of course, as per the annealing design paradigm of Section 3.5.3, we don't expect a blackboard
model to work perfectly the first time it is implemented; the blackboard model will typically be modified
and updated as the implementation is developed.

The equations must be well defined; we don't want any ambiguity or contradictions. The equations can be manipulated and transformed, are subject to proofs, and so forth.

Step 3. Solve the equations. The above differential equation yields the following closed-form expression: $z(t) = z(0) - gt^2/2$. Given an initial value of $z(0) = h$, we find that $z(t) = 0$ when $t = \sqrt{2h/g}$.

Step 4. Determine the physical interpretation of the solution. How do the results relate to the thing being modeled? What is the mathematics telling us? We can make qualitative or numerical predictions. In the example, we see that balls that start higher will take longer to hit, and if gravity were stronger, balls would hit sooner; quantitatively, if the initial height is 3 meters and gravitational acceleration is 9.8 meters/second^2, then the ball will hit in approximately .78 seconds.

(Repeat.) If the results aren't sufficient for our needs, we might start again based on what we have learned. For example, if measurements show that bigger balls take longer to hit, we might choose to include some additional properties, such as mass of the ball and air resistance that depends on the size of the ball, then update the equations, and so on.

The power of this methodology lies in the well-defined mathematical model. Once the equations have been defined, we can draw on the vast body of mathematical knowledge to manipulate them and to solve problems. The equations stand by themselves, irrespective of what the particular problem is. For example, the equation $\frac{d^2}{dt^2}z(t) + g = 0$ in step 2 could perhaps have been derived for a traffic flow model instead of a mechanics problem—it makes no mathematical difference.

One might notice a correspon-

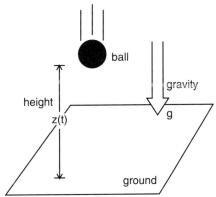

Figure 4.3: A falling ball, used in the text to illustrate the applied mathematical modeling procedure of Fig. 4.2. □

dence between this applied mathematical modeling approach and the ARI structure of a model described in Ch. 3. The correspondence is not accidental[3] and will enter into the discussion in the next sections.

---

[3] The ARI structure was defined by attempting to generalize the mathematical modeling approach.

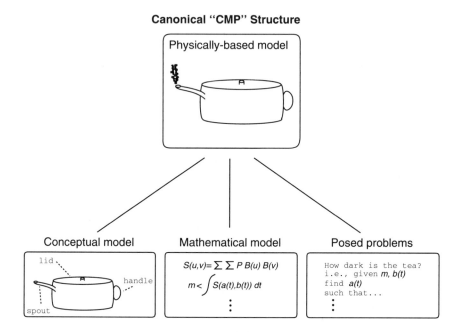

Figure 4.4: Canonical structure of a physically-based model. The conceptual model describes the physical properties of the thing being modeled. The mathematical model is a collection of equations for the behavior of the model. The posed problems include conceptual statements of tasks to be performed, as well as the corresponding mathematical problems. We call this partition the *CMP structure*. □

4.3 Canonical "CMP" Structure of a Physically-Based Model

To a large extent, physically-based modeling is an application of mathematical modeling. Because of the power of the applied mathematical modeling methodology, we strive to build that methodology into our idea of a physically-based model. We thus partition a physically-based model into three distinct parts:

- the *conceptual model,*
- the *mathematical model,* and
- the *posed problems,*

where the parts correspond with the four steps in Section 4.2. We call this partition the conceptual–mathematical–posed-problem structure, or *CMP* structure for short (see Fig. 4.4).

4.3.1   The Conceptual Model ("C")

The *conceptual model* is a description of the properties, features, characteristics, etc., of the thing being modeled, as per step 1 of Section 4.2. According to the ARI terminology of Ch. 3, it is a statement of the abstraction.[4]

In addition to properties that underlie the mathematics, the conceptual model may also contain other information about the thing being modeled. For example, in addition to having terms such as mass and momentum that enter into a mathematical description of classical rigid-body motion, a conceptual model of a dynamic rigid body for computer graphics, would have terms such as surface color and specularity, which do not enter into the equations of motion.

4.3.2   The Mathematical Model ("M")

The *mathematical model* that is part of a CMP structure is directly adopted from mathematical modeling, the result of step 2 in Section 4.2. It is a collection of mathematical equations that describe the behavior of the model. The equations are "context free"—purely mathematical expressions that are complete without needing properties or definitions from the conceptual model. There is of course a correspondence with the conceptual model, but that correspondence is in the mind of the designer of the model, rather than inherent in the mathematics.

Note that we distinguish between a mathematical model and a "math problem": The equations in the model are not "problems" but rather *predicates,* i.e., statements of relationships between entities in the model. For example, the expression

$$\frac{d}{dt}y(t) = f(y(t), t)$$

simply states that the quantity on the left, the rate of change of $y(t)$, is equal to the quantity on the right, the value of $f(\ldots)$. Various problems *could* be posed around the statement—such as an initial-value problem, a boundary-value problem, or testing measured data for agreement—but we don't consider those to be part of the mathematical model (see Fig. 4.5).[5] Phrased from a computer science point of view, the mathematical model is *declarative* rather than *procedural* (this is discussed in Section 5.5.2).

In addition to equations, a mathematical model includes definitions of the terms that go into the equations. For the above example, we would define y to be a

---

[4]Being a statement of the abstraction, it is thus a representation. For a blackboard model, the conceptual model is just a description in words, so the representation is informal; for computer programs (Ch. 6), we have a formal representation as a data structure.

[5]Since we distinguish equations from problems, from our point of view the common phrase *to solve an equation* (such as we used in step 3 of Section 4.2) is unrigorous. We take it to be slang for *to solve the problem that is implied by an equation,* presupposing that only a single problem is implied in the current context.

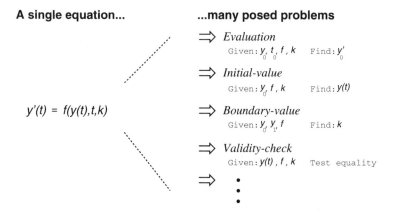

A single equation...　　　　　　**...many posed problems**

$\Rightarrow$ *Evaluation*

Given: y_0, t_0, f, k　　Find: y'_0

$\Rightarrow$ *Initial-value*

Given: y_0, f, k　　Find: $y(t)$

$y'(t) = f(y(t), t, k)$　　　　　$\Rightarrow$ *Boundary-value*

Given: y_0, y_1, f　　Find: k

$\Rightarrow$ *Validity-check*

Given: $y(t)$, f, k　　Test equality

$\Rightarrow$ •
•
•

Figure 4.5: A single mathematical equation or model can lend itself to many posed problems. In this case, a differential equation describes a relationship between various quantities; there are many combinations of knowns and unknowns, which lead to various canonical problems. □

real-valued function of one real argument, f to be a real-valued function of two real arguments, and t to be a real number. It is also often convenient to define named properties, e.g., "a function $T(x)$ is said to be *frumious* when $|T(x)| < x^2 \ldots$"

Creating a mathematical model is not necessarily easy. Note that we don't try to define models that are "minimal"; a model may include any or all definitions and equations that are convenient. For physically-based modeling, we have a set of goals, strategies, and techniques that are relevant, which we discuss in Ch. 5.

4.3.3　The Posed Problems ("P")

We typically want a physically-based model to *do* something, such as make a prediction or simulate some behavior. Mathematically, this translates into solving some problem, as per step 3 of Section 4.2. Thus the third part of a physically-based model, once we've defined the conceptual and mathematical models, is the collection of *posed problems*.

Each posed problem includes both a conceptual notion of a task to perform and the corresponding mathematical problem. The mathematical problems list which terms from the mathematical model have known values, which are unknown, which equations from the mathematical model come into play, and so forth. Sometimes, the mathematical problems may be solved analytically, but in general for physically-based modeling, we will pose problems to be solved numerically, via computer.

The problems can often be stated in a standard canonical form, e.g., as an initial-value differential equation problem: "Find $Y(t)$ where $Y' = f(Y, t)$, given f and the initial value Y_0 at t_0." Notice that, unlike the mathematical model, posed problems are often procedural, e.g., "given x, express y as a function of it, then find z such that. . . ." In general, the problems should be mathematically well posed.[6]

4.3.4   Implementation and Physical Interpretation

To implement a physically-based model, i.e., to make predictions or simulations, we need to solve the posed problems. But how to solve them? We don't offer any specific insights here—that's what the fields of applied mathematics and numerical analysis are about (see, e.g., [Lin,Segel74], [Zwillinger89], [Ralston, Rabinowitz78]). There is also a large body of knowledge and software for solving numerical problems on computers (e.g., [Press *et al.*86], [NAG]). Computer tools exist as well to help with mathematical manipulation and numerical problem solution (e.g., [Wolfram91]).

Most often, the designer of a model has some ideas about how to solve the posed problems; notes along these lines can accompany a description of CMP structure as part of a blackboard model. Given a blackboard model and solution ideas, one can write a special-purpose program that numerically solves the posed problems; this would be an example of modeling by hand, as per Section 3.7.1. Chapter 6 discusses a more general program framework in which to embed the entire CMP structure.

Once a model has been implemented and has produced results, we need to interpret those results, as per step 4 of Section 4.2. The posed problems describe the conceptual tasks that correspond with the mathematical problems, helping one to relate the numerical solutions back to the conceptual model. But ultimately, physical interpretation—how the results relate to the thing being modeled—is a process that is undertaken by the designer or user of the model.

4.4   Discussion of the CMP Structure

4.4.1   CMP and ARI

Just as the ARI structure of Ch. 3 helps us to understand models, we have found that separating the conceptual, mathematical, and posed-problem sections of physically-based modeling techniques makes it easier to understand them. When we read a new article that discusses a model or modeling technique, or when we come up with an idea of our own, it is instructive to ask questions analogous to those in Section 3.2:

---

[6]That is, each problem has a solution that exists, is unique, and depends smoothly on the known values ([Nihon Sugakkai77]).

CMP Structure
(as changes of representation)

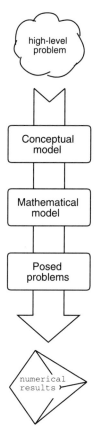

Figure 4.6: The CMP structure of a physically-based model relates to the ARI progression of Ch. 3 (Fig. 3.3). The conceptual model is a statement of the abstraction; the mathematical model is a representation of the behavior; the numerical problems implement a simulation of the model. Taken together, the three parts of the physically-based model can be looked at as a series of changes of representation from a cognitive problem to a numerical simulation. □

- "What is the model or technique trying to do?" (conceptual model)

- "What are the underlying equations?" (mathematical model)

- "What are the knowns and unknowns?" (posed problems)

- "What are the solution techniques?" (implementation)

The CMP structure corresponds closely with the ARI structure: The conceptual model, as we said earlier, is a statement of the abstraction; the mathematical model is a formal representation of the behavior of the model; and the model is implemented (simulated) by solving the posed problems.

We can also view the CMP structure as a sequence of changes of representation, or an ARI progression (see Fig. 4.6). The conceptual model is a representation (albeit informal, in words) of the abstraction. We can transform from the conceptual properties, plus an understanding of the behavior being modeled, to a mathematical representation, i.e., the mathematical model. The posed problems are an alternate representation derived from both the conceptual and mathematical models—this time an "active," task-based representation, rather than "passive" or description-based.

Note that, as mentioned earlier, the conceptual model may contain information that doesn't enter into the mathematical model, thus the transformation from conceptual to mathematical may "throw out" some information. Similarly, the posed problems may not use all the information available in the mathematical model. Note also that the posed problems don't derive directly from the conceptual and mathematical models, but also include our ideas of what we want to do with the model.

4.4.2   Why Separate the Numerical Techniques?

The CMP structure doesn'tbother to include numerical techniques; they are left as implementation details. But sometimes numerical manipulation is presented as an inherent part of a model or method. For example, modeling techniques are sometimes described in ways such as:

> For each frame,[7] update the body positions by adding the velocities. . . .

This description has some appeal: The physical interpretation is immediate; one can intuit why the results are plausible; and it is straightforward to implement. Notice that it mingles the numerical manipulation with the conceptual and mathematical models, as well as with the posed problems. The properties of the body and the animation, a differential equation of motion, and Euler's method for solving an initial-value problem are all stated at once.

Despite the appeals of such mingling, we feel it is best to make a clear separation between the statement of a model and the numerical techniques used to solve the posed mathematical problems.

The most pragmatic reason for the separation is that stating a numerical problem in canonical form allows one to take advantage of existing tools and knowledge. There are many numerical routines, libraries, books, and lore upon which one can

---

[7] An animation *frame* is a single image of the sequence that forms the animation.

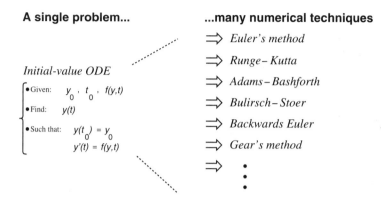

Figure 4.7: A single problem can often be solved by many different numerical techniques. In this case, there is a variety of solvers for initial-value ODE problems; the choice depends on issues such as accuracy, stiffness, speed, ease of implementation, and so forth. The availability of such techniques, and the ability to suit a numerical technique to the particulars of a given problem, are primary reasons not to hardwire a specific technique into one's physically-based model. □

draw, e.g., [Press *et al.*86], [Ralston,Rabinowitz78], [NAG]. There are often tools available that are more robust than the intuitive techniques; for example Euler's method is known to be less accurate than others and unstable for stiff equations ([Press *et al.*86, Ch. 15]).

Furthermore, if the particular numerical solution technique is not *hardwired* into the model, one can choose the technique that is appropriate to the particular circumstances of the problem. For example (see also Fig. 4.7):

> For up to moderately-sized problems, [we use] a Choleski-type matrix factorization procedure.... For large problems [we use] iterative methods such as successive over-relaxation.... Multi-grid methods ... have served well in the largest of our simulations. [Terzopoulos,Fleischer88, p. 275]

Finally, keeping the numerical technique separate helps insure that implementation details such as step sizes, error tolerances, and so forth, don't have significant effects on the conceptual behavior. For example, while we can accept that higher error tolerances may produce less accurate simulations, if we decide to animate at a different frame rate, we wouldn't want to get qualitatively different behavior;[8] see also Fig. 4.8.

Separation of numerical solution techniques from the body of the model is not unique to our CMP structure. In practice it is done quite frequently (hence the existence of the field of numerical analysis). The CMP structure itself, however, is not typically emphasized; the next sections expand on the reasons for the partition.

---

[8]For example, we want the same results whether we make a film (24 frames per second) or a videotape (30 frames per second).

4.4.3   Why Separate Problems from Equations?

The distinction between equations and problems, which we emphasize in Section 4.3.2, may seem like hairsplitting or sophistry. Perhaps interesting to academics, but where is the practical benefit?

The primary benefit is in extensibility and reusability of models. As mentioned earlier, a single mathematical model can imply many numerical problems; if the numerical problems aren't hardwired into the model, we can have the opportunity later to pose modified or new problems.

For example, in our own earlier work [Barzel,Barr88], we hardwired a specific numerical problem into our model: We described the motion of rigid bodies as an initial-value ODE expressed in terms of linear and angular momenta (among other things), with the linear and angular velocities defined as "auxiliary" variables to be computed once the momenta have been determined. After a small amount of experience, we realized that it would be easier for the user if we could specify initial conditions in terms of the velocities rather than the momenta. Unfortunately, because the model (and hence the computer program) had the momenta hardwired as the "more primitive" representation, it required some inelegant patching of the computer program to insert appropriate velocity-to-momentum conversion routines. The mathematical rigid-body model in Ch. 10 of this work, on the other hand, merely describes the relationship between the velocities and momenta, without preferring one to the other; the resulting computer implementation naturally supports user specification of either.

Another reason for the separation of the mathematical model from posed problems is the declarative/procedural distinction between them. Being purely declarative helps make the mathematical model more robust, as is discussed in Ch. 5. And the declarative/procedural distinction is significant to the design of programs to implement physically-based models, as is discussed in Ch. 6.

Note that there is often mathematical manipulation as part of solving a given problem. It is thus possible for ambiguity to exist between an equation that "should" be part of the mathematical model, and one that is "merely" an intermediate result in an analytic solution. For example, many analysis problems are solved via eigenvalues; should the eigenvalue–eigenvector equation be included in the mathematical model? Such questions require judgment calls on the part of the designer of the model. Our general tendency, however, is to include all such equations in the mathematical model; if the equations arise for one posed problem, they may also arise for some later problem, thus we may as well state them up front. Additionally, these equations often have interesting physical interpretations, and thus it can help our understanding of the overall model to include them explicitly. If the intermediate equations are only approximations, however, we are more hesitant to include them in the model (see Fig. 4.8).

Various CMP Decompositions for Flexible-Body Simulation

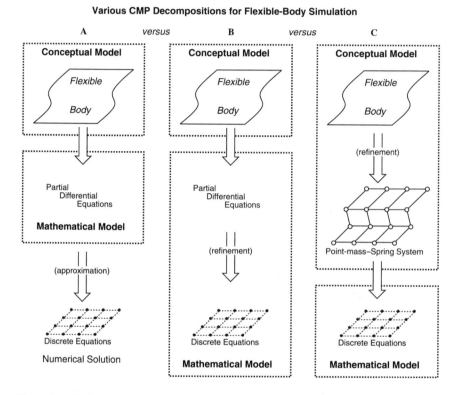

Figure 4.8: Choices in the CMP structure. Example problem: simulating the motion of a flexible body. A flexible body can be described mathematically as a continuous surface governed by partial differential equations (PDEs). PDE solutions are typically approximated by discretizing, yielding numerically soluble equations. We illustrate three ways of organizing the CMP structure:

A. The conceptual model is a flexible body; the mathematical model is a continuous surface; the solution technique requires discretization.

B. The mathematical model includes a refinement to discrete equations.

C. The conceptual model includes a refinement to a mass-point–spring system.

Version *A* is the "cleanest": The numerical solver can automatically/adaptively adjust parameters such as discretization transparently to the high levels of the model, or other solvers can be used. At the other extreme, version *C* has discretization artifacts hardwired into the model (often mixed with other details such as polygonalization for rendering), thus changing solution parameters requires altering the high-level model. Version *C* is in fact used frequently, however, because of its expedience (it can be simple to implement on top of existing rigid-body simulation systems) and mathematical simplicity (there are no PDEs). Flexible bodies are discussed further in Section 14.5. □

4.4.4 Why Separate Concepts from Mathematics?

Having equations that stand alone—without conceptual context—is a source of the power of applied mathematical modeling, as discussed in Section 4.2. This is thus our primary reason for making an explicit distinction between the conceptual and mathematical models.

There are additional benefits incurred by the separation, however. As mentioned in Section 4.3.1, there are properties of the thing being modeled that are important to our overall model but that don't fit into the mathematical model; such properties have a home in the conceptual model.[9] The conceptual model, since it is just a statement in words, can include vague or fuzzy concepts, while the mathematical model must be precise.

The precise nature of the mathematical model lets us examine it for inconsistency, insufficiency, singularities, and so forth. Finding such irregularities in the mathematics can often give us insight into the conceptual model and help identify parts of the overall model that we had neglected conceptually. For example, singularities in a constraint equation can imply physically unrealizable configurations, and having too few quantities to create a well-posed problem implies that our conceptual model isn't rich enough to do what we want. The precision of the mathematical model similarly helps in explaining and debugging a model, as we discuss in Section 4.6.4.

Note that the separation between the concepts and the mathematics can sometimes be hard to specify. For some applications, especially scientific or technical ones, the concepts can be inherently mathematical, e.g., a rigid body's conceptual shape may have a mathematical definition, such as a cone or a sphere. Also, we may introduce a refinement into a model that can be at the conceptual, mathematical, or problem-solution/numerical levels. For example, motion of a flexible body is typically simulated by discretization methods; the discretization might be conceptual, mathematical, or numerical, as illustrated in Fig. 4.8.

4.5 Modularity and Hierarchy

The CMP structure helps us to organize our thoughts about what's what in a model, helps us to understand the mathematical and numerical behavior, and so forth. But CMP doesn't directly address the question of how to handle big models. We need a way to manage their complexity, even within the CMP structure. That's where modularity and hierarchy come in.

Modularity means that we build separate, loosely connected components with well-defined boundaries and interfaces. *Hierarchy* means that each module can

---

[9] In some cases, too, the mathematical model has terms or degrees of freedom that don't map directly back to anything in the conceptual model, e.g., as gauge transformations in classical electromagnetic field theory ([Landau,Lifshitz75]).

Modular Hierarchy of Models

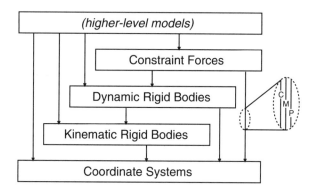

Figure 4.9: Modularity in physically-based models. Individual modules are defined for parts of the overall model domain. Each module may make use of or build on lower-level models for concepts, mathematics, and/or posed problems. The diagram illustrates a hierarchy of modules that describe various aspects of rigid-body motion (the hierarchy corresponds with the prototype library in Part III). □

be built by putting together or invoking simpler modules. These techniques let us work on complex problems by a "divide-and-conquer" approach, breaking down a large problem into simpler ones that are easy to comprehend. At the higher levels, one can focus on the interaction between the modular parts without worrying about the details within them. Furthermore, the modular parts can be reusable—commonly used parts can be designed "once and for all" and kept in public libraries, so that their usage can be consistent, and so that designers won't have to repeatedly reinvent them.

The above is well known from programming, but it applies equally to blackboard physically-based models.[10] Figure 4.9 illustrates a decomposition of rigid-body modeling into separate modules; dynamic rigid bodies, for example, are built from kinematic bodies, but with additional properties such as mass, and their motion is prescribed by Newton's laws.

So how do we make and include modules using the CMP framework? For blackboard models, it's easy: Mostly, just say it's modular, and it's modular—we have no formal mechanisms to deal with. That is, the conceptual model, being just words, can refer in words to concepts from another module, e.g., a high-level model in Fig. 4.9 can say "the swingarm moves as a dynamic rigid body . . . "; the mathematical model of one module can define its quantities and equations in terms

---

[10]If we design our blackboard models modularly, it will then be straightforward to make modular program implementations. This is discussed in Ch. 6.

of those from another module;[11] and a posed problem of one module can require solving a subproblem from another module.

Notice that there's typically parallel modularity and hierarchy in the conceptual–mathematical–posed-problem parts. For example, if one refers to concepts of dynamic rigid bodies, one will typically need to refer also to the corresponding mathematical equations, and one will often pose standard problems. Thus we group all three parts of a CMP structure into a single package or module. Ultimately, we'd like to define libraries of standard, general-purpose CMP modules that can be used repeatedly in many complex modeling tasks; Part III defines a simple prototype library for the domain of rigid-body modeling.

Modularity is a simple concept—there's not really very much that we have to say about it here. It isn't hard to design and build models in a modular manner. What's mostly needed is to *decide* to design models modularly; then, while doing the designs, one pays attention to issues such as generality, ease of use by others, and so forth, that are familiar to most structured programmers.

4.6   Designing a Model

This section discusses some issues for designing a model, i.e., a CMP module. Note that we don't make much of a distinction between "top-level models" and "low-level modules"; we like to design top-level models in the same way as modules intended for inclusion in a library. It's not any harder to design a top-level model as a module, and doing so can help make the model easier to extend or combine with other models later on; furthermore, given a rich library of support modules, the top-level module often doesn't need to do very much.

4.6.1   Separating C from M from P

The most important part of designing a model, we feel, is keeping the concepts separate from the mathematics separate from the posed problems. Various reasons for this separation are expounded in Section 4.4, but they can all be distilled as:

> *A well-defined CMP structure helps a model be robust, reusable, and extensible, and helps us to understand, build, and debug the model.*

There may be choices about what goes into which section (e.g., as per Fig. 4.8), but we insist upon explicitly choosing.[12]

---

[11]Ch. 5 discusses techniques to support modularity of mathematical models.

[12]Note a contrast with the ARI structure: In Section 3.2, we said that it could be hard to define an ARI decomposition precisely, but that such precision wasn't needed. Here, for physically-based modeling, we feel that the problem domain is specific enough that precise CMP separations are possible and should be strongly encouraged.

"Annealing" Design
of a Physically-Based Model

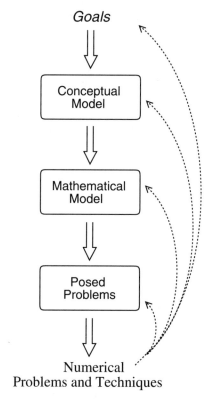

Goals

Conceptual
Model

Mathematical
Model

Posed
Problems

Numerical
Problems and Techniques

Figure 4.10: Design strategy for physically-based models. An idealized top-down approach follows
the progression from goals to numerical implementation. But because implementation details, such as
computability, can influence the choice of CMP structure elements or even restrict the goals, we use a
more pragmatic annealing strategy, as per Fig. 3.5. □

We also want to make sure that implementation details—or things that *ought* to
be implementation details—aren't mixed in with the model. The CMP separation
helps with this somewhat, but one might still mix numerical details with the conceptual task statement in a posed problem. Watch out for statements like "choose
an acceleration to bring the body to rest in one time step" that mix conceptual
properties ("acceleration") with solution parameters ("time step"). Sometimes,
however, implementation details can affect our choice of model, as is discussed in
the next section.

4.6.2 Top-Down versus Bottom-Up versus . . .

How do we go about designing a model? Do we design the conceptual model first, then the mathematical, and finally pose some problems, or do we start with problem tasks, then build the conceptual and mathematical models around them? Do we start with the existing library modules and build upward, or start with the goals and build downward?

The discussion of design strategies in Section 3.5 carries over to the design of physically-based models and modules. In particular, we ultimately agree with the bottom line of that discussion: Use an annealing design strategy, in which we are free to work on the problem in any order and to go back and modify higher-level specifications as we gain understanding about the lower levels, so long as we always make sure to keep an eye on our goals and maintain a structural framework. Here, the framework that we maintain is the CMP structure (see Fig. 4.10).

Top-down design remains our idealized strategy, however. For modularity and hierarchy, top-down means using an approach analogous to structured program design: Start with the top-level module; recognize when submodules can be separated out and designed independently or brought in from a library.

For the CMP structure, a top-down approach—conceptual, then mathematical, then posed problems—corresponds with the mathematical modeling steps of Section 4.2. Notice, however, that mathematical modeling includes a *repeat* step, in which we go back and adjust the top level based upon our experience, and which is consistent with the annealing design strategy.

Often, practical ability to solve the posed problems limits the effectiveness of top-down design. Some difficulties that can arise for numerical problems are

- The solution techniques are unacceptably slow.

- Available subroutine libraries don't have the appropriate solvers.

- It's unknown how to solve a problem, e.g., Fermat's last theorem.

- A problem is probably unsolvable, e.g., the halting problem, or is NP-complete,[13] e.g., the traveling salesman problem.

If we encounter a circumstance similar to one of these, we may need to change the mathematical or conceptual models to produce a more tractable problem. And sometimes, our top-level goals are inherently intractable and cannot be met as stated.

Note that there can be circumstances in which computational details affect the choice of conceptual model without impinging upon our goals. For example, if the falling ball of Fig. 4.3 were to bounce, the traditional linear restitution model

---

[13]For practical purposes, NP-complete problems are computationally intractable; see [Lewis, Papadimitriou81].

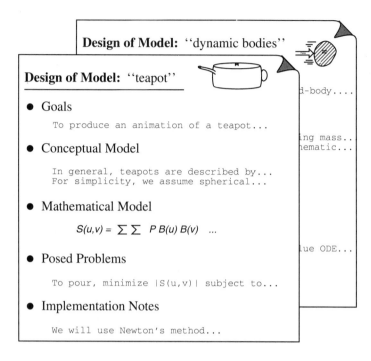

Figure 4.11: Outline of model design. Each module includes a statement of its goals, conceptual model, mathematical model, and posed problems, as well as implementation and other notes. □

for rigid-body collision ([Fox67]) leads to a sort of computational Zeno's paradox, in which the ball takes infinitely many ever-smaller bounces, but never reaches continuous contact with the ground. Switching to a quasilinear restitution model,[14] however, puts a finite bound on the number of bounces. Because the traditional model is merely an axiomatic approximation to empirical evidence, switching to a slightly different model produces equally acceptable simulation of behavior. For another example, [Baraff91] shows that the principle of constraints for mechanical systems leads to a problem that is NP-complete; and while abandoning that principle yields different behavior in indeterminate configurations, the resulting behavior is still consistent with a rigid-body model and, moreover, is computationally tractable. (These two examples can be thought of as consequences of the development of the classical formalisms before computability was a relevant concern, as discussed in Section 2.7.)

---

[14]The traditional equation relating velocity before and after a bounce is $v^+ = -ev^-$, where e is the *coefficient of restitution.* Instead, we use $v^+ = \max(-ev^- - \kappa, 0)$, where κ is a constant velocity-loss term and the final velocity is clamped to 0.

4.6.3   Standard Framework for a Model

To help maintain the structure of a model, we can fill in the blanks of a standard outline (see Fig. 4.11):

- **Goals.** What we are trying to achieve; the high-level problem.

- **Conceptual model.** Includes a list of the physical properties of the thing being modeled, and their corresponding mathematical model terms. Can refer to other modules.

- **Mathematical model.** A collection of definitions and equations; may refer to definitions and equations of other modules. (The mathematical model is discussed at length in Ch. 5.)

- **Posed problems.** Statements of the conceptual tasks to perform and the corresponding mathematical problems, listing the knowns and unknowns for each. A problem may be decomposed into a series of smaller problems that may be posed in other modules.

- **Implementation notes.** Details such as which numerical solvers are used for each problem, numerical parameter settings that produce acceptable results, and so forth.

Note the parallels with the top-down design sequence of Section 3.5.1; for top-down design, we try to fill in the sections in the listed order. For annealing design, we fill in and update the sections as we learn about them. Each module has its own such outline.

4.6.4   Debugging a Model

Suppose we've implemented a model, i.e., solved some numerical problems, and we have understood the physical interpretation of the results. And, unfortunately, the results are wrong: They aren't what we want or expect. What's going wrong? For complex models, it can be hard to figure out the source of the misbehavior; it is often easy to get caught up in wild goose chases, e.g., trying to fix a numerical solver that isn't in fact broken, and so forth—but a CMP structure can make the process easier.

Having a CMP structure helps us locate and isolate bugs. There are typically three cases to consider when the simulated behavior is apparently broken:

1. **The problems are not being solved correctly.** Check to see if the numerical routines are really solving the equations (e.g., verify correctness by substituting solutions back into the original equation, or compare nominal derivative values against actual behavior, etc.). If they aren't solving the equations, there's a bug in the numerical techniques or in how we are using them.

2. They're the wrong problems. If the numerical solvers are correctly doing what they're told, then we must be telling them the wrong things. The problem has not been properly posed: We don't have the desired correspondence between the conceptual task and the mathematical model. There may be a bug in the mathematical model.

3. It's what the model predicts. If the mathematical model does correspond with the conceptual model, and if we are correctly solving the equations, then we are correctly simulating our conceptual model.

If we have identified case 3, the bug isn't "inside" the model. We have a conflict between the behavior that we want or intuitively expect and what the model produces. This can be resolved in two ways:

Change the model. The conceptual model doesn't include the properties that are necessary to elicit the behavior we want. We must rethink our basic abstraction of the thing being modeled.

Change our expectation. Maybe we are wrong and the model is right! A robust model might make surprising predictions that turn out to actually correspond with how the real thing behaves.[15]

Debugging is discussed more concretely in Ch. 6 when we discuss computer implementations of CMP models.

4.7 Communicating Models to Other People

Unsurprisingly, we use the CMP structure to describe a physically-based model. This is of course easiest if the model was designed using the CMP paradigm—then the framework in Section 4.6.3 (Fig. 4.11) serves as an outline for a presentation of the model. The CMP structure directly answers the four questions that are listed in Section 4.4.1, which we have found aids in comprehending a model. Section 3.6's discussion of communicating general models applies here to our physically-based models.

To present a physically-based model clearly, we can flesh out Section 4.6.3's framework with some explanatory material:

- **Background and overview.** Before beginning to explain a model, especially to an audience unfamiliar with the problem domain, it is generally useful to describe the domain in general and provide a few words about what the model will do.

---

[15]I once modeled and simulated a jumprope. I had trouble finding even a single frame that had a nice smooth loop of rope sliding along the floor; it was wiggling and jangling every which way. This was very frustrating until I came across a stroboscopic multi-exposure of a girl jumping rope . . .

- **Goals.** What are the motivations for defining the model? If it is a module intended to be included in a library, what are some anticipated applications?

- **Conceptual model.** What does the model do? Not merely a list of properties, but an overall introduction to the model: an overview of the basic abstraction, descriptions of the expected or common behaviors, and so forth. Diagrams can be helpful.

- **Mathematical model.** Mathematically, the equations should be "context-free"—but to help comprehend them, it helps to explain their physical interpretations alongside them. Chapter 5 has more to say about presenting mathematical models.

- **Posed problems.** In addition to what the problems are, conceptually and mathematically, describe why they are interesting—what are they used for? Also, under what circumstances can and can't the problems be solved, i.e., where are the singularities and so forth, and what are their physical interpretations?

- **Implementation notes.** What solvers are appropriate, what are the numerical issues and parameter settings, etc. Sometimes it may be more convenient to list the numerical techniques for each posed problem directly alongside it, rather than here in a separate section—but be careful not to confuse a particular choice of technique with the statement of the problem.

The modules in Part III are all presented using the above framework. (The reader can judge how effective this approach is!)

For spoken presentations, when fielding questions it can be helpful to identify which part of the framework the question addresses, in the same way as debugging (Section 4.6.4), and as per the discussion in Section 3.6. A common type of question is a "What if ..." question, i.e., asking what the model will do in an unusual circumstance. Here, too, the CMP structure is helpful. Sometimes, the answer is "It's not part of our conceptual model" (e.g., for a question "What if we move the light source close to the jello—does it get hot and melt?). Other times, the question can be mapped into the mathematical model, in which case there's typically one of three answers:

1. "There is no solution to the equations."
2. "There's exactly one solution, which is ... "
3. "There are many solutions."

When there's not exactly one solution, the resulting behavior then depends on the particulars of the numerical solution technique; a techique might report a failure, or might choose an arbitrary result or a result that has some particular numerical properties.

4.8 Summary

We have presented a canonical *CMP* (conceptual–mathematical–posed-problem) structure for physically-based models, which, based on applied mathematical modeling methodology, emphasizes a well-defined mathematical model that is separate from its solution and physical interpretation. Our outlook differs from "straight" applied mathematics in that we take a modular, reusable approach to design of models; we have a heavier emphasis on the separation of the parts, in particular the distinction between an equation and a problem; and our conceptual model can include properties that don't enter into the mathematical model. Because of the importance of the mathematical part of a model, Ch. 5 addresses a structured approach to mathematical modeling, which fits into our CMP framework.

We have found that the CMP structure enhances our ability to discuss, analyze, and understand modeling techniques, helps us to build and debug models, and produces models that are robust, reusable, and extensible. Furthermore, as we show in Ch. 6, it maps well onto programming; the CMP structure can be designed into computer programs.

Despite the presentations in this chapter, there is no cookbook for designing, debugging, and communicating models—those remain creative human processes. However, we do stress the CMP structure for physically-based models. We have used it successfully, for example, for the models in Part III. And even when we don't formally write down a CMP structure in the precise form described in this chapter, we at least *think* about the models in that way.

Related Work

The mathematical modeling methodology we describe in Section 4.2, illustrated in [Boyce81], is reasonably widespread in applied mathematics; see also [Edwards,Hamson90]. Its application to modeling physical systems is discussed, e.g., by [Zeidler88, p. viii], which draws a diagram similar to our Fig. 4.2.

Modularity and hierarchy are basic elements of structured programming (see, e.g., [Dahl *et al.*72]) and object-oriented programming ([Booch91]). □

Chapter 5

Structured Mathematical Modeling

This entire chapter is directed toward solving a single problem: to be able to write down complete explicit mathematical models of complex systems. The task may seem innocuous at first glance, but it is in fact challenging enough to have spawned a chapter that is fairly dense. The chapter has a fair amount of "talk"— philosophy and other discussion—and also defines a few specific mathematical mechanisms that help structure complex models (see Fig. 5.1).

This chapter draws some analogies between mathematical modeling and computer programming to help us take advantage of principles of software design. However, the mathematical techniques we present do not depend on a knowledge of software.

The mathematical exposition does not strictly demand more than a basic familiarity with set theory and functional analysis.[1] The definitions we present are basic, thus somewhat abstract; however, the underlying concepts are quite simple, and we have found that the techniques and notation seem natural after modest exposure. The list of notation, p. xxiii, may be helpful.

The principles and techniques discussed in this chapter are used for the models in Part III. The reader is encouraged to skim Part III in order to see the principles and techniques "in action."

---

[1] "A good treatise on the theory of functions of a real variable does not strictly require of its readers any previous acquaintance of the subject . . . yet a student armed with no more than a naked, virgin mind is unlikely to survive the first few pages. In the same way, although this book does not call upon any previous knowledge . . . " [Truesdell91, p. xvii]

Outline of Chapter 5

Figure 5.1: Outline of this chapter. Sections 5.1–5.5 describe our philosophy and attitudes toward mathematical modeling. Sections 5.6–5.10 present various mathematical mechanisms—definitions, notations, and techniques—that are useful for structured mathematical modeling; Sections 5.11–5.12 contain further discussion and summary. □

5.1   Overview

What is a mathematical model? For our purposes, a mathematical model is a collection of mathematical definitions of terms and equations. For physically-based modeling, we expect a mathematical model to be defined in the context of a CMP (conceptual–mathematical–posed-problem) structure as per Ch. 4. Thus, although problem statements ("given x, find y such that . . . ") and physical interpretation ("z is the width . . . ") are closely related to the mathematical model, we consider them to be separate from it. Chapter 4 details reasons for the separation; in this chapter we take it as a given.

The principles and techniques we discuss in this chapter are "administrative" in nature, directed toward structuring and managing complexity of mathematical models. For most of our applications, we are content to recast classical equations— "model fragments" as per Section 2.7—into our structured form. In order to define such fragments *ab initio,* we refer the reader to [Lin,Segel74].

Since this chapter focuses on mathematical modeling, an unqualified use of "model" can be taken to mean "mathematical model." Similarly, since this chapter focuses on issues significant to structured modeling, an unqualified use of "mathematical modeling" can be taken to mean ". . . from our point of view."

5.2   Motivation for Structured Mathematical Modeling

We adhere to the premise that if we wish to do a simulation, we must first create a well-defined mathematical model; and if a mathematical model is well defined, we ought to be able to write it down (see Section 1.5). Our primary goal for mathematical modeling is therefore:

> *Goal:* To be able to write down complete, explicit equations for complex physically-based models.

The difficulty here lies in the words "complete," "explicit," and "complex." Imagine writing complete, explicit equations for a bicycle drive train: the behavior of each and every link, their interactions with each other and with the gears and derailleurs, etc. Clearly, writing them out longhand in full detail, without the aid of special tricks or techniques, is too cumbersome and ugly to consider seriously.

We notice that computer programming has inherent in it the same difficult components as our goal for mathematical modeling: A computer program must be explicit, must be complete, and can be very complex. Over the past 20 years, techniques for structuring and engineering computer programs have been developed to mitigate these difficulties. We apply many of these proven-successful techniques to mathematical modeling.

The "structured mathematical modeling" techniques in this chapter are intended to help meet our primary goal—complete, explicit, written equations for complex physically-based models. But before developing any specific techniques, we elaborate on various aspects of the goal.

5.2.1   Complex Models

The primary sources of complexity in our models are size and heterogeneity. The mathematical models in [Boyce81] have perhaps a few dozen variables; our computer graphics models can easily have hundreds or thousands, with intricate relationships or interconnections between them.[2] Moreover, we wish to mingle various behavior modes into a single model, where the differing behaviors can be due to different components of a model as well as from individual components that change over time.

Thus, although we adopt the basic mathematical modeling philosophy of [Boyce81] (as discussed in Section 4.2), we also need to develop techniques to handle our unusual complexity requirements.

---

[2]Having merely "thousands" of variables is itself humble, compared to applications such as weather and climate modeling. We emphasize applications, however, in which the many variables cannot be treated statistically or regularly, in that they may have irregular behaviors or interrelationships.

5.2.2 Complete Models

As discussed in Section 2.7, most physical models are expressed as "fragments," i.e., a collection of equations that describe individual components of the model. For example, in presenting techniques for animating dynamic legged locomotion, [Raibert,Hodgins91] contains various equations (taken here out of context):

> Both actuator models have the form $f = k(x - x_r) + b\dot{x}$, where f is ....
> The control system computes the desired foot position as: $x_{fh,d} = $ ....
> The posture control torques are generated by a linear servo: $\tau = $ ....

The article describes how and when the various fragments come into play—but this description is in words: There is no mathematical expression for the model as a whole.[3]

Without mathematical tools that express models completely, it is hard to communicate, analyze, and so forth. Furthermore, when we ultimately want to simulate a model on a computer, it becomes the programmer's job to ascertain or intuit how the various fragments piece together, and build that structure into a computer program. Thus we need to develop techniques to "glue" together separate model fragments.

5.2.3 Explicit Models

In addition to wanting our models to be complete, we also want them to be explicit. That is, we want to minimize ambiguity that might lead to errors occurring through (accidental) inappropriate use of equations. We emphasize two ways of doing this: minimizing tacit dependencies and minimizing tacit assumptions.

Minimizing dependencies when writing equations really means always being careful to write terms as functions that include all their parameters. In addition to minimizing errors in doing mathematical derivations, making all the dependencies explicit greatly eases the ultimate transition to a computer program. Being able to write explicit dependencies requires (and motivates the development of) complexity- and fragment-management techniques as discussed above. For example, in a rigid-body model, the force on a body can depend in principle on the state of all the other bodies at each instant; rather than merely writing "the force f," we want to write "the force function $f(state\text{-}of\text{-}all\text{-}bodies)$"—but using mathematically precise constructs.

Minimizing tacit assumptions is important in the early stages of overall model design, as discussed in Section 4.6. But also, as we write our mathematical equations, we always want to be careful to list what our assumptions are, what

---

[3]No disparagement is intended. We have chosen to cite [Raibert,Hodgins91] precisely because it is an excellent article describing superb work. Thus it illustrates to us not a lack of discipline on the part of the authors, but rather a need for enhanced expressiveness in mathematical models and notation.

conditions are required, and so forth. In this way, each equation can be "globally valid." For example, rather than writing an equation "$x = \ldots$," one would write write "in such-and-such circumstances, $x = \ldots$." This helps in understanding the equations, and again can ease the transition to computer programs.[4] The idea of globally valid equations ties in with modularity (Section 5.4.2) and declarative models (Section 5.5.2).

Unlike our goals of complexity and completeness, for which we identified a need for new techniques, the goal of explicit models to a large extent requires a discipline on the part of the model designer. That is, given techniques that make writing explicit equations feasible, it remains up to the model designer to invest the appropriate effort.

5.2.4   Practical Utility

There is one additional goal that we have not yet mentioned: practical utility. We are not interested in purely academic or theoretical techniques: Not only do we want to develop techniques, we want to be able to use them—and, moreover, we want to be better off for having used them.

That is, we want our mathematical modeling techniques to make it easier to create models. We want the techniques, as well as the models that we create thereby, to be writable and readable. We want to show models to colleagues, who should be able to understand them. We want to scribble models on whiteboards and napkins.

As such, we try to keep to familiar, existing notation, definitions, and terminology as much as possible to avoid abstruseness. We do not attempt to fabricate entirely new mathematical languages, but rather try to augment the existing language with a few simple constructs that have proven to be useful.

Note that it is particularly important that models be understandable to others: Because of structured modeling's modular approach, we will be designing "library" models (or components of models) that are intended to be used by others, often for unforeseen applications. Thus there is a concern for clear and orderly "packaging" and "interfaces," which is familiar to those who design software libraries, but is of lesser significance when one designs a mathematical model purely for one's own one-time use.

Finally, in addition to the above "ergonomic" issues, the techniques we use should be rigorous and robust enough to support derivations, proofs, and so forth.

---

[4] All equations in this chapter and in Part III are careful to include their "givens" and notes in order to help make each be correct and understandable by itself.

5.3   Aesthetics and Design Decisions

A balance often must be struck between the goals discussed in Section 5.2—in particular, between the goal of practical usefulness and all the goals. For instance, if there are too many parameters and parentheses, putting in all the explicit dependencies will make the equations too cumbersome to read and too error-prone to write. Similarly, defining new terms or constructs can clean up an equation, but a plethora of gratuitous definitions can be hard to keep straight and will be particularly inaccessible to newcomers. Or, there can be a tradeoff between full generality (a single model that can do everything) and ease of understanding.

There's no pat answer for what the proper balance is, nor how to strike it. Often, case-by-case decisions will have to be made based on personal aesthetics, individual goals, the levels of experience of the audience and of the designer, and so forth. Thus, doing mathematical modeling involves "design decisions" that are similar in spirit to those made in programming, engineering and other constructive tasks—they are an inherent part of being a designer of mathematical models.

There is one area about which we remain resolute: Even if there's shorthand or whatnot being defined for clarity, we are always careful to make sure that there is an underlying mathematical framework that is solid. Remember the premise that we are trying to make a good and correct mathematical model.

One final tradeoff that needs mentioning is between design effort up front versus ease of use later on. The goal of writing down a complete model before simulating it of course leans heavily toward investing effort in the design in order to create a better product. But we recognize that there can be diminishing returns from excessive time spent designing "blindly," and that often the best way to design is to experiment in order to gain experience and understanding. This tradeoff parallels the top-down versus bottom-up, etc., design strategies of Section 3.5 and Section 4.6.

5.4   Borrowing from Programming

We observed earlier (Section 5.2) that our approach to mathematical modeling bears similarity to programming: Both require complete, explicit descriptions of complex systems. Structured programming and, more recently, object-oriented programming have been developed to help manage the complexity of computer programs; we can apply much of their philosophy and many of their techniques to mathematical modeling as well (see Fig. 5.2).

It would be a shame to clutter up mathematics, which has a traditional ethic and aesthetic of austerity, with excessive or unattractive baggage from the world of programming. As such, although borrowing philosophy of programming is probably harmless, when it comes to specific techniques we try to use a minimal

Programming Concepts

Ideas we embrace for mathematical modeling:	Ideas we eschew for mathematical modeling:
✓ Top-down design	✗ Internal state
✓ Modularity	✗ Procedural definitions
✓ Naming strategies	✗ Polymorphism
✓ Data abstraction	✗ Inflexible syntax

Figure 5.2: Adopting ideas from programming. Many goals and difficulties that we have for mathematical modeling are similar to those of computer programming. As such, we find that several known principles from computer programming are well worth using for mathematical modeling (Section 5.4). Conversely, however, the differences between programming and mathematics compel us to steer clear of some techniques (Section 5.5). □

approach, only bringing in methods that are particularly useful. We'd like to keep our mathematics as familiar, readable, and usable as possible, as per Section 5.2.4.

5.4.1   Top-Down Design

The top-down design strategy calls for first creating a specification, then creating the high levels of a mechanism that meets the specification, and so on, with the final details of implementation saved for last. As discussed in Ch. 3, we find the top-down method to be an appealing ideal, in keeping with our overall goal-oriented approach toward modeling (Section 1.6). For mathematical modeling, the top-down approach mostly enters *before* the design of the mathematical model, i.e., in the specification of goals and physical context for the model, as per the CMP structure discussed in Ch. 4.

It is possible, to some extent, to design the mathematical model itself in a top-down manner. The methods of modularity and data abstraction (which are discussed below) can support specification of the overall structure and relationships within a model, where the details are filled in later.

5.4.2   Modularity

Modularity in programming means that programs are built as a (hierarchical) collection of independent components having well-defined interfaces. It helps us to decompose complex problems into simpler ones that are easier to understand and implement; often, the modular subparts are standardized and kept in libraries. The benefits of modularity apply as well to mathematical modeling.

Mathematics has some modular aspects inherent in it, in that it is based on independent, well-defined axioms and theorems; constructs are defined in terms of more primitive constructs, e.g., a field is defined in terms of sets and a derivative in terms of limits; and often, entire branches of mathematics can be based on earlier branches, e.g., differential geometry is built from linear algebra and calculus ([Millman,Parker77]).

For our purposes, however, modularity in mathematical models will generally coincide with the modular design of physically-based models, as per Section 4.5. For example, in Part III, we have a mathematical module for kinematic rigid-body motion, one for dynamic rigid-body motion, one for force mechanisms, and so forth. Each module defines a consistent set of terms and equations for its model, designed to be useful for a variety of applications, rather than for a specific "end-model." The modules can make use of equations and terms from other modules, e.g., dynamic rigid-body motion is built on top of kinematic.

In order for a module to be widely useful, especially in conjunction with other modules, each module must be designed with a care toward not "stepping on the toes" of others. For example, tacit assumptions should be avoided—they may conflict with assumptions in other modules—but instead assumptions should be listed as explicit preconditions for equations, as per Section 5.2.3. Naming strategies and data abstraction, discussed below, also come into play.

5.4.3 Naming Strategies

In mathematics, as in programming, we assign names to things—the names should be mnemonic and unambiguous. We must be careful to avoid naming conflicts, especially when models are defined modularly and independently.

We adopt several naming strategies from programming for use in mathematical modeling: full-word names, function-name overloading, and namespace scoping. These are discussed in Section 5.6.

5.4.4 Data Abstraction

Data abstraction in programming is analogous to modularity, but for data elements: A collection of related data elements is bundled together as a single logical entity, often called a *data structure* or *abstract data type* (see [Liskov,Guttag86]). Data abstraction provides *encapsulation,* or *information hiding,* in which an abstract data object can be manipulated as a single entity without reference to details of its contents or implementation, and *hierarchy,* in that an abstract data type may be defined in terms of other abstract data types. These capabilities can greatly help to manage complexity.

Object-oriented programming takes data abstraction a step further: An abstract data type (or *class*) is specified along with a well-defined set of the operations that

Programmatic Operation   **Mathematical Operation**

(Changes the contents of an object)   (Maps between elements of sets)

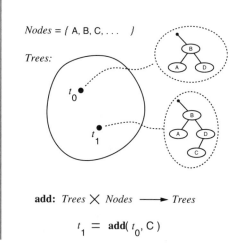

add: $Trees \times Nodes \longrightarrow Trees$

$$t_1 = \mathbf{add}(\, t_0, C\,)$$

Figure 5.3: No "internal state" in mathematical objects. In most computer programming, it is common for objects to have internal states. For example, adding a node to a binary tree object changes the internal state, but it is still considered the "same" object (where objects are typically identified by their memory addresses). In mathematics, however, we will avoid the notion of internal state: A binary tree is an element of the set *Trees* containing all binary trees, whose nodes are elements of the set *Nodes*. We can define a function **add** that, given any tree in *Trees* and any node in *Nodes*, maps onto some other tree in *Trees* that has the appropriate nodes in it. Lack of internal state is a characteristic of functional programming as well (see Section 5.5.1). □

may be performed upon that type of object. Thus the particulars of the elements that make up the data type are implementation details irrelevant to its use and can be changed without affecting the data type's functionality. This separation of implementation from function is another powerful structural tool that aids in maintenance and extensibility of programs.

The field of mathematics has some data abstraction inherent in it. As discussed in Section 5.4.2, types of mathematical objects are often defined hierarchically. Additionally, mathematical "data types"—such as sets, fields, or vectors—are often defined abstractly, via properties and operations, without having any "innards."

For mathematical modeling, we emphasize the use of data abstraction, in the form of *abstract spaces*; this is discussed at length in Section 5.7. We also present, in Section 5.9, a mathematical mechanism for defining *state spaces,* which encapsulate collections of elements and operations into mathematical entities.[5]

---

[5]Our use of abstract spaces is similar to the formal/algebraic treatment of abstract data types in computer science (see [Horebeek,Lewi89], [Cleaveland86]), but note that we have opposite goals: The

5.5 Distinctions from Programming

Lest we get carried away with the parallels between mathematical modeling and software design, we examine differences between them. In particular, there are some ideas from programming that we make a point of *not* borrowing; this section lists several features of mathematical modeling that conflict with common programming methodology (see Fig. 5.2).

5.5.1 No Internal State

One aspect of programming that we find unsuited to mathematical modeling is the idea of "internal state" of an object. As illustrated in Fig. 5.3, a computer-programming object can have variable internal state—in fact, the concept of objects having internal state, with operations to access and modify that state, is the *sine qua non* of object-oriented programming.

In the realm of mathematics, on the other hand, we prefer objects to have no internal state. An operation is merely a map between elements of the domain and elements of the range; "performing" an operation on a given element of the domain just means finding the corresponding element of the range. For example, if we apply the operation "add one" to the number "3," we get "4"—but "3" isn't modified.[6]

Lacking internal state, activities that would be programmatically defined as state changes, are mathematically defined instead as mappings between elements of (abstract) state spaces, as illustrated in Fig. 5.3. We discuss abstract spaces in general in Section 5.7, and a mechanism for state spaces in particular in Section 5.9.

Why not define some mathematical mechanism that supports internal state? Because the lack of internal state is not a drawback but rather a feature: Without internal state, the result of an operation on a given object is single-valued, and we can thus define equations that always apply, without fear of the objects involved being in the wrong state. That is, the lack of internal state is central to the use of globally valid equations, as per Section 5.2.3.

Finally, note that the idea of "globally valid" objects, whose internal state is never modified, does in fact arise in some programming paradigms. For example, for parallel programming, [Chandy,Taylor92] uses *definition variables*, whose values don't change, to insure correctness of otherwise *mutable* variables across parallel composition of program blocks. Another example is functional programming, based on a mathematical function approach in which values are computed

---

study of abstract data types brings mathematical rigor to computer programming constructs, while our use of abstract spaces brings computer programming principles to mathematical modeling.

[6]One is reminded of the applied-mathematicians' joke: "$2 + 2 = 5$, for large values of 2 and small values of 5." Note also the well-known bug in FORTRAN programs: Passing the constant 3 to a routine `addone(x)` might in fact change the value of "3" for the remainder of the program.

but no changes are stored (see, e.g., [Henson87]). Note however that we have not explicitly adopted any techniques or terminology from those realms.

5.5.2   No Procedural Definitions

Traditional programming paradigms are *procedural* (or *imperative*): The programmer specifies a sequence of instructions for the computer to carry out. Our mathematical models, on the other hand, contain no posed problems or instructions for solving problems, but merely state equations (Section 4.3.2). Thus the mathematical models are *declarative*.

Notice that the lack of internal state (Section 5.5.1) goes hand-in-hand with the lack of procedural specification: Not having any state, there can be no notion of the "current instruction." Once again, we have a similarity with the functional programming paradigm:

> One of the great benefits of [functional programming] is that the programs may be considered *declaratively*. It is *not* necessary to attempt a mental execution of the program in order to understand what it "does" . . . . We wish to adopt a more static approach in which it is more appropriate to ask what a program "means" rather than "does." [Henson87, p. 66]

If we replace "programs" with "equations," and "execution" with "solution," the above argument applies as well to mathematical modeling.[7]

In the real world, and hence in our physically-based models, there are often sequential changes of state. Thus we need to be able to express "when *this* happens, do *that*" in a mathematical model—without a procedural specification. In Section 5.10, we discuss "segmented functions," which address this need.

5.5.3   No Polymorphism

One of the most powerful ideas of object-oriented programming is *polymorphism*: A given name may refer to an object of any one of a number of related classes that may respond to a given operation in different ways. This allows a single program to be applied to any of the related classes, even ones that weren't defined when the program was originally written.

We say in Section 5.4.4 that we incorporate the idea of data abstraction—i.e., the definition of classes—into mathematical modeling. Thus we might expect or desire to take advantage of polymorphism as well. Mathematics does contain some simple uses of polymorphism. For example, the expression $a + b$ has slightly different meanings for real numbers, complex numbers, functions, and so forth.

---

[7]The similarity between mathematical modeling and functional programming is unsurprising: Functional programming is designed to allow formal, mathematical manipulation and analysis of programs.

However, as a rule, polymorphism is not suited to mathematical modeling, because it tends to increase ambiguity. That is, the behavior of polymorphic objects isn't completely well defined upon simple inspection of an expression, but will depend on what types of objects are eventually used. For mathematical modeling, we have no compiler or run-time support to identify or disambiguate objects—we just look at the equations, so their meanings should be evident without added context, as discussed in Section 5.2.3.

5.5.4 Human-Friendly Syntax

If we're not careful as we wear our "programmers' hats" when approaching the design of mathematical models, we might end up defining mathematical mechanisms more suited for computers than for people. The ergonomic goals of Section 5.2.4 must be brought into play.

For one thing, the mathematical syntax shouldn't be so subtle or so intricate that it takes a compiler to figure out the intent. That is, important distinctions shouldn't depend on easily confused notation (e.g., tiny subscripted marks), a single symbol shouldn't imply an overly complex or nonintuitive series of operations, and so forth.

Additionally, we don't want to define syntax so rigid or cumbersome that it's inconvenient to use. Sometimes, flexibility can be enhanced by allowing several alternative notations; as in

$$y = \sin(x)$$
$$y = \sin x.$$

Furthermore, when scribbling equations and derivations, one commonly uses shorthand, elisions, and so forth; it should be possible to do so yet still be able to make use of the corresponding mathematical mechanism. On the other side of this same coin, we don't want to invent syntax that is ungainly enough to encourage its elision.

With flexible syntax comes the potential of ambiguity and lack of rigor. If one uses shorthand, leaves off parenthetical arguments, and so forth, one relies on the reader knowing what is meant rather than what is said. This is another "design decision" as per Section 5.3. We generally try to mitigate such ambiguity by appropriate annotation in the accompanying text; Eq. 11.21, for example, has a note, "For clarity, the parameters have been left off $\mathcal{M}_{pq}(Y, t)$. . . ."

This is the end of the Principles *part of Chapter 5. The next part,* Techniques, *presents some mathematical mechanisms that support the structured mathematical modeling approach we have been discussing.*

5.6 Naming Strategies

In mathematical equations, letters are used for names of parameters, functions, and so forth: for example, the letters f, k, t, and x in the equation "$x = f_k(y, t)$." But as more and more equations and terms are written, it's easy to run out of letters.[8] To squeeze more life out of the letters, one can take advantage of various cases and fonts, e.g., r versus R versus $\mathbf{R}$ versus $\mathcal{R}$ versus $\mathfrak{R}$, etc. One can also turn to other alphabets, e.g., ξ, Ψ, $\aleph$, etc. But still, for mathematical models of the complexity we're interested in, running out of letters for names has the potential to be a serious problem. In particular, since we design models as separate modules, we run the risk of having naming conflicts when we combine the modules together. Furthermore, we want names to make sense; with too many letters chosen arbitrarily, it can be hard to remember what's what.

Our concern with mathematical names is analogous to computer programming's concern with variable and function names. We present here three naming strategies from computer programming that can be used as well for mathematical modeling.

5.6.1 Full-Word Names

Instead of using only a single letter for mathematical names one can use a whole word, or at least a multiletter name. This is familiar for many fundamental mathematical functions and operations, such as

$$\sin(x)$$
$$\arccos(x)$$
$$\lim_{n \to \infty} x = 0$$

and so forth, but it is rarer to see multiletter terms in other contexts. ([Misner *et al.*73] is an example of a work that does use a full-word approach, defining, e.g., tensors named **Einstein** and **Riemann**.) In addition to allowing us more names than single letters, multiletter names of course have the advantage of being mnemonic.

As with good programming style, one should generally use longer names for global, important, or infrequently used terms, and use shorter or single-letter names for local and frequently used terms. We use full-word names for most abstract spaces we define (see discussion of abstract spaces in Section 5.7), such as **Locations** in Ch. 8 and **States** in Ch. 9, and even occasional compound-word names, such as **StatePaths** in Ch. 9. However, we maintain standard or historical names where they are familiar, such as m for mass and p for linear momentum in rigid-body dynamics, in Ch. 10.

---

[8]This is "another example of a growing problem with mathematical notation: There aren't enough squiggles to go around." [Blinn92, p. 88]

With multiletter names, one has to be careful that when two names are written next to each other, they don't textually merge into another name. For example, to multiply a term y by a term cat, we might write

$$x = y\, cat$$

but the right-hand side might be mistaken for a single term $ycat$, which might or might not exist.[9] Confusion can be mitigated through use of spacing, different fonts, parentheses or other symbols, and so forth. For example:

$$
\begin{aligned}
x &= y\, cat \\
x &= y\, \text{cat} \\
x &= (y)(cat) \\
x &= y * cat
\end{aligned}
$$

5.6.2 Scoping, Namespaces

How do we avoid "name collisions" when mathematical models are designed as a collection of separate modules? For example, the kinematic rigid-body model in Ch. 9 and the dynamic rigid-body model in Ch. 10 each needs to define an abstract space, and in both cases we would like to use the name "States." Can they both do so? If yes, and we want to mix kinematic and dynamic models, how can we tell which States is being referred to in a given equation? Furthermore, can one model refer to the other's name? We describe here a mechanism inspired by that of Common LISP ([Steele90]).

The basic idea is simple: Each model has its own *scope*, or *namespace*; a name x used in one scope is not the same name x as used in another scope. Thus in each model we are free to use whatever names we want, and by fiat they do not collide with names from other models.

In order to be able to use names from different scopes unambiguously, we give each scope its own *scope name*. For example, the kinematic rigid-body model has scope name KINEMATIC.[10] We can think of the scoping mechanism as follows: When we define terms within a particular model, they are all implicitly "actually" defined with to have *full, or scoped, names* that include the model's scope name. We use the following notation:

---

[9]This is why we like to emphasize full-word names rather than arbitrary mnemonic abbreviations: "$ycat$" is less likely to be accidentally thought of as a defined term if there are no, or few, other non-word names. Of course, one is never entirely safe: consider $x = n\,ever$ versus $x = never$. As well, in practice full words can be unwieldy, so shorter, mnemonic names are necessary. See also [Kernighan,Plauger78] for guidelines for mnemonic names.

[10]We consistently use a small caps font for scope names.

Notation. Double colon "::" for scoped names.

(5.1)

> *If a name, e.g., "States," is defined within a namespace*
> *having a scope name, e.g., "KINEMATIC," its full name*
> *is written using a double colon, as:*
>
> KINEMATIC :: States

Notation 5.1: We write a scoped name by prefixing the short name with the name of the scope, with two colons between them. The colons serve to set the names apart and to emphasize that the name-scoping mechanism is being used. □

When working on a particular model, we generally assume that all names are defined within the scope of that model and there's no need to write out the full names. If we want to use a name from a different model, however, we can use its full name. The dynamic rigid-body model, for example, uses just "States" to refer to its own space and "KINEMATIC :: States" to refer to the kinematic space.

Sometimes we can avoid conflicts, and save writing, by just choosing which namespace is the default for a given name. For example, Ch. 11 starts by stating that "Systems" will be assumed to mean "RIGID :: Systems" (rather than "KINEMATIC :: Systems").

Of course, when there is no conflict, there's no need to use full names. For example, the model named COORDS (Ch. 8) defines several terms (Vectors, Locations, *Lab*, etc.) that are used frequently and widely in other models and are not defined elsewhere—so we do not use the full names. Still, to aid the reader, it is good to start each model by listing where all such "imported" names are defined (this also avoids future ambiguity if a later model provides a different definition of one of these names).

Given that our goal as per Section 5.5.4 is clarity and nonambiguity for the readers, rather than formal syntax, we are not overly strict in our use of namespaces and scoped names. In particular, we find no need to go to the programmatic extremes of Common LISP's mechanism, with its internal versus external names, exporting and shadowing of names, and so forth.

Finally, note that each model must, of course, be given a unique scope name, or we are back to our original name conflicts.[11]

5.6.3   Function Name Overloading

We generally want any given name to have only one meaning (within a given scope) so as to avoid ambiguity, in keeping with the explicitness goal of Section 5.2.3. For example, if we define a function $f(t)$, we don't want to have a parameter

---

[11]One can imagine introducing hierarchy into namespaces so that one might have a fully scoped name such as "CALTECH :: KINEMATIC :: Systems"; we have not (yet?) found this to be necessary, however.

named f as well—especially if we will be in the habit of dropping the parentheses and parameters from functions.[12]

However, sometimes there may be a family of related operators or functions that perform analogous operations, but on different types of parameters. For example, in Ch. 8 we define a family of operators, *Rep*, that yield the coordinate representation of a geometric object; one *Rep* acts on elements of an abstract space Locations to yield an element of $\Re^3$, and a different *Rep* acts on elements of an abstract space Orientations to yield an element of $\Re^{3 \times 3}$.

To eliminate ambiguity, we would give a different name to each operator. Continuing with the earlier example, we might name one operator *RepLoc* and another *RepOrient*. However, doing so can be cumbersome, and it can even be confusing, if we tend to think of all operators in the *Rep* family as essentially the same.

Thus, as an exception to our general policy of nonambiguity, we are willing to allow families of functions to share a single name. We adopt the term *overloading* from programming, where this idea is familiar (in particular *operator overloading* in programming languages—e.g., defining "+" appropriately for various different argument types such as integers, floating-point numbers, or complex numbers—is well known; see [Booch91]). We can give a formal definition of an overloaded mathematical function:

> *Definition.* **Overloaded Functions**

(5.2)

> *An* **overloaded function** *is a function whose domain is the union of the domains of a family of functions (those domains must be disparate), whose range is the union of the ranges of those functions, and whose value for any argument equals that of the member of the family whose domain contains that argument.*

Definition 5.2: An overloaded function is a single function that "chooses" the appropriate function from a family, based on its argument type. See example, Eq. 5.3. □

And an example:

---

[12] In fact, it is not uncommon to see expositions in which a single name is used as a parameter and/or as a function and/or as a value of the function. In fluid mechanics (see, e.g., [Lin,Segel74, Ch. 13]), the name x is commonly used for an independent world-space variable as well as a material-to-world coordinate mapping, $x(a)$. Although there is some benefit—anything named x is always a world-space location—for our purposes we feel that eliminating ambiguity is a strong enough concern that this practice should be discouraged.

(5.3)

> *Given three functions:* $fa: A \rightarrow X$, $fb: B \rightarrow Y$, *and*
> $fc: C \rightarrow Z$, *we can define an overloaded function*
> $f: A \cup B \cup C \rightarrow X \cup Y \cup Z$ *by:*

$$f(x) = \begin{cases} fa(x), & \text{if } x \in A \\ fb(x), & \text{if } x \in B \\ fc(x), & \text{if } x \in C \end{cases}$$

Equation 5.3: Example of an overloaded function. Note that the individual functions don't have to act on only a single parameter or even the same number of parameters. For example, if fb were to take two real-number arguments, its domain would be $B = \Re \times \Re$. We would consider $f(x, y)$ for real x and y to be acting on the pair $(x, y) \in B$, thus $f(x, y) = fb(x, y)$; but for $z \in A$, we would have $f(z) = fa(z)$. □

In practice, we define only the overloaded function name and leave implicit the names of the individual functions in the family (for example, see the definition of *Rep*, Def. 8.5). We have not found it necessary to invent a formal mechanism for naming and referring to the individual functions; as long as we are aware of the underlying unambiguous mechanism, it is sufficient to define the overloaded name and leave it at that.

It is important to remember that overloading is a source of ambiguity—it is a form of polymorphism—and should be used sparingly. One should be careful to define overloaded functions only when it will be obvious which underlying function is implied—that is, we must know to which domain the arguments belong. For example, the function f of Eq. 5.3 is used unambiguously in the expression:

$$a + 1 = f(a), where \ a \in A.$$

Note that if we expect to occasionally leave off function arguments in our expressions, the overloaded functions will be ambiguous. Note also that we do not overload based on the range spaces of the individual functions; that could too easily lead to unresolvable ambiguity.

Function overloading is commonly used in the mathematical world without the fanfare that we have put forth. We prefer, however, that some care be put into the decision of whether or not to overload a particular function; this is a "design decision," as per Section 5.3, where the model designer tries to balance clarity and economy of expression against ambiguous meaning. To help eliminate ambiguity, whenever an overloaded function is defined, the reader should be warned in accompanying text, "Caution: Overloading being done here."

The mathematical function-overloading mechanism we have defined is inspired by the programmatic function-overloading mechanism of the C++ language ([Stroustrup91]); in particular we adopt C++'s choice to overload functions based on argument type, but not on return type, and the implicit creation of individual functions with uniques names for each domain.

5.7   Abstract Spaces

This section describes a basic element of our approach to mathematical modeling: prolific definition of abstract spaces. This leads to the mathematical equivalent of data abstraction, encapsulation, hierarchy, etc., familiar from programming and is thus a powerful tool for the management of complexity.

5.7.1   Defining Abstract Spaces

A primary motivation for the definition of abstract spaces is to have unambiguous meaning. That is, when we define a new abstract space, we are free to assign to it exactly those operators and properties that we need, and no others.[13]   By creating abstract spaces tailored for particular uses, and by stating explicitly what their characteristics are, we attempt to eliminate (or at least mitigate) hidden assumptions or effects. (This is in line with our overall attitude of "do what you're trying to do," as per Section 1.6.)

How does one go about defining an abstract space? At its most basic level, it's easy: One merely says, for example,

Let Things *be an abstract space.*[14]

One would then go on from there and describe various properties of and operations on (elements of) the space. This approach is used for the various geometric objects in Ch. 8.

Often, we can take advantage of existing standard types of abstract spaces. For example, we define a new abstract space to be a vector space, or a Banach algebra. Later in this chapter we define some types of spaces that are particularly useful for our structured modeling purposes: "indexes" in Section 5.8, and "state spaces" in Section 5.9. By using these types of spaces we will ultimately be able to, for example, declare mathematically merely that "x is a rigid-body system" to describe well-defined behavior, properties, etc., for a named collection of rigid bodies that move dynamically.

It may occasionally happen that we will define some new space, and it turns out to be (provably) equivalent to some other, well-known space. For example, in Section 5.9.2 we discuss a space describing rectangles; the space defined there is in fact equivalent to $\Re^2$. If such an equivalence does occur ... great! We can apply whatever properties are known about that existing space to our own space; we've gained an extra body of knowledge about our space "for free."

---

[13] " 'When *I* use a word,' Humpty Dumpty said ... 'it means just what I choose it to mean—neither more nor less.' " In [Carroll60], Martin Gardner discusses Carroll's mathematical philosophy that lies behind "Humpty Dumpty's whimsical discourse on semantics."

[14] We consistently use a sans serif font for abstract spaces. Additionally, we give each space we define a plural name; this makes it easy to read, e.g., "$t \in$ Things" as "t is an element of the set of Things," i.e., "t is a Thing."

One might argue that if it is the case that a new space is equivalent to an existing, well-known space, making our own definition merely confuses things. There is a twofold response:

- With a good name for the space, one can convey a desired connotation. Saying "x is in the space of rectangles" has more intuitive meaning than "x is in $\Re^2$."

- If the model gets refined later on, one can change the properties of the new space without needing to change definitions of other terms. For example, we may later decide to consider orientation in the plane as a property of a rectangle. The expression "x is in the space of rectangles" could still stand, but otherwise we would have to change it to "x is in $\Re^2 \times SO(1)$."

However, there is of course merit to the original argument; too many gratuitous definitions can be obfuscatory. Whether or not to define a new space is often an important "design decision," as discussed in Section 5.3.

Pedantic Interlude

"Abstract space" can mean the universal set of a particular set theory ([Nihon Sugakkai77]); in such usage there can only be a single abstract space under discussion. Our use of "abstract space" is closer to the definition in [James, James76]: "a formal mathematical system consisting of undefined objects and axioms of a geometric nature." However, although most of our applications will in fact be geometric, we don't emphasize the geometric nature. Our working definition is thus "a set of undefined objects," where we invoke naive set theory and the axiom of comprehension ([Nihon Sugakkai77]) to be able to define such sets by fiat, and the axioms of pairing, power set, union, and so forth, to manipulate the sets.

In our use of abstract spaces, we are taking a decidedly nonconstructivist approach; constructivist dogma says: "A set is not an entity which has an ideal existence: a set exists only when ... we prescribe ... what we must do in order to construct an element of the set ... " [Bishop,Bridges85, p. 5]. Our motivation for defining abstract spaces is, as discussed above, to have precise statements of the properties of mathematical objects we will manipulate; in order to encourage such statements, we leave ourselves free to state them without the attendant formal constructivist mechanism. Since the problems we will be dealing with focus on real-world applications, we are less likely to follow chains of inquiry that lead to the sorts of mathematical monsters feared by constructivists. Ultimately, when we implement our models on computer, we will necessarily be constructivist: A computer program always prescribes how its objects are constructed. But we have admittedly left a possible gap in our methodology: We might in principle define models for which constructive formulations can't be created, i.e., that we cannot directly implement on computers. It is intriguing to consider following strict constructivist doctrine in creating mathematical models, leading perhaps to guarantees of computability and so forth. We have not pursued this line of inquiry.

Finally, note that we are perhaps a bit optimistic in our notion that precise statements of properties will lead to "unambiguous meaning." As discussed by [Lakatos76], one always assumes a familiarity with the terms and concepts used in the definitions; to whatever extent those concepts are fluid, ambiguities can arise. Still, in practice, reasonable attempts at precision of meaning can help one go a long way—in particular, a lot farther than one would go without *any* attempts to be precise.[15]

5.7.2   Specializations

Occasionally, we will define (or will be given) an abstract space, but will wish to focus on a subset of it that is particularly interesting, defining operators, properties and so forth that apply only to the subset but not the space as a whole. To formalize this notion, we introduce the idea of a "specialization" (see Fig. 5.4):

Definition. **Specialization**

(5.4)

> A **specialization** *of a given abstract space (called the* **general space***) is a different abstract space that is in one-to-one correspondence with some subset of the general space.*

Definition 5.4: Since the elements of a specialization correspond one-to-one to those of a subset of the general space, properties and operators of the specialization's elements can be thought of as implicitly applying to those of the subset. □

and some attendant notation:

Notation. Subset-like Symbol "⊏" for Specializations

(5.5)

> *If we are given, e.g., spaces named* Specs *and* Gens,
> *and an injection (one-to-one function)*
> f: Specs → Gens, *then we denote the specialization*
> *relationship using the symbol* "⊏":
>
> Specs $\overset{f}{\sqsubset}$ Gens   ≡   *"*Specs *is a specialization of* Gens*"*
>
> f(Specs)   ≡   *The subset of* Gens *corresponding with* Specs

Notation 5.5:   Notation for specializations. If we do not need to name the injection, we simply write Specs ⊏ Gens. □

---

[15] We can claim some kinship with Lakatos, however, in the domain of formalism versus methodology ([Lakatos76, pp. 1–5]). Our approach toward mathematical complexity is not geared toward a formal analysis of complexity, but rather toward methods or heuristics to manage it. For discussion of the complexity of numerical computation, we refer the reader to [Traub *et al.*88].

A "Specialization" of a Space

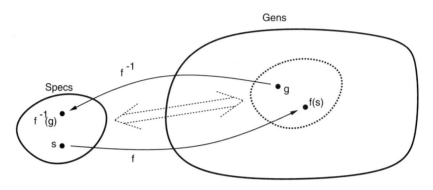

Specs is a specialization of Gens:

$$\text{Specs} \stackrel{f}{\sqsubset} \text{Gens}$$

Figure 5.4: A specialization of an abstract space. Space Specs corresponds one-to-one with a subset of space Gens; the function $f: \text{Specs} \to \text{Gens}$ is an injection (one-to-one function) that determines the subset and the correspondence. Specializations are used, for example, in Ch. 11, to describe some classes of linear functions as specializations of general spaces of arbitrary functions. □

For an element of a specialization, $s \in \text{Specs} \stackrel{f}{\sqsubset} \text{Gens}$, the corresponding element of the general space is given by $f(s)$. Conversely, for an element $g \in f(\text{Specs}) \subseteq \text{Gens}$, the corresponding element of the specialization is given by $f^{-1}(g)$. Note that $f^{-1}(g)$ is not defined for all general elements $g \in \text{Gens}$, only for those elements that actually correspond with elements of Specs.

Since every element of a specialization has exactly one corresponding general element, we commonly (or implicitly) overload all operators on general spaces to act on the specializations:

(5.6)

Given a specialization $\text{Specs} \stackrel{f}{\sqsubset} \text{Gens}$, *and an operator*
$\text{OP}: \text{Gens} \to \text{A}$, *we overload* $\text{OP}: \text{Specs} \to \text{A}$:

$$\text{OP}(s) = \text{OP}(f(s)), \text{ for all } s \in \text{Specs}$$

Equation 5.6: All general-space operators are overloaded onto the specialization. Thus an element of a specialization can act as the corresponding element of the general space. □

In Section 5.9.5 we give a mechanism for specifying new operations and properties just for the specialization.

Our notion of a specialization mechanism is of course patterned after class derivation in object-oriented programming. In principle, we might consider overloading operators so that OP(s) would be different from OP$(f(s))$, thus achieving a mathematical analog of polymorphism. However, as discussed in Section 5.5.3, we think that would introduce excessive ambiguity—our idea behind specializations is to assign extra properties to interesting subsets of a spaces, not to change any existing properties. As an aside, C++ programmers might note that evaluating $f(s)$ is analogous to performing an "upcast" from a derived class to a base class, while $f^{-1}(g)$ is analogous to a "downcast" and is only "type-safe" when $g \in f(\textbf{Specs})$ (see [Stroustrup91]).

5.7.3   Disparate Unions

Generally, when one thinks of a particular space, even an abstract one, the fact that all its elements belong to that space leads one to think of all those elements as being essentially similar in some conceptual way. While this is tautologically true, it will also occasionally be the case that there is a marked *dis*similarity between objects that we have chosen to group together into a single set—in particular, we may group together objects that have different dimensionalities or degrees of freedom (see Fig. 5.5). Thus we define

Definition. **Disparate Union**

(5.7)

> A **disparate union** *is an abstract space that can be partitioned into a collection of disparate sets; each of those sets is called a* **disparate component** *of the union. Two elements of a disparate union are* **agnates** *if they belong to the same disparate component.*

Definition 5.7: A disparate union is a collection of different types of elements. Thus if A is an abstract set, two elements $x, y \in$ A might have no or few common operators or properties—they may be "like apples and oranges." Disparate unions, and paths through disparate unions, will be useful for models of things whose state and makeup can vary qualitatively; see the discussion of segmented functions, Section 5.10. □

A disparate union may be explicitly defined as the union of various different spaces; for example, Def. 8.3 defines a space **GeomObjs** whose elements include locations, scalars, vectors, and others. Or, a space defined in some other manner may nonetheless be a disparate union, for example, the set of all "indexes" of a given space, as is discussed in Section 5.8.2. Trivially, any homogeneous space is a disparate union, comprised of a single disparate component; thus all elements of a homogeneous space are agnates.

We will assume that given an element of a disparate union, we can always know to which disparate component it belongs, either by inspection or by construction—i.e., given any two elements, we can determine if they are agnates. C programmers

Disparate Unions

(a)   (b)

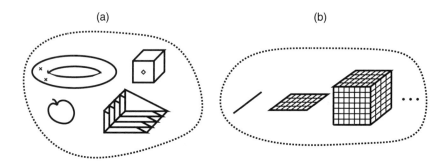

Figure 5.5: Disparate unions. We occasionally define abstract spaces whose elements may be of
various dissimilar types—they needn't even have the same dimensionality or degrees of freedom. Two
elements that are of the same type are said to be "agnates." (a) A disparate union including points on
the surface of a torus, points within the body of a cube, and others. The points marked × are agnates
(both on the torus), but neither is an agnate of the point marked ◇ (in the cube). (b) A disparate union
whose elements have some similarity—all are points from the unit cubes in various dimensions—but
that nonetheless have distinct dimensionality. For this space, arithmetic operations are defined between
agnates, and we can always construct smooth paths between agnates; but we do not have arithmetic or
continuous paths between points that are not agnates. Chapter 8 defines a disparate union of geometric
objects, and disparate unions are central to the segmented function mechanism of Section 5.10 which
is used for the "tennis ball cannon" model of Ch. 13. □

may notice a similarity with the union construct: A union variable may in fact
be of any of its component types, and the programmer must keep track of the type
of any particular value of the union (see [Kernighan,Ritchie88]).

More Pedantry

We are not familiar with existing mathematical mechanisms that emphasize the
manipulation of sets containing elements with varying dimensionality. A related
concept is that of a directed system of sets (see [Spanier66]); that idea, however,
focuses on ordering and maps between the component sets, particularly in the
definition of the direct limit, which defines an equivalence between elements of
each set. We are interested, however, in the fact that the elements of the component
sets *differ*, not in how they can be equated.

For those who are made uneasy by our assumption that we can always determine from which component set an element originates, we can fall back on
[Spanier66]'s definition of *disjoint union* (or *set sum*), in which each element of
the union is a pair containing both an element of a component set and essentially
a tag that indicates which component set.

5.8 Identifiers (IDs) and Indexes

Often a model will need to handle a collection of objects, such as a collection of rigid bodies. This section presents a mechanism that allows us to define a collection of elements, and manipulate it as a single entity, yet also be able to mathematically "access" individual elements within it. We start, in Section 5.8.1, by defining the *identifiers* (*IDs*) that will be used to name objects. Section 5.8.2 defines and gives notation for *indexes,* which are collections of named objects. Section 5.8.3 discusses various operations on indexes.

The mechanism described here is used extensively in the models in Part III; see, e.g., the index **Systems** in Def. 9.6 and its use in Eq. 9.12.

5.8.1 Definition of IDs

The set of identifiers is trivial:

Definition. IDs

$$(5.8) \qquad \text{IDs} \equiv \left(\begin{array}{c} \textit{a discrete space, with an} \\ \textit{equivalence relation to distinguish} \\ \textit{between the elements} \end{array} \right)$$

Definition 5.8: A space of identifiers (IDs). We will use the elements of IDs to label various things. We can think of each ID as a name, like "hansel" or "grendel" or "obj193b." □

Having an equivalence relation simply means that we can tell IDs apart: Given $a, b \in$ IDs, we can tell if $a = b$ or if $a \neq b$. Note that we have no other relations defined for IDs. In particular, we do not define an ordering.[16]

We will use IDs from the one space IDs to name many different types of things. One might be worried about confusion—given a particular ID, what type of thing is it naming? One could partition IDs into disjoint subsets, where each subset corresponds to a different type of thing being named. In practice, we have not found this to be necessary. Note also that the space IDs is infinite; we assume that we can always grab a new ID if we need one.

We will occasionally use sets of IDs. The following definition is convenient:

Definition. IDsets

$$(5.9) \qquad \text{IDsets} \equiv \textit{the space } \left\{ \textit{sets of } \text{IDs} \right\}$$

Definition 5.9: Sets of IDs. If $s \in$ IDsets, then s is a set of IDs; we can speak of the size of the set, $\|s\|$, and whether a given identifier $i \in$ IDs is in the set ($i \in s$) or not ($i \notin s$). □

---

[16]Why go to all this effort? Why not just label objects with integers? The reason is that we don't want to always have an implied ordering between labeled objects if there is no natural ordering. A particular collection of objects may need an ordering (or several orderings); in such a case the orderings would be defined explicitly.

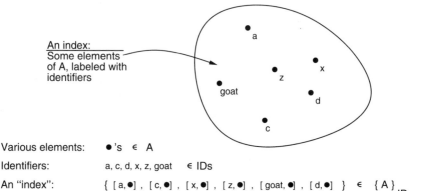

Various elements: •'s ∈ A

Identifiers: a, c, d, x, z, goat   ∈ IDs

An "index":   { [a, •] , [c, •] , [x, •] , [z, •] , [goat, •] , [d, •] } ∈ { A }_{IDs}

Figure 5.6: An index is a collection of elements of some space, each labeled by an identifier; given an index, we can look up elements based on their identifiers. In this illustration, the •'s are various elements of a space A. It is allowable for two of the •'s to be equal—two different identifiers may label the same element—but no single identifier can be used to label two different elements. □

5.8.2 Indexes

We define an index[17] to be a collection of elements from some space, with each element labeled by a unique ID (see Fig. 5.6):

Definition. **Indexes**

(5.10)

> *An **index** of elements of a space A is a set of pairs*
> $[i \in \mathsf{IDs}, a \in \mathsf{A}]$ *such that no two pairs share an ID. That is, if T is an index:*
>
> *For any two pairs $[i, a]$, $[j, b] \in T$,*
> $$i = j \implies a = b$$

Definition 5.10: An index is a collection of paired IDs and values. A given ID can only occur once within the collection; thus each ID uniquely labels its corresponding value. However, any given value may occur several times, labeled by different IDs, i.e., $a = b \not\Rightarrow i = j$. □

We use the following notation for indexes:

---

[17]The word "index" is sometimes used to mean a pointer or indicator that selects a single element from a collection; for instance, in the C programming language expression a[i], the variable i is called an "array index." Our use of "index" is, instead, in the sense of a table; e.g., the index in the back of a book.

Notation. Assorted Notation for Indexes

(5.11)

$$
\begin{aligned}
\{A\}_{IDs} &\equiv \text{\textit{The set of all indexes of elements of space } A} \\
T \in \{A\}_{IDs} &\equiv \text{\textit{``T is an index of elements of space } A\text{''}} \\
Ids(T) &\equiv \text{\textit{The set of IDs used as labels in } T, \textit{ i.e.,}} \\
&\qquad \left\{ i \in IDs \mid \exists a \in A \text{ \textit{such that} } [i, a] \in T \right\} \\
Elts(T) &\equiv \text{\textit{The set of elements of } A \textit{ that are in } T, \textit{ i.e.,}} \\
&\qquad \left\{ a \in A \mid \exists i \in IDs \text{ \textit{such that} } [i, a] \in T \right\} \\
T_i &\equiv \text{\textit{The element of } T \textit{ labeled by } i \in Ids(T), \textit{ i.e.,}} \\
&\qquad a \in A \text{ \textit{such that} } [i, a] \in T
\end{aligned}
$$

Notation 5.11: Notation for indexes. A can be any space. T without subscripts refers to the index as a whole; with a subscript ID, e.g., T_i, refers to a single element. Note that if an ID is not used as a label in T, that is if $i \notin Ids(T)$, then the subscript notation T_i is invalid. □

Sometimes it is convenient to be able to define an index for which we can be careless, and look up an element by ID, without worrying about whether or not the ID is actually used in the index—if it isn't, we will accept 0 as its element. We call these "indexes with 0," and extend the notation:

Notation. Indexes with 0

(5.12)

If space A *has a zero element,* 0*:*

$$
\begin{aligned}
T \in \{A\}^{\circ}_{IDs} &\equiv \text{\textit{``T is an index with zero''}} \\
T_i &\equiv \begin{cases} a \in A \text{ \textit{such that} } [i, a] \in T, & \textit{if } i \in Ids(T) \\ 0, & \textit{if } i \notin Ids(T) \end{cases}
\end{aligned}
$$

Notation 5.12: Indexes with 0. If T is defined to be an index with zero, then the subscript notation is not restricted to IDs that are used as labels in T; for IDs that do not label any element, 0 is used instead. $Ids(T)$ and $Elts(T)$ are the same as in Not. 5.11. □

The remaining discussion of indexes applies also to indexes with zero's.

Note that two indexes $S, T \in \{A\}_{IDs}$ do not necessarily have the same number of entries, or they may have the same number of entries but may use different IDs. Thus the set $\{A\}_{IDs}$ is a disparate union as per Section 5.7.3:

(5.13)

Two indexes $S, T \in \{A\}_{IDs}$ *are agnates if*

$$
Ids(S) = Ids(T)
$$

Equation 5.13: The set of all indexes of A can be partitioned into disparate components so that the indexes in each component have the same IDs. See Def. 5.7. □

Equation 5.35 will illustrate the meaning of *continuity* for index-valued functions.

There is a standard mathematical mechanism similar to our indexes: A mapping from a set Λ to a set A can be called a *family of elements of* A *indexed by* Λ

([Nihon Sugakkai77]). The mapping is commonly written as $\{a_\lambda\}_{\lambda \in \Lambda}$ or just $\{a_\lambda\}$, and Λ is called the *indexing set*. For our purposes, we express the mapping as a set of pairs in order to emphasize its nature as a manipulable mathematical object. Further, we limit our indexes to use IDs as the "indexing set"—but any given index need only be defined over a subset of IDs. LISP programmers will find our indexes to be reminiscent of key-value *association lists* ([Steele90]).

5.8.3   Operations on Indexes

The usual set operations can be applied to indexes, except that we can only perform a union on indexes that don't have any conflicting entries. Several equalities hold.

Given any two indexes $S, T \in \{A\}_{\text{IDs}}$ *of some space* A,

$$Ids(S \cap T) = \left\{ i \in Ids(S) \cap Ids(T) \mid S_i = T_i \right\}$$
$$(S \cap T)_i = S_i, \text{ for } i \in Ids(S \cap T)$$
$$(S \cap T)_i = T_i, \text{ for } i \in Ids(S \cap T)$$

(5.14)
$$Ids(S - T) = Ids(S) - Ids(S \cap T)$$
$$(S - T)_i = S_i, \text{ for } i \in Ids(S - T)$$

If $S_i = T_i$ *for all* $i \in (Ids(S) \cap Ids(T))$,
$$Ids(S \cup T) = Ids(S) \cup Ids(T)$$
$$(S \cup T)_i = \begin{cases} S_i, & \text{if } i \in Ids(S) \\ T_i, & \text{if } i \in Ids(T) \end{cases}$$

Equation 5.14: The intersection of two indexes includes only elements having both the same label and the same value in each index. To subtract from an index, we remove all elements that are in the intersection with the subtrahend. We can only perform a union on two indexes if any IDs that they share are used to label the same value in both. □

We define notation to add and delete elements of an index:[18]

Notation. Index $+$ and $-$

For index $S \in \{A\}_{\text{IDs}}$ *of some space* A, $i \in$ IDs, $x \in$ A,
and $I \in$ IDsets

(5.15)
$$S + [i, x] \equiv S \cup \{[i, x]\}, \qquad i \notin Ids(S)$$
$$S - i \equiv S - \{[i, S_i]\}, \qquad i \in Ids(S)$$
$$S - I \equiv S - \left\{ [i, S_i] \mid i \in I \right\}, \qquad I \subseteq Ids(S)$$

Notation 5.15: Adding and deleting entries from an index. Note that to delete an element, we need only specify the ID. We define "subtraction" for a single ID or for a set of IDs. □

---

[18] We are using sloppy language here; as per Section 5.5.1, we can't "change" an index by adding or deleting elements. More precisely, these are operations that describe a new index given the operands.

Often we will be given an index of elements of A, and an operator that acts on individual elements of A; we will want to apply the operator to the entire index at once, constructing the index of results.[19] Thus, formally:

Definition. Operators on Indexes

(5.16)

> *Given an operator* OP: $A \rightarrow B$ *for some spaces* A *and* B,
> *we overload the operator* OP: $\{A\}_{IDs} \rightarrow \{B\}_{IDs}$ *as*
> *follows: Let* $a \in \{A\}_{IDs}$; $b \in \{B\}_{IDs}$ *be indexes, then*
>
> $$\text{OP}(a) = b \iff \begin{cases} b_i = \text{OP}(a_i), \text{ all } i \in Ids(a) \\ Ids(b) = Ids(a) \end{cases}$$

Definition 5.16: If we apply an operator to an index of elements, we get the index of results of applying the operator to each element. Note that we are implicitly overloading every operator on a space to act on indexes of that space. □

If we have an index of functions,[20] we can always define a corresponding function that returns an index:

Definition. **Implied Function** of an Index of Functions

(5.17)

> *Given an index F whose elements are functions into*
> *some space* A, *i.e.,* $F \in \{functions: \Re \rightarrow A\}_{IDs}$, *the*
> **implied function** *is the unique index-valued function*
> $D: \Re \rightarrow \{A\}_{IDs}$ *such that:*
>
> $$Ids(D(x)) = Ids(F) \quad \text{independent of } x$$
> $$D(x)_i = F_i(x) \quad \text{for all } i \in Ids(F), \ x \in \Re$$

Definition 5.17: A function implied by an index of functions. Given an index F, each of whose elements is a function, there is a unique implied function whose value is the index of results of evaluating each element of F. The domain of the functions doesn't have to be $\Re$, but can be any space. □

Thus we can "evaluate" an index of functions as if it were a function:

Notation. Evaluating an Implied Function Using Parentheses "( )"

(5.18)

> *Given an index of functions into some space* A, *e.g.,*
> $F \in \{functions: \Re \rightarrow A\}_{IDs}$, *parentheses implicitly refer*
> *to F's implied function:*
>
> $$F(x) \equiv D(x), where \ D: \Re \rightarrow \{A\}_{IDs} \text{ is implied by } F$$

Notation 5.18: We can treat an index of functions as if it were the corresponding implied function of indexes. This notation can of course be used for functions other than of reals or of more than one variable; we would write, e.g., $F(x, y, z)$. □

---

[19] In LISP parlance, we are performing a "map" of the operator over the index ([Steele90]).

[20] "Index of functions" — is that kosher? Sure, if one considers each function to be an element of a space of functions. We actually use this frequently in Part III.

5.9   State Spaces

Modeling often involves the manipulation of the *state* of an object: its location, configuration, momentum, and the like, as appropriate—all that describes its condition of existence. To accomplish this, it is often useful to define an abstract space such that a single abstract element corresponds to a unique and complete depiction of the state. This gives us "encapsulation" of information, as discussed in Section 5.4.4—we can manipulate a single entity, rather than having to handle the collection of separate parameter values that make up the state.

Since we will frequently want to define and use abstract "state spaces," this section provides a mechanism—definitions and notation—to aid in the process. Readers with a background in computer programming will observe that the state space mechanism we describe here is reminiscent of data structures or, more strongly, of object-oriented programming. As discussed in Section 5.4, we have intentionally borrowed the object-and-operator paradigm of object-oriented programming for use in mathematical modeling.

5.9.1   Basic Definition and Notation

We want to use abstract spaces whose elements correspond with, or encapsulate, the states of objects. Such spaces will need operators to perform the mapping between the abstract elements and the various parameters and other aspects of the corresponding state. Thus we define

Definition. **State Space, Aspect Operators**

(5.19)

> *A* **state space** *is an abstract space that has an associated collection of named operators into other spaces. These operators are called* **aspect operators** *of the state space.*

Definition 5.19: An element of a state space can be thought of as representing a collection of mathematical values of various types. The "aspect" operators tell us what those values are for any given element. □

An example of a state space might be

(5.20)

$$\begin{aligned} &an\ abstract\ space\ \mathsf{S}\\ &operator\ a : \mathsf{S} \rightarrow \mathsf{A}\\ &operator\ b : \mathsf{S} \rightarrow \mathsf{B}\\ &operator\ c : \mathsf{S} \rightarrow \mathsf{C} \end{aligned}$$

Equation 5.20: A sample state space S having three aspect operators, a, b, and c (see Fig. 5.7). □

We impose the restriction that an element of a state space can be identified by its complete collection of aspect values; all "measurable" or "distinguishing"

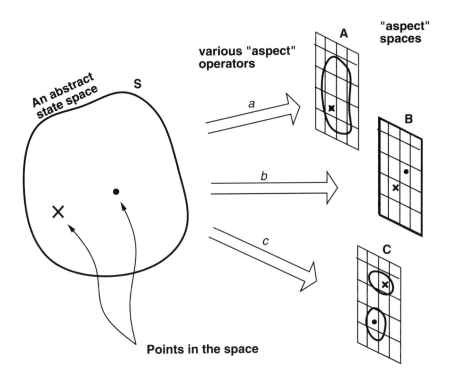

Figure 5.7: A state space is an abstract space with a collection of named "aspect" operators that project into various aspect spaces; here, we illustrate Eq. 5.20. A point in the state space is determined uniquely by its entire collection of aspect values. Note that any given aspect operator may be many-to-one, and the projection of the state space may be a subset of the aspect space. Additionally, aspect values may be nonindependent, e.g., for all points in $s \in \mathsf{S}$, the values of the aspects might always satisfy $a(s) = 1 + 2b(s)$. □

properties of an element of a state space must have aspect operators defined for them.

$$\text{Given a state space } \mathsf{S} \text{ with aspects } a, b, \ldots,$$
$$\text{and } x, y \in \mathsf{S}$$

(5.21)

$$x = y \iff \begin{cases} a(x) = a(y) \\ b(x) = b(y) \\ \vdots \end{cases}$$

Equation 5.21: An element in a state space is uniquely identified by its complete collection of aspect values. There will never be two different elements that "look alike," i.e., have exactly the same aspect values. □

It is convenient to standardize some terminology:

State space. An abstract space, as per Def. 5.19.

Aspect operator. An operator on elements of a state space. (In Eq. 5.20, a, b, and c are aspect operators of S.)

Aspect space. The target space of an aspect operator. (In Eq. 5.20, A, B, and C are aspect spaces.)

Aspect value. The result of applying an aspect operator to a particular element of a state space. (In Eq. 5.20, if $s \in$ S is an element of the state space S, $a(s)$, $b(s)$ and $c(s)$ are its aspect values.)

Point in a space. We use "point in a space" interchangeably with "element of a space." However, "point" tends to have a connotation that the space is continuous, while "element" has a connotation that the space is discrete.

For a more tangible example of a state space, suppose we wish to have a space of geometric arcs, Arcs. Every element in the space Arcs corresponds to a particular geometric arc. We use operators on the space Arcs to examine the properties of the arcs; each operator specifies a geometric property of the arc that corresponds with a given element of Arcs. Thus, we might have operators to tell us the radius and subtended angle of each arc. Rather than list the space and name the operators in long form as in Eq. 5.20, we use a shorthand:

Notation. Brackets "[ ]" and Arrows "$\mapsto$" for a State Space

(5.22)

Notation 5.22: The notation on the left is shorthand for the collection of statements on the right to define a state space. Note that if we define several state spaces that share aspect names, we are implicitly overloading the aspect operators (see Section 5.6.3). □

Generally, we think of and visualize elements of state spaces as points or dots in some nebulous region, as illustrated in Fig. 5.7. However, it is also possible to think of concrete values: By Eq. 5.21, each element of a state space S has a unique tuple of aspect values. Thus a state space S can be embedded in the Cartesian product of its aspect spaces:

(5.23)

Given a state space S *with aspect operators* $a, b, \ldots$
and corresponding aspect spaces A, B, $\ldots$,
where S *is isomorphic to a set* $C \subseteq$ A $\times$ B $\times \ldots$,

$$C = \left\{ [a(s), b(s), \ldots] \mid s \in \mathsf{S} \right\}$$

Equation 5.23: An embedding of a state space. The state space S is isomorphic to the set C comprised of the tuples of aspect values. The isomorphism of the spaces S and C comes directly from the definition of identity of elements of S, in Eq. 5.21. □

That is, when it is more convenient, we can think of an element as its equivalent tuple of aspect values (hence Not. 5.22 looks like a tuple written vertically). If we wish to define an element of a state space by specifying its tuple of aspect values, we use the following notation:

Notation. Brackets "[ ]" and Backarrows "↤" for a Tuple

(5.24)

$$\begin{bmatrix} r & \leftarrowtail & r \\ angle & \leftarrowtail & a \end{bmatrix} \quad \equiv \quad \begin{array}{c} c \in \mathsf{Arcs} \; such \; that \\ r(c) = r, \\ angle(c) = a \end{array}$$

Notation 5.24: Shorthand notation to specify an element of a state space by a tuple of aspect values. Note that this notation leaves implicit to which space the element belongs—it needs to be clear from context. The notation is not well defined if there is not a unique element corresponding with the tuple. It is not always necessary to include values for all the aspect operators, however; this is discussed in Section 5.9.2. □

5.9.2 Internal Properties of a State Space

For a particular state space it may be true that only certain combinations of aspect values are possible. Aspects may be redundant (e.g., two aspects—one describes a length in yards, the other describes the same length in meters); more generally, there may be arbitrary relationships between possible aspect values, reflecting the inherent structure and "topology" of the aspect space. According to the terms of Eq. 5.23, C would be a proper subset of the embedding space $A \times B \times \ldots$; often, C is a low-dimensionality manifold in the higher-dimensionality embedding space.

We define the *internal properties* of a space to be the aspect value relationships that are guaranteed to hold for all elements of the space. It is convenient to note the internal properties explicitly, at once when the space is defined. Thus we extend Not. 5.22:

Notation. Internal Properties below a Line "—"

(5.25)

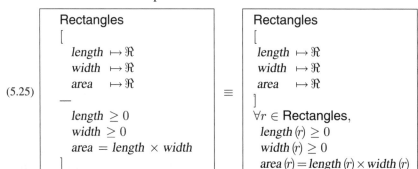

Notation 5.25: The notation on the left is shorthand for the statements on the right, which define a state space (Not. 5.22) and list its collection of internal properties. Note the shorthand leaves implicit the "for all" qualifier—internal properties are by definition true for every element of the space. □

The internal properties defined for a state space are not restrictions that describe acceptable or interesting elements, or those that solve some problem. Rather, as we said above, the properties indicate the internal "topology" of the space.[21]

Equation 5.21 says that, in general, one needs the complete collection of aspect values to identify an element of a state space. For spaces with internal properties, however, it is often true that the values of only a few aspect operators—or even a single aspect operator—are in fact sufficient to identify uniquely a point in the space. For example, in Not. 5.25, the values of any two of $length(r)$, $width(r)$, and $area(r)$ are sufficient to identify an element $r \in$ Rectangles. We call a collection of only some aspect values a *sub-tuple* for an element (and for clarity we will occasionally refer to the complete tuple of values as a *full tuple*) and define

Definition. **Identifying Sub-tuple**

(5.26)

> *A sub-tuple of aspect values that is sufficient to identify an element of a state space is called an* **identifying sub-tuple.** *If eliminating any value guarantees that the remaining values will be insufficient to identify an element, it is called a* **minimal identifying sub-tuple.**

Definition 5.26: An identifying sub-tuple means that there is only a single element in the space that has those particular aspect values. The remaining values of the element's full tuple can be determined by the internal properties of the space. □

When defining a state space, it is often useful to describe the minimal identifying sub-tuples. Minimal identifying sub-tuples are typically the easiest way to specify

---

[21] However, one might imagine a computer program that numerically computes elements of a state space, representing elements by tuples of values; such a program may in fact use the internal properties to restrict the solution to lie on the proper manifold in the embedding space.

particular elements of a space. Note that Not. 5.24 allows us to describe an element
using an identifying sub-tuple, leaving out the unnecessary aspect values; since the
notation includes aspect names, there's no ambiguity about which aspect operator
values are part of the sub-tuple.

5.9.3   Subscript Notation for Aspect Operators

An aspect operator is just an operator, and we can use ordinary parenthetical
notation to evaluate it, as in Eq. 5.21. However, sometimes parentheses can get
cumbersome—when equations get complex or, in particular, when an aspect value
is itself a function. We find it convenient to define an alternative notation:

Notation. Subscripts for Aspect Values

(5.27)

> *Given a state space* S *with an aspect operator* a *and an*
> *element* $s \in$ S, *the following notations are equivalent:*
>
> $a(s)$ *[standard parenthetical notation]*
> a_s *[new subscript notation]*
>
> $$a_s \equiv a(s)$$

Notation 5.27: Subscript notation for aspect operators. In any given expression, we use
whichever notation seems clearer. □

Often, we consider functions into state spaces. Again, to alleviate difficulties with
parentheses, we define an alternate subscript notation:

Notation. Subscripts for Aspect-Valued Functions

(5.28)

> *Given a state space* S *with an aspect operator* a *and a*
> *function* $s: \Re \to$ S, *the following notations are equivalent:*
>
> $a(s(t))$ *[standard parenthetical notation]*
> $a_{s(t)}$ *[subscript notation of Not. 5.27]*
> $a_s(t)$ *[new subscript notation]*
> $(a \circ s)(t)$ *[function composition notation]*
>
> $$a_s(t) \equiv a_{s(t)} \equiv a(s(t)) \equiv (a \circ s)(t)$$

Notation 5.28: Subscript notation for functions into state space. The new subscript notation
$a_s(t)$ emphasizes the composite result: an aspect value as a function of t. In any given
expression, we use whichever notation seems clearer. This notation can of course be
used for functions other than of reals or of more than one variable; we would write, e.g.,
$a_s(x, y, z) \equiv a(s(x, y, z))$. □

The different notations in Not. 5.28 have the common feature that from left to right,
they all list a then s then t, so even if we get lost among the various parentheses
and subscripts, we can get the idea of what's happening.

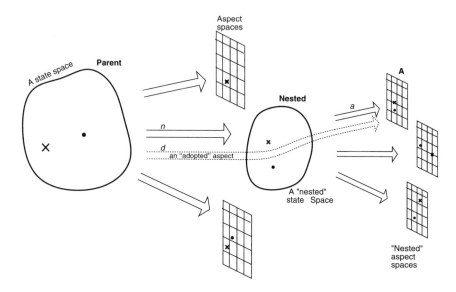

Figure 5.8: Nested state spaces. An aspect space of a state space may be another state space. The aspects of the nested space may be "adopted" as aspects of the parent space through composition of aspect operators; here we illustrate aspect operator n being adopted into the parent space as aspect operator d. □

5.9.4   Nested State Spaces

An aspect space of a state space may be another state space. That is, one state space may be "nested" inside of another; this is illustrated in Fig. 5.8. The parent space can "adopt" aspects from the nested space to be its own aspects as well:

Definition. **Adopt** an Aspect

(5.29)

> *Given a space* A, *a state space* Nested *with an aspect operator* a: Nested → A, *and a state space* Parent *with aspect operators* n: Parent → Nested *and*
> d: Parent → A,
>
> **Parent adopts** a *as* d *iff:*
>
> $$d(p) = a(n(p)), \text{ for all } p \in \textsf{Parent}$$

Definition 5.29: Adopting an aspect from a nested space. The parent space's aspect operator is equivalent to the composition of the nested space's aspect operator with the aspect operator that yields the nested space element (see Fig. 5.8). □

Using Not. 5.25, we can rewrite Def. 5.29, perhaps more clearly:

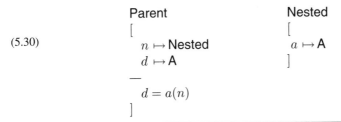

State space **Parent** *adopts an aspect* a *of state space*
Nested *as its own aspect* d *if, for some space* **A***:*

(5.30)

$$
\begin{array}{ll}
\textbf{Parent} & \textbf{Nested} \\
[& [\\
\quad n \mapsto \textbf{Nested} & \quad a \mapsto \textbf{A} \\
\quad d \mapsto \textbf{A} &] \\
\\
\overline{} \\
\quad d = a(n) \\
]
\end{array}
$$

Equation 5.30: Adopting an aspect from a nested space. The adoption equivalence in Def. 5.29 is expressed as a property of the parent space **Parent**. □

Frequently, we choose to keep the same name for the adopted aspect in the parent space as it has in the nested space. We extend Not. 5.25 to allow easy definition of adopted aspects:

Notation. Ellipsis "..." for an Adopted Aspect

(5.31)

$$
\begin{array}{l}
\textbf{Bricks} \\
[\\
\quad height \mapsto \Re \\
\quad base \quad \mapsto \textbf{Rectangles} \\
\quad depth \quad \dots length \mapsto \Re \\
\quad width \quad \dots width \mapsto \Re \\
\quad volume \mapsto \Re \\
\\
\overline{} \\
\quad height > 0 \\
\quad volume = height \cdot area\,(base) \\
]
\end{array}
\quad \equiv \quad
\begin{array}{l}
\textbf{Bricks} \\
[\\
\quad height \quad \mapsto \Re \\
\quad base \quad \mapsto \textbf{Rectangles} \\
\quad depth \quad \mapsto \Re \\
\quad width \quad \mapsto \Re \\
\quad volume \mapsto \Re \\
\\
\overline{} \\
\quad height > 0 \\
\quad volume = height \cdot area\,(base) \\
\quad depth = length\,(base) \\
\quad width = width\,(base) \\
]
\end{array}
$$

Notation 5.31:   The notation on the left is shorthand for the definition on the right, in which the nested space's *length* and *width* aspects are adopted into the parent space. In the shorthand notation, each adoption is listed directly underneath the nested space, with ellipses leading from the parent aspect name to the adopted aspect name. The names may be the same or different. **Rectangles** is used here as defined in Not. 5.25. □

The examples in Not. 5.25 and Not. 5.31 let us derive a corollary from the properties of the spaces **Bricks** and **Rectangles**:

$$\forall b \in \textbf{Bricks}, \; volume_b = depth_b \times width_b \times height_b.$$

A final note on nested spaces: We want to avoid circularity—we disallow a parent state space that nests itself or that nests a space that directly or indirectly nests the parent.

5.9.5   State Space Specializations

In Section 5.7.2, we discussed the idea of a *specialization,* i.e., a subset of a general space that has additional properties and operators. The state space mechanism can be used to define these additional properties.

To define a state space **Specs** as a specialization of some general space **Gens** with an injection f: **Specs** → **Gens**, we need only list f as an aspect operator of **Specs** and include internal properties that insure f is one-to-one. However, we define notation to make the specialization explicitly visible:

Notation. Specialization Symbol "⊏" for State Spaces

(5.32)

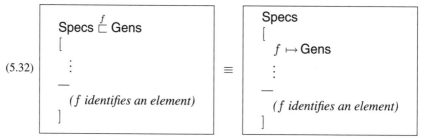

Notation 5.32:   The definitions on the right-hand side define **Specs** as a specialization of **Gens**, as per Def. 5.4 and Fig. 5.4; the notation on the left is a shorthand form. Note that since f is one-to-one, each element $s \in$ **Specs** has a unique value of f_s; thus a value of f comprises an identifying tuple for an element of **Specs**. □

If the general space is itself a state space, then the specialization implicitly adopts all of its aspects, by Eq. 5.6 and Def. 5.29. That is, we have

Notation. Specialization of a State Space

(5.33)

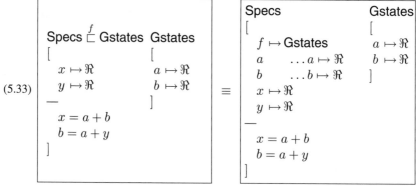

Notation 5.33:   A specialization of a state space implicitly adopts all aspects. Note that in this example the internal properties of **Specs** are sufficient to determine x and y from the adopted aspect values a and b, thus f is sufficient to identify an element of **Specs**. If no name is needed for the injection aspect operator, we can write just **Specs** ⊏ **Gstates**. □

Several examples of state space specializations can be found in Ch. 11.

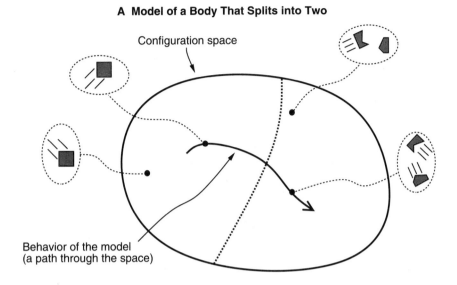

A Model of a Body That Splits into Two

Configuration space

Behavior of the model
(a path through the space)

Figure 5.9: Example of a segmented function. Consider a model of a body that splits into two bodies. When there is only one body, we describe the model with 6 degrees of freedom (3D position and orientation), but when there are two bodies, 12 degrees of freedom are needed. The model's behavior over time is described by a *segmented function:* a piecewise-continuous function into a disparate union. □

5.10   Segmented Functions

Suppose we want to create a model of a thing whose behavior over time includes discontinuous changes in its configuration or properties. For example, as illustrated in Fig. 5.9, the number of bodies in a model may change as bodies are created or destroyed; [Brockett90] describes a formal language for robotic motion that includes discrete changes in force function; and [Kalra90] allows the behavior of a model to change discretely between nodes of a directed graph.

We would like to define a single function of time that completely describes a model's behavior. But at each discontinuous change, the model may switch between incompatible configurations having different dimensionality or degrees of freedom—how can we have one function that spans these changes?

The answer is simple: Consider the overall configuration space of the model to be the *disparate union* (Section 5.7.3) of the various individual configuration spaces—then define the behavior as a path through that overall configuration space. This section introduces the idea of a *segmented function* to describe such paths. The mechanism we define here is used, for example, in the "tennis ball cannon" model of Ch. 13.

5.10.1   Definition of a Segmented Function

We'd like a path through a disparate union to be "continuous," but continuity can't be defined in general for disparate unions. A path that stays within a single disparate component of the union can be continuous, however—but to make a transition between components, there must be a discontinuity. Thus we define

Definition. **Segmented Function**

(5.34)

> *A* **segmented function** *is a piecewise-continuous function from the real numbers to a disparate union. Each continuous piece is called a* **segment,** *and we refer to each discontinuity as an* **event.**

Definition 5.34: Each segment of a segmented function stays within a disparate component of the union; i.e., all points along the segment are agnates. The transition from one segment to the next may cross into a different component. Note that we define segmented functions only as paths, i.e., functions from the real numbers, rather than as functions from arbitrary spaces. □

The definition assumes that *continuous* is well defined within each component of the disparate union. For a space that is discrete, we take *continuous* to mean *constant.* And thus, for a space that is (equivalent to) a Cartesian product of discrete and smooth spaces, *continuous* means that the discrete parts stay constant and the smooth parts can vary continuously.

A common use of segmented functions is for paths into a space of indexes (Section 5.8.2). First, we'll look at what continuity means for index-valued functions:

(5.35)

> *For an index-valued function* $f: \Re \to \{A\}_{IDs}$ *to be continuous, we must have*
>
> • *the composite function* $(Ids \circ f): \Re \to IDsets$ *is constant, and*
> • *each composite function* $f_i: \Re \to A$ *is continuous, for* $i \in Ids(f(t))$.

Equation 5.35: Continuous index-valued functions. For f to be continuous, we must have a given collection of elements, each of which varies continuously (we assume that continuity is defined for the space A). □

A segmented function is made from continuous pieces, and thus:

(5.36)

> *For a segmented index-valued function* $f: \Re \to \{A\}_{IDs}$,
> *we have*
>
> • $(Ids \circ f): \Re \to IDsets$ *is constant in each segment, and*
> • *each* $f_i: \Re \to A$ *is continuous in each segment, for* $i \in Ids(f(t))$.

Equation 5.36: Segmented index-valued functions. Each segment may have a different set of IDs. If two adjacent segments share an ID i, the value $f(t)_i$ might or might not vary continuously across the event. □

A Segmented Function $Y(t)$ **Represented by a Sequence**

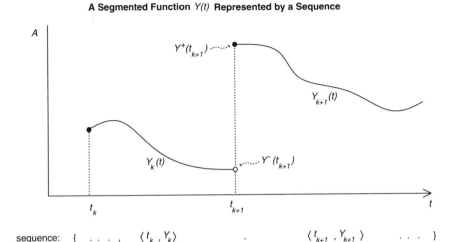

Figure 5.10: Sequential representation of a segmented function. Each element in the sequence is a pair containing the corresponding segment's left bound and continuous function. The diagram illustrates two adjacent segments. ☐

5.10.2 Sequential Representation of a Segmented Function

We'd like to represent segmented functions concretely in order to be able to manipulate and evaluate them. Mathematical and numerical methods are most often designed for continuous functions and don't robustly handle discontinuities. Thus we isolate the continuous parts of a segmented function, expressing it as a sequence of continuous functions with bounded domains (see Fig. 5.10):

Definition. **Sequential Representation**

(5.37)

> *The* **sequential representation** *of a segmented function* $Y: \Re \rightarrow A$ *for some space* A *is a sequence of real/function pairs:* $\{\ldots, \langle t_{k-1}, Y_{k-1} \rangle, \langle t_k, Y_k \rangle, \langle t_{k+1}, Y_{k+1} \rangle, \ldots\}$ *such that for each pair* $\langle t_k, Y_k \rangle$,
>
> $t_k \in \Re$ *increasing with* k
> $Y_k: [t_k, t_{t+1}] \rightarrow A$ *continuous function on the interval*
> $Y(t) = Y_k(t),$ *where* $t_k \leq t < t_{k+1}$

Definition 5.37: Sequential form of a segmented function. The t_k's in the sequence are the values of t for which there are events. Each function Y_k need only be defined on the interval corresponding to its segment but must be continuous, thus its values must stay within a single disparate component of A. ☐

In order for a segmented function to be defined and single-valued everywhere, including the points of discontinuity, Def. 5.37 defines (arbitrarily) that $Y(t)$ take the value of the segment on the right-hand side of each discontinuity. Thus we have not used the rightmost value of each segment's function. Sometimes, however, we will want to examine "both" values at the discontinuity:

Notation. Superscript "$-$" and "$+$" for Left and Right Values

(5.38)

$$\begin{array}{l} \textit{Given a segmented function } Y : \Re \to \mathsf{A} \textit{ represented} \\ \textit{sequentially by a sequence } \{\langle t_k, Y_k \rangle\}, \textit{ define} \end{array}$$

$$Y^-(t) \equiv \begin{cases} Y(t), & t \neq t_k \textit{ for any } k \\ Y_{k-1}(t_k) & t = t_k \textit{ for some } k \end{cases}$$

$$Y^+(t) \equiv \begin{cases} Y(t), & t \neq t_k \textit{ for any } k \\ Y_k(t_k) & t = t_k \textit{ for some } k \end{cases}$$

Notation 5.38: $Y^+(t_k)$ is the value of the segmented function on the right-hand side of the discontinuity at t_k, and $Y^-(t_k)$ is the value on the left-hand side. For convenience, away from discontinuities, both are defined to be the same as Y. $\square$

Note that Def. 5.37 and Not. 5.38 assume and imply an infinite number of segments. Often, however, the sequence will be finite on either end: The end segments may extend to $\pm\infty$ if there are no farther events, or we may only be interested in $Y(t)$ for a bounded domain.

5.10.3   Functional Characterization of a Segmented Function

The sequential representation describes a segmented function by enumerating all the segments, i.e., listing the event times t_k and the continuous functions Y_k. We would also like to describe a segmented function "all at once." But, as mentioned in Section 5.10.2, we want a mechanism that isolates the discontinuities.

We define here a predicate-based method to characterize segmented functions. In addition to locating the events between segments, this method emphasizes the relationship that links one segment to the next.

Definition. **Functional Characterization**

The **functional characterization** *of a segmented function* $Y: \Re \to A$ *is a triple of predicates:*

(5.39)

The **functional characterization** *of a segmented function* $Y: \Re \to A$ *is a triple of predicates:*

$\quad$ *a* **body function** $\qquad F: \Re \times A \to \text{Boolean}$
$\qquad\qquad\qquad\qquad\quad$ *that describes the continuous parts of Y,*
$\quad$ *an* **event function** $\qquad G: \Re \times A \to \text{Boolean}$
$\qquad\qquad\qquad\qquad\quad$ *that isolates the events (discontinuities) in Y*
$\quad$ *a* **transition relation** $\quad H: A \times \Re \times A \to \text{Boolean}$
$\qquad\qquad\qquad\qquad\quad$ *that describes the events in Y,*

such that for each segment $\langle t_k, Y_k \rangle$,

$\qquad F(t, Y_k(t))$ *is true* $\qquad\qquad$ *for* $t_k < t < t_{k+1}$
$\qquad G(t, Y^-(t))$ *is true* $\qquad\qquad$ *iff* $t = t_k$
$\qquad H(Y^-(t_k), t_k, Y^+(t_k))$ *is true* $\quad$ *(for each t_k)*

Definition 5.39: A segmented function characterized by three predicates. The body function is true[22] along each continuous segment; the event function is true only at the events; and the transition relation is true where the function crosses an event. □

Notice that we refer to Def. 5.39 as a *characterization*, rather than a *representation*. The predicates are not necessarily "tight": We have not specified their values for arguments that are off the path of $Y(t)$, and furthermore, for the body function and transition relation, constant true predicates would always suffice. Thus a single segmented function can be characterized by many predicate triples, and a single predicate triple can characterize many functions.

Still, the functional characterization provides a canonical form that is often useful—and in many circumstances, we can define predicates that *are* tight. For example, Appendix C uses a functional characterization to define segmented functions as solutions to piecewise-continuous ODEs. Notice that the functional characterization gives a declarative way of encapsulating the procedural instruction *"when x happens, do z"*: If we increase t, the value of the event function, $G(t, Y^-(t))$, remains false until an event occurs, i.e., until *"x happens"*; and in describing the transition from $Y^-(t)$ to $Y^+(t)$ at the event, the transition relation $H(\ldots)$ embodies *"do z."*

This is the end of the Techniques *part of Chapter 5. The next part,* Discussion, *contains some notes on designing models, as well as an overall summary of the chapter.*

---

[22]For predicate calculus purists, writing "$F(\ldots)$ is true" is inelegant; one would just write "$F(\ldots)$." But since we use predicates rarely, we will be explicit.

5.11   Designing a Model

Thus far, this chapter has discussed philosophy and goals for modeling and has presented assorted techniques for mathematical modeling. In this section, we try to give a feel of how these all fit together.

We would like to emphasize again that there is no unique "right" way of defining any particular mathematical model. As discussed in Section 5.3, there are design decisions involved that are often not cut-and-dried, but can be based on aesthetics, experience, goals, and so forth. Thus we don't attempt to provide a specific recipe for model design, but just a collection of notes on creating models.

The kinematic rigid-body module in Ch. 9 is small and serves as a good example of many ideas here; we encourage the reader to refer to it while reading this section. We use the following notation to point to specific examples:

> [§9.3]   = "see Section 9.3 for an example"
> [Eq9.1] = "see Eqn. (or Defn. or Notn.) 9.1 for an example"

5.11.1   Writing a Model

A mathematical model is just a collection of equations and definitions written down with some explanatory text. [§9.3]

Context. We write each mathematical model within the context of the overall physically-based model, as per Section 4.6.3. That is, the mathematical model is preceded by a description of the *conceptual model* [§9.2], i.e., an explanation of the thing being modeled in terms of the behavior and properties of interest, and is followed by statements of *posed problems* [§9.4], i.e., tasks described in words and as the corresponding mathematical problems.

Exposition. The intention of the written mathematical model is to be understandable by human readers. Thus, although the mathematics of the model should be complete and well defined without any extra material, we should also include suitable explanatory text or diagrams to help make the mathematics understandable. In particular, we should explain the physical interpretations of the terms and equations that we write.

Framework. Each mathematical model is intended to be used as a module and may invoke terms and equations from other modules. This leads to the following framework for writing a model:

> **Names and notation.** We start each model by stating its scope name,[23] and also list terms from other modules that we will reference, as per Section 5.6.2.

---

[23]Generally, the scope name does not need to appear anywhere else within the model. This is like the children's riddle: *Q.* "What belongs to you but is used more by everybody else?" *A.* "Your name."

We may also describe other naming conventions, notation that will be used, and so forth. [§9.3.1]

Main body. The definitions and equations that describe the thing being modeled. This may be divided into several sections and is often presented in a form paralleling the conceptual model. [§9.3.2–9.3.5]

Derivations and proofs. We put derivations and proofs, if any are needed, in a separate section. Thus the main body of the model contains the "bottom-line" equations that are of practical use for other modules, while this section contains supplementary material that is of interest to "maintainers" of the model. [§8.7]

5.11.2   What Is in a Typical Model?

Things that are commonly found in models:

State spaces. Typically, the thing being modeled, or objects therein, has some sort of configuration, or state. We use the state space mechanism of Section 5.9 to define the abstract configuration space [Eq9.1]. Note that we're not minimalist about the choice of aspects in state spaces: We include any quantity that defines or is defined by the configuration [Eq10.4]; in order to be able to specify individual elements, we describe what combinations of aspect values comprise identifying tuples. In many cases, it may be useful to define a *metric* for a state space ([Hughes92]), i.e., a definition of a distance between two elements. State spaces are also convenient to bundle a collection of quantities into a single entity [Eq9.8].

Indexes. Whenever there are several of a thing—numbers, vectors, functions, sets, etc.—in a model, we use the index mechanism of Section 5.8.2 to be able to manipulate a collection of the things as a single entity. Particularly common is to have an index of states. [Eq9.6]

Predicates. It is often convenient to define a predicate that is true when a particular relationship or property holds for certain values. [Eq9.9]

Functions. We often define abstract spaces, each element of which is a function. Probably the most common functions are those used for the behavior of a thing over time [Eq9.2], but they can be arbitrary [Eq10.16]. Sometimes we define a space that includes all possible functions from one space to another [Eq8.19], and sometimes we define a space containing only functions that we find interesting or useful [Eq9.2].

5.11.3 Things to Do

"Tactical" ideas for designing models:

Modular design. We don't want to define "global" quantities, but rather always encapsulate them in a state space—even for a top-level model. Thus, we wouldn't write *"let y be the number of yaks, and z the number of zebras."* Instead, we define a state space:

> ZooStates
> [
> $y \mapsto$ *Integers*   *number of yaks*
> $z \mapsto$ *Integers*   *number of zebras*
> $\vdots$
>]

then we can write *"for a zoo having state $s \in$ ZooStates . . . , the number of yaks, y_s, is equal to . . . ."* [§13.3]

Temporal behavior. For behavior of objects over time, we don't want to have a "current" configuration. Instead, we define the entire path of a function over time as a single object [Eq9.2]. We often define predicates that describe interesting paths, or paths that are consistent with other items in the model [Eq10.10].

Layered design. We like to take a layered approach, first defining general properties, then building on them to include more details. For example, Def. 10.10 describes a path of a rigid body that is consistent with respect to arbitrary net force/torque functions; Def. 10.18 refines this to net force/torque fields; and Def. 10.25 refines this further to collections of individual force/torque "motives."

Validity tests. When defining a model, it can be helpful to include theorems or redundancies, i.e., "if *those* are true, then *this* must be true as well." For example, the rigid body model includes an energy formulation so that if the bodies' motions are consistent with the applied forces, an energy conservation equation, Eq. 10.32, must hold. In addition to providing a consistency check on the model, it can be a powerful debugging aid when implementing models, by specifying what to double-check to determine if the solution techniques are working (as discussed in Section 4.6.4).

5.11.4 Things to Think About

Some things to bear in mind while creating a model:

Remember the context. In designing a model, we want to find a balance between definitions that are intuitive and close to the conceptual model, and those that are well suited to the particular problems we expect to pose. Sometimes it all might fit together well, but occasionally there is some tension. We have no specific advice other than to try to keep an eye on "both ends" at once.

Declarative model. We have emphasized the importance of a mathematical model being declarative, a statement of relationships rather than a problem to solve. However, it is easy to slip into a problem-posing mode, especially when we expect to program/simulate a particular problem. One might define a model that's technically declarative, but only via declarations such as "$x = solution\text{-}to\text{-}the\text{-}problem$." As we write equations that define objects, we try to ask ourselves:

- Does the equation describe *what* the object is?

- Or does it just describe *how* to create one?

There is, of course, no hard dividing line, but it is something to think about. We have found that as we gain experience, it becomes easier and more natural to create declarative models.

Relationships in the model. There is an aspect of designing a structured mathematical model that is not unlike programming. In order for the expressions to be complete, we want every function to have arguments for everything it depends on—there should be no hidden parameters. This often involves thinking about how to represent and encapsulate relevant information, what the underlying relationships are between entities, how to define functions so that the right information gets to the right place, and so forth. The design process for the "fancy forces" model in Ch. 11 was an exercise in this type of thinking.

5.12 Summary

This chapter was motivated by the idea that having written, well-defined mathematical formulations leads to more robust models. Traditional mathematical techniques and methods facilitate the creation of what we call "model fragments" (Section 2.7), but do not focus on creating well-defined complex models that include the "glue" between these fragments.

This chapter thus presented techniques and methods that help organize and structure complex mathematical models in a well-defined, writable way. Many of the ideas were inspired by computer programming methodology that has been developed to meet similar needs. The techniques fall into five groups:

Naming strategies (Section 5.6). Techniques for naming mathematical entities. Most notably, we introduce *scoped names*, e.g.,

$$\text{KINEMATIC} :: \textsf{States}$$

Abstract spaces (Section 5.7). Discussion and methods for defining abstract spaces of mathematical entities. Includes the ability to define *specializations*, e.g.,

$$\text{Specs} \sqsubseteq \text{Gens}$$

Indexes (Section 5.8). A mechanism to manipulate collections of named entities, e.g.,

$$\{\text{Things}\}_{\text{IDs}}$$

State spaces (Section 5.9). A mechanism to encapsulate a collection of properties into a single entity, e.g.,

$$
\begin{array}{l}
\text{Arcs} \\
[\\
\quad r \qquad\; \mapsto \Re \\
\quad angle \; \mapsto \Re \\
]
\end{array}
$$

Segmented functions (Section 5.10). A mechanism to describe functions whose values may have discontinuous changes in dimensionality, e.g.,

$$\{\ldots, \langle t_k, Y_k \rangle, \ldots\}$$

We have actually used these mechanisms, informally on whiteboards and on napkins as we developed mathematical models, as well as more formally for the expositions in Part III. They were designed (and refined and re-designed) in order to be practical and effective. We have found that with some experience they are natural and easy to use. Of course, we don't claim that these specific techniques are the best or only ones to meet our goals. Different or additional structuring techniques might well be useful.

Related Work

We are not familiar with other work that follows our approach of creating "complete, explicit models" with a focus on the relationships and administration of model fragments. For basic applied mathematical modeling exposition, we refer the reader to [Lin,Segel74], [Boyce81], and [Edwards, Hamson90]. □

Chapter 6

Computer Programming for Structured Modeling

This chapter puts together various elements discussed so far, to form the basis of a physically-based modeling system:

- Changes of representation and "the computer as a modeling medium" as per Ch. 3
- Conceptual–mathematical–posed-problem structure and modularity as per Ch. 4
- Mathematical models as per Ch. 5

In this chapter, we go from the blackboard to the keyboard: That is, we assume that the designer has made (a first pass at) a "blackboard" version of the model, as per Ch. 4, and now is ready to sit down at a computer and write some code to implement it. Note that in Ch. 4, numerical solution techniques are largely dismissed as an implementation detail and are left out of the CMP structure. Here, however, we're focusing on implementation, so the numerical techniques are on an equal footing.

We describe a framework for the structure of modeling programs and how to implement a CMP model within that framework. Several design issues are discussed, including questions of debugging and efficiency.

The prototype models in Part III include descriptions of their implementations, in accordance with the framework described in this chapter. Appendix B provides a background description of our prototype modeling environment.

Framework for Program Structure

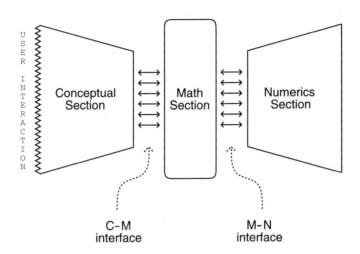

Figure 6.1: Framework for program structure. The structure for a program follows the canonical conceptual–mathematical–posed-problem structure discussed in Ch. 4. The program is divided into three separate sections. The "conceptual section" is the front end, maintaining the data structures that represent the user's conceptual model. The "math section" contains data structures that represent the mathematical model. The "numerics section" contains various numerical problem solvers; the posed problems themselves are embodied in the interfaces between the three sections. □

6.1   Overview

For computer graphics modeling, we want extensible, reusable modeling tools (as discussed in Section 2.4). This chapter discusses a modeling "system" or "environment" containing a collection of such tools from which a particular model or modeling program can be built. Note that the tools we build are for implementors—programmers—rather than for end-users.[1]

The modeling system follows the "computer as a modeling medium" approach of Section 3.7.3. The modules and techniques that comprise the collection of tools are at various levels of representation; they can be mixed as appropriate for a given application. We emphasize that we are not defining a "standard interface" for physically-based modeling (as, e.g., RenderMan [Upstill90] does for scene description), but rather just an extensible toolbox.

A particular design goal for the system is to decouple the state of a model

---

[1] A programmer could use the tools as the "guts" of an end-user modeling workstation or environment, but we are not directly describing such an application.

from the state of the program. A mathematical model as per Ch. 5 can be a single formulation that spans discontinuities and state changes in the thing being modeled; the computer program should do the same. That is, it should be possible to "random access" the model over time, with the model's state reflecting the correct configuration for each access. This is discussed further in Section 6.7.

A note on terminology: We use *environment* or *system* to refer to the collection of modules, techniques, and so forth. We use *program* to refer to a (hypothetical) computer program built using tools from the environment; a program might implement a single model, some small class of models, or a general end-user modeling workstation.

6.2   Framework for Program Structure

The conceptual–mathematical–posed-problem decomposition of a physically-based model that is discussed in Ch. 4 translates into a framework for programs. We divide a program into three distinct sections (see Fig. 6.1):

- the conceptual section,
- the math section, and
- the numerics section.

The *conceptual section* supports the user's conceptual model. It maintains data structures describing the objects being modeled, interacts with the user, and so forth. The *math section* embodies mathematical models as per Ch. 5. It contains various data elements and structures that represent the mathematical objects and equations. The *numerics section* is responsible for numerical solution of specific equations and problems. Notice that the posed problems of the model do not have a section of their own in the program; they are embodied in the interfaces between the three sections.

Putting it all together, a program has the following sequence of functionality:

1. The conceptual section defines a formalized conceptual model, based on user input.

2. The conceptual section creates a mathematical model based on the conceptual model, using items from the math section.

3. For posed problems, the appropriate mathematical problems are created based on the mathematical model.

4. For posed problems, the numerics section computes solutions to the problems, which get relayed back to the mathematical model, from there to the conceptual model, and finally back to the user.

Notice that the program maintains two separate data structures that represent the overall model: one for the conceptual model, and one for the mathematical model.[2]

The program is composed of modules that "live" within each section, as well as interface modules that bridge between the sections. The math and numerics sections are mostly just libraries of routines and objects; they have no autonomous operation. The conceptual section, however, administrates the operation of the entire program.

6.2.1 Conceptual Section

The conceptual section maintains the formal version of the user's conceptual model. This is typically a data structure containing objects that the user understands and manipulates, corresponding to entities in the thing being modeled. For example, a rigid-body modeling system might have objects for the primitive body, objects for forces that act on the bodies, and objects for "control points" at which the forces are attached, all grouped hierarchically (see Fig. 6.2). Note that in Ch. 4 the conceptual model was expressed as words; here we formalize the representation as a data structure.

The conceptual model data structure includes sufficient information to construct the corresponding mathematical

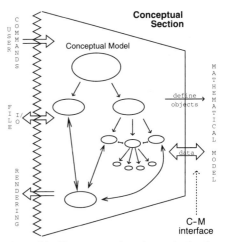

Figure 6.2: The conceptual section maintains the data structure representing the conceptual model, i.e., the objects, properties, relationships, etc., in the model. The section handles input/output interactions and, via the C–M interface, defines and exchanges data with the mathematical model. □

model data structure (via the C–M interface). In addition, it includes information such as rendering details, user-interaction constructs, hierarchical groupings, and so forth, that are conceptually important, i.e., part of the abstraction, but may be invisible or irrelevant to the mathematical simulation.

Many tasks performed by the conceptual section are the same as those of a traditional (kinematic) modeling program, such as reading and writing model description files, sending frames to a renderer, interacting with the user, etc.[3] The

---

[2]Actually, there's no reason to limit it to two models. One can imagine having separate graphical/interaction/etc. models, as well as the mathematical and conceptual models. For this discussion, however, we will just toss all but the mathematical into the conceptual model; thus the conceptual model we describe is perhaps not as well structured as it ought to be.

[3]For this discussion, we assume that rendering is purely a conceptual task. In principle, however, a mathematical formulation for rendering could be part of the mathematical model, and the task of producing an image would then be a posed problem.

only traditional modeling program task that is not performed is the computation of the objects' behavior—that part is offloaded to the mathematical section, which is used as an "equation engine."

The conceptual model may actually include some snippets of mathematical equation or knowledge, especially when the high-level abstraction is inherently mathematical (see Section 4.4.4). For example, the shape of a body may be defined via a parametric function, as in [Snyder92].

6.2.2 Numerics Section

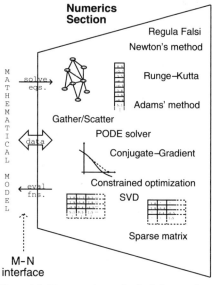

The numerics section is the "back end" of a physically-based modeling program. It is a collection of program objects whose role is straightforward: to solve numerical problems (on request), such as integrating ordinary differential equations (ODEs), finding roots of functions, solving linear systems of equations, and so forth, without regard to any larger context these problems may be embedded in.

The underlying functionality of the numerics section can be provided by numerical software packages, such as [Press *et al.*86] or [NAG]. However, the subroutines in such packages typically act at a simple level of representation, such as arrays of numbers, and the interface is often procedural, e.g., for an ODE

Figure 6.3: The numerics section includes a variety of numerical solution modules. The bottom-level subroutines can usually be taken from books or libraries. Above those lie various modules that perform changes of representation between low-level subroutines and the higher, interface level. □

integrator, one steps the solution forward by repeatedly calling a subroutine.

A collection of modules is built on top of the bottom-level subroutines. These perform transformations to higher-level representations, such as from procedural interfaces to functional, from arrays to arbitrary data objects, and so forth. These modules are designed in an object-oriented manner, allowing different solution techniques to be "swapped in" based on circumstances (as per Section 4.4.2).

Numerical solution subroutines often require that the caller provide problem-specific subroutines to evaluate various functions (such as the derivative function of a differential equation). The higher-level modules in the numerics section provide the appropriate items to the underlying numerical subroutines, but the modules must in turn be "fed" routines by the M–N interface.

6.2.3 Math Section

The math section fits between the conceptual and numerics sections. It contains definitions of computer objects that represent elements of mathematical models, such as sets, various kinds of functions, state spaces, IDs and indexes, and so forth (see Fig. 6.4). The objects support simple operations that access their values. Note that each object's value is constant[4] over the lifetime of the object—as discussed in Section 5.5.1, mathematical objects have no changeable internal state. However, the value of an object may be a function which can be evaluated on different arguments as needed; in order to determine the value of a function, the math section may do

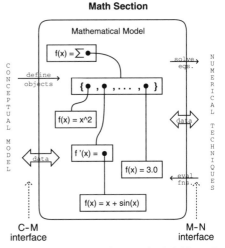

Figure 6.4: The math section contains definitions of objects that support mathematical entities, allowing construction of data structures that represent mathematical models as per Ch. 5. The figure illustrates a function whose value is equal to the sum of the values of a set of other functions. □

simple symbolic or arithmetic computation, or may call on the numerics section (via the M–N interface) to solve the appropriate problems.

Remember that a mathematical model as per Ch. 5 is declarative rather than procedural (Section 5.5.2). Translating this to the program, it means that the objects in the math section don't "do" anything—they just "are." They don't manage control flow in the program: At most, they merely evaluate functions on demand. Thus the math section is written in a functional-programming style.

In addition to definitions of various types of math objects, the math section contains utility routines to help create and manipulate objects. For example, a utility routine might define a function object whose value is the sum of the values of a given set of other function objects.

The modeling environment can pre-define some math section objects, such as IDs and numbers, as basic primitive elements. However, for the most part, each implementation of a blackboard mathematical model requires definitions of its own abstract spaces, functions, indexes, and so forth.[5] To help in writing new models, the environment can provide math section utilities such as templates and run-time support for these elements; Appendix B discusses the utilities provided in our prototype system.

---

[4] Ideally. In Sections 6.8 and B.3.2 we discuss relaxing this requirement for efficiency reasons.

[5] Thus programmers must be "toolmakers" as well as users of tools. We follow the design philosophy that to write a program, one should write a module library, then call it (see, e.g., [Strauss85]).

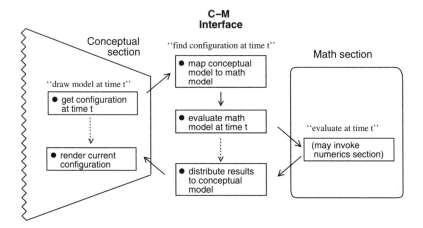

Figure 6.5: Outline of control flow across the C–M interface for a sample task. The conceptual section uses the math section as a "computation engine," via the C–M interface. Here, the posed problem is to draw the model at a particular instant of time. If the task will be performed repeatedly with minor variation, such as drawing the model for each frame of an animation, the initial mapping may be performed just once in a "setup" phase. □

6.2.4   C–M and M–N Interfaces

Between the *C*onceptual and *M*ath sections lies the *C–M interface,* and between the *M*ath and *N*umerics sections lies the *M–N interface.* The interfaces are the part of the program that arrange for posed problems to be solved.

C–M Interface

The C–M interface contains the "know-how" to construct a mathematical model from a conceptual model and to transfer data between them. Thus, the C–M interface is the high-level instrument by which posed problems are solved: It converts a conceptual task into the appropriate mathematical problem statement, constructing (via the M–N interface) mathematical objects whose values are solutions to the problem. In transferring the resulting data from the mathematical to the conceptual model, the C–M interface implements part of the physical interpretation phase of physically-based modeling (Section 4.3.4). For example, Fig. 6.5 illustrates the control flow to draw the conceptual model at a particular instant of time. For models in which objects are created and destroyed over time, the C–M interface will know how to create/destroy or activate/deactivate conceptual-model objects based on mathematical results.

The C–M interface's "know-how" does not have to be completely hardwired. An object-oriented design for the conceptual section can allow each type of concep-

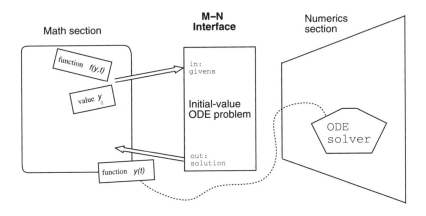

Figure 6.6: Role of the M–N interface, for a sample task. The M–N interface maps between mathematical model objects and numerical solution techniques. Here, an M–N interface routine constructs a function object, $y(t)$, that solves an initial-value ODE, $\frac{d}{dt}y(t) = f(y,t)$, $y(0) = y_0$; the function object is "tethered" to a numerical ODE solver, so that if evaluated, the function will implicitly invoke the numerical routine to compute the result. $\square$

tual object to define methods relating to its corresponding math section elements. The C–M interface may provide "callback" functions to the mathematical section which evaluate whatever mathematical equations reside in the conceptual model.

M–N Interface

The M–N interface contains the "know-how" to map between mathematical model objects and numerical modules. Thus, the M–N interface is the low-level instrument by which posed problems are solved: Given mathematical model objects containing the "knowns" for a particular problem, the M–N interface constructs objects for the solution.

For problems whose solutions are simple values (e.g., "find $x \in \Re$ that minimizes ... "), the M–N interface can immediately call a numerical solver to compute the result. For problems whose solutions are functions, however, the M–N interface might construct a function object that is "tethered" to a numerical routine; for example, Fig. 6.6 illustrates a function whose evaluation gets handed off to a numerical ODE solver.

The "tethering" can be implemented via object-oriented programming; each of the various types of function objects implements evaluation by calling the appropriate numerical solver. The M–N interface may provide "callback" functions to the numerical techniques; for example, the ODE solver in Fig. 6.6 needs to evaluate $f(y, t)$ during the course of its computation.

6.3   How to Implement a CMP Model

Suppose we have a CMP blackboard model worked out—now what? This section goes over the steps involved in creating an implementation of the model.

A CMP module translates into a collection of definitions of data structures, objects, routines, and so forth. Remember that we're not trying to make an end-user program, but trying to add a collection of tools to our toolbox, as discussed in Section 6.1. Here's what to do:

Conceptual model. Define a data structure that represents the conceptual model, including all properties, relationships, and so forth, that are relevant, as per Section 6.2.1. Build appropriate user interface tools to read/write files, send scenes to a renderer, etc.

Mathematical model. Define a class of objects for each abstract space—with associated operators to perform evaluations, access elements of sets, and so forth—and also perhaps utility routines that perform simple symbolic tasks, such as defining a function object that computes the sum of the values of other function objects, as per Section 6.2.3.

Posed problems. Each posed problem consists of a conceptual task and a corresponding mathematical problem.

• Define conceptual-section routines to provide a high-level interface to the conceptual task; for example, a routine `draw(t)` that draws the model at time `t`, as per Fig. 6.5.

• Define C–M interface routines that construct the appropriate "known" mathematical objects based on the conceptual data structure, and that can map the data from the "solution" object back into the conceptual data structure, as per Section 6.2.4.

• Define M–N interface routines that construct "solution" objects from "known" objects, linking the solution to modules in the numerical section, as per Section 6.2.4.

• Choose the numerics section modules to use. If necessary, write modules to transform between the high-level representations used in the mathematical objects to lower-level representations needed by the numerical solvers, as per Section 6.2.2. If necessary, write new low-level numerical solvers, or incorporate techniques from books or public-domain or commercial packages; these might be specific to the particular CMP module, or (ideally) might be suitable for incorporation into the common numerics section library.

We don't necessarily do all the above in the listed order. Most commonly, we start with the mathematical model definitions, then work bottom-up through the posed problem, and finally put the high-level conceptual interface on top.

Note that if the blackboard CMP model was designed modularly (Section 4.5), based on existing CMP modules, we can correspondingly use existing tools in building the new tools. This can be done at any or all levels: math objects that include other math objects; C–M routines that call other C–M routines; and so forth. Additionally, the environment can include basic support for common mathematical constructs (e.g., indexes and state spaces as per Ch. 5) and conceptual tasks (e.g., animation loops that call a `draw(t)` routine for each frame), as well as a rich numerics library; Appendix B describes the tools in our prototype system.

Note also that occasionally not all the above items need to be created. For example, the geometric objects (locations, vectors, scalars, etc.) defined in Ch. 8 need no M–N interface; all their operations can be performed symbolically or arithmetically. For another example, in Fig. 4.8's version C of a flexible-body model, the conceptual model includes a refinement to a collection of rigid bodies; thus given pre-existing rigid-body tools, the flexible-body conceptual tasks could translate directly into rigid-body conceptual tasks, and no new math, numerics, or interface routines would need to be written.

6.4   Procedural Outlook

The math section objects, as we said in Section 6.2.3, don't "do" anything; that is, they are functional rather than procedural. Thus the procedural elements in the program are the two ends: the conceptual section and the numerics section.

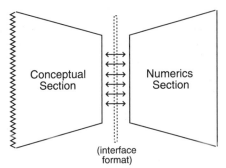

Figure 6.7: From a procedural point of view, the mathematical model is just an intermediate interface format between the conceptual and numerics sections of the program. □

Let's look at what happens when the conceptual section performs a task: The C–M interface bundles up the relevant information into a data structure (the mathematical model) and passes it to the M–N interface; then the M–N interface unbundles the information to invoke the numerical solvers, bundles the result back into mathematical data structure objects, and passes it back to the C–M interface; finally, the C–M interface unbundles the result for the conceptual section to use.

Thus, from a procedural point of view, the mathematical model is essentially just an interface format between the conceptual and numerics sections. (Or even just an interface format between the C–M and M–N interfaces.)

6.5   Why Have a Math Section?

Since, as we discovered in Section 6.4, the math section objects in some sense just comprise an intricate interface format between the conceptual and numerics sections, one might wonder why we bother to define them. Why not just let the conceptual section call the numerical routines directly? There are several reasons for having a separate mathematical model.

First, having a separate, explicit mathematical model allows the program to correspond directly with the CMP structure discussed in Ch. 4. This helps eliminate "transcription" errors in developing the program from the blackboard model. Conversely, when the program points out flaws in our model and sends us back to the drawing board, we will have an easier time updating the CMP model.

Furthermore, although the mathematical model is derived from the conceptual model, it is not necessarily a simplification of the conceptual model; it is likely to be organized differently. For example, in the mathematical model, the states of all the bodies that have the same equations of behavior may be grouped into a single index, regardless of the hierarchical relationship of the bodies in the conceptual model. Thus the task of the C–M interface can be complex, and if we were to try to merge the mathematical model organization into the conceptual model, it could end up a tangled mess. Along the same lines, having a separate mathematical model also makes it easier for us to decouple the state of the model from the state of the program, as is discussed in Section 6.7.

Finally, the math section can be sufficiently large and intricate to justify being designed, implemented, tested and debugged independently or with just the M–N interface. Once it is working, it can be incorporated into the higher levels of the program. (See also the discussion of debugging, Section 6.9.)

We can think of the math section as providing a programmatic mathematical manipulation and computation package for the given model. Consider a programmatic package that supports rational numbers or infinite-precision arithmetic: It would include definitions of the primitive data objects, and operators and subroutines to manipulate the objects and perform numerical computations. The math section for a given model does the same, but the "primitive objects" represent not just numbers, but indexes (Section 5.8.2), elements of state spaces (Section 5.9), and so forth; and the M–N interface provides the computational support.

6.6   Representational Outlook

A program that provides a high-level model to the user and also uses "number-crunching" routines to compute simulations must by necessity transform data between the form of the high-level representation and that of the numerical routines. This transformation can typically be decomposed into a series of separate steps, as per the discussion of progressive decomposition in Sections 3.3 and 4.4.1.

Representations in the Program

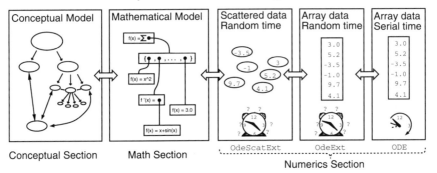

Figure 6.8: A sequence of changes of representation, from the high level that the user interacts with, down to the number-crunching format used by the numerical solvers. The illustration shows several steps within modules in the numerics section: The module OdeScatExt evaluates the solution $y(t)$ to an ODE at arbitrary values of t, distributing the results into mathematical model objects; OdeExt evaluates $y(t)$ at arbitrary values of t, transferring the result as an array of values; and ODE is a traditional step-wise ODE solver that computes array-valued results for increasing values of t. These modules are described further in Section B.4. □

We prefer to design programs such that those changes of representation are explicit; hence the separation between the conceptual, math, and numerics sections in the program framework. The C–M and M–N routines are the agents that perform the changes. The changes of representation continue within the numerics section as well. Figure 6.8 illustrates the changes of representation that we commonly carry out to simulate a model as a function of time. Notice that the whole program can be viewed as a "pipeline," analogous to the well-known rendering pipeline for computer graphics imaging ([Foley *et al.*90]).[6]

Changing representations is not often considered to be a major functional component of a program. The "meat" of the program might be identified as the number-crunching or rendering or user interface, while the code that links various modules together often seems like it's not "doing" anything, merely housekeeping. However, we have found that changing representations can often be the trickiest part of a program. Housekeeping tasks, such as gathering/scattering data between a collection of separate objects and a single array, are often fraught with bugs.

By identifying representation-change tasks explicitly, we can often separate them out from the "meat" and build separate modules that perform the changes. The changes of representation can thus be designed and debugged independently, and the remaining routines are freed from the need to do the housekeeping. Appendix B describes change-of-representation modules for array gather/scatter, full-to-sparse matrix, and sequential-to-random access of data.

---

[6] Just as computer hardware is often built to support the rendering pipeline directly, we can imagine hardware support of a modeling pipeline for some classes of posed problems.

6.7   Decoupling Model State from Program State

For computer graphics modeling, the most commonly posed problem for a model is *simulate the model's behavior over time.* Mathematically, this means we define a function $Y(t)$ that we evaluate to yield the behavior at any given time t. The most common form for the results of a simulation is a sequence of frames for an animation; that is, we sample the function Y(t) at times $t_0, t_0 + \Delta, t_0 + 2\Delta, \ldots$, rendering and recording an image for each sample. Thus, programs are often designed to evaluate $Y(t)$ only at a sequence of increasing times.

Given that we've expressed our model's behavior mathematically as a function $Y(t)$, however, we don't want to limit ourselves to sampling it sequentially. We would like to "random access" the function, i.e., evaluate it at any arbitrary time values, in arbitrary order. This would allow, for example:

- "shuttling" back and forth in interactive output

- rendering using motion-blur techniques that need arbitrary time samples, e.g., distributed ray tracing ([Cook *et al.*84])

- solving numerical problems that may span events, such as multipoint boundary-value problems ([Press *et al.*86])

Random access of the model is particularly appealing, and difficult, when the model includes events that change its structure, such as adding new bodies or relationships. Mathematically, the function $Y(t)$ would be a *segmented function* as per Section 5.10. In the conceptual section of the program, we need to "decouple" the program's state from the state of the model; the next few paragraphs illustrate what we mean by this.

Consider a program that simulates the model's behavior by Euler's method: The program data structures describe the state of the body at some time t_k. The program computes the derivatives and uses them to take a small step forward, updating the data structures for time t_{k+1}; when discontinuous events are encountered, the program's data structures are modified, and simulation continues. Thus the program directly "acts out" the behavior of the model over time (see Fig. 6.9a).

Sophisticated ODE solution techniques, which are more robust than Euler's method ([Press *et al.*86, Ch. 15]), need to be able to explore the state space: They require a user-provided subroutine that computes derivatives based on *hypothetical* states and times and will call that subroutine repeatedly for many arbitrary values in arbitrary order,[7] before settling on and returning what the model's state *really* is for some time t. In order to use these techniques, one must make a leap in how one thinks about one's program: The program no longer has a "current state" that is always correct, but needs to be able to evaluate arbitrary states and times, that

---

[7] John Platt has coined the apt name "numerics dance" to describe this process [Platt87].

Decoupling Model State from Program State

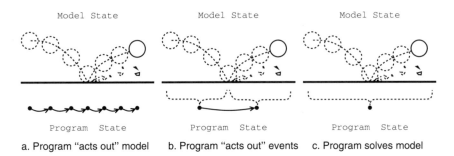

a. Program "acts out" model   b. Program "acts out" events   c. Program solves model

Figure 6.9: State of the simulated model versus state of the program. We illustrate three programming paradigms, for a model of a ball that bounces and kicks up some shrapnel: (a) Each step of program execution moves the model forward in simulation time. (b) The program computes continuous behavior as a mathematical function of simulation time, but if there are changes in the structure of the model, the state of the program must be altered. (c) The program computes the behavior as a mathematical function that spans discontinuities; the state of the program need not be altered to evaluate the model in any of its states. □

might be off the solution manifold. The program is not acting out the model, but rather calculating a function that describes how the model varies over time.

Using sophisticated numerical solvers thus forces a certain amount of decoupling of program state from model state. However, that decoupling is typically for continuous changes in state only; programs still typically solve forward in time; when an event happens, the program's data structures are changed, and a new continuous problem is solved forward from there. Thus the program is still "acting out" the discrete events (see Fig. 6.9b.)

We go one step further: Solve a mathematical segmented function, which spans discontinuous, state-changing events, and evaluate that solution anywhere. This requires that the conceptual model data structures can be adjusted based on the value of the function: The number of bodies, etc., isn't known a priori. It also requires numerical solvers that can compute them. The example "tennis ball cannon" model in Ch. 13 illustrates a model described by a segmented function that is solved using the piecewise-continuous ODE solver described in Appendix C.[8]

---

[8] Another approach to random access of models is to compute sequentially, but save the "history" so that we can play back prior states as needed—this would work even for Euler's method. However, as mentioned earlier, defining the mathematical model as a segmented function can let us solve problems that span events, such as multipoint boundary-value problems. During the "numerics dance," solvers might need to explore possible states of the model across discontinuous events—and whether or not any individual event *really* occurs won't be known until the solution is complete.

6.8 Efficiency

The conversion to and from a math section data structure, and the overall emphasis on changes of representation, can give us pause: This approach has some advantages in terms of modularity and so forth, but if it makes our programs too slow or memory-intensive, we won't be able to use it. We take a brief look at efficiency.

Start by considering the far extreme: Assume that efficiency is not a concern. Since the mathematical model is defined based on the conceptual model, and has no changeable internal state of its own, in principle it doesn't need to be maintained all the time. Whenever the conceptual model needs some numbers, such as the state of the model at a particular instant of time, it can whip up a mathematical model, evaluate it, get the results, and toss it out.

But, since we often solve the same problem over and over again, we can be more frugal than that. Commonly, the solution is a function object; we don't throw it away but rather keep it and evaluate it repeatedly. This allows the back end to maintain previous values, cache results, take advantage of coherence, and so forth.

In general, the changes of representation involve a structural setup phase, which builds data structures, sets up memory address pointers, and so forth. The actual transfer of data can just follow those pointers, often "leapfrogging" past several changes of representation to place the data in its final destination.

Note also that for numerically intensive computations, most of the inner loops are inside of the low-level numerical routines—thus efficiency of the higher levels of the program is not critical. Often, however, there are "callback" routines that must be used in an inner loop, e.g., a routine to compute derivatives for an ODE solver; but these don't necessarily have to go all the way back up the representational pipeline, and also, as before, can be set up once then quickly accessed later.

Our overall approach to dealing with efficiency in our system is as espoused by [Kernighan,Plauger78]: "Make it right before you make it faster." That is, we first design and prototype in an idealized, modular form, written to optimize cleanliness of concept. Once it's written and working, if it turns out to be insufficiently efficient, we can use "profilers" and other diagnostic techniques to determine what needs to be optimized. It's always relatively easy to go back and cut corners to provide speedups (for special cases) when necessary—but if it's originally designed and built with those corners cut, it would be harder to go back and modularize later. Remember that one of our goals is to define general, reusable tools, not optimized special-purpose simulations.[9]

---

[9]"My refusal to regard efficiency considerations as the programmer's prime concern is not meant to imply that I disregard them. . . . My point, however, is that we can only afford to optimise (whatever that may be) provided that the program remains sufficiently manageable." [Dijkstra72, p. 6]

6.9 Debugging

As we implement physically-based models as computer programs, we can encounter two types of bugs:

- *bugs in the program,* and
- *bugs in the model.*

Bugs in the program mean that it doesn't faithfully implement the blackboard model; bugs in the blackboard model means that we goofed in our CMP design. It is important to recognize the difference between these two types of bugs, or we might spend lots of time and effort on wild goose chases: For example, we might pore over trace output, single-step through program execution, and so forth, trying to find out where we've made a "typo" in an expression, but the real problem is a "thinko" in the conceptual model. Conversely, we might keep trying to re-derive or re-express a mathematical equation, but the problem turns out to be an a[i] that should be an a[j].

Of course, it's not always easy to determine what type of bug we're dealing with—that can be a major part of the debugging task. However, the CMP structure of the model can help us to isolate and identify bugs in the model, as is discussed in Section 4.6.4. Similarly, the modular design of the program framework can help us isolate bugs in the program: Are the numerical modules working correctly? Are the results being properly represented as math section objects? and so forth.

In blackboard mathematical models, there are often redundancies, or multiple ways of expressing a quantity; we can take advantage of this to help find bugs in programs. For example, the state of a dynamic rigid body (Ch. 10) includes mass m, momentum p, velocity v, and position x; when we create or use a state object, we can double-check to make sure that the relation $p = mv$ holds (i.e., check that the internal properties of the state space are maintained, as per Section B.3.6), and for a body whose behavior is computed numerically, we can double-check that $v = \frac{d}{dt}x$ (by finite differencing) as expected.[10]

Double-checking can happen at a very broad scope—we can "swap in" additional problems to solve in order to double-check our simulation, i.e., the C–M interface can create additional elements in the mathematical model, and request additional solution objects from the M–N interface. The ability to do this "swap-

---

[10]Because of finite precision and approximate solutions to problems, we can't expect values that are analytically equivalent to be exactly equal in the program, thus we can only check to see if the values are "close enough" within some tolerance. But how to choose that tolerance? The tolerance doesn't have to be tight—it doesn't affect the accuracy of simulation, it's only a guard against errors. When there's a bug, the results are often **very** wrong, so they will exceed any small tolerance. Also common is buggy behavior that causes the different quantities to diverge as the simulation progresses, so that even if the tolerance is too loose to catch the error initially, after a short time the tolerance will be exceeded.

ping" is a benefit of the modular framework in general and the separation of the mathematical model in particular.

It can also be useful to put "assertions" in the program to check for things that the model says can't happen: two disjoint events that happen simultaneously, or singularities in equations, and so forth. When such things do occur, it can often be easy to determine by inspection if they are merely bugs in the program, or if they have uncovered gaps in our conceptual understanding of the problem (see Section 4.4.4).

6.10   Summary

This chapter described an approach to implementing physically-based models that are defined via the CMP structure of Ch. 4. The focus is on an overall framework for the creation of tools in a modular and extensible manner. The tools are intended as basic reusable support for programmers to create end-user applications.

The program framework parallels the CMP structure; in particular it emphasizes that the role of the program is to define and solve mathematical problems, then convey the results back to the user. Thus there is an emphasis on a separate and explicit definition of a programmatic mathematical model and of numerical solution techniques.

The framework also emphasizes the simulation of a model as a change between various representations of the model and data. The changes of representation are performed in a series of well-defined, modularized steps.

A feature of the framework is that it allows a decoupling of the state of a program from the state of the model that is simulated; thus the program can explore the state space of the model to produce solutions and can "random access" the solution in various states—even spanning discontinuities.

Related Work

[Zeleznik *et al.*91] presents an interactive modeling system that, although not specifically focused on physically-based modeling, is similarly based on the specification of an extensible, object-oriented framework.

[Kalra90] provides a unified scheme for solving arbitrary constraint problems; in the lingo of our own work, it discusses how to transform a mathematical representation to a numerical representation.

[Blaauw,Brooks93] takes a view similar to ours, of computation as a series of changes of representation. □

PART III

PROTOTYPE PHYSICALLY-BASED MODEL LIBRARY

Description of a prototype modeling system: A small library of physically-based model modules plus examples of models built using the library. The system is designed using the principles of Part II.

- **Ch. 7. Overview**
  Overview of the goals, features, organization, and presentation of the prototype system.

- **Chs. 8–11. Prototype Library Modules**
  Each module of the prototype library is presented in a separate chapter.

- **Chs. 12–13. Sample Models**
  Examples of models that use the prototype library.

- **Ch. 14. Extensions to the Prototype Library**
  Some ideas about how the prototype library could be enhanced to support additional capabilities.

Chapter 7

Overview of Model Library

The preceding chapters (Part II) present a structured strategy for designing and implementing physically-based models. The main ideas of the strategy are:

- Decomposition of a model into conceptual–mathematical–posed-problem parts (Ch. 4).

- Modular hierarchy of models (Ch. 4).

- Mathematical modeling techniques and notation (Ch. 5).

- A program framework having separate conceptual–math–numerics sections (Ch. 6).

We move now (Part III) from theory and philosophy to practice and applications. This chapter gives an overview of a prototype library for rigid-body modeling, which was designed using the structured strategy and is discussed in detail in the upcoming chapters. The prototype library (Chs. 8–11) supports classical dynamic rigid-body motion, with geometric constraints. Sample models built using the library are described in Chs. 12 and 13. The library and models have been implemented as described; implementation notes are included in the upcoming chapters, and Appendix B has an overview of the prototype implementation environment. Some possible extensions to the library are outlined in Ch. 14.

Overview of prototype library

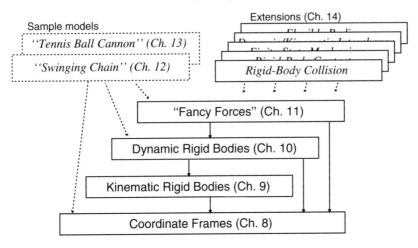

Figure 7.1: Modules in the prototype library. The coordinate frames module provides us with a common framework for working with 3D coordinate geometry. The kinematic rigid bodies module defines our idea of rigid-body motion. The dynamic rigid bodies module adds classical Newtonian mechanics. The "fancy forces" module provides a mechanism to specify forces for the Newtonian model, which supports geometric constraints on bodies. Sample models illustrate the use of the library. We also discuss ideas for extending this library. □

7.1 Goals for the Prototype Library

The prototype library has three major goals:

- **To demonstrate the structured design strategy.**
  The development of the strategy, in Chs. 3–6, included an assortment of philosophy and techniques. Here, we illustrate how we bring them all together, by developing (and using) an extensible library, from initial concept through implementation details.

- **To test the feasibility of the design strategy.**
  The strategy is experimental: an idea that we are putting forth for consideration, but which has not yet passed "the test of time." The prototype library will test the practicality of the strategy, e.g.: Do our models fit into a CMP structure? Does modularity work for us? Are the mathematical techniques practicable?, etc. (Chapter 15 includes an evaluation of our experience.)

- **To provide a rigid-body modeling library.**
  This prototype library attempts to serve as a first step toward a general, reusable, and extensible library for rigid-body dynamics, as espoused by the design strategy.

We have attempted to design and present the smallest possible example of a library that would reasonably meet the above goals—our intent is to be illustrative, rather than encyclopedic. However, we try not to cut any corners: In order to demonstrate and test the strategy validly, the prototype was developed, structured, implemented, and presented in accordance with the stated design strategy. Thus we've ended up with "just a simple example" that fills more pages than the description of the strategy itself.[1]

Note also that we present only the result of the design process, rather than chronicle the design process itself. The reader may rest assured that the prototype library was not initially conceived in exactly its final form, but rather we designed, modified, implemented, re-designed, and so forth, as per the annealing paradigm discussed in Section 3.5.3.

7.2   Features of the Library

The library includes the following features for rigid-body modeling:

- Basic Newtonian motion of rigid bodies, in response to forces and torques.

- The ability to measure work done by each force and torque, and balance it against the kinetic energy of the bodies.

- Support for various kinds of forces to apply to bodies, including "dynamic constraint" forces ([Barzel,Barr88]) to allow constraint-based control.[2]

- The ability to handle discontinuities in a model.

- The ability to be extended, both by enhancing the modules we describe and by adding additional modules.

To give a feel for how the library could be extended, Ch. 14 discusses several possible additions: rigid-body collision and contact, finite-state control mechanisms, transitions between kinematic and dynamic behavior, and flexible bodies.

---

[1] From Dijkstra's *Notes on Structured Programming:* "I am faced with a basic problem of presentation. What I am really concerned about it the composition of large programs, the text of which may be, say, of the same size as the whole text of this chapter. . . . For practical reasons, the demonstration programs must be small, many times smaller than the 'lifesize' programs I have in mind." [Dijkstra72, p. 1]

[2] We don't intend to be self-serving by describing our own "dynamic constraints" work, nor to imply that it is the primary method of control that should be supported by a rigid-body modeling library. Rather, it comprises a reasonably intricate test case for the design strategy and has the advantage (to us) that we are experienced with it and thus were able to focus on the structure of the model rather than on getting the technique to work.

7.3   Outline of the Library

The prototype library includes four modules, each implementing a different "sub-model" within the overall domain of rigid-body modeling. Each module builds on the previous modules (see Fig. 7.1).

1. **Coordinate Frames Model** (Ch. 8): Defines the basic 3D Euclidean world space in which our models exist, and provides support for manipulating co-ordinate system frames and geometric objects such as orientations, locations, and vectors.

2. **Kinematic Rigid Bodies Model** (Ch. 9): Defines our abstraction for kinematic motion (i.e., motion without regard to force or inertia) and provides a simple descriptive mechanism.

3. **Dynamic Rigid Bodies Model** (Ch. 10): Provides support for bodies moving under the influence of arbitrary forces and torques. Includes an energy-balance mechanism.

4. **"Fancy Forces" Model** (Ch. 11): Provides a mechanism to define forces and torques, and apply them to arbitrary bodies. Integrated with the "dynamic constraints" force mechanism.

We provide examples of models built using the library:

"Swinging Chain" (Ch. 12): Bodies linked and suspended to form a chain swing-ing in gravity. Illustrates continuous dynamic motion, using the constraints mechanism.

"Tennis Ball Cannon" (Ch. 13): An oscillating cannon fires a stream of balls that bounce, change size, and disappear. Illustrates discontinuous changes in state and configuration of a model.

The "model fragments" (Section 2.7), i.e., the low-level equations of behavior, that are embodied in the library are quite simple, as compared with, say, flexible-body mechanics, or fluid dynamics. Our emphasis for this prototype is on modularity in the models, the ability to pose multiple problems from a single model, the interrelationships between the bodies, and other design issues, rather than on particularly complex behaviors.

7.4   Common Mathematical Idioms

Because of our emphasis on explicit statement of assumptions and properties, the expositions in our modules follow a rather axiomatic approach that is more common in pure mathematics than in physics or mechanics: Each module has a series of definitions of abstract spaces and properties, then provides further equations that are derivable from those definitions.[3]

Note that the principles and equations that underlie the various modules in our library are well known; there will be no fundamentally new or surprising equations or derivations. Thus the mathematical models in the libraries serve mostly to recast the known equations into a form convenient for our structured, modular outlook. Because we will be covering well-trodden ground, we will not in general include detailed proofs or derivations, but rather refer interested readers to appropriate references.

The modules include definitions of various state spaces (Section 5.9) to describe the configurations of objects. Often, a state space will include a description of the motion as well—in which case the space is a generalization of a physicists' *phase space* ([Marion70]). Note that each point in a state space typically describes the state of an object *at an instant*—the object's behavior over time is described by a path through state space. If the state space includes motion information, we will often explicitly define a *consistent* path to be such that the motion description at each state along the path actually agrees with the trajectory described by the path.

Expositions of physics commonly use a single name as a value or as a function. For example, "x" may be defined as the location of a particle, and later "$x(t)$" would be used to describe the location as a function of time. However, as discussed in Section 5.6.3, we prefer a name to have only one meaning. Thus, if we define a value

$$x \in \textsf{States}$$

for some space $\textsf{States}$, we will *never* use it as a function; if we are interested in a function, we will always define one explicitly, e.g.,

$$p\colon \Re \to \textsf{States},$$

in which case "p" refers to the function as a whole, and "$p(t)$" refers to the value of the function for some $t \in \Re$. We will often define a space of functions, such as

$$\textsf{StatePaths} \equiv \textit{the set of functions } \{\Re \to \textsf{States}\},$$

and we will then use

$$p \in \textsf{StatePaths}$$

to denote a function p.

Finally, all of the bodies in the prototype models exist in a 3D Euclidean world; all "vectors" and so forth are thus three-space objects, as defined in the coordinate frames model, Ch. 8.

---

[3]In this, we are similar to the field of *Rational Mechanics*: "The traditional approach to mechanics is in no way incorrect, but it fails to satisfy modern standards of criticism and explicitness. Therefore, some parts of the foundations of mechanics heretofore left in the penumbrae of intuition and metaphysics I shall here present in an explicit, compact mathematical style. . . ." [Truesdell91, p. 6]

7.5   Presentation of Each Module

Each of the upcoming chapters describes a single CMP module. We consistently use the following organization for each chapter, combining the CMP framework of Section 4.7 with the mathematical modeling framework of Section 5.11.1:

Introduction. A small blurb at the front of each chapter, giving an overview of the domain and use of the module in the chapter. More extensive background may be given as an initial section of the chapter, if needed.

Goals. A description of our purpose or desired features for the module.

Conceptual model. A description of the conceptual model, as per Section 4.3.1. Our focus in these prototype modules is on behavior as defined mathematically; thus the conceptual models include little beyond those elements that are described by the mathematical models.

Mathematical model

> **Names and notation.** The scope name (Section 5.6.2) for the module, a list of names used from other modules, and a description of any unusual notations that will be used.

> **Definitions and equations.** These are broken up into multiple sections as appropriate.

Posed problems. As discussed in Section 4.4.3, there are potentially many interesting problems that can be posed for a given model. We typically include only one or two interesting or common problems.

Implementation notes. These describe the prototype implementation; the implementation follows Ch. 6's program framework: separate conceptual, math, and numerics sections, along with C–M and M–N interfaces. Appendix B gives some details of our particular implementation, and discusses the terminology and notation we use in the notes for each model. Since our focus in this prototype is on the mathematical models, the notes emphasize the math section and, to a lesser extent, the C–M and M–N interfaces; the conceptual section is simply sketched at a high level.

Derivations and proofs. We put these at the end (rather than within the mathematical model) so as not to get in the way.

Related Work

[Fox67] and [Goldstein80] are two classic classical mechanics references. [Marion70] gives a good introduction to the dynamics of particles and rigid bodies. We will refer also to [Craig89] for kinematics and 3D geometry. □

Chapter 8

Coordinate Frames Model

Computer graphics models commonly deal with three-dimensional geometric objects such as locations, vectors, etc., often working with several different coordinate systems. This module contains some basic definitions and notation for manipulating these objects and representing them in arbitrary orthonormal coordinate frames.

The mathematics for 3D objects and coordinate systems is well known; see, e.g., [Craig89] and [Foley *et al.*90]. We assume that the reader has at least a passing familiarity with the ideas of vectors, matrices, tensors, and so forth; although we define all our terms axiomatically, this exposition would not suffice as an introductory text in linear algebra.

This module is intended to give us a standard, convenient, and consistent form for using Euclidean 3D coordinate objects within our modeling environment. It does not address curvilinear coordinate systems, such as cylindrical or spherical coordinates. It also does not address geometry in homogeneous coordinates (which is common in computer graphics—see [Foley *et al.*90, Ch. 5]), nor in curved spaces.

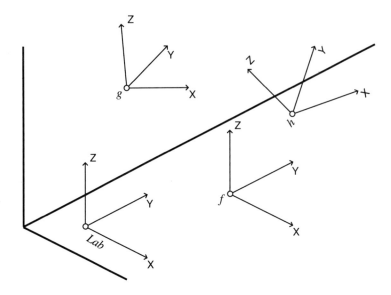

Figure 8.1: Multiple coordinate frames. We illustrate several different right-handed, orthonormal coordinate frames, labeled f, g, h, and Lab, all defined in an absolute, uniform, 3D world space. Lab is an arbitrary frame that is chosen to be a fixed standard. □

8.1   Background

Conceptually, the ideas of geometric objects such as coordinate systems, vectors, locations, and so forth, are often conveyed via diagrams (e.g., Figs. 8.1, 8.2, etc.). Mathematically, however, one needs a formal definition and algebra. There are two common approaches to the definition and use of geometric objects:

- **Numerical coordinates.** Objects are defined as collections of coordinate values (also called *components*), along with rules that describe how the values change if one switches coordinate systems. Arithmetic and other operations are defined by matrix operations on the coordinate values.

- **Abstract entities.** Objects are defined as elements of abstract spaces. Arithmetic and other operations are defined in a manner independent of coordinate systems. When coordinate values are needed, mappings are defined from the abstract spaces to any desired coordinate system.

The abstract approach has a simple, compact notation and can extend to arbitrary manifolds in non-Euclidean spaces. It is thus the approach of choice for studying differential geometry (e.g., [Millman,Parker77]). However, the details of numerical computation are typically hidden or implicit.

The coordinate-based approach, on the other hand, keeps track of numerical values in particular frames of reference. The equations tend to be cumbersome—full of "bookkeeping" of coordinate frames and components—but they apply immediately to numerical computation. It is thus the common approach used for practical applications, e.g., robotics ([Craig89]) or computer graphics ([Foley *et al.*90]).

For our purposes, we want elegant mathematical models—thus we want the convenience and expressive power of the abstract approach. But we also need to perform numerical computations—thus we want the applicability of coordinate-based formulations.[1] Our approach is therefore to define the geometric objects as abstract concepts, and define the corresponding abstract mathematical notation, but also provide a notation that lets us express the objects in arbitrary coordinate systems and perform numerical manipulations.

8.2 Goals

We have several goals for this module:

- To have a standard model and notation for geometric objects, which encapsulates coordinate systems and coordinate transformations.

- To support useful geometric objects, be they tensors or nontensors.[2]

- To be able to use coordinate-free notation and expressions.

- To be able to use coordinate notation and expressions for arbitrary coordinate systems.

- To support objects and coordinate systems that change as functions of time. A particular special case is an object that has a constant representation in changing coordinate systems, such as a piece of material that is fixed to a rigid body and is carried with it as the body moves.

The emphasis for the above goals is on basic support for mathematical models and corresponding program implementations, rather than on any a priori conceptual model.

---

[1]*"Pictorial* treatment of geometry ... is tied conceptually as closely as possible to the world. ... *Abstract* differential geometry ... is the quickest, simplest mathematical scheme. ... *Components* [are] indispensible in programming. ... Today, no one has full power to communicate with others about [geometry] who cannot express himself in all three languages." [Misner *et al.*73, p. 199]

[2]A *tensor* is an object that obeys certain transformation rules when we switch between coordinate systems (see Eq. 8.11).

8.3   Conceptual Model

We assume the existence of an absolute three-dimensional Euclidean space, some-times called *world space*. The space is homogeneous and isotropic, i.e., has no preferred directions or locations. We also assume that *time* is homogeneous.

We can place x, y, and z axes anywhere we like in space, to define a coordinate system which can be used to represent geometric objects. We refer to each triple of axes as a *coordinate frame*, or just *frame* (see Fig. 8.1). Each frame gives us a coordinate system for measuring objects in the world—i.e., the frame gives us a particular vantage to "look at" the world. We restrict ourselves to frames that are orthonormal, i.e., the x, y, and z axes are perpendicular and all frames have the same scale for distance, and that are right-handed, i.e., if x points to the right and y points forward, then z points upward.

We define several types of abstract geometric objects. Each object can be described in a given frame by a collection of coordinate numbers, which we call the object's *numerical representation*, or just *representation*. We emphasize the distinction between an abstract object and its representations: A single abstract object may have different representations in different frames. A collection of numbers, along with a frame, can uniquely describe a particular type of object; but a collection of numbers without a coordinate frame to go with them doesn't "mean" anything, geometrically.

This module includes several types of geometric objects (of course, these are not all possible geometric objects; we merely define some objects that we have found to be useful for our applications):

Location.[3] An absolute location in space, represented numerically as a 3×1 matrix containing its x, y, and z coordinates (distances from the origin of the frame). Pictorially, we draw a dot (see Fig. 8.2).

Orientation. An absolute orientation in space. Can be represented in a variety of ways: Pictorially, we draw an orthonormal triple of vectors (see Fig. 8.3); numerically we most commonly use a 3×3 rotation matrix, whose columns are the representations of the corresponding vectors.

Scalar. A frame-independent value (zero-order tensor). Represented numerically as a single real number.

Vector. A direction with magnitude (first-order tensor). Represented numerically as a 3×1 matrix containing its x, y, and z coordinates (displacements along each axis). Pictorially, we draw an arrow (see Fig. 8.2); the position of the arrow is irrelevant; only its direction and length are significant.

---

[3][Craig89] uses the term *position vector* for these; we prefer to reserve the word *vector* for the first-order tensor object only.

A Location versus a Vector

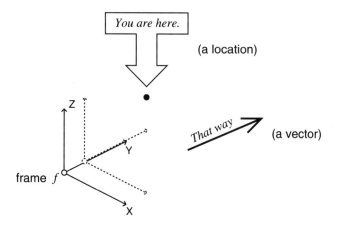

Figure 8.2: We distinguish between a *location*, which describes a position in absolute space, and a *vector*, which describes a direction (and distance). Both are represented by x, y, and z coordinate values in any given frame; but if we translate the frame, the coordinates of a location will vary, but the coordinates of a direction will stay the same. We similarly distinguish between *orientations*, which describe fixed alignments in space, and *rotations*, which describe operations on vectors. □

2Tensor. An abstract object (second-order tensor) that corresponds with a linear operation on vectors; the operation can be performed by "multiplying" (arithmetic is discussed in Def. 8.14) a vector by a 2tensor to yield the new vector. Represented numerically as a 3×3 matrix, where each column represents the result of the operation on an axis. Pictorially, the operation can be illustrated by showing "before" and "after" drawings of a triple of vectors (see Fig. 8.3).

Rotations. 2tensors, whose corresponding operations preserve length and angles.

Basis.[4] A generalization of an orientation; corresponds with a triple of three arbitrary vectors. Represented as the 3×3 matrix whose columns represent the corresponding vectors.

Frame. A coordinate frame is defined by the location of its origin, P, and the orientation of its axes, R. We choose one arbitrary frame, which we call the *lab frame*, to be a fixed standard for reference. The coordinate system defined by the lab frame is called *lab coords* or *world coords*. Pictorially, we draw the frame's orientation situated at the frame's origin.

---

[4]Basis objects are not often used conceptually; we include them for mathematical completeness.

Orientations: A 2tensor operation:

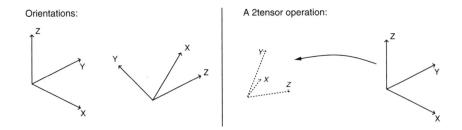

Figure 8.3: We draw an orientation as a triple of vectors, all drawn from the same spot—but the position of that spot is irrelevant. To illustrate a 2tensor, we draw an arc linking an orthonormal triple of vectors to the triple that results when each vector is multiplied by the 2tensor. □

We stress the conceptual distinction between locations and vectors: A location corresponds with a fixed position in absolute space, while a vector corresponds with a magnitude and direction but has no specific position[5] (see Fig. 8.2). Similarly, we distinguish between an absolute orientation in space and a rotation operation that one might use to align any particular frame to it. (In any given frame, however, there is a correspondence between locations and vectors, and between orientations and rotations; see Section 8.4.6 and Fig. 8.6.)

Notice that we consider a frame to be a type of geometric object. Thus there is circularity in our definitions: Locations and orientations are described by their representations in frames, but a frame is defined by a location–orientation pair. The lab frame serves to break this circularity.

We use the term *moving object* (location, vector, etc.) to refer to one that varies over time. Moving objects can have associated velocity objects; in particular, we define an *instantaneous frame* to be a frame with associated linear and angular velocity vectors. A moving object may be *fixed in a moving frame*, i.e., it follows the frame's motion so that its coordinates never change as seen from that frame.

A Note on Units and Dimension

The conceptual objects described here often have physical *dimension* associated with them, such as length, mass, and time, and are measured in terms of *units*, such as centimeters, grams, and seconds. The terms in the mathematical model, however, are dimensionless—just numbers. [Lin,Segel74, Ch. 6] discusses the *nondimensionalization* process, which is beyond our scope; we just point out the need for (at least) consistency of units within a given model.

---

[5]Differential-geometers may comment that a "direction" (tangent vector) for an arbitrary surface or manifold is an element of the space tangent to the manifold *at a particular point* ([Millman,Parker77, pp. 93, 213]). For our Euclidean formalism, however, all tangent spaces are isomorphic to each other, thus we are safe in our use of tangent vectors without associated positions in space.

8.4   Mathematical Model

8.4.1   Names and Notation

The scope name for this module is

COORDS.

We don't use definitions from any other module. In this module, we define and extensively use a prefix-superscript notation:

$$^{f}x \qquad \text{(Not. 8.6)}$$

8.4.2   Definitions

We start by defining abstract spaces for various types of objects; we refer to these as the *primitive* objects:

Definition. (Primitive Geometric Spaces)

(8.1)
$$
\begin{aligned}
\text{Scalars} &\equiv \textit{the set}\ \big\{\, \textbf{scalar}\ \textit{objects} \,\big\} \\
\text{Vectors} &\equiv \textit{the set}\ \big\{\, \textbf{vector}\ \textit{objects} \,\big\} \\
\text{2Tensors} &\equiv \textit{the set}\ \big\{\, \textbf{2tensor}\ \textit{objects} \,\big\} \\
\text{Rotations} &\equiv \textit{the set}\ \big\{\, \textbf{rotation}\ \textit{objects} \,\big\} \subset \text{2Tensors} \\
\text{Locations} &\equiv \textit{the set}\ \big\{\, \textbf{location}\ \textit{objects} \,\big\} \\
\text{Bases} &\equiv \textit{the set}\ \big\{\, \textbf{basis}\ \textit{objects} \,\big\} \\
\text{Orientations} &\equiv \textit{the set}\ \big\{\, \textbf{orientation}\ \textit{objects} \,\big\} \subset \text{Bases}
\end{aligned}
$$

Definition 8.1: We define an abstract space for each type of geometric object.   Note that orientations are types of bases whose corresponding vectors are orthonormal. □

The space of coordinate frames is defined as a state space, using the mechanism of Section 5.9:

Definition. Frames

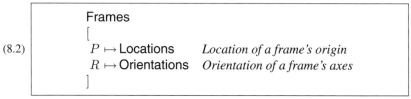

(8.2)

```
Frames
[
    P ↦ Locations        Location of a frame's origin
    R ↦ Orientations     Orientation of a frame's axes
]
```

Definition 8.2: Space of coordinate frames.   Each frame $f \in$ Frames has an origin P_f at some location, and an orientation R_f. (The use of subscripted aspect values is as per Not. 5.27.) □

It is convenient to define a single set for the primitive geometric objects:

Definition. GeomObjs

(8.3)

$$\text{GeomObjs} \quad \equiv \quad \text{Locations} \cup \text{Bases} \cup \text{Scalars} \\ \cup \text{Vectors} \cup \text{2Tensors}$$

Definition 8.3: All primitive geometric objects. A geometric object $x \in$ GeomObjs can be a location, basis, scalar, vector, or 2tensor. Thus the space GeomObjs is a disparate union as per Section 5.7.3, where two objects are *agnates* if they are both of the same primitive geometric type. □

We define a lab frame, to give us a standard set of coordinates, as per Section 8.3.

Definition. $\mathcal{L}ab$

(8.4)

$$\mathcal{L}ab \in \text{Frames}$$

Definition 8.4: The fixed lab frame $\mathcal{L}ab$ is a unique element of Frames. It has no special properties other than being agreed upon by everybody. □

8.4.3 Representation and Notation

An element from one of the above spaces is an abstract object; to make it seem concrete, we can produce a *representation* of the object. The representation depends, of course, on a choice of coordinate frame. Thus we define the representation operator *Rep*:

Definition. Rep

(8.5)

We define an overloaded operator
$$Rep: \text{Frames} \times \text{GeomObjs} \rightarrow \Re \cup \Re^3 \cup \Re^{3 \times 3} \textit{ that}$$
yields the coordinates of an object in a given frame.

$Rep: \text{Frames} \times \text{Scalars} \rightarrow \Re$	*a single number*
$Rep: \text{Frames} \times \text{Vectors} \rightarrow \Re^3$	*a 3×1 matrix*
$Rep: \text{Frames} \times \text{2Tensors} \rightarrow \Re^{3 \times 3}$	*a 3×3 matrix*
$Rep: \text{Frames} \times \text{Locations} \rightarrow \Re^3$	*a 3×1 matrix*
$Rep: \text{Frames} \times \text{Bases} \rightarrow \Re^{3 \times 3}$	*a 3×3 matrix*

Definition 8.5: Representation operators convert from an abstract geometric object to a collection of real numbers, given a choice of frame. Note that *Rep* is overloaded (Section 5.6.3) to act on elements of the various different spaces. □

Because we commonly work with representations of objects, we define a shorthand notation for representations:

Notation. Prefix-Superscripts for Representation in a Frame

(8.6)

> *For any f ∈* Frames *and any x ∈* GeomObjs,
>
> $${}^{f}x \;\equiv\; Rep\,(f, x)$$

Notation 8.6: Representation of a geometric object in a given frame. The above terms can be read as "x represented numerically in frame f" or just as "x in f." We most commonly use the prefix-superscript notation. □

Note that while x is an abstract geometric object, ${}^{f}x$ is always just a collection of numbers. The representation functions are one-to-one and thus can be used to determine identity:

(8.7)

> *For any objects x, y ∈* GeomObjs *that are agnates (i.e.,*
> *of the same primitive type), and any f ∈* Frames
>
> $${}^{f}x = {}^{f}y \;\Longleftrightarrow\; x = y$$

Equation 8.7: Given a fixed frame, the representation of a geometric element of a given type is sufficient to identify the element. □

Thus, for any given frame f, there is an equivalence between geometric objects and their numerical representations. Also, since locations and vectors share a representational space, for a given frame there is a natural correspondence between them; and similarly for orientations and rotations (see Section 8.4.6).

The *Rep* operators for orientations and rotations yield orthonormal rotation matrices. (An orientation's matrix corresponds with the rotation that aligns the frame axes to it.) Rotations and orientations may be represented in other ways as well, such as by Euler angles, in angle–axis form, or as unit quaternions (see [Craig89, Ch. 2]). We give a definition for the latter:[6]

Definition. Repq

(8.8)

> *The quaternion representation of orientations and*
> *rotations is given by:*
>
> *Repq*: Frames × Orientations → $\Re^{4}$
> *Repq*: Frames × Rotations → $\Re^{4}$

Definition 8.8: Quaternion representation, overloaded for orientations and rotations. For any $r \in$ Orientations $\cup$ Rotations and any $f \in$ Frames, we have $|Repq\,(f, r)| = 1$, i.e., the representation is as a unit quaternion. The quaternion representation can be computed from the matrix representation $Rep\,(f, r)$ as described, e.g., in [Shoemake85].[7] □

We don't have a direct representation for frames; however, the location and

---

[6]Quaternions can themselves be defined as abstract objects. For the purposes of this module, however, we treat them simply as four-component arrays having the appropriate arithmetic rules.

[7][Shoemake85] uses left-handed quaternion rotations; the matrix conversion therein describes the transpose of the right-handed matrix we would use.

Representation of a Frame

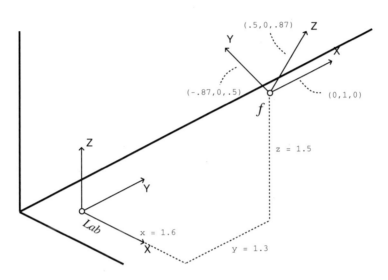

Figure 8.4: Any frame f is defined by its location P_f and orientation R_f, which can in turn be represented in any frame. Here, frame f is at location ${}^{\mathcal{L}ab}P_f = \begin{bmatrix} 1.6 \\ 1.3 \\ 1.5 \end{bmatrix}$ in the lab, and its orientation in the lab is ${}^{\mathcal{L}ab}R_f = \begin{bmatrix} 0 & -.87 & .5 \\ 1 & 0 & 0 \\ 0 & .5 & .87 \end{bmatrix}$. Represented in itself, f is at location ${}^{f}P_f = \begin{bmatrix} 0 \\ 0 \\ 0 \end{bmatrix}$ with orientation ${}^{f}R_f = \begin{bmatrix} 1 & 0 & 0 \\ 0 & 1 & 0 \\ 0 & 0 & 1 \end{bmatrix}$ as per Eq. 8.10. □

orientation of a frame can of course be represented numerically in any frame (see Fig. 8.4). Combining P_f and R_f, defined in Def. 8.2, with Not. 8.6, gives us:

For $f, g \in$ **Frames**

(8.9)
$$
{}^{g}P_f = \left(\begin{array}{c} \textit{Frame f's location,} \\ \textit{represented numerically in} \\ \textit{frame g} \end{array} \right)
$$

$$
{}^{g}R_f = \left(\begin{array}{c} \textit{Frame f's orientation,} \\ \textit{represented numerically in} \\ \textit{frame g} \end{array} \right)
$$

Equation 8.9: The position and orientation of frame f, as "seen from" frame g. □

Since the location of a frame is defined to be the location of its origin, and since the orientation of a frame is defined to be the orientation of its axes (Section 8.3), a frame's representation of its own location and orientation is always trivial:

For any $f \in$ Frames

(8.10)
$$^f P_f = \begin{bmatrix} 0 \\ 0 \\ 0 \end{bmatrix}, \quad ^f R_f = \begin{bmatrix} 1 & 0 & 0 \\ 0 & 1 & 0 \\ 0 & 0 & 1 \end{bmatrix}$$

Equation 8.10: A frame represented in terms of itself. The frame's origin is always at its own coordinates (0,0,0), and its orientation representation is the identity. □

8.4.4   Transforming Representations between Frames

Often, we know the representation of an object in one frame, and we'd like to determine the representation in some other frame. We define the transformation rules:

For $f, g \in$ Frames

(8.11)
$$^g s = {}^f s \qquad\qquad s \in \text{Scalars}$$
$$^g v = ({}^g R_f)\, {}^f v \qquad\qquad v \in \text{Vectors}$$
$$^g a = ({}^g R_f)\, {}^f a\, ({}^g R_f)^T \qquad a \in \text{2Tensors}$$
$$^g p = {}^g P_f + ({}^g R_f)\, {}^f p \qquad p \in \text{Locations}$$
$$^g b = ({}^g R_f)\, {}^f b \qquad\qquad r \in \text{Bases}$$

Equation 8.11: Transformation rules. We emphasize that these rules do not transform geometric objects—rather, they change between two different representations *of the same object*. All operations in the above are performed via matrix arithmetic. □

In Eq. 8.11, the tensor objects—scalars, vectors, and 2tensors— employ the standard tensor transformation rules. Locations, however, take into account the origin of the frame in which they are represented; bases transform like vectors.

Notice that if we transform from a frame to itself, we can use Eq. 8.10 to reduce each equality in Eq. 8.11 to the trivial identity:

Given any $f, g \in$ Frames, and any $x \in$ GeomObjs,

(8.12)
$$f = g \implies {}^f x = {}^g x$$

Equation 8.12: The transformation rules are consistent. If we "transform" a representation between a frame and the same frame, the representation doesn't change. Note that the converse isn't true, i.e., ${}^f x = {}^g x \not\Rightarrow f = g$; for example, a vector will have the same representation in two frames that have the same orientation but different origin locations. □

We occasionally want to consider the representation of a frame's location and orientation in a second frame, as compared with the second frame's representation in the first. We have the following equalities:

For any $f, g \in$ Frames

(8.13)
$$
\begin{aligned}
{}^{g}P_f &= -{}^{g}R_f \, {}^{f}P_g \\
{}^{g}R_f &= ({}^{f}R_g)^T
\end{aligned}
$$

Equation 8.13: The relationship between two frames' representations. If we "look at" frame f from within frame g, we get "opposite" representations from those we get if we look at g from within f. These equalities derive from Eqs. 8.10 and 8.11 (see Section 8.7). □

8.4.5 Arithmetic Operations

We can perform arithmetic operations on the representations of objects, using standard matrix arithmetic, as in Eqs. 8.11 and 8.13. However, doing so requires picking a choice of frame and can lead to cumbersome equations.

We want to define arithmetic operations directly on the abstract geometric objects; the abstract operations should correspond with the matrix operations on the objects' representations. A purist's approach might be to define the arithmetic operations abstractly, then prove that (with proper choice of representation) the representations follow the corresponding matrix arithmetic—in any frame. For our purposes, however, we define the abstract operations "through the back door," i.e., define them such that they agree with the representations:

Definition. **Arithmetic Operations**

(8.14)

> *For any binary matrix arithmetic operation $\star$ or unary matrix operation $\diamond$, we define the corresponding abstract geometric operations, for any $x, y \in$ GeomObjs, by:*
>
> $$
> \begin{aligned}
> {}^{f}(x \star y) &\equiv ({}^{f}x) \star ({}^{f}y) \\
> {}^{f}(\diamond y) &\equiv \diamond({}^{f}y)
> \end{aligned}
> \left. \vphantom{\begin{aligned} a \\ b \end{aligned}} \right\}
> \begin{aligned} &\textit{when independent of the} \\ &\textit{choice of } f \in \text{Frames} \end{aligned}
> $$

Definition 8.14: Arithmetic operations between geometric objects, $x \star y$, are defined by the corresponding matrix arithmetic operations between their representations ${}^{f}x$ and ${}^{f}y$—but only where those operations yield frame-invariant results. Note that x and y are not necessarily agnates, e.g., a matrix may be multiplied by a vector. □

Figure 8.5 lists the arithmetic operations. Note in particular that there is no meaning to the sum of two locations, or to the negation of a location—but a vector can be added to a location, and the difference between two locations can be found. We list some of the usual arithmetic properties:

Arithmetic Operations on Abstract Objects

Binary operations:

addition	Scalars $+$ Scalars $\rightarrow$ Scalars
subtraction	Scalars $-$ Scalars $\rightarrow$ Scalars
multiplication	Scalars $*$ Scalars $\rightarrow$ Scalars
scale	Scalars $*$ Vectors $\rightarrow$ Vectors
scale	Scalars $*$ 2Tensors $\rightarrow$ 2Tensors
scale	Scalars $*$ Bases $\rightarrow$ Bases
scale	Vectors $*$ Scalars $\rightarrow$ Vectors
addition	Vectors $+$ Vectors $\rightarrow$ Vectors
subtraction	Vectors $-$ Vectors $\rightarrow$ Vectors
inner product	Vectors $\cdot$ Vectors $\rightarrow$ Scalars
cross product	Vectors $\times$ Vectors $\rightarrow$ Vectors
outer product	Vectors $*$ Vectors $\rightarrow$ 2Tensors
displacement	Vectors $+$Locations $\rightarrow$ Locations
cross product	Vectors $\times$ 2Tensors $\rightarrow$ 2Tensors
cross product	Vectors $\times$ Bases $\rightarrow$ Bases
scale	2Tensors $*$ Scalars $\rightarrow$ 2Tensors
product	2Tensors $\cdot$ Vectors $\rightarrow$ Vectors
addition	2Tensors $+$ 2Tensors $\rightarrow$ 2Tensors
subtraction	2Tensors $-$ 2Tensors $\rightarrow$ 2Tensors
product	2Tensors $\cdot$ 2Tensors $\rightarrow$ 2Tensors
product	2Tensors $\cdot$ Bases $\rightarrow$ Bases
displacement	Locations$+$ Vectors $\rightarrow$ Locations
difference	Locations$-$Locations $\rightarrow$ Vectors
scale	Bases $*$ Scalars $\rightarrow$ Bases
cross product	Bases $*$ Vectors $\rightarrow$ Bases
addition	Bases $+$ Bases $\rightarrow$ Bases
subtraction	Bases $-$ Bases $\rightarrow$ Bases

Unary operations:

inverse	Scalars^{-1} $\rightarrow$ Scalars
negation	$-$Scalars $\rightarrow$ Scalars
antisymmetric dual	Vectors* $\rightarrow$ 2Tensors
negation	$-$Vectors $\rightarrow$ Vectors
transpose	2Tensors^{T} $\rightarrow$ 2Tensors
inverse	2Tensors^{-1} $\rightarrow$ 2Tensors
negation	$-$2Tensors $\rightarrow$ 2Tensors
negation	$-$Bases $\rightarrow$ Bases

Figure 8.5: The arithmetic operations on abstract geometric objects, in accordance with Def. 8.14. All the usual operations on tensors are defined. Note, however, that locations may only be subtracted from each other or added to vectors, and bases may be left-multiplied by 2tensors, but not right-multiplied. □

For all $a \in$ 2Tensors, $r \in$ Rotations,
$n \in$ Orientations, and $v, w \in$ Vectors, we have the
following properties:

(8.15)
$$a^{-1} a = a a^{-1} = 1$$
$$r^{-1} = r^T$$
$$r n \in \text{Orientations}$$
$$v^* w = v \times w$$

Equation 8.15: The inverse of a 2tensor is both a right- and left-inverse. The inverse of a rotation is its transpose. Orientations are closed under left-multiplication by rotations. The antisymmetric dual,[8] v^*, of a vector v performs a cross product on another vector. □

The following "special" objects are defined, with the usual properties:

(8.16)

Object	Name	Rep.	Properties
$1 \in$ Scalars	*one*	1	$1 * x = x$
$0 \in$ Scalars	*zero*	0	$0 + x = x, 0 * x = 0$
$0 \in$ Vectors	*zero vector*	$\begin{bmatrix} 0 \\ 0 \\ 0 \end{bmatrix}$	$0 + x = x$
$0 \in$ 2Tensors	*zero 2tensor*	$\begin{bmatrix} 0\,0\,0 \\ 0\,0\,0 \\ 0\,0\,0 \end{bmatrix}$	$0 * x = 0$
$1 \in$ 2Tensors	*identity*	$\begin{bmatrix} 1\,0\,0 \\ 0\,1\,0 \\ 0\,0\,1 \end{bmatrix}$	$1 * x = x$
$0 \in$ Bases	*zero basis*	$\begin{bmatrix} 0\,0\,0 \\ 0\,0\,0 \\ 0\,0\,0 \end{bmatrix}$	$x * 0 = 0$

For any $f, g \in$ Frames: ${}^f 0 = {}^g 0$, and ${}^f 1 = {}^g 1$

Equation 8.16: Objects with special properties. The representations of these objects are the same in all frames, as can be shown by substituting into Eq. 8.11. □

8.4.6   Correspondence between Objects

Given a choice of frame, there is a natural correspondence between locations and vectors, and between orientations and rotations, based on equality of representation (see Fig. 8.6):

---

[8]The antisymmetric dual v^* of a vector v may be unfamiliar: The dual of $\begin{bmatrix} x \\ y \\ z \end{bmatrix}$ is $\begin{bmatrix} 0 & -z & y \\ z & 0 & -x \\ -y & x & 0 \end{bmatrix}$.

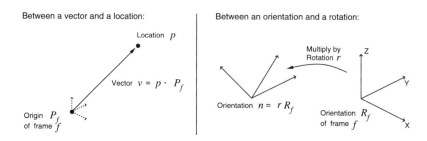

**Correspondences between Objects
in a Given Frame** f

Figure 8.6: For a given frame f, there is a natural correspondence between a location $p \in$ Locations and the vector $v \in$ Vectors from the frame's origin to p; both are represented by the same three coordinate values in frame f. Similarly, there is a natural correspondence between a rotation $r \in$ Rotations and the orientation $n \in$ Orientations that results when multiplying the frame's orientation by r. □

For any $f \in$ Frames, $p \in$ Locations, $v \in$ Vectors,
$r \in$ Rotations, $n \in$ Orientations, $a \in$ 2Tensors,
$b \in$ Bases, *we have the following correspondences:*

(8.17)

$$v = p - P_f \quad \Longleftrightarrow \quad {}^f v = {}^f p$$
$$n = r\,R_f \quad \Longleftrightarrow \quad {}^f n = {}^f r$$
$$b = a\,R_f \quad \Longleftrightarrow \quad {}^f b = {}^f a$$

Equation 8.17: In any given frame, the representation of a location is the same as the representation of the vector from the origin to that location. Similarly, the representation of an orientation corresponds with the rotation that aligns the frame with that orientation. More generally, given a frame, there is a correspondence between bases and 2tensors. □

Due to this correspondence (and perhaps also because the common emphasis is on tensor objects only), many expositions don't define locations and orientations as separate entities. However, we prefer to define them separately, because the correspondence is only valid for a single frame; e.g., if a vector and location correspond in some frame f, they won't necessarily correspond to each other in some other frame g, because of their different transformation rules in Eq. 8.11.

The correspondence is useful when switching between numerical and abstract forms of an equation; this is illustrated in Section 8.7 (for the derivation of Eq. 8.30).

8.4.7   Using Scalars as Real Numbers

Since the representation of a scalar is independent of the choice of frame (Eq. 8.11), there is a natural isomorphism between scalars and real numbers. Thus, to make things simple we eliminate the distinction between the two spaces:[9]

(8.18)
$$\text{Scalars} = \Re$$
$$\underset{s}{f} = s \begin{cases} \textit{for all } s \in \textbf{Scalars} \\ \textit{independently of } f \in \textbf{Frames} \end{cases}$$

Equation 8.18: We can use **Scalars** and $\Re$ interchangeably. The representation operator is trivial: A scalar is represented as itself. We can freely add or drop frame-superscripts on scalars. □

We will continue to use **Scalars** and the superscript notation in this module, for consistency with the other primitive geometric objects. In general, however, there is little reason to define equations in terms of **Scalars** rather than reals.

8.4.8   Moving Objects

What we think of conceptually as a *moving object* is mathematically just a function from the reals, i.e., time or path parameters, onto the geometric objects (see Fig. 8.7). Thus we define the following spaces:

Definition. ScalarPaths, VectorPaths, etc.

(8.19)
$$\begin{aligned}
\textbf{ScalarPaths} &\equiv \textit{the set of functions } \left\{ \Re \to \textbf{Scalars} \right\} \\
\textbf{VectorPaths} &\equiv \textit{the set of functions } \left\{ \Re \to \textbf{Vectors} \right\} \\
\textbf{2TensorPaths} &\equiv \textit{the set of functions } \left\{ \Re \to \textbf{2Tensors} \right\} \\
\textbf{RotationPaths} &\equiv \textit{the set of functions } \left\{ \Re \to \textbf{Rotations} \right\} \\
\textbf{LocationPaths} &\equiv \textit{the set of functions } \left\{ \Re \to \textbf{Locations} \right\} \\
\textbf{BasisPaths} &\equiv \textit{the set of functions } \left\{ \Re \to \textbf{Bases} \right\} \\
\textbf{OrientationPaths} &\equiv \textit{the set of functions } \left\{ \Re \to \textbf{Orientations} \right\} \\
\textbf{GeomPaths} &\equiv \textbf{LocationPaths} \cup \textbf{BasisPaths} \\
& \cup \textbf{ScalarPaths} \cup \textbf{VectorPaths} \\
& \cup \textbf{2TensorPaths}
\end{aligned}$$

Definition 8.19: Spaces of functions, for moving objects. Note that RotationPaths ⊂ 2TensorPaths, and OrientationPaths ⊂ BasisPaths. We define a disparate union GeomPaths analogously to GeomObjs, Def. 8.3. □

[9]The specific space COORDS :: **Scalars** that we define in this module is interchangeable with $\Re$, but a more general notion of scalars would encompass quantities such as complex numbers.

Moving Objects

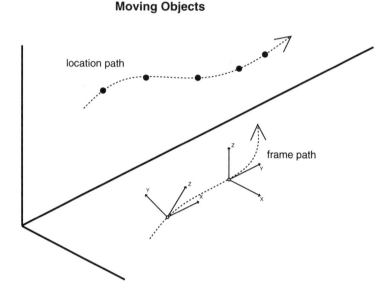

Figure 8.7: A "moving object" is described by a path, i.e., a function from reals to the object's space. We illustrate a location path and a frame path, but one can define paths for any geometric object. □

We can define derivatives for these paths by extension from the arithmetic operations (Def. 8.14). Note that because the difference of two locations is a vector, the derivative of a location path is a vector path. Note also that the derivative of a location is a vector, and that in general, the derivative of a rotation is a 2tensor (not a rotation) and the derivative of an orientation is a basis (not an orientation). We have the following identity:

Definition. $\frac{d}{dt}$ (derivatives of paths)

(8.20)

> *For a path* $x \in$ **GeomPaths**, *and constant frame* $f \in$ **Frames**,
>
> $$^f\!\left(\tfrac{d}{dt}x(t)\right) = \tfrac{d}{dt}\left(^f\!x(t)\right), \quad t \in \Re$$

Definition 8.20: For a fixed frame, the derivative and representation operators commute. Note that if f varies as a function of t, the operators no longer commute. □

For rotations and orientations, the following identities hold and can be used to define an angular velocity:

Definition. **Angular Velocity**

(8.21)

> *For any differentiable function* $r \in$ RotationPaths *or*
> $r \in$ OrientationPaths, *there exists a unique* **angular**
> **velocity** *function* $\omega \in$ VectorPaths *such that*
>
> $$\tfrac{d}{dt}r(t) = \omega^*(t)r(t), \quad t \in \Re$$

Definition 8.21: The derivatives of rotations and orientations always obey these identities. The angular velocity, ω, is a vector function; at each instant its value is a vector that lies along the instantaneous axis of rotation and whose magnitude is the instantaneous rate of rotation (radians per unit time). □

An analogous equation holds for quaternion representations (Def. 8.8):

(8.22)

> *For any differentiable function* $r \in$ RotationPaths *or*
> $r \in$ OrientationPaths, *if* $\omega \in$ VectorPaths *is the*
> *angular velocity function, then for any constant*
> $f \in$ Frames,
>
> $$\tfrac{d}{dt}Repq\,(f, r(t)) = \tfrac{1}{2}\,\overset{f}{\omega}(t)Repq\,(f, r(t)), \quad t \in \Re$$

Equation 8.22: The angular velocity equation in Def. 8.21 has an analog in quaternion representations, using quaternion arithmetic. □

If a frame "moves," it will have associated with it linear and angular velocities. We define a space that associates two velocity vectors with a frame:

Definition. InstFrames

(8.23)

> InstFrames
> [
> $\quad F \mapsto$ Frames $\qquad\qquad$ *a frame*
> $\quad P \quad \ldots P \mapsto$ Locations
> $\quad R \quad \ldots R \mapsto$ Orientations
> $\quad V \mapsto$ Vectors $\qquad\qquad$ *a linear velocity*
> $\quad \omega \mapsto$ Vectors $\qquad\qquad$ *an angular velocity*
>]

Definition 8.23: Each "instantaneous frame" is a frame along with a linear velocity vector and an angular velocity vector. Note that InstFrames is not a specialization of Frames; it is possible to have two instantaneous frames that have the same frame but different velocities. □

If we consider paths in the space InstFrames, we are most interested in ones whose velocity aspects actually agree with their motion, as per Def. 8.21. Thus we define

Definition. **Consistent** *Frame Function*

(8.24)

> *Given a differentiable function* $f: \Re \rightarrow$ InstFrames, *we*
> *say* f *is* **consistent** *iff:*
>
> $$\frac{d}{dt} P_f(t) = V_f(t), \qquad t \in \Re$$
> $$\frac{d}{dt} R_f(t) = \omega_f^*(t) R_f(t), \quad t \in \Re$$

Definition 8.24: A path through instantaneous frame space is consistent if at each point on the path, the velocity vectors at that point correspond with the actual derivatives of the function. (The use of subscripted aspects of functions is as per Not. 5.28.) □

Notice that we can trivially construct an ordinary frame from an instantaneous frame by projecting the F aspect operator of the instantaneous frame:

(8.25)

Given $j \in$ InstFrames, *define* $f \in$ Frames *by*

$$f = F_j$$

Equation 8.25: Given an instantaneous frame, the corresponding ordinary frame is trivially available. □

Thus we will implicitly overload all functions and notations that expect frames to accept instantaneous frames as well. In particular, the representation operator $Rep(f, x)$ and notation ${}^f x$ are defined for $f \in$ InstFrames.

Similarly, extending Eq. 8.25, we can be careless and blur the distinction between differentiable functions to frames and consistent functions to instantaneous frames, since one can be trivially constructed from the other:

For differentiable $f: \Re \rightarrow$ Frames *and consistent* $j: \Re \rightarrow$ InstFrames

(8.26)

$$
\begin{aligned}
\text{Given } f, \text{ define } j \text{ by:} & \\
F_j(t) &= f(t), & t \in \Re \\
V_f(t) &= \tfrac{d}{dt} P_f(t), & t \in \Re \\
\omega_f^*(t) &= (\tfrac{d}{dt} R_f(t))(R_f(t)),^T & t \in \Re \\
\text{Or, given } j, \text{ define } f \text{ by:} & \\
f(t) &= F_j(t), & t \in \Re
\end{aligned}
$$

Equation 8.26: Switching between differentiable frame functions and consistent instantaneous frame functions. Because one can be constructed from the other, we will blur the distinction between them. □

We define a space of consistent functions:

Definition. FramePaths

(8.27) $\text{FramePaths} \equiv \textit{the set of functions} \left\{ \begin{array}{c} f\colon \Re \to \text{InstFrames } \textit{such} \\ \textit{that } f \textit{ is consistent} \end{array} \right\}$

Definition 8.27: Space of moving frames. We restrict the space to consistent (Def. 8.24) functions. As per Eq. 8.26 we can interchange consistent instantaneous and ordinary frame functions, so for brevity we name this space "FramePaths" rather than "InstFramePaths." □

A moving frame "carries" its coordinates system along with it:

Given a moving frame $f \in$ FramePaths,

(8.28)
$$^{f(t)}P_f(t) = 0 \qquad \frac{d}{dt}\,^{f(t)}P_f(t) = 0 \text{ (constant)}$$
$$^{f(t)}R_f(t) = 1 \qquad \frac{d}{dt}\,^{f(t)}R_f(t) = 0 \text{ (constant)}$$
$$^{f(t)}V_f(t) = \textit{not constant, in general}$$
$$^{f(t)}\omega_f(t) = \textit{not constant, in general}$$

Equation 8.28: Represented in itself, a moving frame's origin is always at (0,0,0) and its orientation is the identity, as per Eq. 8.10. The velocities can have any values, however. □

But notice that if we equate velocities with derivatives in Eq. 8.28, we get the following "paradox," i.e., a seeming violation of Def. 8.24:

Given a moving frame $f \in$ FramePaths, *in general:*

(8.29)
$$^{f(t)}V_f(t) \quad \neq \quad \frac{d}{dt}(^{f(t)}P_f(t))$$
$$^{f(t)}\omega_f^*(t) \quad \neq \quad \frac{d}{dt}(^{f(t)}R_f(t))(^{f(t)}R_f(t))^T$$

Equation 8.29: Moving-frame "paradox." A moving frame can have nonzero velocity coordinates, but the origin is always at zero as per Eq. 8.28—thus the velocity is apparently not the derivative of the location. However, the offending inequalities are not equivalent to Def. 8.24: differentiation and representation do not commute for a nonconstant frame (Def. 8.20). □

8.4.9 Derivatives in Moving Frames

Suppose that we have a constant object, but we represent it in a moving frame. Thus though the object itself does not change, the representation of it might. The derivatives for the various types of constant objects represented in a moving frame are

For moving frame $f \in$ FramePaths and constant
objects $s \in$ Scalars, $v \in$ Vectors, $a \in$ 2Tensors,
$p \in$ Locations, $n \in$ Orientations

(8.30)

$$\frac{d}{dt}\left(^{f(t)}s\right) = 0$$

$$\frac{d}{dt}\left(^{f(t)}v\right) = -\,^{f(t)}[\omega_f(t) \times v]$$

$$\frac{d}{dt}\left(^{f(t)}a\right) = -\,^{f(t)}[\omega_f^*(t)\,a + a\,\omega_f^{*T}(t)]$$

$$\frac{d}{dt}\left(^{f(t)}p\right) = -\,^{f(t)}[V_f(t) + \omega_f(t) \times (p - P_f(t))]$$

$$\frac{d}{dt}\left(^{f(t)}n\right) = -\,^{f(t)}[\omega_f^*(t)\,n]$$

Equation 8.30: These equations describe behavior of the representation of an object if the object is constant but the frame we represent it in changes. (See derivation in Section 8.7.) □

Suppose now that we have an object that is moving and we represent it in a moving frame. This is a more general case of Eq. 8.30:

For moving frame $f \in$ FramePaths and moving objects
$s \in$ ScalarPaths, $v \in$ VectorPaths,
$a \in$ 2TensorPaths, $p \in$ LocationPaths,
$n \in$ OrientationPaths

(8.31)

$$\frac{d}{dt}\left(^{f(t)}s(t)\right) = \,^{f(t)}[\tfrac{d}{dt}s(t)]$$

$$\frac{d}{dt}\left(^{f(t)}v(t)\right) = \,^{f(t)}[\tfrac{d}{dt}v(t) - \omega_f(t) \times v(t)]$$

$$\frac{d}{dt}\left(^{f(t)}a(t)\right) = \,^{f(t)}[\tfrac{d}{dt}a(t) - \omega_f^*(t)\,a(t) - a(t)\,\omega_f^{*T}(t)]$$

$$\frac{d}{dt}\left(^{f(t)}p(t)\right) = \,^{f(t)}[\tfrac{d}{dt}p(t) - V_f(t) - \omega_f(t) \times (p(t) - P_f(t))]$$

$$\frac{d}{dt}\left(^{f(t)}n(t)\right) = \,^{f(t)}[\tfrac{d}{dt}n(t) - \omega_f^*(t)\,n(t)]$$

Equation 8.31: These equations describe the behavior of the representation of an object if both the object and the frame to represent it in are changing. □

Now consider an object that is moving and that we represent in a moving frame—but its representation in that frame is constant. Thus the object "moves with" or "is carried by" or just "is fixed in" that moving frame; we define

Definition. **Fixed in a Moving Frame**

(8.32)

> *A moving object* $x: \Re \rightarrow$ GeomObjs
> *is* **fixed in a moving frame** $f \in$ FramePaths *iff:*
>
> $$\frac{d}{dt}^{f(t)} x(t) = 0, \text{ for all } t$$

Definition 8.32: A moving object is fixed in a frame if its representation in that frame is constant or, equivalently, the derivative of its representation is zero. □

The representations of fixed objects in other frames are given directly by Eq. 8.11. The derivatives can be defined as abstract objects:

For moving objects $s \in$ ScalarPaths,
$v \in$ VectorPaths, $a \in$ 2TensorPaths,
$p \in$ LocationPaths, $n \in$ OrientationPaths, *fixed in
moving frame* $f \in$ FramePaths

(8.33)

$$\frac{d}{dt} s(t) = 0$$
$$\frac{d}{dt} v(t) = \omega_f(t) \times v(t)$$
$$\frac{d}{dt} a(t) = \omega_f^*(t)\, a(t) + a(t)\, \omega_f^{*T}(t)$$
$$\frac{d}{dt} p(t) = V_f(t) + \omega_f(t) \times (p(t) - P_f(t))$$
$$\frac{d}{dt} n(t) = \omega_f^*(t)\, n(t)$$

Equation 8.33: These equations describe the behavior of an object that is fixed in a moving frame. The derivatives are computed using abstract geometric operations on the various quantities. □

Note that the latter above implies that an orientation that is fixed in a moving frame f has an angular velocity ω that is the same as f's angular velocity ω_f (see Def. 8.21).

8.5   Posed Problems

The conceptual and mathematical models that we have defined do not immediately imply any complicated numerical problems. However, there are many simple "evaluation" tasks that may often need to be performed. To list a few:

- Define an object given its representation in a particular frame.
- Given an object, evaluate its representation in a particular frame.
- Find the motion of an object fixed in a moving frame.
- Given a location path, find its velocity (also a path).
- Given an orientation path, find its angular velocity (also a path).

8.6   Implementation Notes[†]

The implementation of this module lies entirely in the math section of the program—in the conceptual section, we typically manipulate arrays of numbers, corresponding to the representations in conceptually natural frames, thus no intricate C–M interface is needed; and since we have defined no complicated numerical problems, there is no M–N interface. The math section has scope name MCO ("Math COordinates"). Figure 8.8 lists the definitions for the module.

Primitive objects. The implementation maintains the distinction between abstract geometric objects and their representations: An object is not tied to a particular frame. For each class of object, a method, rep(Frame), yields the representation in any specified frame (which is specified via an instance of class Frame, described below). Thus:

class Vector :
    constructors: (Frame, double[3])   *construct from coords in given frame*
    methods: rep(Frame) : double[3]   *represent as coords in given frame*

class Orientation :
    constructors: (Frame, double[3][3])   *construct from matrix in given frame*
                (Frame, double[4])   *construct from quaternion in given frame*
    methods: rep(Frame) : double[3][3]   *represent as matrix in given frame*
                repq(Frame) : double[4]   *represent as quaternion in given frame*

To construct an instance of a primitive object, one provides a frame along with the representation in that frame, as per Eq. 8.7. Notice that an Orientation can be constructed/represented via matrices or quaternions (Def. 8.8); the same is true for the Rotation class. Classes 2tensor and Location are defined similarly to Vector. Scalar is implemented simply as an alias for double, as per Eq. 8.18. The various arithmetic operators, +, *, cross, etc., are defined for these classes as appropriate (see Fig. 8.5).

Internally, our implementation stores these objects as their lab-frame representations: When an instance is constructed or represented, the appropriate transformation (Eq. 8.11) is performed; arithmetic is performed directly in lab coordinates. The implementation could perhaps be optimized in various ways, however; for example, the representation in the most recently requested frame might be stored to avoid repeatedly performing the transformation calculations to the same frame.

Frames.   The classes for state spaces Frames (Def. 8.2) and InstFrames (Def. 8.23) are defined in the standard manner (Section B.3.6):

class Frame :
    constructors: (Location P, Orientation R)
                (InstFrame)   *trivial, as per Eq. 8.25*
    members: P : Location
                R : Orientation

[†] See Appendix B for discussion of the terminology, notation, and overall approach used here.

Program Definitions in Scope MC0:		
class name	*abstract space*	
2tensor	2Tensors	*(Def. 8.1)*
2tensorPath	2TensorPaths	*(Def. 8.19)*
Frame	Frames	*(Def. 8.2)*
FramePath	FramePaths	*(Def. 8.27)*
InstFrame	InstFrames	*(Def. 8.23)*
Location	Locations	*(Def. 8.1)*
LocationPath	LocationPaths	*(Def. 8.19)*
Orientation	Locations	*(Def. 8.1)*
OrientationPath	OrientationPaths	*(Def. 8.19)*
Rotation	Rotations	*(Def. 8.1)*
RotationPath	RotationPaths	*(Def. 8.19)*
Scalar	Scalars	*(Def. 8.1)*
ScalarIdx	$\{\text{Scalars}\}_{\text{IDs}}$	*index of scalars (Not. 5.11)*
ScalarPath	ScalarPaths	*(Def. 8.19)*
ScalarPathIdx	$\{\text{ScalarPaths}\}_{\text{IDs}}$	*index of scalar paths (Not. 5.11)*
Vector	Vectors	*(Def. 8.1)*
VectorIdx	$\{\text{Vectors}\}_{\text{IDs}}$	*index of vectors (Not. 5.11)*
VectorPath	VectorPaths	*(Def. 8.19)*
global constant	*mathematical object*	
Lab_Frame	$\mathcal{L}ab \in$ Frames	*(Def. 8.4)*
Zero_Vector	$0 \in$ Vectors	*(Eq. 8.16)*
Zero_2tensor	$0 \in$ 2Tensors	*(Eq. 8.16)*
Identity_2tensor	$1 \in$ 2Tensors	*(Eq. 8.16)*

Figure 8.8: Math section definitions in the prototype implementation. In addition to classes for the abstract spaces that we use, we define a few constant global variables. □

```
class InstFrame :
  constructors:  (Location P, Orientation R, Vector v)
                 (Frame f, Vector v)
  members:       f : Frame
                 P : Location
                 R : Orientation
                 v : Vector
                 w : Vector
```

Notice the circularity discussed in Section 8.3: We need a location and an orientation to construct a frame, but we need a frame to construct a location or orientation. The pre-defined constant frame Lab_Frame provides a starting point.

Paths. Classes for object paths (Def. 8.19) are defined in the standard manner (Section B.3.7):

```
class LocationPath :
  constructors:  (Location)                  constant path
                 (FramePath, double[3])      fixed in given moving frame
  methods:       eval(double t) : Location
                 velocity()     : VectorPath
```

The classes 2tensorPath, OrientationPath, RotationPath, ScalarPath, and VectorPath are defined similarly. In addition to constant paths and fixed paths as shown, there is support for paths that are algebraic combinations of given paths, and for paths that are evaluated by calling arbitrary user-supplied subroutines. Some paths support the velocity method, which returns a path whose value is the derivative of the given path, e.g., as per Eq. 8.33. We additionally define the class FramePath, the standard manner for paths into state spaces (Section B.3.7).

8.7 Derivations

Since the mathematics of geometric objects is well known, there are no surprises in this chapter. Hence, we refer the reader to [Craig89] and [Foley *et al*.90] for further discussion of 3D geometry and linear algebra, or the reader may simply "take our word for it." To illustrate the use of our notation, however, we provide derivations of Eq. 8.13 and one equality in Eq. 8.30.

- Equation 8.13

> Given: two frames $f, g \in$ Frames.
> For any location $p \in$ Locations, we have
> $$^g p \;=\; ^g P_f + (^g R_f)\,^f p ; \qquad\qquad (Eq.\ 8.11)$$
> substitute P_g (the origin of frame g) for p to get
> $$^g P_g \;=\; ^g P_f + (^g R_f)\,^f P_g$$
> $$0 \;=\; ^g P_f + (^g R_f)\,^f P_g \qquad\qquad (via\ Eq.\ 8.10)$$
> $$^g P_f \;=\; -\,^g R_f\,^f P_g .$$
>
> For any orientation $n \in$ Orientations, we have
> $$^g n \;=\; (^g R_f)\,^f n ; \qquad\qquad (Eq.\ 8.11)$$
> substitute R_g (the orientation of frame g) for n to get
> $$^g R_g \;=\; (^g R_f)(^f R_g)$$
> $$1 \;=\; (^g R_f)(^f R_g) \qquad\qquad (via\ Eq.\ 8.10)$$
> $$^g R_f \;=\; (^f R_g)^T . \qquad\qquad (via\ Eq.\ 8.15)$$

• Equation 8.30

Given: constant location $p \in$ Locations and moving frame $f \in$ FramePaths.
For any constant frame $g \in$ Frames, we have

$$^g p = {}^g P_{f(t)} + ({}^g R_{f(t)})\, {}^{f(t)}p \qquad\qquad (Eq.\ 8.11)$$

$$\frac{d}{dt}({}^g p) = \frac{d}{dt}({}^g P_{f(t)} + ({}^g R_{f(t)})\, {}^{f(t)}p)$$

$$^g(\tfrac{d}{dt}p) = \qquad\qquad\qquad\qquad (via\ Def.\ 8.20)$$

$$0 = \qquad\qquad\qquad\qquad (p\ is\ constant)$$

$$= \frac{d}{dt}({}^g P_{f(t)}) + [\frac{d}{dt}({}^g R_{f(t)})]\, {}^{f(t)}p + {}^g R_{f(t)} \frac{d}{dt}({}^{f(t)}p) \quad (product\ rule)$$

$$-{}^g R_{f(t)} \frac{d}{dt}({}^{f(t)}p) = \frac{d}{dt}({}^g P_{f(t)}) + [\frac{d}{dt}({}^g R_{f(t)})]\, {}^{f(t)}p$$

$$= {}^g(\tfrac{d}{dt}P_{f(t)}) + {}^g(\tfrac{d}{dt}R_{f(t)})\, {}^{f(t)}p \qquad (via\ Def.\ 8.20)$$

$$= {}^g V_{f(t)} + {}^g \omega^*_{f(t)}\, {}^g R_{f(t)}\, {}^{f(t)}p \qquad (via\ Def.\ 8.24)$$

$$\frac{d}{dt}({}^{f(t)}p) = -({}^g R_{f(t)})^T\, {}^g V_{f(t)} - ({}^g R_{f(t)})^T\, {}^g \omega^*_{f(t)}\, {}^g R_{f(t)}\, {}^{f(t)}p \quad (mult.\ by\ -R^T)$$

$$= -{}^{f(t)}R_g\, {}^g V_{f(t)} - {}^{f(t)}R_g\, {}^g \omega^*_{f(t)}({}^{f(t)}R_g)^T\, {}^{f(t)}p \qquad (via\ Eq.\ 8.13)$$

$$\dagger \qquad = -{}^{f(t)}V_{f(t)} - {}^{f(t)}\omega^*_{f(t)}\, {}^{f(t)}p \qquad (via\ Eq.\ 8.11)$$

$$= -{}^{f(t)}V_{f(t)} - {}^{f(t)}\omega^*_{f(t)}({}^{f(t)}p - {}^{f(t)}P_{f(t)}) \qquad (via\ Eq.\ 8.10)$$

$$\ddagger \qquad = -{}^{f(t)}[V_{f(t)} + \omega^*_{f(t)}(p - P_{f(t)})] \qquad (via\ Def.\ 8.14)$$

$$= -{}^{f(t)}[V_{f(t)} + \omega_{f(t)} \times (p - P_{f(t)})] \qquad (via\ Eq.\ 8.15)$$

Notice in line $\dagger$ that ${}^f\omega^*_f\, {}^f p$ is a valid matrix product, but there is no corresponding abstract operation—we can't multiply a 2tensor, ω^*_f, by a location, p. But, by subtracting zero in the form ${}^f P_f$, we essentially replace p with its corresponding vector in frame f (Eq. 8.17). Since a product between a 2tensor, ω^*_f, and a vector, $(p - P_f)$, *is* a valid abstract operation, we can make the transition to line $\ddagger$.

Chapter 9

Kinematic Rigid-Bodies Model

"Kinematic" motion is motion without considerations of mass and force. This includes, e.g., motion described by keyframe animations systems, geometric constraints, and direct user manipulation.

This module provides a basic expression of the kinematic motion of rigid bodies. It provides a simple structure for describing collections of bodies and a mechanism for describing bodies constrained in fixed hierarchies. The module is administrative rather than technical. We do not give any specific methods or techniques for manipulating bodies; we merely provide a framework within which to express such techniques.

The "traditional" computer graphics animation techniques are kinematic, as discussed in Ch. 2; see also, e.g., [Magnenat-Thalmann,Thalmann85]. An extensive discussion of kinematics, in the context of robotics, can be found in [Craig89].

a. A moving rigid body...   b. ... is abstracted as a moving coordinate frame

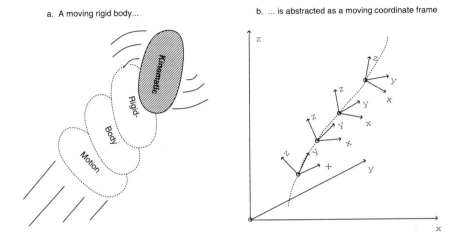

Figure 9.1: The motion of a rigid body is described by the motion of an orthonormal coordinate frame that is fixed relative to the body. Each body's frame is called its "body coordinates." □

9.1   Goals

We have a few simple goals for this module:

- To provide a basic model and notation for rigidly moving bodies

- To describe kinematic relationships between bodies, e.g., as a hierarchy

- To describe behavior of points fixed on a body

The intent is not to define any particular techniques for kinematic rigid-body motion, but to give a common framework and terminology that can be built upon by other, higher-level models and techniques, such as dynamics or articulated key-frame animation.

9.2   Conceptual Model

Our conceptual model for kinematic rigid bodies is quite simple. We describe our basic abstraction of a *body,* as well as two other useful notions, that of a *body point* and that of a *hierarchical configuration* of bodies. All bodies exist in the fixed, Euclidean 3D world space of Ch. 8.

Bodies

A rigid body doesn't change its shape—that is what we mean by "rigid"—thus a body's motion can be described by its position and orientation. In other words, we think of a rigid body as "carrying" with it a coordinate frame, as per Section 8.3. We call that frame the *body frame* (see Fig. 9.1). Note that a moving body has a velocity and angular velocity at each instant of time.

The body frame is fixed relative to the body and serves to define *body coordinates* that can be used in particular to describe the shape or configuration of the body. In this module, we make no restrictions on the body shape, other than that it be constant in body coordinates; nor do we provide any mechanism for describing the shape.[1] Presumably, in most cases, the origin of body coordinates is at some "natural" spot relative to the body shape (e.g., the center or the corner or the apex, depending on the shape), and the body coordinate axes are aligned with the axes of symmetry of the shape—but this is not required.

Each body in a model is given a unique "name" of some sort so that we can identify and distinguish the bodies.

Body Points

Frequently, in addition to defining a primitive body, we are interested in specifying "interesting" points on the body. For example, we might specify a point at which to attach a constraint. We define a *body point* to be a location that is fixed in the body frame, as per Section 8.3, i.e., its body coordinates are constant. Thus, as the body moves, it "carries" the body point with it.

For the most part, we think of a body point as being the location of a specific piece of "material" within the body or on its surface. But we don't require this; one could define a body point in the middle of a donut's hole, for example. The origin of the body frame is a body point, at coordinates $(0, 0, 0)$.

Hierarchical Configurations

We're often interested in describing kinematic relationships between groups of bodies; for example, it is common to model humans, animals, and robot manipulators as *articulated figures,* i.e., collections of segments connected at joints (see [Badler *et al.*91], [Craig89]).

This module defines a *hierarchical configuration,* i.e., a collection of bodies organized into a tree hierarchy, with the position and orientation of each body's frame described in the coordinates of its parent (see Fig. 9.2). An articulated figure can be described by a hierarchical configuration in which each body's origin is fixed in its parent's frame, but the body's orientation can be adjusted.

---

[1] The description of shape is a fundamental part of computer graphics; we refer readers to [Foley *et al.*90] and [Snyder92].

Hierarchical Configuration

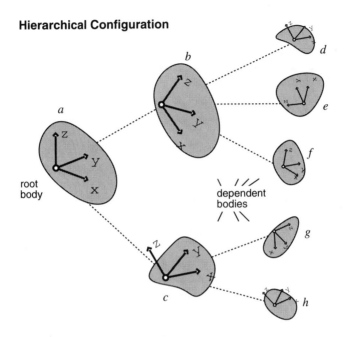

Figure 9.2: A *hierarchical configuration* is a collection of bodies organized into a hierarchical structure. Each body's configuration is specified in the body coordinates of its parent; thus if, e.g., body *b* is moved or rotated, bodies *d*, *e*, and *f* will be carried with it, and if the root body *a* is moved, the entire collection moves with it. A common type of hierarchical configuration is an *articulated figure,* in which primitive body segments are connected at joints. □

9.3   Mathematical Model

9.3.1   Names and Notation

The scope name for this module is

KINEMATIC.

We make use of the following definitions from other modules:

IDforests	(Def. A.1)	Locations	(Def. 8.1)
IDs	(Def. 5.8)	LocationPaths	(Def. 8.19)
FramePaths	(Def. 8.27)	Orientations	(Def. 8.1)
InstFrames	(Def. 8.23)	Vectors	(Def. 8.1)

We also use superscript frame-representation notation:

$$^{f}x \quad \text{(Not. 8.6)}$$

9.3.2 Body State

We define the space of possible configurations of a rigidly moving kinematic body, States. Note that the space includes only coordinate-frame information; we are not including any shape description.

Definition. States

(9.1)

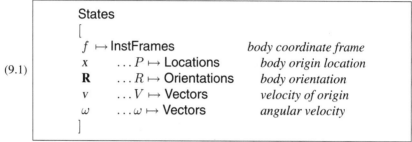

> States
> [
> | $f \mapsto$ InstFrames | *body coordinate frame* |
> | x $\ldots P \mapsto$ Locations | *body origin location* |
> | R $\ldots R \mapsto$ Orientations | *body orientation* |
> | v $\ldots V \mapsto$ Vectors | *velocity of origin* |
> | ω $\ldots \omega \mapsto$ Vectors | *angular velocity* |
>]

Definition 9.1: Kinematic rigid-body state space. The state of a rigid body at an instant is just its instantaneous coordinate frame (which includes linear and angular velocities). Note that we have renamed the origin to be x and velocity v, in keeping with common usage for rigid-body modeling. □

A moving body can be described by its trajectory, i.e., a path through state space. Based on Section 8.4.8, we define a space StatePaths, each of whose elements is a path of a moving body:

Definition. StatePaths

(9.2)

$$\text{StatePaths} \equiv \textit{the set of functions} \left\{ \begin{array}{l} s\colon \Re \to \text{States } \textit{such that} \\ (f \circ s) \in \text{FramePaths} \end{array} \right\}$$

Definition 9.2: The space of paths through state space. For a path $s \in$ StatePaths, the composite function $(f \circ s)$, which describes the body frame's motion, must be an element of FramePaths; this means that it is consistent as per Def. 8.24, i.e., that the velocity vectors at each instant agree with the trajectory of the body. □

The moving-frame "paradox," Eq. 8.29, applies directly to moving bodies:

For $s \in$ StatePaths

(9.3)

$$\frac{d}{dt} x_s(t) = v_s(t)$$
$$0 = \frac{d}{dt}{}^{f_s(t)} x_s(t) \neq {}^{f_s(t)} v_s(t)$$

Equation 9.3: The moving-body "paradox." The velocity vector can be nonzero in body coordinates, even though the origin is always at (0,0,0). The velocity vector describes the motion of the body relative to the fixed world space; thus the body "knows" that it is moving, unlike special-relativistic formulations of motion, in which there is no local way to distinguish a frame at rest from one moving with constant velocity. □

9.3.3 Body Points

We define the space of states of body points, **Bodypts**, analogous to the states of bodies, to define the configuration of a body point.

Definition. **Bodypts**

(9.4)

$$
\begin{array}{l}
\textbf{Bodypts} \\
[\\
\quad x \mapsto \textbf{Locations} \quad \textit{location of body point} \\
\quad v \mapsto \textbf{Vectors} \quad\ \ \textit{velocity of body point} \\
]
\end{array}
$$

Definition 9.4: Body point state space. A body point has a location x and a velocity v. The velocity v is the point's velocity in space. □

We can specify a body point state given its body-frame coordinates and the state of the body it belongs to:

Definition. **Bodypt**

(9.5)

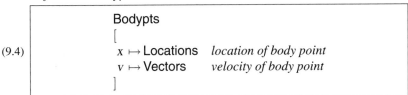

Define a function Bodypt: **States** $\times\ \Re^{3\times3} \to$ **Bodypts**
such that, for all $s \in$ **States** *and coords* $\in \Re^{3\times3}$,

$$
{}^{f(s)}x(Bodypt(s, coords)) = coords
$$
$$
v(Bodypt(s, coords)) = v_s + \omega_s \times (x(Bodypt(s, coords)) - x_s)
$$

Definition 9.5: A function that yields the state of a body point given its body-frame coordinates. The expression for the point's velocity comes from Eq. 8.33, which gives derivates of objects fixed in moving frames. □

9.3.4 Collections of Bodies

The definitions in Section 9.3.2 are generic, without the concept of *which* body. Here, we provide definitions allowing us to name and identify bodies. We define a *system* to be a collection of names (IDs) of bodies and their corresponding states:

Definition. **Systems**

(9.6)

$$
\textbf{Systems} \equiv \{\textbf{States}\}_{\textbf{IDs}}
$$

Definition 9.6: Each system is an index of states (as per Section 5.8.2). That is, it is a collection of body states elements, each labeled with a different "name," or ID. Given a system $Y \in$ **Systems**, the state of a body labeled with $b \in$ **IDs** is given by Y_b. □

The above describes the state of a collection of bodies at a single instant of time. For a collection of bodies that are moving over time, we define a *system path:*

Definition. SysPaths

(9.7) | $$\text{SysPaths} \equiv \{\text{StatePaths}\}_{\text{IDs}}$$

Definition 9.7: Each system is an index of state paths. Note that each element in the index is a function. That is, for a system path $\mathcal{Y} \in$ SysPaths, the state of body b at an instant of time t is given by $\mathcal{Y}_b(t)$. $\square$

To construct a system $Y \in$ **Systems** given a system $\mathcal{Y} \in$ **SysPaths**, we evaluate all the paths in $\mathcal{Y}$ at a common time t. This is written as $Y = \mathcal{Y}(t)$, as per Not. 5.18.

9.3.5   Hierarchical Configurations

A hierarchical model consists of the tree hierarchy that organizes the bodies, along with the specification of each child's state relative to that of its parent. Section A.1 defines the IDforests mechanism for hierarchies of names. All that remains for us is to define a mechanism to specify each body's frame relative to its parent.

We start by defining a space that encapsulates representations of frames.[2]

Definition. FrameReps

(9.8)

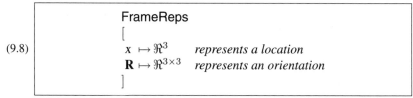

Definition 9.8: Each "frame rep" will be used to specify the representation of a frame in some other frame. Note that x and $\mathbf{R}$ are numbers—they will be representations of abstract geometric objects, rather than the abstract objects themselves. $\square$

We have a notion of two bodies that are "aligned" by a given frame representation:

---

[2]This is the most general way of describing a frame relative to some coordinate system. But for specific applications, other representations might be more convenient. For example, articulated figures are typically described in terms of joint angles. Such descriptions could be defined as specializations (Section 5.7.2) of FrameReps.

Definition. **Aligned Bodies,** Given a Frame Representation

(9.9)

> *A body state $b \in$* States *is* **aligned** *to a body state*
> *$a \in$* States *given a frame representation*
> *$c \in$* FrameReps *iff:*
>
> $$^{f(a)}x(b) = x(c)$$
> $$^{f(a)}\mathbf{R}(b) = \mathbf{R}(c)$$

Definition 9.9: The numbers in frame rep $c \in$ FrameReps give the coordinate values for body b when "looked at" from body a. Note that given any two of a, b, or c, the third is uniquely determined. □

A hierarchical configuration bundles together a collection of frame-representation constraints along with a forest (collection of trees) of body names:

Definition. HierConfigs

(9.10)

> HierConfigs
> [
>
> | | | |
> |---|---|---|
> | forest | $\mapsto$ IDforests | *the ID hierarchy* |
> | roots | ... roots $\mapsto$ IDsets | *independent bodies* |
> | nonroots | ... nonroots $\mapsto$ IDsets | *dependent bodies* |
> | leaves | ... leaves $\mapsto$ IDsets | *bodies having no children* |
> | parent | ... parent $\mapsto \{$IDs$\}_{\text{IDs}}$ | *parent of each dependent* |
> | config | $\mapsto \{$FrameReps$\}_{\text{IDs}}$ | *the frame representations* |
>
> —
>
> $Ids(config) = nonroots$
>
>]

Definition 9.10: A hierarchical model. *forest* is a forest of body IDs. For each body $c \in nonroots$, we will use frame rep $config_c$ to align body c in its parent's coordinates. The internal property $Ids(config) = nonroots$ guarantees that every nonroot body has a corresponding frame rep. □

Putting together Defs. 9.9 and 9.10, we tell if a particular collection of body states satisfies a given hierarchical configuration:

Definition. **Satisfies**

(9.11)

> *A collection of body states $Y \in$* Systems **satisfies** *a*
> *hierarchical configuration $m \in$* HierConfigs *iff, for all*
> *$c \in nonroots(m)$,*
>
> *$Y_c(t)$ is aligned to $Y_{parent(m)_c}$ given $config(m)_c$*

Definition 9.11: A given system satisfies a model if each child body is properly aligned to its parent. Note that no top-level restrictions are placed on the roots. □

9.4   Posed Problems

A well-known problem in modeling is the *forward kinematics problem*: Given a
static hierarchical configuration and the states at the roots, determine the states of
all the bodies (see [Craig89, Ch. 3]). This can be expressed using our constructs
as:

$$
\begin{array}{rl}
\textit{given:} & B \in \textsf{Systems } \textit{and} \\
& H \in \textsf{HierConfigs}, \\
& \textit{such that } \mathrm{Ids}(B) = \mathrm{roots}(H) \\
\textit{find:} & Y \in \textsf{Systems} \\
\textit{such that:} & \left\{ \begin{array}{l} Y_b = B_b \textit{ for all } b \in \mathrm{Ids}(B) \\ Y \textit{ satisfies } H \end{array} \right.
\end{array}
$$

(9.12)

Equation 9.12: The forward kinematics problem. We are given B, the states of the roots
of the hierarchy H. We want to determine the states of all the children as well. The solution system Y includes the states of all the bodies, roots (directly as given) and nonroots
(determined from H). □

Solving this problem is straightforward. One proceeds top-down from the roots,
at each node constructing the frame that is aligned with its parent.

The complementary problem to the above is an *inverse kinematics problem:*
Given the states of the roots and leaves of the hierarchy, determine the relationships
between the bodies:

$$
\begin{array}{rl}
\textit{given:} & B \in \textsf{Systems } \textit{and} \\
& F \in \textsf{IDforests}, \\
& \textit{such that } \mathrm{Ids}(B) = \mathrm{roots}(F) \cup \mathrm{leaves}(F) \\
\textit{find:} & Y \in \textsf{Systems } \textit{and} \\
& H \in \textsf{HierConfigs}, \\
\textit{such that:} & \left\{ \begin{array}{l} Y_b = B_b \textit{ for all } b \in \mathrm{Ids}(B) \\ \mathrm{forest}(H) = F \\ Y \textit{ satisfies } H \end{array} \right.
\end{array}
$$

(9.13)

Equation 9.13: An inverse kinematics problem. We are given the hierarchical structure
of body names F, but no configuration specifications, and we are given B, the states of the
roots and leaves. We want to determine the states of all the intermediate bodies as well. The
solution includes the system Y and the complete hierarchical configuration H. For specific
types of models we may be given additional input or restrictions, such as given segment
lengths for articulated figures. □

Program Definitions in Scope `MKIN`:		
class name	*abstract space*	
`Bodypt`	Bodypts	*(Def. 9.5)*
`FrameRep`	FrameReps	*(Def. 9.8)*
`FrameRepIdx`	{FrameReps}$_{IDs}$	*index of frame reps (Not. 5.11)*
`HierConfig`	HierConfigs	*(Def. 9.10)*
`State`	States	*(Def. 9.1)*
`StatePath`	StatePaths	*(Def. 9.2)*
`SysPath`	SysPaths	*(Def. 9.7)*
`System`	Systems	*(Def. 9.6)*

Figure 9.3: Math section definitions in the prototype implementation. □

Unlike the forward kinematics problem, solving inverse problems can be difficult. There is not necessarily a unique solution; there may be none or many. [Craig89, Ch. 4] discusses this problem in detail.

9.5   Implementation Notes[†]

9.5.1   Conceptual Section Constructs

The conceptual bodies can be defined using an object-oriented method: A base class Body includes the body's name, position and orientation data members; various derived classes, e.g., `Sphere`, `Cylinder`, `Banana`, etc., implement their own `draw` methods to draw the body at its current position and orientation. The base class can also maintain a list of body points associated with the body.

9.5.2   Math Section Constructs

The scope name for this module's math section is `MKIN`; Fig. 9.3 lists the class definitions. The classes for the state spaces States, Bodypts, FrameReps, and HierConfigs are defined in the standard manner (Section B.3.6):

```
class State :
  constructors:  (MCO::InstFrame ff)
  members:       f : MCO::InstFrame
                 x : MCO::Location
                 R : MCO::Orientation
                 v : MCO::Vector
                 w : MCO::Vector
```

[†] See Appendix B for discussion of the terminology, notation, and overall approach used here.

```
class Bodypt :
  constructors:  (State s, double c[3])    computes Bodypt(s, c), Def. 9.5
  members:       x : MCO::Location
                 v : MCO::Vector


class FrameRep :
  constructors:  (double[3], double[4])
  members:       x : double[3]
                 r : double[4]


class HierConfig :
  constructors:  (MMISC::Forest, FrameRepIdx)
  members:       forest   : MMISC::Forest
                 config   : FrameRepIdx
                 roots    : MM::IdSet
                 nonroots : MM::IdSet
```

Notice that the function *Bodypt* (Def. 9.5) is implemented as a constructor for Bodypt. The class for **StatePaths** is defined in the standard manner for paths (Section B.3.7):

```
class StatePath :
  constructors:  (MCO::FramePath ff)
  members:       f : MCO::FramePath
                 x : MCO::LocationPath
                 R : MCO::OrientationPath
                 v : MCO::VectorPath
                 w : MCO::VectorPath
```

9.5.3 M–N Interface

The scope name for the M–N interface is NKIN. We define a routine to compute the system that solves the forward kinematics problem. It is implemented using the routine NMISC::IdForestPreorder(...) of Section A.3.1 to traverse the hierarchy.

```
SolveForward(System, HierConfig) : System
```

9.5.4   C–M Interface

The C–M interface routines must be able to do the following:

- Map between conceptual body names and math IDs
- Map between `MKIN::State` objects and conceptual body objects
- Map between `MKIN::System` objects and the conceptual data structures
- Construct an `MKIN::HierConfig` from the conceptual data structures

Chapter 10

Dynamic Rigid-Bodies Model

This model describes classical dynamics of rigid bodies, i.e., motion of rigid bodies based on inertia and the influence of applied forces and torques, in accordance with Newton's laws. For collections of bodies, each body's motion is due directly only to the forces and torques acting on it; interaction between bodies is mediated by forces and torques.

The force-based paradigm of motion is simple, reasonably intuitive, and uniform across applications. We don't address other paradigms, such as Lagrangian or Hamiltonian, that are based upon energy and generalized or canonical coordinates. Generalized coordinates are useful for deriving equations of motion for specific problems with constrained motion and limited degrees of freedom; using the force-based paradigm, we constrain the motion through explicit introduction of forces, as is discussed in Ch. 11.

The presentation in this module, while axiomatic, assumes that the concepts of mass, force, and so forth are familiar to the reader. Detailed discussion and analysis can be found in [Fox67] and [Goldstein80].

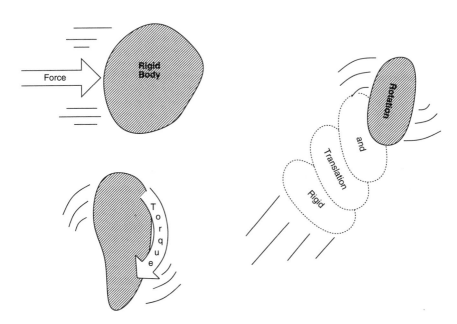

Figure 10.1: Rigid-body motion. A body moves under the influence of forces and torques, in accordance with Newton's laws of motion. The motion of a body can be separated into the linear velocity of the center of mass of the body and the angular velocity of the body's rotation about the center of mass. The body features are encapsulated as a constant net mass and an inertia tensor that is fixed in the body frame. □

10.1   Goals

Our goals for this model are

- To describe bodies that move under the influence of forces and torques

- To keep track of energy expenditures for analysis and debugging

- To provide support for higher-level modules that implement collisions, constraints, force mechanisms, etc.

At this level, we do not provide any mechanism for describing how individual forces and torques arise; we take forces and torques as "givens" from a higher-level module.

10.2   Conceptual Model

The dynamic rigid-bodies model is built on the kinematic rigid-bodies model of Ch. 9, set in the fixed 3D world space of Ch. 8. To the kinematic model, we add the notion of *dynamics,* i.e., motion in accordance with forces and inertia, as per Newton's laws and the classical paradigm.[1]

10.2.1   Bodies

We assume that each body is completely rigid, i.e., does not flex or deform in any circumstances, and that each body has a constant mass that is distributed throughout the body. This abstraction is not unreasonable for many real-world objects, so long as they are subject to relatively mild pressures and accelerations.

A dynamic body is a kinematic body as per Ch. 9—i.e., is uniquely identifiable and has a *body frame* associated with it—along with a *mass distribution.* We don't need to know the details of the mass distribution; it is encapsulated into an *inertia tensor* and a location of the *center of mass.* Note that the center of mass does not have to be at the origin of the body frame. Since the body is rigid, the mass distribution is fixed in the body frame.

A body moves in response to *forces* and *torques* acting on it, in accordance with Newton's laws (see Fig. 10.1). Motion is separable into translational motion of the center of mass (linear velocity) and rotation of the body about the center of mass (angular velocity). In the absence of any applied forces or torques, the center of mass moves in a straight line—but the body frame origin may rotate about it if the body is spinning. Forces and torques are discussed in greater detail below (Section 10.2.2).

As in the kinematic model, this model includes no explicit description of the shape of a body (the body doesn't even need to be contiguous). The inertia tensor depends on the shape, but not uniquely: Bodies with different shapes may share the same inertia tensor. In practice a body's behavior often does depend on details of its shape or mass distribution, e.g., wind resistance or gravitational field variation. We don't disallow such effects in this model, but merely observe that for our purposes, they are indirect and can be encapsulated (by higher-level modules) into net forces and torques acting on our abstracted rigid bodies. This model does disallow, however, bodies that don't have constant mass, such as a rocket that loses mass as it burns propellant.

For collections of bodies, each moves independently in world space, reacting only to the forces and torques applied to it. All interactions between bodies are thus mediated by forces. Notice that unless suitable forces are applied, there is nothing preventing bodies from overlapping, occupying the same locations in space.

---

[1] Actually, the classical rigid-body paradigm, and Newton's laws, can be derived from more basic postulates known as Euler's laws; see [Fox67].

Types of "Motives"

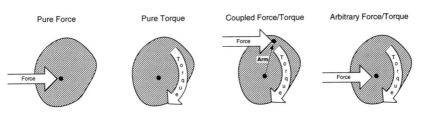

Figure 10.2: There are four types of motives: pure forces, which cause translation but not rotation; pure torques, which cause rotation about the center of mass, but not translation; coupled force/torque, in which a force applied to a body at some distance from the center of mass yields a corresponding torque about the center of mass; and arbitrary force/torque pairs, each of which can be thought of as a pure force and a pure torque acting simultaneously. □

We assume finite forces and torques for this module, so the motion is always continuous. For discontinuities in velocity, such as those caused by collisions between rigid bodies, the idea of *impulses*—infinite forces applied instantaneously— would be introduced; we leave this for higher-level modules (see discussion in Section 14.1). Note, however, that this module could still be used to describe the continuous motion between discontinuities, as in the "tennis ball cannon" example of Ch. 13.

10.2.2 "Motives"—Force/Torque Objects

We assume the existence of forces and torques, which are primitive objects that can be described by vectors and which, when applied to bodies, cause them to move.[2]

We find it convenient to bundle a single force and/or a single torque into an object that we call a *motive*. The most common type of motive is a *coupled force/ torque,* in which a force applied away from the center of mass of a body induces a torque on the body (the vector from the center of mass to the point of application is called the *moment arm*). We can also have a *pure force* or *pure torque,* which can be thought of as applied to the center of mass, and for generality, an arbitrary *force/torque pair* (see Fig. 10.2).

Motives exist in themselves as abstract objects, but to be used, a motive must be applied to some specific body: An *applied motive* is a motive along with (the name of) the body it acts on. If the motive is a coupled force/torque, its moment arm describes the point of application on the body. We typically give each applied motive a unique name in order to identify it.

---

[2]It is not strictly necessary to define torques as primitive objects—the effect of any torque can be mimicked by a suitably chosen pair of forces—but it is a convenient abstraction.

Any number of motives can be applied to a body simultaneously. The forces and torques from each can be added, to produce a single *net force* and *net torque* on the body. The behavior of the body under the influence of the collection of motives is the same as if only the net force and torque were applied to it.

Motives are typically described at any instant by a force/torque *field*, i.e., a function of the configuration of the model.[3] For example, a Hooke's-law spring applies a force that is proportional to how much the spring is stretched. The fields are defined over hypothetical configurations—i.e., they describe what the motive would be *if* the model were in any given state—not just for the path taken by a particular simulation.[4] Note that a single field can depend on the configuration of the entire model—thus the force on a given body can depend on the configurations of the other bodies in the model, giving us an avenue to create interactions between bodies.

10.2.3   Point Masses

A *point mass* is a hypothetical object: a body that has all of its mass concentrated at a single mathematical point (see Fig. 10.3). A point mass has a location and velocity and will move under the influence of forces in the same manner as an ordinary body. Point masses have a zero inertia tensor and have no associated orientation or angular velocity. We do not define the application of a torque to a point mass.

Figure 10.3: A point mass is a body that has all its mass at a single point. Point masses move under the influence of forces, but not torques. □

Point masses provide a simple abstraction of rigid-body motion when orientation is not an issue. They are often used as experimental "test particles." Many flexible-body models are comprised of networks of point masses and interconnecting forces. In addition, the center of mass of any arbitrary deforming (nonrigid) body moves in the same way as a point mass experiencing the sum of all forces acting on the body.

---

[3]This use of the term "field" is in the geometric sense, "function over some manifold," rather than the abstract algebraic sense, "set having addition and multiplication operations."

[4]It is particularly important that fields be defined off the solution path for a particular simulation, because most numerical solvers must explore the configuration space in order to determine that path.

10.2.4 Body Points

A dynamic body point is essentially the same as a kinematic body point (Section 9.2), i.e., a location that moves with a body, fixed in the body's coordinate system (see Fig. 10.4). As with kinematic body points, since we have no explicit description of the shape of a body, we do not care whether a body point is "in" or "on" the body.

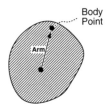

Body points provide convenient "handles" at which to apply forces. Since a force applied at a body point

Figure 10.4: A body point is fixed in body coordinates. Each body point has an associated moment arm, which is the vector from the center of mass. □

yields a coupled torque, we associate a *moment arm* with each body point, as per Section 10.2.2. Note that the moment arm is the vector from the center of mass, not from the body origin.

10.2.5 Energy

It is a fundamental property of classical mechanics that energy is always conserved, or at least accounted for. Thus, although we are using a force-based paradigm rather than energy-based (i.e., Newtonian rather than Lagrangian), we can still keep track of energy in our models.

Each body has an associated *kinetic energy*, based on its linear and angular motion. When a body is acted upon by motives, its kinetic energy can change. The *work* done by each motive is the kinetic energy it adds to the body (negative work means that the force removes kinetic energy, i.e., slows the body).[5]

We can analyze the behavior of a model by examining the work done by each motive. In addition, we can test for consistency of the model by checking that the kinetic energy of each body agrees with the work done by all motives acting on it.

Often, a motive field is *conservative*, i.e., has a *potential energy* field associated with it such that the potential energy and work done by the motive add up to a constant—energy taken from a body is "stored" in the potential energy field, and vice versa. Examples include a gravitational field and a Hooke's-law spring.

Nonconservative motives are *dissipative* if they remove energy from the bodies, or are *active* if they add energy. The work done by these motives corresponds with a conversion between mechanical (kinetic) energy and other forms of energy, such as heat, electromagnetic, or chemical, that are out of the ken of this model.

---

[5] Although the motive may arise from a field over possible configurations (Section 10.2.2), the actual work done by a motive depends on the particular path taken by the body.

10.3   Mathematical Model

10.3.1   Names and Notation

The scope name (see Section 5.6.2) for this module is

RIGID.

We use the following terms from other modules:

IDs	(Def. 5.8)	$\mathcal{L}ab$	(Def. 8.4)
InstFrames	(Def. 8.23)	Locations	(Def. 8.1)
KINEMATIC :: *Bodypt*	(Def. 9.5)	2Tensors	(Def. 8.1)
KINEMATIC :: Bodypts	(Def. 9.4)	Orientations	(Def. 8.1)
KINEMATIC :: StatePaths	(Def. 9.2)	Scalars	(Def. 8.1)
KINEMATIC :: States	(Def. 9.1)	Vectors	(Def. 8.1)

We also extensively use subscript notation for state spaces, and prefix-superscript frame representation notation:

$$x_s \qquad \text{(Not. 5.27)}$$
$$x_s(t) \qquad \text{(Not. 5.28)}$$
$$^f x \qquad \text{(Not. 8.6)}$$

10.3.2   Mass Distributions

If we know the shape of a body and the mass density everywhere within it, we can compute the mass distribution values.

(10.1)

If a body occupying volume V has
mass density $\rho\colon \Re^3 \to \Re$, we compute the mass $\mathtt{m} \in \Re$,
center of mass $\mathtt{xc} \in \Re^3$, and
inertia tensor matrix $\mathtt{I} \in \Re^{3\times3}$ by:

$$\mathtt{m} = \int_V \rho(r)\, d^3 r$$
$$\mathtt{xc}_i = \tfrac{1}{\mathtt{m}} \int_V r_i\, \rho(r)\, d^3 r$$
$$\mathtt{I}_{ij} = \int_V (|r|^2 \mathbf{1}_{ij} - r_i r_j)\, \rho(r)\, d^3 r \; - \; \mathtt{m}\left(|\mathtt{xc}|^2 \mathbf{1}_{ij} - \mathtt{xc}_i \mathtt{xc}_j\right)$$

Equation 10.1: Mass distribution equations. The variable of integration, $r \in \Re^3$, is a point in body coordinates, within the volume V. Note that we transfer the inertia tensor to be about the center of mass, rather than about the origin of body coordinates. Full discussion of these equations is beyond our scope; see, e.g., [Fox67, App. B]. □

Because our model does not include a description of the shape of a body, we generally take the mass distribution values to be primitive values that are given to us "precomputed" by a higher-level model.[6] We encapsulate the rigid mass distribution properties of a body into a single space MassDists so that each element of MassDists corresponds with a particular mass distribution:

Definition. MassDists

(10.2)
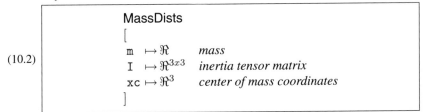

Definition 10.2: A space describing mass distributions of rigid bodies. xc gives the offset of the center of mass from the origin of the body's coordinate system. I is the inertia tensor about the center of mass. Note that each element is a collection of numbers, not geometric objects (we use a typewriter font to remind us of this). These numbers describe the mass distribution of a body in its own coordinate system. □

A point mass (Section 10.2.3) has all its mass concentrated at its origin. We can think of it as the end result of a limiting process in which we keep the mass of a body constant while shrinking the shape to a zero volume located at the origin. We see in Eq. 10.1 that both xc and I go to zero. Thus we define the set of point mass distributions to be a subset of all mass distributions:

Definition. PtMassDists

(10.3)
$$\text{PtMassDists} \equiv \left\{ \text{M} \in \text{MassDists} \;\middle|\; \begin{array}{l} \text{I}(\text{M}) = 0 \\ \text{xc}(\text{M}) = 0 \end{array} \right\}$$

Definition 10.3: The set of point masses. A point mass has all of its mass concentrated at its origin. Its inertia tensor I is thus 0, and its center of mass xc is at its origin. □

10.3.3   State of a Single Body

The instantaneous dynamic state of a body is completely determined by its mass distribution and its kinematic state. However, there are assorted useful geometric, momentum, and energy terms that also describe various properties of the body's dynamic state. We group all the terms into a single state space, States, which has internal properties that ensure the appropriate relationships hold amongst the

---

[6][Fox67] includes a table giving the mass properties for a variety of homogeneous bodies in canonical shapes; [Lien,Kajiya84] computes integral properties of arbitrary nonconvex polyhedra; [Snyder92] computes the mass properties for homogeneous bodies described by parametric surfaces. The net mass properties of a rigid body formed as a compound of simpler bodies are described in [Fox67, App. B].

various terms. Thus each element of **States** encapsulates a complete dynamic
state:

Definition. **States**

(10.4)

States

[

M	$\mapsto$ MassDists	*mass distribution*
m	$\dots m \mapsto \Re$	*mass*
I	$\mapsto$ 2Tensors	*inertia tensor*
k	$\mapsto$ KINEMATIC :: States	*kinematic state*
f	$\dots f \mapsto$ InstFrames	*body coordinate frame*
x	$\dots x \mapsto$ Locations	*location of body coords origin*
R	$\dots \mathbf{R} \mapsto$ Orientations	*body orientation*
v	$\dots v \mapsto$ Vectors	*body velocity*
ω	$\dots \omega \mapsto$ Vectors	*body angular velocity*
arm	$\mapsto$ Vectors	*moment arm of body origin*
xc	$\mapsto$ Locations	*location of center of mass*
vc	$\mapsto$ Vectors	*velocity of center of mass*
p	$\mapsto$ Vectors	*linear momentum*
L	$\mapsto$ Vectors	*angular momentum*
$KEv \mapsto \Re$		*linear kinetic energy*
$KE\omega \mapsto \Re$		*angular kinetic energy*
$KE \mapsto \Re$		*net kinetic energy*

—

$$^f\mathbf{I} = \mathbf{I}(\mathrm{M}) \qquad \text{arm} = x - xc$$
$$-(^f\text{arm}) = {}^f xc = xc(\mathrm{M}) \qquad v = vc + \omega \times \text{arm}$$
$$KEv = \tfrac{1}{2} m \, vc \cdot vc \qquad p = m \, vc$$
$$KE\omega = \tfrac{1}{2} \omega \cdot \mathbf{I}\omega \qquad L = \mathbf{I}\omega$$
$$KEv + KE\omega = KE$$
$$\mathrm{M} \in \text{PtMassDists} \implies \begin{cases} \mathbf{R} = R_{\mathcal{L}ab} \\ \omega = 0 \end{cases}$$

]

Definition 10.4: Instantaneous dynamic state of a rigid body. Note that a body has separate
position and velocity information for its body frame origin (x and v) versus for its center
of mass (xc and vc). The vector *arm* is the displacement of the origin relative to the center
of mass; it is fixed in body coordinates, given by the mass distribution. Identifying tuples
for the space include [M, k]—mass distribution and kinematic state; [M, xc, **R**, p, L]—mass
distribution and dynamic state; [M, f, xc, vc]—mass distribution and mixed state. □

Notice that we use the single space **States** to encompass both bodies and point
masses; since a point mass has no intrinsic notion of orientation, we (arbitrarily)
choose to define that a point mass has the lab's orientation $R = R_{\mathcal{L}ab}$, and zero

angular velocity, $\omega = 0$. From the above and from Def. 10.3 we have the following corollary properties of a point mass:

Given $p \in$ States with $\mathrm{M}_p \in$ PtMassDists,

$$(10.5) \qquad \begin{array}{ll} \mathbf{I}_p = 0, & \mathbf{R}_p = Lab, \\ \omega_p = 0, & xc_p = x_p, \\ arm_p = 0, & vc_p = v_p, \\ L_p = 0, & KE_p = KEv_p, \\ KE\omega_p = 0 & \end{array}$$

Equation 10.5: Various properties of point masses. □

It may seem like overkill to use States for point masses: Mightn't it be "cleaner" to have a separate, simpler space just for point masses? However, by having a single space, the remaining discussion will apply uniformly both to bodies and to point masses.

10.3.4   Motion of a Single Body

A moving body varies its state over time; that is, a moving body is described by a path through States space. Thus we define the space:

Definition. StatePaths

$$(10.6) \qquad \text{StatePaths} \equiv \begin{array}{l} \textit{the set of functions} \\ \left\{ \begin{array}{c} s\colon \Re \to \text{States } \textit{such that} \\ (k \circ s) \in \text{KINEMATIC}\colon\colon\text{StatePaths, } \textit{and} \\ \mathrm{M}_s(t) \textit{ is constant} \end{array} \right\} \end{array}$$

Definition 10.6: The set of paths through state space. We only consider functions s for which the resulting kinematic state function $k_s(t)$ is a kinematic state path (Def. 9.2). Additionally, we require that the mass distribution $\mathrm{M}_s(t)$ doesn't change. □

Since we require that the mass distribution of a state path be constant, we can drop the path parameter when using the mass distribution aspects:

Notation. Dropping the Parameter (t) for a State Path

$$(10.7) \qquad \begin{array}{c} \textit{For a state path } s \in \text{StatePaths} \\[4pt] \mathrm{M}_s \equiv \mathrm{M}_s(t) \\ m_s \equiv m_s(t) \end{array}$$

Notation 10.7: Since, by definition, the mass distribution of a state path doesn't depend on the path parameter, we usually leave it off for clarity. □

From Defs. 10.4 and 10.6, we have

Given a state path $s \in$ **StatePaths**

(10.8)
$$
\begin{aligned}
{}^{f_s(t)}\mathbf{I}_s(t) &= \mathbf{I}(\mathrm{M}_s), \; constant \\
{}^{f_s(t)}xc_s(t) &= m_s, \; constant
\end{aligned}
$$

Equation 10.8: For a state path s, the inertia tensor $\mathbf{I}_s(t)$ and location of center of mass $xc_s(t)$ are **not** constant—they move with the body, changing over time. But their representations in the body's moving coordinate frame are constant, given by the constant mass distribution. Using the parlance of Section 8.4.9, they are "fixed" in the moving body frame. □

Definition 10.6 requires that the motion be continuous and that the mass distribution in the body be constant. That, along with Defs. 9.2 and 8.24, ensures that, as expected:

Given a state path $s \in$ **StatePaths**,

(10.9)
$$
\begin{aligned}
\tfrac{d}{dt}x_s(t) &= v_s(t) \\
\tfrac{d}{dt}xc_s(t) &= vc_s(t) \\
\tfrac{d}{dt}\mathbf{R}_s(t) &= \omega_s^*(t)\mathbf{R}_s(t)
\end{aligned}
$$

Equation 10.9: Velocities of a state path agree with the derivatives as expected. Note that the "moving-body paradox," Eq. 9.3, applies to dynamic rigid bodies' origins, orientations, and centers of mass. □

In addition to moving continuously and rigidly, we want a body to move dynamically under the influence of forces and torques. Thus we define (see Fig. 10.5):

Definition. **Consistent** (path, net force, net torque)

*A state path $s \in$ **StatePaths** is **consistent** with net force and torque functions $F, T\colon \Re \to$ **Vectors** iff:*
(10.10) $\tfrac{d}{dt}p_s(t) = F(t)$ *(force equals change in momentum)*
$\tfrac{d}{dt}L_s(t) = T(t)$ *(torque equals change in angular momentum)*
$\mathrm{M}_s \in$ **PtMassDists** $\implies T(t) = 0$

Definition 10.10: Dynamic behavior of a rigid body. At each instant of time, the change in momenta is due to the *net force* $F(t)$ and *net torque* $T(t)$. As discussed in Section 10.2.3, we don't apply torques to point masses. □

By Def. 10.4 and Eq. 10.9 we have, for a path $s \in$ **StatePaths**, $\tfrac{d}{dt}p_s(t) = \tfrac{d}{dt}m_s vc_s(t) = m\tfrac{d^2}{dt^2}x_s(t)$. Thus Def. 10.10 is equivalent to the common "$F = m\,a$" second-order Newtonian equation of motion.

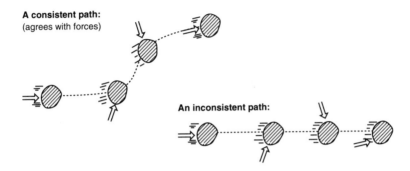

Figure 10.5: Consistent versus inconsistent paths. A state path is an arbitrary function that describes physically realizable motion of a rigid body. If we have a net force function and a net torque function (torque not illustrated), we say that the path and functions are *consistent* if the motion of the body agrees with the force and torque, as per "$F = m\,a$." □

10.3.5 Body Points

A dynamic body point is similar to a kinematic body point, but we find it convenient to include the point's moment arm as part of its instantaneous state.

Definition. **Bodypts**

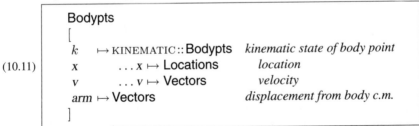

Definition 10.11: Body point state space. The state of a body point includes its kinematic description as well as a moment arm, i.e., a vector from the center of mass of the body to the point location. Note, however, that there is no explicit indication of *which* body. □

We can specify a body point state by giving its body-frame coordinates and the state of the body it belongs to:

Definition. Bodypt

(10.12)

> *Define a function Bodypt:* States $\times \Re^{3\times3} \to$ Bodypts
> *such that, for all $s \in$* States *and coords $\in \Re^{3\times3}$,*
>
> $k(Bodypt(s, coords)) = \text{KINEMATIC} :: Bodypt(k_s, coords)$
> $\text{arm}(Bodypt(s, coords)) = x(Bodypt(s, coords)) - xc_s$

Definition 10.12: A function that yields the state of a body point given its body-frame coordinates. The kinematic state of the body point is specified via KINEMATIC :: *Bodypt* (Def. 9.5). The moment arm is the vector from the body center of mass to the body point. □

Some properties of a body point:

(10.13)

> *Given a body state $s \in$* States *and*
> *body point $p \in$* Bodypts, *where $p = Bodypt(s, coords)$*
> *for some coords $\in \Re^{3\times3}$, we have*
>
> $$^{f(s)}x_p = coords$$
> $$^{f(s)}\text{arm}_p = coords + {}^{f(s)}\text{arm}_s$$
> $$= coords + \text{xc}(M_s)$$
> $$v_p = v_s + \omega_s \times (x_p - x_p)$$
> $$= vc_s + \omega_s \times \text{arm}_p$$

Equation 10.13: The location and moment arm of a body point defined via *Bodypt* (Def. 10.12) can easily be expressed in body coordinates. The velocity can be expressed geometrically in terms of either the body's origin or the body's center of mass. These equalities are derived from from Defs. 9.5 and 10.12, and the properties in Def. 10.4. □

10.3.6   A Collection of Bodies

For a collection of continuously moving dynamic bodies, the interaction between the bodies is mediated by forces, as discussed in Section 10.2.1. That is, each body doesn't directly "see" any other bodies, it just responds to the forces it "feels," in accordance with Def. 10.10. However, we are free to define whatever force functions we like—in particular, the force function for any given body may at any instant be determined by the states of all the bodies. In this way, the motion of a body may be determined (indirectly) by interaction with other bodies.

In order to manage collections of bodies, we proceed analogously to the scheme used for kinematic bodies (Section 9.3.4). We define an instantaneous *system*:

Definition. Systems

(10.14)

> Systems $\equiv \{$States$\}_{\text{IDs}}$

Definition 10.14: Each instantaneous system is an index of states (as per Section 5.8.2). That is, it is a collection of body state elements, each labeled with a different "name," or ID. Given a system $Y \in$ Systems, the state of a body labeled with $b \in$ IDs is given by Y_b. □

Each point in the space **Systems** describes the state of a collection of bodies at an instant of time. For moving bodies, we analogously define a *system path* to be a labeled collection of paths:

Definition. **SysPaths**

(10.15)
$$\mathsf{SysPaths} \equiv \{\mathsf{StatePaths}\}_{\mathsf{IDs}}$$

Definition 10.15: Each system path is an index of state paths. Note that each element in the index is a function. That is, for a system path $\mathcal{Y} \in$ **SysPaths**, the state of body b at an instant of time t is given by $\mathcal{Y}_b(t)$. □

Given $\mathcal{Y} \in$ **SysPaths**, the instantaneous state of the system at a time t is given by evaluating all paths in $\mathcal{Y}$ at t; this is written as $\mathcal{Y}(t)$ as per Not. 5.18.

We define a few types of *fields*, i.e., functions over instantaneous systems:

Definition. (fields)

(10.16)
$$\mathsf{SysScalarFields} \equiv \left\{ \begin{array}{l} \textit{the set of functions} \\ \mathsf{Systems} \times \Re \to \mathsf{Scalars} \end{array} \right\}$$

$$\mathsf{SysVectorFields} \equiv \left\{ \begin{array}{l} \textit{the set of functions} \\ \mathsf{Systems} \times \Re \to \mathsf{Vectors} \end{array} \right\}$$

$$\mathsf{SysLocationFields} \equiv \left\{ \begin{array}{l} \textit{the set of functions} \\ \mathsf{Systems} \times \Re \to \mathsf{Locations} \end{array} \right\}$$

Definition 10.16: Scalar, vector, and location fields are functions on instantaneous systems and time. Since an instantaneous system $Y \in$ **Systems** labels each state with the ID naming its body, an individual field function $F(Y, t)$ can depend on particular named bodies. □

For an example of a field, we can define a vector field *velA* that yields the velocity of the body named *bodyA*:

(10.17)
> *Given an identifier bodyA* $\in$ **IDs***, we can define a*
> *vector field velA* $\in$ **SysVectorFields** *by:*
>
> $$velA(Y, t) = v(Y_{bodyA})$$

Equation 10.17: Sample vector field that gives the velocity of a body named *bodyA*. Note that the field is only well defined for systems that include this body, i.e., for *bodyA* $\in Ids(Y)$. Note also that the field is independent of any bodies other than *bodyA* that may be in the system, as well as the time t. □

Having made the above definitions, we can extend Def. 10.10 to apply to a collection of bodies acting under the influence of corresponding labeled collections of force and torque fields (see Fig. 10.6):

**A Consistent Path
in a Force Field**

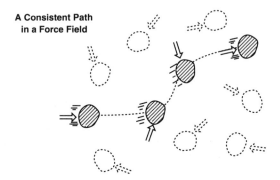

Figure 10.6: A consistent path in a force field. A force field defines what the force would be on a body for any possible state it may be in. A path is consistent with a force field and a torque field (not shown) if it is consistent with the forces traced out as the body path moves through the field. Note that if there are several bodies in a system, the force/torque on any one of them can depend on the state of all of them; thus the consistency of each individual path can depend on all the other paths. $\square$

Definition. **Consistent** (system path, net force index, net torque index)

(10.18)

$$
\begin{array}{c}
\textit{A system path } \mathcal{Y} \in \mathsf{SysPaths} \textit{ is } \textbf{consistent} \textit{ with} \\
F, T \in \{\mathsf{SysVectorFields}\}_{\mathsf{IDs}} \textit{ iff:} \\[1mm]
\mathit{Ids}(\mathcal{Y}) = \mathit{Ids}(F) = \mathit{Ids}(T) \\
\mathcal{Y}_b \textit{ is consistent with } (F_b \circ \mathcal{Y}) \textit{ and } (T_b \circ \mathcal{Y}), \textit{ for all } b \in \mathit{Ids}(\mathcal{Y})
\end{array}
$$

Definition 10.18: A system path is consistent if each individual path is consistent (Def. 10.10) with its corresponding composite net force and torque functions. For each ID b, the net force and torque acting on body b are given by $F_b(\mathcal{Y}(t), t)$ and $T_b(\mathcal{Y}(t), t)$, respectively. Notice the force/torque on each body can depend on the state of all the other bodies. $\square$

10.3.7   Motives

The description of rigid-body motion in Def. 10.18 assumes the existence of fields giving the net force and torque on each body in a system. Here, we use the idea of *motives*—force/torque objects—as per Section 10.2.2, and allow a collection of separate motives to apply to each body: We derive the net force and torque fields on each body by adding the contributions from a collection of motive fields.

We start by defining a space of motives. Each element in the space is a value of a force and/or torque, along with the corresponding moment arm:

Definition. Motives

(10.19)

> Motives
> [
> F $\mapsto$ Vectors *force*
> T $\mapsto$ Vectors *torque*
> arm $\mapsto$ Vectors *moment arm*
> ───
> $T = \text{arm} \times F$ *or* $\text{arm} = 0$
>]

Definition 10.19: The space of motives. For a *coupled force/torque,* we have a nonzero force and moment arm, yielding the corresponding torque $T = \text{arm} \times F$. A *pure force* has force but no torque ($F \neq 0$, arm $= T = 0$). A *pure torque* has torque but no force ($F = \text{arm} = 0$, $T \neq 0$). An arbitrary *force/torque pair* has ($F \neq 0$, $T \neq 0$, arm $= 0$). (See Fig. 10.2.) □

A pure force is, of course, equivalent to a force applied at the center of mass (arm$=0$). Since we have no notion of body shape here, there is no requirement that the moment arm actually be "in" or "on" the body.

An *applied motive* describes a motive that is applied to a particular body name. Thus we define

Definition. AppliedMotives

(10.20)

> AppliedMotives
> [
> motive $\mapsto$ Motives   *motive*
> F $\ldots F \mapsto$ Vectors   *force*
> T $\ldots T \mapsto$ Vectors   *torque*
> arm $\ldots$ arm $\mapsto$ Vectors   *moment arm*
> body $\mapsto$ IDs   *body that the motive is applied to*
>]

Definition 10.20: Motives applied to bodies. Each element defines a particular motive and the ID of a body at which it is applied. □

We define fields of motives and applied motives, analogous to the fields in Def. 10.16:

Definition. (motive fields)

(10.21)

SysMotiveFields ≡ *the set of functions*
$$\{\text{Systems} \times \Re \rightarrow \text{Motives}\}$$

AppliedMotiveFields ≡ *the set of functions*
$$\left\{ \begin{array}{l} a\colon \text{Systems} \times \Re \rightarrow \text{AppliedMotives} \\ \textit{such that } body(a(Y,t)) \textit{ is constant} \end{array} \right\}$$

Definition 10.21: Motive and applied motive fields. For applied motive fields, we restrict the definition to those functions whose body ID doesn't vary, no matter what parameters it's given. □

We require that each applied motive field correspond with the application of a motive field to a single body. Thus the *body* aspect of an applied motive field is independent of the parameters, and we typically drop them:

Notation. Dropping Parameters (Y, t) for Applied Motive Field Body

(10.22)

For $a \in$ AppliedMotiveFields

$$body(a) \equiv body(a(Y,t))$$

Notation 10.22: Since, by definition, the body of an applied motive field doesn't depend on the parameters, we usually leave them off for clarity. □

A common occurrence in models is a force that is applied to a body at a particular body point. For example, we might attach a spring force to a body point at one end of a cylinder; as the cylinder moves, the spring follows it, always acting on the given point of the body. In terms of motives, this means

(10.23)

If an applied motive field $a \in$ AppliedMotiveFields
describes a force applied to a
body named $body(a) \in$ IDs *in system $\mathcal{Y} \in$* SysPaths *at*
body coordinates $coords \in \Re^{3 \times 3}$, we have

$$arm_a(\mathcal{Y}(t), t) = arm(Bodypt(\mathcal{Y}_{body(a)}(t), coords)), \quad \textit{for all } t \in \Re$$

Equation 10.23: For us to say that a force is "applied to a body point," the applied motive field's *arm* aspect must always agree with the body point's *arm* aspect as the body moves over time. □

Typically, a model will contain many applied motive fields acting on the various bodies in the model. Since each applied motive field specifies the body it's applied to, we don't need to explicitly organize the various motive fields by body. We group all the applied motive fields into an index; this will let us refer to them by ID later, e.g., for the energy expressions in Section 10.3.8.

The following functions extract the net force and torque on each body given an index of applied motives.

Definition. Fnet, Tnet

(10.24)

$$
\begin{aligned}
&\textit{We define the net force and torque functions,}\\
&Fnet: \{\mathsf{AppliedMotives}\}_{\mathsf{IDs}} \to \{\mathsf{Vectors}\}^{\circ}_{\mathsf{IDs}}\\
&Tnet: \{\mathsf{AppliedMotives}\}_{\mathsf{IDs}} \to \{\mathsf{Vectors}\}^{\circ}_{\mathsf{IDs}} \text{ such}\\
&\textit{that, for all } A \in \{\mathsf{AppliedMotives}\}_{\mathsf{IDs}},
\end{aligned}
$$

$$
Fnet(A)_b \equiv \sum_{\substack{a \in Elts(A)\\ body(a)=b}} F_a
$$

$$
Tnet(A)_b \equiv \sum_{\substack{a \in Elts(A)\\ body(a)=b}} T_a
$$

$$
Ids(Fnet(A)) \equiv Ids(Tnet(A)) \equiv \Big\{ body(a) \ \Big| \ a \in Elts(A) \Big\}
$$

Definition 10.24: Net force and torque, given an index of applied motives. For each body b, $Fnet(A)_b$ yields the sum of all the individual motive forces that are applied to body b. Note that $Fnet(A)$ is defined to be an index with zero, so that if A doesn't apply any forces to a particular body, the body will be assigned a net force of 0. Note that we don't need to refer to the elements of A by their ID labels. (Similarly for $Tnet$.) □

Using the above definition, we can extend Def. 10.18's specification of consistent system paths to handle a collection of applied motives; this is the "bottom line" specification of rigid-body motion in our model:

Definition. **Consistent** (system path, applied motive index)

(10.25)

$$
\begin{aligned}
&A \textit{ system path } \mathcal{Y} \in \mathsf{SysPaths} \textit{ is } \textbf{consistent}\\
&\textit{with } \mathcal{A} \in \{\mathsf{AppliedMotiveFields}\}_{\mathsf{IDs}} \textit{ iff:}\\[4pt]
&\mathcal{Y} \textit{ is consistent with } (Fnet \circ \mathcal{A}), (Tnet \circ \mathcal{A})
\end{aligned}
$$

Definition 10.25: A system is consistent with an index of applied motives if it is consistent (Def. 10.18) with the net force and torque implied by the motives. Here, as in Def. 10.24, the IDs that label elements of the index of applied motive fields, $\mathcal{A}$, are not needed. □

10.3.8 Energy

The following expression describes the rate of change of energy of a body, in relation to the force and torque applied to it:

(10.26)

*For any state path $s \in$ StatePaths consistent with net
force and torque functions $F, T: \Re \rightarrow$ Vectors,*

$$\tfrac{d}{dt}KE_s(t) = F(t) \cdot vc_s(t) + T(t) \cdot \omega_s(t)$$

Equation 10.26: Energy balance. The rate of change of the body's kinetic energy is equal to the power applied by the net force and torque acting on it, for a consistent system. This equation can be derived from Defs. 10.4 and 10.10. □

Thus we describe the instantaneous *power* being applied by a force and torque:

(10.27)

*Given a body with state $b \in$ States that is acted on by a
force and torque $F, T \in$ Vectors, the power $P \in \Re$
being applied is given by:*

$$P = F_m \cdot vc_b + T_m \cdot \omega_b$$

Equation 10.27: The instantaneous power applied to a body by an applied force and torque. □

To measure the energy imparted to a body by a motive, we need to keep track of the power and work associated with the motive as the body moves along its path. We start by defining a *power motive* (or just *pmotive*) that extends a motive to include power-related terms:

Definition. Pmotives, PmotivePaths

(10.28)

Pmotives
[

M	$\mapsto$ Motives	*a motive*
F	$\ldots F \mapsto$ Vectors	
T	$\ldots T \mapsto$ Vectors	
arm	$\ldots$ arm $\mapsto$ Vectors	
v	$\mapsto$ Vectors	*a body velocity*
ω	$\mapsto$ Vectors	*a body angular velocity*
P	$\mapsto \Re$	*power applied by motive*
W	$\mapsto \Re$	*work done*

—

$$P \equiv F \cdot v + T \cdot \omega$$

]

PmotivePaths $\equiv$ *the set of functions* $\{\Re \rightarrow$ Pmotives$\}$

Definition 10.28: Each pmotive element of Pmotives describes the instantaneous application of a motive M to a body with velocities v and ω. P is the power exerted. W is an additional parameter, which will be used to accumulate the work done by the motive over time. We also define the set of pmotive-valued paths, PmotivePaths, without any a priori restrictions. □

For a given system path, we can associate a pmotive path with an applied motive field; this pmotive path keeps track of the work done by that applied motive field on its body in the system:

Definition. **Consistent** (pmotive path, applied motive field, system path)

(10.29)

> *A power motive path $p \in$* PmotivePaths *is* **consistent**
> *with $a \in$* AppliedMotiveFields *and $\mathcal{Y} \in$* SysPaths *iff:*
>
> $$
> \begin{aligned}
> M_p(t) &= motive_a(\mathcal{Y}(t), t) \\
> v_p(t) &= vc(\mathcal{Y}_{body(a)}(t)) \\
> \omega_p(t) &= \omega(\mathcal{Y}_{body(a)}(t)) \\
> \tfrac{d}{dt} W_p(t) &= P_p(t)
> \end{aligned}
> $$

Definition 10.29:   We describe a power motive path p that corresponds with an applied motive field, for a given system. The first three equations signify that the power motive path p continually describes the actual application of the motive, i.e., the motive and velocity aspects agree. The final equation further restricts the path p to the one in which the rate of change of work is equal at each instant to the applied power (this is analogous to Def. 8.24's restricting frame paths to those with a velocity matching the change in location). Thus $W_p(t)$ is the total work done by a in system $\mathcal{Y}$, up to time t. □

The above definition relates a single applied motive field to a single corresponding pmotive path. For an index of applied motive fields, we can create a corresponding index of pmotive paths, where the label of each applied motive field is used to label its corresponding pmotive path. Thus we extend the above definition:

Definition. **Consistent** (pmotive paths, appl. motive fields, system path)

(10.30)

> *An index of pmotive paths $\mathcal{P} \in \{$* PmotivePaths $\}_{\text{IDs}}$ *is*
> **consistent** *with $\mathcal{A} \in \{$* AppliedMotiveFields $\}_{\text{IDs}}$ *and*
> *$\mathcal{Y} \in$* SysPaths *iff:*
>
> $$
> Ids(\mathcal{P}) = Ids(\mathcal{A}),
> $$
> *$\mathcal{Y}$ is consistent with $\mathcal{A}$,*
> *P_f is consistent with $\mathcal{A}_f$ and $\mathcal{Y}$, for all $f \in Ids(\mathcal{A})$*

Definition 10.30: For an index of motive paths $\mathcal{P}$ to be consistent with an index of applied motive fields $\mathcal{A}$, for a given system of bodies $\mathcal{Y}$: First, each path in $\mathcal{P}$ must have the same ID as a field in $\mathcal{A}$; second, the $\mathcal{Y}$ and $\mathcal{A}$ must themselves be consistent, as per Def. 10.25; finally, each pmotive path in $\mathcal{P}$ must be consistent with its corresponding field in $\mathcal{A}$, as per Def. 10.29. □

Putting together Eq. 10.26 through Def. 10.30, we have balance of energy for an entire system of bodies:

(10.31)

$$Given \; \mathcal{P} \in \{\text{PmotivePaths}\}_{\text{IDs}} \; consistent \; with$$
$$\mathcal{A} \in \{\text{AppliedMotiveFields}\}_{\text{IDs}} \; and \; \mathcal{Y} \in \text{SysPaths},$$
$$then \; for \; all \; b \in Ids(\mathcal{Y}):$$

$$KE(\mathcal{Y}_b(t)) - \sum_{\substack{f \, \in \, Ids(\mathcal{A}) \\ body(\mathcal{A}_f) = b}} W(\mathcal{P}_f(t)) \; is \; constant$$

Equation 10.31: Energy balance. For each body in a consistent system, the total kinetic energy of the body is balanced by the sum of the work done by all the motives acting on it. Note that we don't have a precise value (e.g., zero, as one might expect) for this equation, because W is only specified up to a constant offset, by the differential equation in Def. 10.29. □

Note that Eq. 10.31 is merely Eq. 10.26 applied independently and simultaneously to each body in the system. That is, no energy is transferred directly between bodies. Rather, the energy added to or removed from each body is due only to the forces acting on it. However, we can sum them together to make a single equation for the entire system:

(10.32)

$$Given \; \mathcal{P} \in \{\text{PmotivePaths}\}_{\text{IDs}} \; consistent \; with$$
$$\mathcal{A} \in \{\text{AppliedMotiveFields}\}_{\text{IDs}} \; and \; \mathcal{Y} \in \text{SysPaths},$$
$$we \; have$$

$$\sum_{a \, \in \, Ids(\mathcal{Y})} KE(\mathcal{Y}_a(t)) - \sum_{f \, \in \, Ids(\mathcal{A})} W(\mathcal{P}_f(t)) \; is \; constant$$

Equation 10.32: Net energy balance for a system. The total kinetic energy of the bodies is balanced by the total work done by the motives. □

As discussed in Section 10.2.2, some motive fields are *conservative,* and we know a potential energy associated with the motive. In such a case, the potential energy must balance the work done by the motive:

(10.33)

$$Given \; \mathcal{P} \in \{\text{PmotivePaths}\}_{\text{IDs}} \; consistent \; with$$
$$\mathcal{A} \in \{\text{AppliedMotiveFields}\}_{\text{IDs}}, \; and \; \mathcal{Y} \in \text{SysPaths},$$
$$if \; we \; have \; a \; potential \; energy$$
$$field \; U_f \in \text{SysScalarFields} \; for \; applied \; motive \; field \; \mathcal{A}_f,$$

$$U_f(\mathcal{Y}(t), t) + W(P_f(t)) \; is \; constant$$

Equation 10.33: If a motive field $\mathcal{A}_f$ has a potential energy U_f associated with it, then as a system evolves over time, any lost potential energy is transferred to work done by the motive, and vice versa. □

Furthermore, for a conservative motive field, the force/torque is given by the gradient of the potential energy field.

10.4 Posed Problems

Forward Dynamics

The most common problem we solve is to determine the behavior of a collection
of bodies that start out in some configuration and are acted on by some collection
of force fields. This is the *forward dynamics problem*.

(10.34)

$$
\begin{aligned}
\textit{Given:}\quad & t_0 \in \Re, \\
& Y_0 \in \textsf{Systems}, \\
& \mathcal{A} \in \{\textsf{AppliedMotiveFields}\}_{\textsf{IDs}}, \\
\textit{find:}\quad & \mathcal{Y} \in \textsf{SysPaths} \\
\textit{such that:}\quad & \begin{cases} \mathcal{Y}(t_0) = Y_0 \\ \mathcal{Y} \textit{ is consistent with } A \end{cases}
\end{aligned}
$$

Equation 10.34: The forward dynamics problem. Given an initial condition of a collection of bodies (at time t_0 the state is Y_0) and a collection of motive fields applied to the
bodies, determine the behavior of the bodies for other values of t. The resulting system
$\mathcal{Y}$ must match the initial conditions and must be consistent with the applied motives as per
Def. 10.25. □

The definition of *consistent* (Def. 10.25) can be expanded to yield a first-order
ordinary differential equation in canonical, numerical form:

(10.35)

For a system path $\mathcal{Y} \in \textsf{SysPaths}$ *consistent with*
$$\mathcal{A} \in \{\textsf{AppliedMotiveFields}\}_{\textsf{IDs}}, \textit{ if}$$
$$Ids(\mathcal{Y}) = \{a, b, \dots\}, \textit{ then:}$$

$$
\begin{aligned}
\tfrac{d}{dt}{}^{\mathcal{L}ab}xc(\mathcal{Y}_a(t)) &= {}^{\mathcal{L}ab}vc(\mathcal{Y}_a(t)) \\
\tfrac{d}{dt}{}^{\mathcal{L}ab}\mathbf{R}(\mathcal{Y}_a(t)) &= {}^{\mathcal{L}ab}\omega^*(\mathcal{Y}_a(t))\mathbf{R}(\mathcal{Y}_a(t)) \\
\tfrac{d}{dt}{}^{\mathcal{L}ab}p(\mathcal{Y}_a(t)) &= {}^{\mathcal{L}ab}Fnet(\mathcal{A}(\mathcal{Y}(t),t))_a \\
\tfrac{d}{dt}{}^{\mathcal{L}ab}L(\mathcal{Y}_a(t)) &= {}^{\mathcal{L}ab}Tnet(\mathcal{A}(\mathcal{Y}(t),t))_a \\
\tfrac{d}{dt}{}^{\mathcal{L}ab}xc(\mathcal{Y}_b(t)) &= {}^{\mathcal{L}ab}vc(\mathcal{Y}_b(t)) \\
&\vdots
\end{aligned}
$$

$$\textit{i.e.,} \quad Y' = F_{\mathcal{A}}(Y, t)$$

Equation 10.35: Canonical numerical ODE form for rigid-body motion. The dynamic
state of all the bodies can be expressed in lab coordinates and collected into a single linear
array "Y." The derivative of Y is a function of Y and time t—the function can be constructed
from $\mathcal{A}$, along with the bodies' mass distributions and the rigid-body equations of motion.
Note that, as per Def. 10.4, the values of xc, $\mathbf{R}$, p and L are sufficient to identify the state of
a body, given that we know its (constant) mass distribution. □

To solve the forward dynamics problem, we start with an initial value for Y, then numerically integrate the above ODE, using any convenient numerical integrator. For any body in the system that is a point mass, we can make Y smaller by eliminating the $\mathbf{R}$ and L entries. Note that if Eq. 10.35 is integrated as written, numerical inaccuracies will soon cause $^{cab}\mathbf{R}(\mathcal{Y}_a(t))$ to diverge from a rotation matrix; instead, we commonly use the quaternion representation of the rotation, Eq. 8.22; inaccuracies can still creep into the solution, but they are less significant.

Forward Dynamics and Work

A corollary problem to forward dynamics is to compute the amount of work done by each motive in the model; this means finding the consistent power motive paths. That is, we extend Eq. 10.34:

(10.36)
$$
\begin{aligned}
&\textit{Given:}\quad t_0 \in \Re, \\
&\qquad\qquad Y_0 \in \mathsf{Systems}, \\
&\qquad\qquad \mathcal{A} \in \{\mathsf{AppliedMotiveFields}\}_{\mathsf{IDs}}, \\
&\textit{find:}\quad \mathcal{Y} \in \mathsf{SysPaths} \\
&\qquad\qquad \mathcal{P} \in \{\mathsf{PmotivePaths}\}_{\mathsf{IDs}} \\
&\textit{such that:}\quad \begin{cases} \mathcal{Y}(t_0) = Y_0 \\ \mathcal{P} \text{ is consistent with } \mathcal{A} \text{ and } \mathcal{Y} \end{cases}
\end{aligned}
$$

Equation 10.36: An augmented forward dynamics problem. Solve the forward dynamics problem (Eq. 10.34), but also find the corresponding consistent (Def. 10.30) index of pmotive paths. Then the total work done by an applied motive labeled $i \in Ids(\mathcal{A})$ up to time t is given by $W(\mathcal{P}_i(t))$. □

Expanding the definition of *consistent* for pmotive paths (Def. 10.30) gives

For a pmotive path index $\mathcal{Y} \in \{\mathsf{PmotivePaths}\}_{\mathsf{IDs}}$
consistent with $\mathcal{A} \in \{\mathsf{AppliedMotiveFields}\}_{\mathsf{IDs}}$ and
$\mathcal{Y} \in \mathsf{SysPaths}$, if $Ids(\mathcal{A}) = \{j, k, \ldots\}$, then we
augment Eq. 10.35:

(10.37)
$$
\begin{aligned}
\tfrac{d}{dt} W(\mathcal{P}_j(t)) = P(\mathcal{P}_j(t)) \quad &= F(\mathcal{A}_j(\mathcal{Y}(t),t)) \cdot vc(\mathcal{Y}_{body(\mathcal{A}_j)}(t)) \\
&\quad + T(\mathcal{A}_j(\mathcal{Y}(t),t)) \cdot \omega(\mathcal{Y}_{body(\mathcal{A}_j)}(t)) \\
\tfrac{d}{dt} W(\mathcal{P}_k(t)) = P(\mathcal{P}_k(t)) \quad &= F(\mathcal{A}_k(\mathcal{Y}(t),t)) \cdot vc(\mathcal{Y}_{body(\mathcal{A}_k)}(t)) \\
&\quad + T(\mathcal{A}_k(\mathcal{Y}(t),t)) \cdot \omega(\mathcal{Y}_{body(\mathcal{A}_k)}(t))
\end{aligned}
$$

$$\vdots$$

i.e.,
$$
\begin{aligned}
Y' &= F_{\mathcal{A}}(Y, t) \\
P' &= G_{\mathcal{A}}(P, Y, t)
\end{aligned}
$$

Equation 10.37: Canonical numerical ODE form for work done by motives. We append equations for the work to the rigid-body motion ODE of Eq. 10.35. □

As a "sanity check" for our simulations, we can plug the solution results into the energy-balance equations, Eqs. 10.31 and 10.32. For conservative motives, we can check against the potential energy as per Eq. 10.33. Note that initial values for the work terms can be chosen arbitrarily since the energy balance equations are specified only up to a constant. We commonly use an initial work value of zero, or, for conservative forces, $-U_f(Y_0, t_0)$, so that Eq. 10.33 will always sum to zero.

Piecewise-continuous Forward Dynamics

The forward dynamics problem as expressed above is continuous (for finite motives). However, a model that includes discontinuities can use the above ODEs to describe the continuous parts of the behavior; for example, the "tennis ball cannon" example in Ch. 13 sets up a forward dynamics problem as an initial-value piecewise-continuous ODE problem.

Other Posed Problems

Other problems can be posed as well. *Inverse dynamics problems* compute forces and torques that yield given desired behaviors or constraints on behavior. Often, the resulting forces and torques are then used in a forward dynamics formulation to yield the complete behavior, as in [Isaacs,Cohen87] or [Barzel,Barr88] (the latter of which we incorporate into the "fancy forces" module, Ch. 11).

[Witkin,Kass88] finds behavior that optimizes objectives such as energy, for motion that can be constrained at multiple points. They pose a constrained optimization problem in which the dynamics of body motion (Def. 10.10 in our formulation) is treated as an additional constraint on discretized force and motion functions; force function parameters are found that optimize the given objective functions.

	Program Definitions in Scope `MRIG`:	
class name	*abstract space*	
`ApplMotive`	AppliedMotives	*(Def. 10.20)*
`ApplMotiveField`	AppliedMotiveFields	*(Def. 10.21)*
`ApplMotiveFieldIdx`	{AppliedMotiveFields}$_{IDs}$	*index of fields*
`ApplMotiveIdx`	{AppliedMotives}$_{IDs}$	*index of applied motives*
`ApplMotiveIdxField`	Systems $\times \Re \rightarrow$ {AppliedMotives}$_{IDs}$	*field that yields an index*
`Bodypt`	Bodypts	*(Def. 10.11)*
`MassDist`	MassDists	*(Def. 10.2)*
`Motive`	Motives	*(Def. 10.19)*
`Pmotive`	Pmotives	*(Def. 10.28)*
`PmotivePath`	PmotivePaths	*(Def. 10.28)*
`PmotivePathIdx`	{PmotivePaths}$_{IDs}$	*index of pmotive paths*
`State`	States	*(Def. 10.4)*
`StatePath`	StatePaths	*(Def. 10.6)*
`SysLocationField`	SysLocationFields	*(Def. 10.16)*
`SysLocationFieldIdx`	{SysLocationFields}$_{IDs}$	*index of location fields*
`SysMotiveField`	SysMotiveFields	*(Def. 10.16)*
`SysPath`	SysPaths	*(Def. 10.15)*
`SysScalarField`	SysScalarFields	*(Def. 10.16)*
`SysScalarFieldIdx`	{SysScalarFields}$_{IDs}$	*index of location fields*
`SysVectorField`	SysVectorFields	*(Def. 10.16)*
`SysVectorFieldIdx`	{SysVectorFields}$_{IDs}$	*index of location fields*
`System`	Systems	*(Def. 10.14)*

Figure 10.7: Math section definitions in the prototype implementation. □

10.5 Implementation Notes[†]

10.5.1 Conceptual Section Constructs

In the conceptual section of a program, a conceptual body object can be built from kinematic conceptual bodies (Section 9.5.1), which maintain the position and orientation and "know" how to draw the body, augmented with mass distribution values.

This module supports a few simple motives; classes are defined for Hookean springs, constant fields, viscous damping, and so forth. Each class defines a routine to compute the associated field function (or a pair of routines that compute equal-and-opposite fields, e.g., for a spring linking two bodies). Motive classes also support a "draw" method that can draw arrows or otherwise illustrate the force.

[†] See Appendix B for discussion of the terminology, notation, and overall approach used here.

10.5.2   Math Section Constructs

The math section for this module has scope name MRIG ("Math RIGid-body dynamics"); Fig. 10.7 lists the classes that are defined. All are defined straightforwardly, as described in Section B.3. We give a few notes.

- Class definition for **MassDists** (Def. 10.2):

class MassDist :
constructors: (double m,I[3][3], double cm[3])   *construct arbitrary body*
                  (double m)   *construct point mass*
members: m   : double   *net mass*
                  minv   : double   *inverse of the mass, i.e.,* $1/m$
                  I   : double[3][3] *inertia tensor matrix*
                  Iinv   : double[3][3] *inverse of the inertia matrix, i.e.,* I^{-1}
                  cm   : double[3]   *body coords of center of mass*
                  is_ptmass : int   *true if is a point mass, Def. 10.3*

The state space class MassDist, defined in the standard manner (Section B.3.6), has two constructors: The constructor for point masses sets I and cm to zero; conversely, the constructor for arbitrary bodies signals an error if zero is given for I. Both constructors precompute the inverses of m and I so that they won't need to be computed repeatedly during execution. Notice that we add an extra member that lets us easily distinguish point masses.

- Class definition for **States** (Def. 10.4):

class State :
constructors: (MassDist, MKIN::State)
                  (MassDist, MCO::Location xc, MCO::Orientation R, MCO::Vector p,L)
                  (MassDist, MCO::Location xc, MCO::Vector p)
                  (MassDist, MCO::Frame, MCO::Vector vc,w)
                  (MassDist, MKIN::State, MCO::Vector p,L)
members: mdist : MassDist
                  m   : double
                  minv : double
                  I   : MCO::2tensor
                  Iinv : MCO::2tensor
                  k   : MKIN::State
                  f   : MCO::InstFrame
                  x   : MCO::Location
                  R   : MCO::Orientation
                  v   : MCO::Vector
                  w   : MCO::Vector
                  arm   : MCO::Vector
                  xc   : MCO::Location
                  vc   : MCO::Vector
                  p   : MCO::Vector
                  L   : MCO::Vector
                  KEv   : double
                  KEw   : double
                  KE   : double

The state space class State has several constructors that define elements based on the various identifying tuples discussed in Def. 10.4. In addition, there is a constructor that takes a nonminimal tuple—a mass distribution, a kinematic state, and momentum vectors p and L—and checks that the given values are consistent with the internal properties of the space ($p = m\,vc$, etc.).

• Class definitions for fields (Def. 10.16):

```
class SysVectorField :
   constructors:  (MCO::Vector v)            constant
                  (Fieldcode, MM::Id id)     extract property of a body
   methods:       eval(System, double t) : MCO::Vector
```

(The classes SysScalarField and SysVectorField are similar.) The first constructor above creates a constant field. The second creates a field that extracts a vector property of an individual body, where the Fieldcode parameter chooses which property; for example, the *velA* field in Eq. 10.17 would be constructed via the parameter pair (BODY_VEL, *bodyA*). In addition to these, there is support for fields that are algebraic combinations of other fields, for fields that are evaluated by calling arbitrary user-supplied subroutines, and so forth.

10.5.3 M–N Interface

The scope name for the M–N interface is NRIG. We define a routine to solve the forward dynamics problem, Eq. 10.34, given initial conditions and a field that computes an applied motive index.

```
SolveForward(double t0, System Y0, ApplMotiveIdxField A) : SysPath
```

This function returns a SysPath object—which can then be evaluated at arbitrary values of time t. The object is set up internally so that the ODE solver NUM::OdeScatExt (Section B.4.6) is invoked to integrate Eq. 10.35 as necessary to perform the evaluation. Notice that this routine does *not* take an index of applied motive fields, i.e., $\mathcal{A} \in \{\text{AppliedMotiveFields}\}_{\text{IDs}}$ of Eq. 10.35, but rather the implied function (Def. 5.17) that returns an index; an instance of the implied function's class, ApplMotiveIdxField, can be created trivially from the index of applied motive fields, as per Section B.3.7. (Using the implied function allows the numerical solver to perform a single evaluation to compute all the motives; this is convenient when the motives must be computed simultaneously, as in the fancy force mechanism of Ch. 11.)

A similar routine

```
SolveForwardEnergy(...) : PmotivePathIdx
```

returns a PmotivePathIdx object that solves the augmented forward dynamics problem, Eq. 10.36.

Both the above routines can also be used to define the continuous behavior of an initial-value piecewise-continuous ODE problem; the returned paths invoke the NUM::podeScatExt solver (Section B.4.9).

10.5.4 C–M Interface

To solve a forward dynamics problem, the C–M interface performs the following initial setup:

- Construct a System instance, Y0, from the initial conceptual model state. (This defines a map from conceptual body objects to math IDs.)
- Construct an ApplMotiveFieldIdx instance, A, from the conceptual motive objects. (This defines a map from conceptual force objects to math IDs.)
- Construct the solution object: Y = NRIG::SolveForward(t0, Y0, A).
- For energy computation, construct the solution object: P = NRIG::SolveForwardEnergy(...).

To set the conceptual model state for any time t, the C–M interface does

- Compute the System instance Yt = Y(t).
- For each ID i in Yt, set the state of the corresponding conceptual body object based on Yt[i].
- For energy computation, similarly set the state of each force object based on P(t).

The conceptual section can then draw the bodies, print the energy values, check energy balance, etc.

It can be convenient to allow the conceptual model to associate dimensional units with the various quantities. For example, mass may be specified in grams or kilograms, and distance in meters or inches. The mathematical model, as discussed in Section 8.3, must be expressed using uniform units. Thus the C–M interface should perform the proper scaling. Note in particular that the inertia tensor is in units of mass-length^2, thus varies quadratically with changes in length scale.

Chapter 11

"Fancy Forces" Model

The rigid-body model in Ch. 10 is force-based: By assumption, all interactions between bodies and all environmental effects on a body are mediated by the forces (and torques) applied to the bodies. In particular, if we—as creators and users of a model—wish to influence the behavior of the bodies, we must do so through application of forces. Chapter 10 assumes the existence of forces and force fields, but does not discuss how to create them.

This chapter presents a mechanism to create forces and apply them to bodies. It supports forces due explicitly to things in the model, such as springs and gravity, as well as *constraint forces* that can be introduced in order to connect bodies together, specify their motion, and so forth. All the forces fit into a common mathematical model.

The constraint forces in this model use the "dynamic constraints" method described in [Barzel,Barr88]. Indeed, this entire chapter essentially rephrases that work to use the structured design strategy. In particular, the original work defined mathematical "model fragments" for the individual constraints and relied on textual and pseudocode descriptions to combine them—here, we create a complete mathematical model that includes the "glue" between the fragments.

For an example of the "fancy forces" mechanism in use, see the "swinging chain" model in Ch. 12. Although the material in this chapter is self-contained, we refer readers to [Barzel,Barr88] for fuller discussion; and more extensive treatment of the topic can be found in [Barzel88].

212

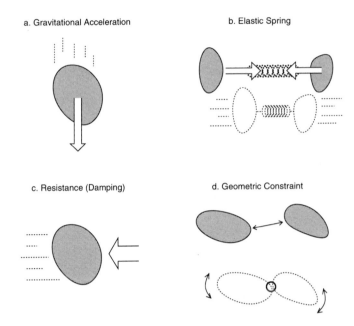

Figure 11.1: Various types of force objects. (a) Gravitational acceleration yields a constant force on a body, proportional to its mass. (b) An elastic spring yields equal-and-opposite forces on a pair of bodies based on their separation distance. (c) Damping yields a force negatively proportional to the body velocity, thus resisting motion. (d) Geometric constraints (a "point-to-point" constraint is illustrated) induce forces whose values are not known explicitly, but instead adapt so as to maintain the constraints no matter what other motions and forces affect the bodies. □

11.1   Goals

Our goals for this model are

- To predefine various types of force objects, which can later be applied to arbitrary bodies

- To allow a single force object to generate related forces on several bodies; e.g., an elastic spring would exert equal-and-opposite forces on two bodies

- To support geometric constraints (via the "dynamic constraints" mechanism of [Barzel,Barr88])

- To have a uniform mathematical formulation that can accommodate the various types of forces

11.2   Conceptual Model

This module describes a mechanism for creating force and torque objects for use in conjunction with the rigid-body dynamics model of Ch. 10. Note that Ch. 10 defines a *motive* to be a force and/or torque vector, and a *motive field* to be a function that yields a single motive given the configuration of a collection of bodies. Here, we return to the word *force*, but with a more general connotation:

- A *force object* is a conceptual entity that is a source of motives, i.e., a thing that creates forces and torques.

A force object may be defined to act on one, two, or more bodies. When a force object is applied to a specific set of bodies (at a specified point on each body), it determines a motive field on each body. Figure 11.1 illustrates several examples.

11.2.1   Force Pairs

If a force object acts on one body, it will typically apply a force along with the corresponding coupled torque (due to the moment arm of the point of application; see Section 10.2.2). A force object that acts on several bodies will apply a separate coupled force/torque to each.

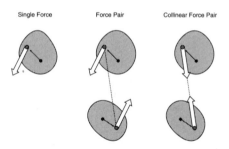

Commonly, a force object that acts on two bodies will apply forces to the bodies that are equal-and-opposite. Such a *force pair* adds no net linear momentum to the system

Figure 11.2: A force object acting on several bodies applies a different force to each. Commonly, a force object acting on two bodies will apply an equal-and-opposite pair of forces. (The corresponding torques are not illustrated.) □

as a whole—the position of the aggregate center of mass isn't affected—though it may add angular momentum, unless the points of application on the two bodies are at the same location in space, i.e., the bodies are touching.

A force pair that points along the line connecting the application points is called a *collinear force pair*—these force objects embody Newton's third law ("every action has an equal and opposite reaction") and are thus consistent with many natural sources of force, such as elastic springs, gravitational and electrostatic attraction, surface contact, and so forth.[1]

In the general case, we allow a force object to apply an arbitrary force/torque to each body that it acts on.

---

[1] If a collinear force pair acts on the bodies' centers of mass, it is called a *central force* ([Goldstein80]).

11.2.2   Explicit Forces

For our model of rigid-body dynamics, forces are the medium by which bodies interact with each other and the environment. In many cases, we can abstract away the underlying physical mechanism and simply express a force as an explicit function of the configuration of the model. We give a few examples:

Gravitational acceleration. (Fig. 11.1a) For laboratory-scale environments on the surface of the earth, we can express the earth's gravitational attraction on a body as a constant downward acceleration, i.e., a force proportional to the body mass, acting at the center of mass. At larger scales, we would need to use Newton's radial, inverse-square law of gravitation.

Damping. (Fig. 11.1c) Newton's first law tells us that objects in motion tend to stay in motion. However, in practice, bodies are almost always affected by friction and air resistance. When we create models, it is often convenient to gloss over the details and essentially use the pre-Newtonian law "a body in motion tends to come to rest." To do so, we introduce a damping force that is opposite to the body's velocity (and similarly, a damping torque that is opposite to the body's angular velocity). Damping forces are *dissipative* (Section 10.2.5)—they always remove energy from the bodies they act on.

Damping that is linearly proportional to body speed is called *viscous;* it can quickly bring a body to rest, resisting motion as if the body were slogging through goo. Quadratic damping—proportional to the square of the speed—is a rough approximation for air resistance: It opposes motion at high speeds, but is negligible at low speeds. Reasonable results can often be achieved by combining small amounts of viscous and quadratic damping.[2]

Elastic spring. (Fig. 11.1b) It is often convenient to model the effect of attaching two bodies by a spring (or a rubber band). We assume that the mass and motion of the spring itself are unimportant—thus we don't introduce the spring into the model as a body, but merely as a force object that acts on the bodies it attaches. A spring always pulls or pushes along its own length, thus yielding a collinear force pair (Section 11.2.1). The strength is usually based on Hooke's law, i.e., is proportional to the displacement of the spring from its rest length.

Often, there is friction or other dissipation in the spring; we can add a damping term that opposes change in the length of the spring, to yield a *spring-and-dashpot* (analogous to an automotive shock absorber). Damping helps to limit oscillations that springs induce in a model.

---

[2]We must stress that applying a motion-resisting damping force to a body is a very simple ad hoc approximation to real-world effects. A more studied approximation to air resistance would take into account the shape of the body and the profile that it offers to the air; and, of course, the resulting disturbance of the air is significant as well.

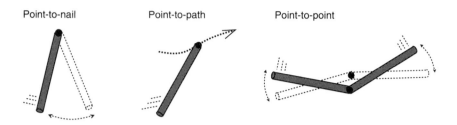

Point-to-nail   Point-to-path   Point-to-point

Figure 11.3: Some geometric constraints. The *point-to-nail* constraint requires that a body point be at a constant location in space; the body is free to swing and rotate about that point. More generally, the *point-to-path* constraint specifies a kinematic path for a body point to follow. Two bodies may be assembled via a *point-to-point* constraint; the specified body points must stay attached, but the bodies may otherwise move freely. □

11.2.3   Geometric Constraints

A powerful way to control models is to specify constraints on the geometric configuration of the bodies. Figure 11.3 illustrates three basic constraints on the locations of body points: *point-to-nail, point-to-path,* and *point-to-point.* Other constraints might involve the orientations or surfaces of bodies.

In order to effect the constraints, forces must be applied to the bodies. Thus a geometric constraint is a type of force object; the resulting forces are called *constraint forces.* Unlike explicit force objects (Section 11.2.2), we can't know in advance precisely what the forces should be—the constraint forces need to take into account the influences of other forces that act on the bodies.

But what is the "meaning," or physical interpretation, of the constraint objects? There are two outlooks:

- *An abstraction of mechanical mechanisms.* For example, a point-to-point constraint can be thought of as an idealized ball-and-socket joint: The resulting constraint forces are equipollent[3] to those that a frictionless physical joint would exert, but we don't need to model the details of the joint.
- *"The hand of God."* Sometimes, we don't have or need an underlying physical mechanism. For example, we may perform an experiment in which we presuppose that one point on a body follows a given path, in order to determine the dynamic response of the rest of the system.

Note that it is possible to *overconstrain* a model by describing a physically unrealizable assemblage of a collection of bodies. As a trivial example, one might constrain different parts of a rigid body to be at the same location in space. We would like the implementation to inform us when a model has unrealizable constraints—but we place no restrictions on the resulting behavior.

---

[3]Forces are *equipollent* if they result in the same net force and torque ([Fox67, p. 67]).

11.3 Mathematical Model

The mathematical model for this module has a few features that bear mentioning:

- *Generality.* We have opted for generality in the design of the mathematical model to support not just the specific examples of force objects listed in Section 11.2, but a wide class of explicit or implicit (constraint) forces. The resulting model is thus somewhat abstract.

- *Housekeeping.* The mathematical model follows the philosophy of Ch. 5: All dependencies between quantities in the model are made explicit. This requires a fair amount of "housekeeping," because each force object can apply to arbitrary bodies, and furthermore because the values of the constraint forces can depend on all the other forces in the system. The resulting model is thus somewhat arcane.

- *Infrastructure.* Unlike those of Chs. 8–10, the mathematical model here does not immediately follow the conceptual model: Instead, we first define a mathematical infrastructure. That infrastructure is then used to define the mathematical elements that correspond with the conceptual objects of Section 11.2.

We therefore include an overview of the mathematical, in Sections 11.3.1–11.3.3, before going on to the full exposition in the remaining sections.

11.3.1 Overview: Connection with Rigid-Body Model

The link between this model and the dynamic rigid-body model (Ch. 10) is via Def. 10.25, which defines the behavior of a collection of bodies via an applied motive index

$$\mathcal{A} \in \{\mathsf{AppliedMotiveFields}\}_{\mathsf{IDs}},$$

i.e., a function which given the state of a system, $Y \in \mathsf{Systems}$ at time $t \in \Re$, yields an index of applied motives[4] $A \in \{\mathsf{AppliedMotives}\}_{\mathsf{IDs}}$:

$$A = \mathcal{A}(Y, t).$$

Recall that each element of A is an applied motive, i.e., a motive and the name of the body it applies to.

The role of the "fancy forces" model is thus to define a function $\mathcal{A}$—i.e., to relate a state Y and time t with a collection A of motives that are applied to bodies—consistent with any given collection of force objects acting on bodies in a model. We provide an abstract definition of $\mathcal{A}$ in Def. 11.15; and the equation that ultimately relates A, Y, and t is given in Eq. 11.21.

---

[4]Formally, $\mathcal{A}$ is an index of functions, and we are discussing its *implied function* as per Def. 5.17.

11.3.2   Overview: Contrast with Previous Formulation

The exposition of the "dynamic constraints" method in [Barzel88] (and more compactly in [Barzel,Barr88]) starts with a statement of an inverse dynamics problem—determine the unknown constraint forces given requirements for behavior—and proceeds to derive a linear equation for the constraint forces.

Here, we take the opposite approach. We axiomatically define a series of abstract constructs and mechanisms for defining and constraining motives, and refine and build on them—until we have constructed essentially the same linear constraint equation as the original work.

The most significant feature of the current mathematical model is that it is complete and explicit, in keeping with the goals and philosophy discussed in Section 5.2. The original work, in contrast, described the various "model fragments" in isolation and described the resulting linear constraint equation, but the details of which constraints applied to which bodies were left implicit.

11.3.3   Overview: Decomposition of Force Objects

We decompose a force object into three parts: a *proto-motive*, which is an array of "knobs" that can be tweaked; a *motive-generator function* that creates motives based on the settings of those knobs; and a *constraint function* that examines the results to see if they are appropriate (see Fig. 11.4):

Proto-motive. The forces and torques that are applied by a force object are often interrelated and thus have limited degrees of freedom (d.o.f.). For example: on a body is often due to the force acting at a fxed moment arm (three d.o.f.); or, the forces on two bodies may be a collinear equal-and-opposite pair (only one d.o.f. for the two forces). The proto-motive is an array of real numbers (a "vec" as per Section A.2) having as many dimensions as there are degrees of freedom.

Motive-generator function. Given the names of the bodies, and the points of application on each, the motive-generator function maps from proto-motive values to a collection of applied motives. For example, a single force on a single body has three d.o.f., and the three proto-motive values can be used directly as the coordinates of the force vector. A force pair on two bodies also has three d.o.f.: The three proto-motive values can be used as the coordinates of the force on one body, and their negation as the coordinates of the force on the other body. (In both cases the torque follows from the fixed moment arm, so adds no d.o.f.)

Definition 11.6 defines $\mathsf{ProtoGens}[n, k]$ to be the space of motive-generator functions that act on n bodies and have k degrees of freedom. Ultimately, in Section 11.3.8, we define several common motive-generator functions: a

Proto-Motives   **Applied Motives**

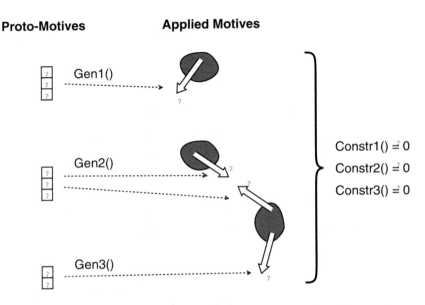

Figure 11.4: Outline of proto-motive mechanism. Each *proto-motive* is a real-number array of some size. Each *motive-generator function* (labeled "Gen1," etc.) converts a proto-motive into one or more applied motives. *Constraint functions* ("Constr1," etc.) examine the entire state of the system of bodies and collection of applied motives. To make a system be consistent we choose values for the proto-motives such that the motive-generator functions yield applied motives that cause the constraint functions to evaluate to zero. □

single pure force, a single pure torque, a single coupled force/torque, a force pair, and a collinear force pair.

Constraint function. The proto-motives provide us with "knobs" to tweak in order to adjust the forces and torques—but we need to choose the settings for those knobs. Thus we define a *constraint function*, which examines a collection of applied motives, and the state of the system, and tells us whether or not they are acceptable—the function yields an array of reals that are all equal to zero if the motives are OK. A constraint function may examine all the motives and bodies in the system in order to decide whether they are acceptable. Thus the value of a constraint function for one force object may be influenced by the settings of other force objects.

Definition 11.7 defines $\mathsf{ProtoConstrs}[n, k]$ to be the space of constraint functions that check n bodies and yield k values. Sections 11.3.9 and 11.3.10 define constraint functions for several force objects in Section 11.2: gravitational acceleration, damping, and elastic spring forces, and point-to-nail, point-to-path, and point-to-point constraints.

11.3.4   Names and Notation

The scope name for this module is

FORCES.

We make use of the following terms from other modules:

AppliedMotiveFields	(Def. 10.21)	*Fnet*	(Def. 10.24)
AppliedMotives	(Def. 10.20)	*Tnet*	(Def. 10.24)
Bodypt	(Def. 10.12)	StatePaths	(Def. 10.6)
Bodypts	(Def. 10.12)	SysPaths	(Def. 10.15)
IDs	(Def. 5.8)	Systems	(Def. 10.14)
Lab	(Def. 8.4)	Vectors	(Def. 8.1)
Locations	(Def. 8.1)	Vecs	(Def. A.2)
Mats	(Def. A.2)		

We use Systems to mean RIGID :: Systems rather than KINEMATIC :: Systems, and similarly for Bodypts, etc. We also extensively use subscript notation for indexes and state spaces, and specializations of state spaces:

$\mathcal{X}_i$	(Not. 5.11, for an index $\mathcal{X}$ and ID i)
x_s	(Not. 5.27, for aspect x of state space element s)
A ⊏ B	(Not. 5.32 and Not. 5.33)

11.3.5   Application Information

In order to specify to which bodies a particular force object will be applied, and what the IDs of the resulting motives should be, we define a state space containing *application information* elements:

Definition. ApplicInfos

(11.1)

ApplicInfos
[
$a \mapsto$ IDs   *ID of an applied motive*
$b \mapsto$ IDs   *ID of a body*
$pt \mapsto \Re^3$ *body coordinates of application point*
]

Definition 11.1: Each application info $p \in$ ApplicInfos contains the ID of an applied motive, the ID of a body that the motive acts on, and the body coordinates of the point at which the force should be applied (for coupled force/torque motives). □

Because a force object may act on several bodies, we define *application sets* of information elements:

Definition. ApplicSets

$$
\begin{aligned}
\textsf{ApplicSets} &\equiv \text{the space } \left\{ \text{ordered sets of } \textsf{ApplicInfos} \right\} \\
\textsf{ApplicSets}[n] &\equiv \left\{ s \in \textsf{ApplicSets} \ \Big| \ \|s\| = n \right\}
\end{aligned}
$$

(11.2)

Definition 11.2: An application set $s \in \textsf{ApplicSets}[n]$ has size $s = n$, i.e., contains n elements; since the set is ordered, we can examine its elements by number: $s_0, s_1, \ldots s_{n-1}$. □

We would like to identify when the motives listed in an application set are to be found in a given index of applied motives. Thus we define

Definition. **Compatible** (motive index, application set)

(11.3)

An applied motive index $A \in \{\textsf{AppliedMotives}\}_{\textsf{IDs}}$ and an application set $s \in \textsf{ApplicSets}$ are **compatible** *iff:*

$$
\begin{aligned}
a(r) &\in Ids(A), & \text{all } r \in s \\
b(r) &= body(A_{a(r)}), & \text{all } r \in s
\end{aligned}
$$

Definition 11.3: An application set s is compatible with an index of applied motives A if each application info $r \in s$ corresponds with an applied motive in A. That is, the ID $a(r)$ must be the label of an element of A; that element must be applied to body ID $b(r)$, where a and b are as per Def. 11.1. Note that A may also have additional elements that are not specified by any pair in s. □

Furthermore, we would like to identify when a collection of application sets accounts for all the motives in an index:

Definition. **Compatible** (motive index, application set index)

(11.4)

An applied motive index $A \in \{\textsf{AppliedMotives}\}_{\textsf{IDs}}$ and an application set index $S \in \{\textsf{ApplicSets}\}_{\textsf{IDs}}$ are **compatible** *iff:*

- *A is compatible with s, for all $s \in Elts(S)$*
- $\|A\| = \displaystyle\sum_{s \in Elts(S)} \|s\|$

Definition 11.4: Compatible index of applied motives and index of application sets. The applied motive index must be compatible (Def. 11.3) with each application set. The total number of applied motives must agree with the total number of application infos—this implies that each application info and each application set is unique. □

It will be convenient to have some notation for various quantities relating to the point of application of a body force, as specified by application info:

Notation. Point of Application

(11.5)

$$
\begin{aligned}
&\textit{Given application info } r \in \mathsf{ApplicInfos} \textit{ and}\\
&\quad \textit{system state } Y \in \mathsf{Systems}, \textit{ we write}\\[4pt]
&\textit{with } s = Y_{b(r)} \textit{ and } d = Bodypt(s, pt(r)),
\end{aligned}
$$

$$
\begin{aligned}
x(Y, r) &\equiv {}^{\mathcal{L}ab}x_d && \textit{location}\\[4pt]
v(Y, r) &\equiv {}^{\mathcal{L}ab}v_d && \textit{velocity}\\[4pt]
\mathrm{arm}(Y, r) &\equiv {}^{\mathcal{L}ab}\mathrm{arm}_d && \textit{moment arm}\\[4pt]
\mathrm{acc}_0(Y, r) &\equiv {}^{\mathcal{L}ab}\!\left(\mathrm{arm}_d^* \, \mathbf{I}^{-1}(\omega_s \times L_s) + \omega_s \times (\omega_s \times \mathrm{arm}_d)\right)\\
& && \textit{free acceleration}\\[4pt]
\mathrm{acc}_F(Y, r) &\equiv \tfrac{1}{m_s} && \textit{acceleration force-dependence}\\[4pt]
\mathrm{acc}_T(Y, r) &\equiv -{}^{\mathcal{L}ab}\mathrm{arm}_d^* \mathbf{I}^{-1} && \textit{acceleration torque-dependence}
\end{aligned}
$$

Notation 11.5: Quantities for a point of application. The acceleration acc_0 is due to the rotation of the body; acc_F and acc_T are coefficients that yield acceleration due to force and torque. *Bodypt* maps from body point coordinates to a dynamic body point state element (Def. 10.12). Derivations for the acceleration terms are given in Section 11.6.1. $\square$

11.3.6 Proto-Motive Mechanism

This section defines the proto-motive mechanism that is outlined in Section 11.3.3. Motive-generator and constraint functions are defined so that any given function can be applied to arbitrary bodies; the details of a particular application are sepcified via an application set (Def. 11.2).

First, we define the class of motive-generator functions, which map from "vec"-valued proto-motives to applied motives:

Definition. ProtoGens

(11.6)

$$
\mathsf{ProtoGens}[n, k] \equiv \textit{the set of functions}
$$
$$
\left\{ f \colon \begin{pmatrix} \mathsf{Systems} \times \Re \times \\ \mathsf{ApplicSets}[n] \times \\ \mathsf{Vecs}[k] \end{pmatrix} \to \{\mathsf{AppliedMotives}\}_{\mathsf{IDs}} \;\middle|\; \textit{such that } f(Y, t, s, x) \textit{ and } s \textit{ are compatible} \right\}
$$

Definition 11.6: Motive-generator functions for n motives, using k degrees of freedom. Given a system $Y \in$ at time $t \in \Re$, and an application set $s \in \mathsf{ApplicSets}[n]$ naming the n motives to generate and the bodies to apply them to, a motive-generator function maps from a proto-motive value $x \in \mathsf{Vecs}[k]$ to an index of applied motives. $\square$

And next, the class of constraint functions, which yield constraint residues given an index of applied motives:

Definition. ProtoConstrs

(11.7)
$$\text{ProtoConstrs}[n, k] = set\ of\ functions$$
$$\left\{ \left(\begin{array}{c} \text{Systems} \times \Re \times \\ \text{ApplicSets}[n] \times \\ \{\text{AppliedMotives}\}_{\text{IDs}} \end{array} \right) \rightarrow \text{Vecs}[k] \right\}$$

Definition 11.7: Constraint functions for n motives, yielding k residues. Given a system $Y \in$ at time $t \in \Re$, and an application set $s \in$ ApplicSets$[n]$ naming the n motives and bodies of interest, a constraint function maps from an index of applied motives $A \in \{\text{AppliedMotives}\}_{\text{IDs}}$ to a size-k vec of values that are zero if the constraint is met. □

We bundle together a constraint function and motive-generator function into a *proto-specifier,* which describes a *force object* as per Section 11.2:

Definition. ProtoSpecs

(11.8)
ProtoSpecs
[

n	$\mapsto$ *Integers*	*number of motives*
cz	$\mapsto$ *Integers*	*size of the constraint*
pz	$\mapsto$ *Integers*	*size of the proto-motive*
Constr	$\mapsto$ ProtoConstrs$[n, cz]$	*constraint function*
Gen	$\mapsto$ ProtoGens$[n, pz]$	*motive-generator function*

]

Definition 11.8: Each proto-specifier $p \in$ ProtoSpecs has a constraint function and a motive-generator function.[5] Commonly, we will have $cz_p = pz_p$, i.e., the number of degrees of freedom agrees with the number of constraint equations, but we do not require this. □

A proto-specifier takes a proto-motive as input and yields a constraint residue as output, with an applied motives index as the intermediate result (see Fig. 11.4). Note that all proto-specifiers in a model share a common applied motive index.

Note that a proto-specifier is defined independently of Do a given proto-specifier index and application set index jibe? We define

Definition. **Compatible** (proto-specifier index, application set index)

(11.9)
A proto-specifier index $\mathcal{P} \in \{\text{ProtoSpecs}\}_{\text{IDs}}$ *and an application set index* $\mathcal{S} \in \{\text{ApplicSets}\}_{\text{IDs}}$ *are* **compatible** *iff:*

$$Ids(\mathcal{P}) = Ids(\mathcal{S})$$
$$\|\mathcal{S}_i\| = n(\mathcal{P}_i),\ all\ i \in Ids(\mathcal{P})$$

Definition 11.9: Compatible proto-specifier and application set indexes. Each application set has the number of elements that is appropriate for its corresponding proto-specifier. □

---

[5]Notice that we have slightly extended the state-space notation of Section 5.9, by specifying the sizes of the functions, n, cz, and pz, "inline" rather than via separate explicit properties.

Similarly, does a proto-specifier index agree with a proto-motive index?

Definition. **Compatible** (proto-specifier index, proto-motive index)

(11.10)

> *A proto-specifier index* $\mathcal{P} \in \{\mathsf{ProtoSpecs}\}_{\mathsf{IDs}}$ *and a proto-motive index* $\mathcal{X} \in \{\mathsf{Vecs}\}_{\mathsf{IDs}}$ *are* **compatible** *iff:*
>
> $$Ids(\mathcal{P}) = Ids(\mathcal{X})$$
> $$sz(\mathcal{X}_i) = pz(\mathcal{P}_i), \text{ all } i \in Ids(\mathcal{P})$$

Definition 11.10: Compatible proto-specifier and proto-motive indexes. Each proto-motive is the appropriate size for its corresponding proto-specifier. □

Putting together the various types of compatibility, we define

Definition. **Compatible ensemble**

(11.11)

> *A group of indexes* $\mathcal{P} \in \{\mathsf{ProtoSpecs}\}_{\mathsf{IDs}},$ $\mathcal{X} \in \{\mathsf{Vecs}\}_{\mathsf{IDs}}, \mathcal{S} \in \{\mathsf{ApplicSets}\}_{\mathsf{IDs}},$ *and* $A \in \{\mathsf{AppliedMotives}\}_{\mathsf{IDs}}$ *form a* **compatible ensemble** *iff:*
>
> - $\mathcal{P}$ *is compatible (Def. 11.10) with* $\mathcal{X}$,
> - $\mathcal{P}$ *is compatible (Def. 11.9) with* $\mathcal{S}$, *and*
> - $\mathcal{S}$ *is compatible (Def. 11.4) with* A

Definition 11.11: Structurally compatible ensemble. Each proto-specifier $\mathcal{P}_i$ maps its corresponding proto-motive $\mathcal{X}_i$ to the applied motives listed in its corresponding application set $\mathcal{S}_i$. All the resulting applied motives are gathered in A. □

From Def. 11.4, we know that the elements of $\mathcal{S}$ in a compatible ensemble are unique. Thus we can use them as subscripts, instead of IDs.

Notation. Application Sets as Subscripts

(11.12)

> *Given a compatible ensemble* $\mathcal{P} \in \{\mathsf{ProtoSpecs}\}_{\mathsf{IDs}},$ $\mathcal{X} \in \{\mathsf{Vecs}\}_{\mathsf{IDs}}, \mathcal{S} \in \{\mathsf{ApplicSets}\}_{\mathsf{IDs}},$ *and* $A \in \{\mathsf{AppliedMotives}\}_{\mathsf{IDs}}$: *If* $s \in \mathsf{ApplicSets}$ *and* $i \in Ids(\mathcal{S})$ *are such that* $s = \mathcal{S}_i$, *we write*
>
> $$\mathcal{X}_s \equiv \mathcal{X}_i$$
> $$\mathcal{P}_s \equiv \mathcal{P}_i$$
> $$cz_s \equiv cz(\mathcal{P}_i)$$
> $$pz_s \equiv pz(\mathcal{P}_i)$$
> $$Constr_s \equiv Constr(\mathcal{P}_i)$$
> $$Gen_s \equiv Gen(\mathcal{P}_i)$$

Notation 11.12: Subscript notation for compatible sets. In a compatible ensemble, the elements $\mathcal{S}$ are unique (Def. 11.4), so we can use them as subscripts to refer to the corresponding elements of $\mathcal{X}$ and $\mathcal{P}$. For further shorthand, we also use those subscripts directly for the aspects of elements of $\mathcal{P}$. □

The components of a compatible ensemble (Def. 11.11) have the proper structure—all the right sizes, the right IDs in the right places, etc.—but we also want to have the proper values:

Definition. **Consistent**

(11.13)

> A compatible ensemble $\mathcal{P} \in \{\mathsf{ProtoSpecs}\}_{\mathsf{IDs}}$, $\mathcal{X} \in \{\mathsf{Vecs}\}_{\mathsf{IDs}}$, $\mathcal{S} \in \{\mathsf{ApplicSets}\}_{\mathsf{IDs}}$, and $A \in \{\mathsf{AppliedMotives}\}_{\mathsf{IDs}}$ is **consistent** with $Y \in \mathsf{Systems}$ and $t \in \Re$ iff:
>
> For all $s \in Elts(\mathcal{S})$:
> - $Constr_s(Y, t, s, A) = 0$
> - $Gen_s(Y, t, s, \mathcal{X}_s) \subseteq A$

Definition 11.13: A compatible ensemble is consistent with an instantaneous state if all the constraints are met and if all the applied motives agree with the motive-generator functions (see Fig. 11.4). □

Note, from Defs. 11.4 and 11.6, the latter equation above is equivalent to:

(11.14)

> *[Given same as Def. 11.13], for all $s \in Elts(\mathcal{S})$ and all $i \in Ids(Gen_s(Y, t, s, \mathcal{X}_s))$,*
>
> $Gen_s(Y, t, s, \mathcal{X}_s)_i = A_i$

Equation 11.14: Each motive-generator function Gen_s yields an index of applied motives; and each applied motive in that index is labeled by the same ID in the overall applied motive index A. □

We are now in a position to define an index of applied motive fields (as per the discussion in Section 11.3.1), based on an index of proto-specifiers and an index of application sets:

Definition. **Consistent** (applied motive field, proto-specifier index)

(11.15)

> *An index of applied motive fields $A \in \{\mathsf{AppliedMotiveFields}\}_{\mathsf{IDs}}$ is **consistent** with $\mathcal{P} \in \{\mathsf{ProtoSpecs}\}_{\mathsf{IDs}}$ and $\mathcal{S} \in \{\mathsf{ApplicSets}\}_{\mathsf{IDs}}$ iff:*
>
> *for any $Y \in \mathsf{Systems}$ and $t \in \Re$, there exists $\mathcal{X} \in \{\mathsf{Vecs}\}_{\mathsf{IDs}}$, such that the ensemble $\mathcal{P}, \mathcal{X}, \mathcal{S}, A(Y, t)$ is consistent with Y and t.*

Definition 11.15: The field A is consistent with $\mathcal{P}$ and $\mathcal{S}$ if at each point in space and time it maps to a collection of motives that are consistent with $\mathcal{P}$ and $\mathcal{S}$. □

The definitions in this section provide us with a useful framework, but they are too general to perform computations. The next section looks at a restricted class of proto-specifiers whose functions are linear.

11.3.7   Linear Proto-Motive Mechanism

Section 11.3.6 defines the structural relationships between the components for arbitrary proto-specifiers. Here, we examine proto-specifiers whose constraint and motive-generator functions are linear; these will be sufficient to handle both explicit force objects (Section 11.2.2) and "dynamic constraint" force objects (Section 11.2.3).

The presentation in this section defines canonical forms for linear proto-motive and constraint functions. These forms are inserted into the definition of a consistent ensemble, Def. 11.13, resulting in a constraint equation, Eq. 11.21, that is linear in the proto-motives.

We start by defining fields analogous to the location, vector, and scalar fields of Def. 10.16, except that these fields also take application sets as parameters:

Definition. (fields)

$$(11.16)$$

$$\mathsf{SysVecFields}[n, k] \equiv \textit{the set of functions}$$
$$\left\{ \begin{pmatrix} \mathsf{Systems} \times \Re \\ \times \mathsf{ApplicSets}[n] \end{pmatrix} \to \mathsf{Vecs}[k] \right\}$$

$$\mathsf{SysMatidxFields}[n, j, k] \equiv \textit{the set of functions}$$
$$\left\{ \begin{pmatrix} \mathsf{Systems} \times \Re \\ \times \mathsf{ApplicSets}[n] \end{pmatrix} \to \{\mathsf{Mats}[j, k]\}^{\circ}_{\mathsf{IDs}} \right\}$$

$$\mathsf{SysMatidxAFields}[n, j, k] \equiv \textit{the set of functions}$$
$$\left\{ \begin{matrix} f \in \mathsf{SysMatidxFields}[n, j, k] \textit{ such that} \\ \mathit{Ids}(f(Y, t, s)) = \{a(r) \mid r \in s\} \end{matrix} \right\}$$

$$\mathsf{SysMatidxBFields}[n, j, k] \equiv \textit{the set of functions}$$
$$\left\{ \begin{matrix} f \in \mathsf{SysMatidxFields}[n, j, k] \textit{ such that} \\ \mathit{Ids}(f(Y, t, s)) = \{b(r) \mid r \in s\} \end{matrix} \right\}$$

Definition 11.16: Fields over instantaneous state, which are additionally parametrized by applications sets. Note that elements of SysMatidxFields$[n, j, k]$ are functions that yield indexes with zero. The spaces SysMatidxAFields$[n, j, k]$ and SysMatidxBFields$[n, j, k]$ are subsets of SysMatidxFields$[n, j, k]$ that yield indexes whose IDs are specified by the application set parameter $s \in$ ApplicSets; the former uses the applied motive IDs listed in s, while the latter uses the body IDs. □

We define the set of motive-generator functions that are linear in the proto-motives—this is a subset of the general class of motive-generator functions (Def. 11.6). Notice the use of a state space specialization, as per Not. 5.32, to define aspect operators on the subset.

Definition. Lgens

(11.17)

$$\mathsf{Lgens}[n,k] \overset{gen}{\sqsubset} \mathsf{ProtoGens}[n,k]$$

[

$G \mapsto \mathsf{SysMatidxAFields}[n,3,k]$ *force coefficients*
$H \mapsto \mathsf{SysMatidxAFields}[n,3,k]$ *torque coefficients*
$J \mapsto \mathsf{SysMatidxAFields}[n,3,1]$ *motive arms*

$\overline{}$ *For* $Y \in \mathsf{Systems}$, $t \in \Re$, $s \in \mathsf{ApplicSets}[n]$ *and* $X \in \mathsf{Vecs}[k]$,

$$\overset{lab}{}F(gen(Y,t,s,X)_{a(r)}) = G(Y,t,s)_{a(r)}\,X, \quad \textit{for all } r \in s$$

$$\overset{lab}{}T(gen(Y,t,s,X)_{a(r)}) = H(Y,t,s)_{a(r)}\,X, \quad \textit{for all } r \in s$$

$$\overset{lab}{}arm(gen(Y,t,s,X)_{a(r)}) = J(Y,t,s)_{a(r)} \quad\quad \textit{for all } r \in s$$

]

Definition 11.17: Linear motive-generator functions. Each generated force vector is the product of a matrix in G and the proto-motive X (when represented in lab coords); similarly for the torque vectors. The motive arms are independent of X. Note that we must have either $J(Y,t,s)_{a(r)} = 0$ or $H(Y,t,s)_{a(r)} = J(Y,t,s)^*_{a(r)}G(Y,t,s)_{a(r)}$, by Def. 10.19. □

Similarly, we define the subset of constraint functions (Def. 11.7) that depend linearly on the forces and torques in the applied motive index:

Definition. Lconstrs

(11.18)

$$\mathsf{Lconstrs}[n,k] \overset{constr}{\sqsubset} \mathsf{ProtoConstrs}[n,k]$$

[

$K \mapsto \mathsf{SysVecFields}[n,k]$ *independent term*
$\Gamma \mapsto \mathsf{SysMatidxBFields}[n,k,3]$ *force-dependency coefficients*
$\Lambda \mapsto \mathsf{SysMatidxBFields}[n,k,3]$ *torque-dependency coefficients*
$all \mapsto \{0,1\}$ *all-or-some selector*

$\overline{}$ *For* $Y \in \mathsf{Systems}, t \in \Re, s \in \mathsf{ApplicSets}[n], A \in \{\mathsf{AppliedMotives}\}_{\mathsf{IDs}}$,

$$constr(Y,t,s,A,all) =$$

$$K(Y,t,s) + \begin{cases} \displaystyle\sum_{a \,\in\, Elts(A)} \begin{pmatrix} \Gamma(Y,t,s)_{body(a)}\overset{lab}{}F_a + \\ \Lambda(Y,t,s)_{body(a)}\overset{lab}{}T_a \end{pmatrix}, & all = 1 \\[2em] \displaystyle\sum_{r \,\in\, s} \begin{pmatrix} \Gamma(Y,t,s)_{b(r)}\overset{lab}{}F(A_{a(r)}) + \\ \Lambda(Y,t,s)_{b(r)}\overset{lab}{}T(A_{a(r)})) \end{pmatrix}, & all = 0 \end{cases}$$

]

Definition 11.18: Linear constraint functions. The constraint is the sum of a force- and torque-independent term K and products of coefficients with forces and torques. The *all* selector chooses whether to perform the summation over all applied motives in a given index (A), or only over those motives specified in the given application set (s). □

Notice that by Def. 11.16, $\Gamma(Y, t, s)_b$ and $\Lambda(Y, t, s)_b$ will be zero for body IDs b that are not listed in s. Thus the $all = 1$ and $all = 0$ cases are similar in structure: Both examine only the bodies listed in s, accumulating $\Gamma(Y, t, s)_b$ times a force and $\Lambda(Y, t, s)_b$ times a torque for each body b—but in the $all = 0$ case, the force and torque are from the motive listed in s, while in the $all = 1$ case, they are the *net force* and *net torque* on the body.

We define the set of linear proto-specifiers (Def. 11.8):

Definition. LprotoSpecs

(11.19)

$$\text{LprotoSpecs} \overset{P}{\sqsubseteq} \text{ProtoSpecs}$$
[

Lconstr $\mapsto$ Lconstrs$[n, cz]$		*linear constraint function*
K	$\dots K \mapsto$ SysVecFields$[n, cz]$	
Γ	$\dots \Gamma \mapsto$ SysMatidxBFields$[n, cz, 3]$	
Λ	$\dots \Lambda \mapsto$ SysMatidxBFields$[n, cz, 3]$	
all	$\dots all \mapsto \{0, 1\}$	
Lgen $\mapsto$ Lgens$[n, pz]$		*linear generator function*
G	$\dots G \mapsto$ SysMatidxAFields$[n, 3, pz]$	
H	$\dots H \mapsto$ SysMatidxAFields$[n, 3, pz]$	

—

Constr $= constr(Lconstr)$
Gen $= gen(Lgen)$
]

Definition 11.19: A linear proto-specifier is a special case of a proto-specifier, having functions that are linear as per Defs. 11.17 and 11.18. □

Continuing with the shorthand notation defined in Not. 11.12, we use application sets as subscripts when we have a compatible ensemble:

Notation. Application Sets as Subscripts

(11.20)

[Given same as Not. 11.12], if $s \in$ ApplicSets and $p \in$ LprotoSpecs are such that $s = \mathcal{S}_i$ and $P(p) = \mathcal{P}_i$, we write

$$
\begin{aligned}
K_s &\equiv K(p) \\
\Gamma_s &\equiv \Gamma(p) \\
\Lambda_s &\equiv \Lambda(p) \\
G_s &\equiv G(p) \\
H_s &\equiv H(p) \\
all_s &\equiv all(p)
\end{aligned}
$$

Notation 11.20: For a compatible ensemble, we use subscripts to refer to the aspect values of any linear proto-specs. □

Definitions 11.13, 11.17, and 11.18 lead to a linear equation for compatible proto-specifiers and motives (written using Not. 11.20). Section 11.6.2 contains the derivation of the following:

> *If a compatible ensemble* $\mathcal{P} \in \{\textsf{LprotoSpecs}\}_{\textsf{IDs}}$,
> $\mathcal{X} \in \{\textsf{Vecs}\}_{\textsf{IDs}}$, $\mathcal{S} \in \{\textsf{ApplicSets}\}_{\textsf{IDs}}$,
> $A \in \{\textsf{AppliedMotives}\}_{\textsf{IDs}}$ *is consistent with*
> $Y \in \textsf{Systems}$ *and* $t \in \Re$, *then*

(11.21)
$$\forall p \in Elts(\mathcal{S}), \qquad K_p(Y,t,p) + \sum_{q \in Elts(\mathcal{S})} \mathcal{M}_{pq}(Y,t)\, \mathcal{X}_q = 0$$

where
$$\mathcal{M}_{pq} \in \textsf{Mats}[cz_p, pz_q]$$
$$= \begin{cases} 0, & all_p = 0 \,\&\, p \neq q \\ \sum_{r \in q} ([\Gamma_p]_{b_r}[G_q]_{a_r} + [\Lambda_p]_{b_r}[H_q]_{a_r}), & otherwise \end{cases}$$

Equation 11.21: A consistent collection of linear proto-motives is based on an array equation, linear in the proto-motives. For clarity the parameters have been left off of $\mathcal{M}_{pq}(Y,t)$, $\Gamma_p(Y,t,p)$, $\Lambda_p(Y,t,p)$, $G_q(Y,t,q)$, and $H_q(Y,t,q)$. See derivation in Section 11.6.2. □

Equation 11.21 is the *linear constraint-force equation* of [Barzel,Barr88]. We discuss it further in Section 11.4.

The definitions in this section provide canonical forms for motive-generator functions, constraint functions, and proto-specifiers. In the coming sections, we fill in those forms for the various types of force objects discussed in Section 11.2.

11.3.8 Motive-Generator Functions

This section defines several commonly useful motive-generator functions. These are all linear functions as per Def. 11.17, thus each is defined by a pair of functions $G, H \in \textsf{SysMatidxAFields}[n,3,k]$, where k is the number of degrees of freedom in the resulting motives. Each function yields an index containing one entry per motive. We will define motive-generator functions for one and for two motives.

For one arbitrary pure force:

Definition. $\mathcal{G}pure\mathcal{F}$

(11.22)

> *Define* $\mathcal{G}pure\mathcal{F} \in \textsf{Lgens}[1,3]$ *by:*
>
> $$G_{\mathcal{G}pure\mathcal{F}}(Y,t,s)_{a(s_0)} \quad \equiv \quad 1$$
> $$H_{\mathcal{G}pure\mathcal{F}}(Y,t,s)_{a(s_0)} \quad \equiv \quad 0$$

Definition 11.22: Motive-generator function for a pure force. The three values of a proto-motive are used directly as the components of the force; the torque and motive arm are zero. Note that $G(Y,t,s)$ and $H(Y,t,s)$ are independent of Y and t. $J(Y,t,s)$ must be zero, by Def. 11.17. □

For one arbitrary pure torque:

Definition. $\mathcal{G}pureT$

(11.23)

$Define \ \mathcal{G}pureT \in \mathsf{Lgens}[1,3] \ by:$
$G_{\mathcal{G}pureT}(Y,t,s)_{a(s_0)} \ \equiv \ 0$
$H_{\mathcal{G}pureT}(Y,t,s)_{a(s_0)} \ \equiv \ 1$

Definition 11.23: Motive-generator function for a pure torque. Analogous to Def. 11.22 but with opposite values for G and H. □

Most often, we will generate a motive consisting of a coupled force/torque, where the force is applied at a specified point in body coordinates:

Definition. $\mathcal{G}coupled$

(11.24)

$Define \ \mathcal{G}coupled \in \mathsf{Lgens}[1,3] \ by:$
$G_{\mathcal{G}coupled}(Y,t,s)_{a(s_0)} \ \equiv \ 1$
$J_{\mathcal{G}pureF}(Y,t,s)_{a(s_0)} \ \equiv \ \mathrm{arm}(Y,s_0)$

Definition 11.24: Motive-generator function for a coupled force/torque. The three values of the proto-motive are used directly as the components of the force; the moment arm is as specified by s_0, and the torque is coupled. □

In the most general case for one motive, we may wish to generate an arbitrary force and torque; this requires six degrees of freedom:

Definition. $\mathcal{G}arbit$

(11.25)

$Define \ \mathcal{G}arbit \in \mathsf{Lgens}[1,6] \ by:$
$G_{\mathcal{G}arbit}(Y,t,s)_{a(s_0)} \ \equiv \ \begin{bmatrix} 1\,0\,0\,0\,0\,0 \\ 0\,1\,0\,0\,0\,0 \\ 0\,0\,1\,0\,0\,0 \end{bmatrix}$
$H_{\mathcal{G}arbit}(Y,t,s)_{a(s_0)} \ \equiv \ \begin{bmatrix} 0\,0\,0\,1\,0\,0 \\ 0\,0\,0\,0\,1\,0 \\ 0\,0\,0\,0\,0\,1 \end{bmatrix}$
$J_{\mathcal{G}pureF}(Y,t,s)_{a(s_0)} \ \equiv \ 0$

Definition 11.25: Motive-generator function for an arbitrary force/torque. This acts on a proto-motive vec with six values: The first three values of the proto-motive are used for the components of the force, and the last three are used for the components of the torque. □

For a force object that acts on two bodies, we most commonly generate an equal-and-opposite force pair (Section 11.2.1); this requires three degrees of freedom:

Definition. $\mathcal{G}$*pair*

$$\text{Define } \mathcal{G}\text{pair} \in \mathsf{Lgens}[2, 3] \text{ by:}$$

(11.26)
$$
\begin{aligned}
G_{\mathcal{G}pair}(Y, t, s)_{a(s_0)} &\equiv 1 \\
G_{\mathcal{G}pair}(Y, t, s)_{a(s_1)} &\equiv -1 \\
J_{\mathcal{G}pure\mathcal{F}}(Y, t, s)_{a(s_0)} &\equiv \text{arm}(Y, s_0) \\
J_{\mathcal{G}pure\mathcal{F}}(Y, t, s)_{a(s_1)} &\equiv \text{arm}(Y, s_1)
\end{aligned}
$$

Definition 11.26: Motive-generator function for a force pair. The proto-motive values are used directly as the components of the force for application s_0, and the negation is used for s_1. The moment arms are as specified by s, and the torques are coupled. □

For a collinear force pair, in which the paired forces lie on the line connecting the application points (Section 11.2.1), only one degree of freedom is needed:

Definition. $\mathcal{G}$*collinear*

$$\text{Define } \mathcal{G}\text{collinear} \in \mathsf{Lgens}[2, 1] \text{ by:}$$

(11.27)
$$
\begin{aligned}
G_{\mathcal{G}collinear}(Y, t, s)_{a(s_0)} &\equiv x(Y, s_0) - x(Y, s_1) \\
G_{\mathcal{G}collinear}(Y, t, s)_{a(s_1)} &\equiv -G_{\mathcal{G}collinear}(Y, t, s)_{a(s_0)} \\
J_{\mathcal{G}pure\mathcal{F}}(Y, t, s)_{a(s_0)} &\equiv \text{arm}(Y, s_0) \\
J_{\mathcal{G}pure\mathcal{F}}(Y, t, s)_{a(s_1)} &\equiv \text{arm}(Y, s_1)
\end{aligned}
$$

Definition 11.27: Motive-generator function for a collinear force pair. There is only one degree of freedom: The force is determined by scaling the line segment that separates the application points. The moment arms are as specified by s, and the torques are coupled to the forces. □

11.3.9   Constraint Functions for Explicit Force Objects

This section discusses explicit force objects (Section 11.2.2); we discuss geometric constraint objects (Section 11.2.3) in Section 11.3.10.

Constraint functions for explicit force objects are expressed directly in terms of Def. 11.18, by specifying values for $K \in \mathsf{SysVecFields}[n, k]$ and $\Gamma, \Lambda \in \mathsf{SysMatidxBFields}[n, k, 3]$. We define constraint functions for the objects described in Section 11.2.2; functions for other objects can be defined analogously.

For a gravitational acceleration force:

Definition. Cgrav

(11.28)

$$
\begin{array}{c}
\textit{Define the family of functions } \mathcal{C}grav[g] \in \mathsf{Lconstrs}[1,3] \\
\textit{for } g \in \Re \textit{ by:} \\[1em]
\text{all}_{cgrav} \equiv 0 \\
\Gamma_{cgrav}(Y,t,s)_{b(s_0)} \equiv -1 \\
\Lambda_{cgrav}(Y,t,s)_{b(s_0)} \equiv 0 \\
K_{cgrav}(Y,t,s) \equiv \begin{bmatrix} 0 \\ 0 \\ -g\, m(Y_b(s_0)) \end{bmatrix}
\end{array}
$$

Definition 11.28: Constraint functions for gravitational acceleration. The values of Γ and Λ are such that Defs. 11.13 and 11.18 imply that the lab coordinates of the force are given directly by K, when this constraint is met. K itself yields a downward value proportional to the body mass and the gravitational acceleration parameter. Here, we assume that the lab frame z-axis points "up." □

For a damping force and torque:

Definition. Cdamp

(11.29)

$$
\begin{array}{c}
\textit{Define the family of functions} \\
\mathcal{C}damp[\mu_v, \mu_w, \nu_v, \nu_w] \in \mathsf{Lconstrs}[1,6] \textit{ for} \\
\mu_v, \mu_\omega, \nu_v, \nu_\omega \in \Re \textit{ by:} \\[1em]
\text{all}_{cdamp} \equiv 0 \\[0.5em]
\Gamma_{cdamp}(Y,t,s)_{b(s_0)} \equiv \begin{bmatrix} -1 & 0 & 0 & 0 & 0 & 0 \\ 0 & -1 & 0 & 0 & 0 & 0 \\ 0 & 0 & -1 & 0 & 0 & 0 \end{bmatrix} \\[1em]
\Lambda_{cdamp}(Y,t,s)_{b(s_0)} \equiv \begin{bmatrix} 0 & 0 & 0 & -1 & 0 & 0 \\ 0 & 0 & 0 & 0 & -1 & 0 \\ 0 & 0 & 0 & 0 & 0 & -1 \end{bmatrix} \\[1em]
K_{cdamp}(Y,t,s) \equiv \begin{bmatrix} -(\mu_v + \nu_v \| \text{vc}(Y_{b(s_0)}) \|)\ ^{\mathcal{L}ab}\text{vc}(Y_{b(s_0)}) \\ -(\mu_\omega + \nu_\omega \| \omega(Y_{b(s_0)}) \|)\ ^{\mathcal{L}ab}\omega(Y_{b(s_0)}) \end{bmatrix}
\end{array}
$$

Definition 11.29: Constraint functions for viscous and quadratic damping. μ_v and ν_v are the coefficients of viscous and quadratic damping for the linear velocity, and μ_ω and ν_ω are for the rotation. The first three values of K give the force, and the last three give the torque, in a manner similar to Def. 11.28. □

For a Hooke's-law spring with viscous damping:

Definition. Cspring

Define the family of functions
$Cspring[l_0, k, \mu] \in \mathsf{Lconstrs}[2, 3]$ *for* $l_0, k, \mu \in \Re$ *by:*

(11.30)

$$
\begin{aligned}
\mathrm{all}_{Cspring} &\equiv 0 \\
\Gamma_{Cspring}(Y, t, s)_{b(s_0)} &\equiv -1 \\
\Gamma_{Cspring}(Y, t, s)_{b(s_1)} &\equiv 0 \\
\Lambda_{Cspring}(Y, t, s)_{b(s_0)} &\equiv 0 \\
\Lambda_{Cspring}(Y, t, s)_{b(s_1)} &\equiv 0 \\
K_{Cspring}(Y, t, s) &\equiv (k(l - l_0) + \mu\, v \cdot \hat{r})\, \hat{r}, \\
\mathrm{where} \quad r &= x(Y, s_1) - x(Y, s_0) \\
v &= v(Y, s_1) - v(Y, s_0) \\
l &= \|r\| \\
\hat{r} &= r/l
\end{aligned}
$$

Definition 11.30: Constraint functions for damped spring forces. The value of K constrains the force of application point s_0 to point toward the application point of s_1, based on rest length l_0, spring constant k, and damping coefficient μ. $\hat{r}$ is the unit vector from application point s_0 to s_1, and $v \cdot \hat{r}$ is the rate of change of separation between the bodies. This function is not well defined if the two application points coincide in space, unless $l_0 = \mu = 0$. (No constraint is placed on application s_1; presumably an opposite force will be generated for it.) □

11.3.10 Constraint Functions for Geometric Constraints

We model geometric constraints via the "dynamic constraints" method described in [Barzel,Barr88]. We recap that method here, before defining some specific constraint functions.

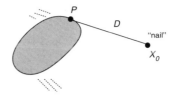

For any geometric constraint, we define a "deviation measure" that equals zero when the constraint is met (see Fig. 11.5). The deviation measure is a function of the state of the system and the bodies the constraint acts on; i.e., it is a vec field

Figure 11.5: The "deviation measure" for a geometric constraint is a function D whose value is zero when the constraint is met. Here, we show a point-to-nail constraint, whose deviation is given by $^{\mathcal{L}ab}(X_p - X_0)$ for body point p constrained to a nail at X_0. □

$D \in \mathsf{SysVecFields}[n, k]$, as per Def. 11.16. We allow a deviation measure to be applied to any number of bodies, n, and have any fixed size k. In general D may have explicit dependence on time (such as for a point-to-path constraint), but in many cases D is purely geometric.

To express the requirement that a deviation measure equal zero, we use

(11.31)

*Given a deviation measure $D \in$ SysVecFields$[n, k]$, an
application set $s \in$ ApplicSets$[n]$, a system path
$\mathcal{Y} \in$ SysPaths, and a constant $\tau \in \Re$, we require*

$$\frac{d^2}{dt^2}D(\mathcal{Y}(t), t, s) + \frac{2}{\tau}\frac{d}{dt}D(\mathcal{Y}(t), t, s) + \frac{1}{\tau^2}D(\mathcal{Y}(t), t, s) = 0$$

Equation 11.31: Required behavior for the value of deviation measure D as a model moves over time. We have picked a second-order differential equation that describes critical damping: From any initial condition, the value decays smoothly down to zero, "assembling" the model.[6] The *time constant*, τ, controls the rate of assembly; τ must be positive. (See, e.g., [Boyce,DePrima77] for discussion of critically damped differential equations.) □

Equations other than Eq. 11.31 could perhaps be used to describe the constraint; we choose Eq. 11.31 because it describes "assembly" of a model from an initial condition in which the constraint isn't met, and also because it results in an expression for the constraint as an equation that is linear in the forces and torques on the bodies, and that is numerically tractable when we implement the model.

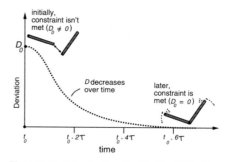

Figure 11.6: Behavior described by Eq. 11.31. □

To convert Eq. 11.31 into a form having explicit dependence on motives, we create auxiliary functions that describe the behavior of the deviation measure over time, for a dynamic system of bodies:

(11.32)

*Given a deviation measure $D \in$ SysVecFields$[n, k]$, an
application set $s \in$ ApplicSets$[n]$, and a
system path $\mathcal{Y} \in$ SysPaths consistent with
applied motive fields $\mathcal{A} \in$ {AppliedMotiveFields}$_{\text{IDs}}$,
we create auxiliary functions
$D^{(1)} \in$ SysVecFields$[n, k]$ and
$D^{(2)} \in$ ProtoConstrs$[n, k]$ such that:*

$$\begin{aligned}
D^{(1)}(\mathcal{Y}(t), t, s) &\equiv \frac{d}{dt}D(\mathcal{Y}(t), t, s) \\
D^{(2)}(\mathcal{Y}(t), t, s, \mathcal{A}(t)) &\equiv \frac{d^2}{dt^2}D(\mathcal{Y}(t), t, s)
\end{aligned}$$

Equation 11.32: Auxiliary deviation measure functions. $D^{(1)}$ yields the instantaneous rate of change of the deviation; $D^{(2)}$ yields the instantaneous acceleration. □

Notice in Eq. 11.32 that since D is geometric, it depends only on positions and

---

[6]Analytically, the value of D asymptotically approaches zero, but doesn't ever reach exactly zero. When implemented numerically, however, it soon reaches zero within error tolerances.

orientation information in $\mathcal{Y}(t)$. But $D^{(1)}$ will depend also on the velocities in $\mathcal{Y}(t)$ (Eq. 10.9), and $D^{(2)}$ will depend further on the net force and torque applied to each body (Def. 10.10), since $\mathcal{Y}$ is consistent with $\mathcal{A}$ (Def. 10.25). By the chain rule for differentiation, the dependency of $D^{(2)}$ on the net forces and torques is linear. Thus we can expand $D^{(2)}$:

(11.33)

> *Given $D^{(2)}$ of Eq. 11.32, we create auxiliary functions*
> $\Gamma, \Lambda \in \mathsf{SysMatidxBFields}[n, k, 3]$ *and*
> $\beta \in \mathsf{SysVecFields}[n, k]$ *such that, then for any*
> $Y \in \mathsf{Systems}, t \in \mathfrak{R}, s \in \mathsf{ApplicSets}[n],$ *and*
> $A \in \{\mathsf{AppliedMotives}\}_{\mathsf{IDs}},$

$$D^{(2)}(Y, t, s, A) = \beta(Y, t, s) + \sum_{r \in s} \Gamma(Y, t, s)_{b(r)} \mathit{Fnet}(A)_{b(r)}$$
$$+ \sum_{r \in s} \Lambda(Y, t, s)_{b(r)} \mathit{Tnet}(A)_{b(r)}$$

Equation 11.33: Auxiliary deviation measure functions. $D^{(2)}$, which describes the acceleration of the deviation measure, depends linearly on the net force and net torque on each body; Γ gives the coefficients for the forces, Λ gives the coefficients for the torques, and β gives the part of $D^{(2)}$ that is independent of the forces and torques. *Fnet* and *Tnet* are as per Def. 10.24. □

The auxiliary definitions of Eqs. 11.32 and 11.33 are in a form allowing us to define a specialization of linear constraint functions to express Eq. 11.31:

Definition. $\mathsf{GeomConstrs}[n, k]$

(11.34)

$\mathsf{GeomConstrs}[n, k] \sqsubset \mathsf{Lconstrs}[n, k]$
[
τ	$\mapsto \mathfrak{R}$	*time constant*
D	$\mapsto \mathsf{SysVecFields}[n, k]$	*deviation measure*
$D^{(1)}$	$\mapsto \mathsf{SysVecFields}[n, k]$	*rate of change*
β	$\mapsto \mathsf{SysVecFields}[n, k]$	*acceleration w/o forces*

—

$all = 1$
$\tau > 0$
$D, D^{(1)}, \beta, \Gamma,$ *and* Λ *relate by Eqs. 11.32, 11.33*
$K(Y, t, s) = \beta(Y, t, s) + \frac{2}{\tau} D^{(1)}(Y, t, s) + \frac{1}{\tau^2} D(Y, t, s)$
]

Definition 11.34: Constraint functions for geometric constraints, using the "dynamic constraints" method. For a constraint function $f \in \mathsf{GeomConstrs}[n, k]$, the constraint requirement $f(Y, t, s, A) = 0$ (Def. 11.13) is met when Eq. 11.31 holds. □

Now we can define various constraint functions that are elements of $\mathsf{GeomConstrs}[n, k]$; in each case, we define a family of functions that is parametrized by the time constant τ. We will define functions for the three body point constraints described in Section 11.2.3; functions for other objects can be defined analogously.

For a point-to-nail constraint:

Definition. Cptnail

(11.35)

> *Define the family of functions*
> $Cptnail[\tau, X_0] \in$ GeomConstrs$[1, 3]$ *for*
> $\tau \in \Re$ *and* $X_0 \in$ Locations *by:*
>
> $$\begin{aligned}
D_{cptnail}(Y, t, s) &= x(Y, s_0) - {}^{\mathcal{L}ab}X_0 \\
D^{(1)}_{cptnail}(Y, t, s) &= v(Y, s_0) \\
\beta_{cptnail}(Y, t, s) &= acc_0(Y, s_0) \\
\Gamma_{cptnail}(Y, t, s)_{b(s_0)} &= acc_F(Y, s_0) \\
\Lambda_{cptnail}(Y, t, s)_{b(s_0)} &= acc_T(Y, s_0)
\end{aligned}$$

Definition 11.35: Point-to-nail constraint function. The deviation measure is thus simply the difference between the point location and the nail location X_0. The rate of change and acceleration of the deviation are just those of the point (as per Not. 11.5). □

For a point-to-point constraint:

Definition. Cptpt

(11.36)

> *Define the family of functions*
> $Cptpt[\tau] \in$ GeomConstrs$[2, 3]$ *for* $\tau \in \Re$ *by:*
>
> $$\begin{aligned}
D_{cptpt}(Y, t, s) &= x(Y, s_0) - x(Y, s_1) \\
D^{(1)}_{cptpt}(Y, t, s) &= v(Y, s_0) - v(Y, s_1) \\
\beta_{cptpt}(Y, t, s) &= acc_0(Y, s_0) - acc_0(Y, s_1) \\
\Gamma_{cptpt}(Y, t, s)_{b(s_0)} &= acc_F(Y, s_0) \\
\Gamma_{cptpt}(Y, t, s)_{b(s_1)} &= -acc_F(Y, s_1) \\
\Lambda_{cptpt}(Y, t, s)_{b(s_0)} &= acc_T(Y, s_0) \\
\Lambda_{cptpt}(Y, t, s)_{b(s_1)} &= -acc_T(Y, s_1)
\end{aligned}$$

Definition 11.36: Point-to-point constraint function. The deviation measure is the difference between the locations of the two points of application. The remainder of the terms are analogous to Def. 11.35. Each body point's force- and torque-dependence for acceleration, acc_F and acc_T, result in a separate entry in Γ and Λ. □

For a point-to-path constraint:

Definition. $\mathcal{C}$*ptpath*

$$
\begin{array}{c}
\textit{Define the family of functions} \\
\mathcal{C}ptpath[\tau, P] \in \mathsf{GeomConstrs}[1, 3] \textit{ for} \\
\tau \in \Re \textit{ and path } P \colon \Re \to \mathsf{Locations} \textit{ by:}
\end{array}
$$

(11.37)

$$
\begin{aligned}
D_{\mathcal{C}ptpath}(Y, t, s) &= x(Y, s_0) - {}^{\mathcal{L}ab}P(t) \\
D^{(1)}_{\mathcal{C}ptnail}(Y, t, s) &= v(Y, s_0) - \tfrac{d}{dt}{}^{\mathcal{L}ab}P(t) \\
\beta_{\mathcal{C}ptnail}(Y, t, s) &= acc_0(Y, s_0) - \tfrac{d^2}{dt^2}{}^{\mathcal{L}ab}P(t) \\
\Gamma_{\mathcal{C}ptnail}(Y, t, s)_{b(s_0)} &= acc_F(Y, s_0) \\
\Lambda_{\mathcal{C}ptnail}(Y, t, s)_{b(s_0)} &= acc_T(Y, s_0)
\end{aligned}
$$

Definition 11.37: Point-to-path constraint function. A generalization of the point-to-nail constraint, Def. 11.35, but for a "moving nail." □

11.3.11 Proto-Specifiers

Given the definitions in the previous sections, all that remains in order to specify a force object is to match up a motive-generator function of Section 11.3.8 with a constraint function of Sections 11.3.9 or 11.3.10 to form a proto-specifier as per Defs. 11.8 and 11.19. We define proto-specifiers for the conceptual force objects described in Section 11.2:

Definition. (various proto-specifiers)

We define several families of proto-specifiers, all elements of $\mathsf{LprotoSpecs}$:

(11.38)

p	$[n_p,$	$pz_p,$	$cz_p,$	$Lgen_p$	$, Lconstr_p$	$]$
$Gravity[g]$	$=[1$	$, 3$	$, 3$	$, \mathcal{G}pure\mathcal{F}$	$, \mathcal{C}grav[g]$	$]$
$Damp[\mu_v, \mu_w, \nu_v, \nu_w]$	$=[1$	$, 6$	$, 6$	$, \mathcal{G}arbit$	$, \mathcal{C}damp[\mu_v, \mu_w, \nu_v, \nu_w]]$	$]$
$Spring[l_0, k, \mu]$	$=[2$	$, 1$	$, 3$	$, \mathcal{G}collinear,$	$\mathcal{C}spring[l_0, k, \mu]$	$]$
$Point\mathcal{T}o\mathcal{N}ail[\tau, X_0]$	$=[1$	$, 3$	$, 3$	$, \mathcal{G}coupled$	$, \mathcal{C}ptnail[\tau, X_0]$	$]$
$Point\mathcal{T}o Point[\tau]$	$=[2$	$, 3$	$, 3$	$, \mathcal{G}pair$	$, \mathcal{C}ptpt[\tau]$	$]$
$Point\mathcal{T}o Path[\tau, P]$	$=[1$	$, 3$	$, 3$	$, \mathcal{G}coupled$	$, \mathcal{C}ptpath[\tau, P]$	$]$

Definition 11.38: Various proto-specifiers. Each is defined by specifying its motive-generator function, *Lgen*, and constraint function, *Lconstr*. In most cases, the number of degrees of freedom (*pz*) is equal to the number of constraint terms (*cz*); see discussion in Section 11.4. □

Usually, a constraint function has a natural or intended motive-generator function that goes with it. For example, the point-to-point constraint function $\mathcal{C}ptpt$ is paired with the equal-and-opposite force pair motive generator $\mathcal{G}pair$ to form

PointToPoint. But we can also mix and match. For example, if we pair constraint *Cptpt* with generator *Gcoupled*—which applies a force to only one body—then we have a constraint in which a body "follows" or "shadows" another without affecting its motion.[7] Or, we could apply a pure force to meet a point-to-path constraint, thus the body will translate but not rotate in order to follow the path.

11.4   Posed Problems

We have one prominent posed problem for this model: to create the forces and torques that are described by a given set of linear proto-specifiers, i.e., that are due to the motive-generator functions and that satisfy the constraint functions. That is, as discussed in Section 11.3.1,

(11.39)

$$
\begin{aligned}
\textit{Given:} \quad & \mathcal{P} \in \{\mathsf{LprotoSpecs}\}_{|\mathsf{IDs}}, \textit{ compatible with} \\
& \mathcal{S} \in \{\mathsf{ApplicSets}\}_{|\mathsf{IDs}}, \\
\textit{define:} \quad & \mathcal{A} \in \{\mathsf{AppliedMotiveFields}\}_{|\mathsf{IDs}} \\
& \textit{where } \mathcal{A} \textit{ is consistent with } \mathcal{P} \textit{ and } \mathcal{S} \\
\textit{evaluate:} \quad & \mathcal{A}(Y,t) \\
& \textit{for any } Y \in \mathsf{Systems} \textit{ and } t \in \Re
\end{aligned}
$$

Equation 11.39: Motive evaluation. The indexes $\mathcal{P}$ and $\mathcal{S}$ describe the force objects in the model and how they are applied to the bodies. They determine a motive field index $\mathcal{A}$ (Def. 11.13). During the course of a simulation, we will want to evaluate $\mathcal{A}$ for many different values of Y and t. □

Because we are using linear proto-specifiers, to evaluate $\mathcal{A}(Y,t)$ as per Def. 11.13 we use Eq. 11.21, which we paraphrase:

$$
\begin{aligned}
\forall p, \quad & K_p(Y,t,p) + \sum_q \mathcal{M}_{pq}(Y,t)\, \mathcal{X}_q = 0 \\
\textit{where} \quad & \mathcal{M}_{pq} \in \mathsf{Mats}[cz_p, pz_q] \\
& K_p \in \mathsf{Vecs}[cz_p] \\
& \mathcal{X}_q \in \mathsf{Vecs}[pz_q].
\end{aligned}
$$

We can express the above in matrix form, if we arbitrarily assign an order to the elements of the proto-motive ensemble:

$$
\begin{bmatrix}
\mathcal{M}_{11}(Y,t) & \mathcal{M}_{12}(Y,t) & \cdots & \mathcal{M}_{1n}(Y,t) \\
\mathcal{M}_{21}(Y,t) & \mathcal{M}_{22}(Y,t) & \cdots & \mathcal{M}_{2n}(Y,t) \\
& & \vdots & \\
\mathcal{M}_{n1}(Y,t) & \mathcal{M}_{n2}(Y,t) & \cdots & \mathcal{M}_{nn}(Y,t)
\end{bmatrix}
\begin{bmatrix}
\mathcal{X}_1 \\ \mathcal{X}_2 \\ \vdots \\ \mathcal{X}_n
\end{bmatrix}
+
\begin{bmatrix}
K_1(Y,t,p_1) \\ K_2(Y,t,p_2) \\ \vdots \\ K_n(Y,t,p_n)
\end{bmatrix}
= 0
$$

---

[7] Strictly speaking, since *Gcoupled*(Y,t,s,X) requires an application set $s \in$ ApplicSets[1] while *Cptpt*(Y,t,s,A) requires an application set in $s \in$ ApplicSets[2], they can't be used together, as per Def. 11.19. However, we can trivially extend *Gcoupled* to act on elements $s \in$ ApplicSets[2] by ignoring s_1.

Each element in the above is an array; we can consider the above to be a block matrix form[8] of a $\left(\sum_p cz_p \right) \times \left(\sum_q pz_q \right)$ matrix equation:

$$\mathbf{M}(Y, t)\, \mathbf{X} + \mathbf{K}(Y, t) = 0.$$

For any Y and t, we can compute $\mathbf{M}(Y, t)$ and $\mathbf{K}(Y, t)$ and then solve for $\mathbf{X}$ using one of many standard numerical techniques (see [Press *et al.*86]). We note some characteristics of $\mathbf{M}$ that can be taken into account:

- $\mathbf{M}$ is generally sparse.
- $\mathbf{M}$ is not necessarily square; a proto-specifier p may have $pz_p \neq cz_p$. If there are fewer degrees of freedom than constraints ($pz_p < cz_p$), there won't in general be a solution unless the constraints are redundant (as is true for the proto-specifier *Spring*).
- The explicit force objects ($all_p = 0$) have only diagonal entries; the corresponding values $\mathcal{X}_p$ can be found first, and the remaining matrix can be reduced.[9]
- $\mathbf{M}$ can often be partitioned into independent blocks, which can be solved separately; each block corresponds with a group of bodies that may be constrained with respect to each other, but there are no constraints between the blocks.
- The structure of $\mathbf{M}$ is due to the indexes $\mathcal{P}$ and $\mathcal{S}$ and is independent of Y and t. Thus the partitioning and so forth can be performed once per collection of force objects and then used for each evaluation of $\mathcal{A}(Y, t)$. Furthermore, many of the functions Γ, Λ, G, and H defined in Sections 11.3.8–11.3.10 are constants, which can be folded once per collection of force objects, to minimize repeated computation.
- $\mathbf{M}$ may be singular or ill-conditioned, implying the lack of a unique solution. If there are multiple solutions, any solution is acceptable; this may occur through extraneous degrees of freedom in the proto-specifiers, through redundancies in the constraints specified in the model, or through the existence of equipollent sets of forces that meet the constraints. If there are no solutions, it can indicate improperly constructed proto-specifiers (e.g., an orientation-based constraint function paired with a pure force motive-generator function) or an overconstrained system as discussed in Section 11.2.3. Additionally, if using the constraints to "assemble" models as discussed in Section 11.3.10, the path implied by Eq. 11.31 may be physically unrealizable; see discussion in [Barzel,Barr88]. A least-squares solution is often practicable.

---

[8] We refer readers to [Horn,Johnson85] and [Golub,Van Loan85] for discussion of matrices.

[9] In [Barzel,Barr88], the explicit forces are treated as a special case a priori and are not entered into the matrix. Here, we prefer a more uniform mathematical treatment and leave it to the implementation to special-case the computation of the diagonal entries.

Once we've computed **X**, and hence the proto-motives, $\mathcal{X}$, we can determine the actual motives, i.e., the forces and torques, by evaluating all the motive-generator functions, as per Eq. 11.14:

$$\mathcal{A}(Y, t) = \bigcup_{s \in \mathcal{S}} Gen_s(Y, t, s, \mathcal{X}_s).$$

The generator functions are evaluated by multiplying each $\mathcal{X}_s$ by the values of $G_s(Y, t, s)$ and $H_s(Y, t, s)$, as per Def. 11.17; these values were already computed to construct **M**, and can be reused.

11.5 Implementation Notes[†]

11.5.1 Conceptual Section Constructs

The conceptual section of a program supports various types of force objects. Each instance of a force object includes the name(s) of the body (bodies) that it acts on and the body points of application, along with the time constant τ for geometric constraints and other type-specific parameters.

Each type of force object knows how to draw itself, for illustration or debugging, e.g., a helix between points attached by a spring, or the curve of a point-to-path constraint.

Paths for point-to-path constraints can be defined symbolically or via a curve editor, as described in [Snyder92].

11.5.2 Math Section Constructs

The math section for this module has scope name MFRC ("Math fancy FoRCes"). Figure 11.7 lists the objects that are defined. Classes for the various state spaces, sets, and indexes are defined as per Section B.3. We give a few additional notes.

- Class definitions for ProtoGens$[n, k]$ and Lgens$[n, k]$:

```
class ProtoGen :
   constructors:  (int n,k)
   members:       n : int
                  k : int
   methods:       eval(MRIG::System Y, double t, ApplicSet S, MMISC::Vec x)
                       : MRIG::ApplMotiveIdx
```

[†]See Appendix B for discussion of the terminology, notation, and overall approach used here.

Program Definitions in Scope MFRC:		
class name	*abstract space*	
ApplicInfo	ApplicInfos	*(Def. 11.1)*
ApplicSet	ApplicSets	*(Def. 11.2)*
ApplicSetIdx	{ApplicSets}$_{\text{IDs}}$	*index of application sets*
GeomConstr	GeomConstrs	*(Def. 11.34)*
Lconstr	Lconstrs	*(Def. 11.18)*
Lgen	Lgens	*(Def. 11.17)*
LprotoSpec	LprotoSpecs	*(Def. 11.19)*
LprotoSpecIdx	{LprotoSpecs}$_{\text{IDs}}$	*index of linear proto-specs*
ProtoConstr	ProtoConstrs	*(Def. 11.7)*
ProtoGen	ProtoGens	*(Def. 11.6)*
ProtoSpec	ProtoSpecs	*(Def. 11.8)*
SysMatIdxAField	SysMatidxAFields	*(Def. 11.16)*
SysMatIdxBField	SysMatidxBFields	*(Def. 11.16)*
SysMatIdxField	SysMatidxFields	*(Def. 11.16)*
SysVecField	SysVecFields	*(Def. 11.16)*
global constant	*function*	
Garbit	$\mathcal{G}$arbit	*(Def. 11.25)*
Gcollinear	$\mathcal{G}$collinear	*(Def. 11.27)*
Gcoupled	$\mathcal{G}$coupled	*(Def. 11.24)*
Gpair	$\mathcal{G}$pair	*(Def. 11.26)*
GpureF	$\mathcal{G}$pure$\mathcal{F}$	*(Def. 11.22)*
GpureT	$\mathcal{G}$pure$\mathcal{T}$	*(Def. 11.23)*
class name	*function family*	
Cdamp	$\mathcal{C}$damp	*(Def. 11.29)*
Cgrav	$\mathcal{C}$grav	*(Def. 11.28)*
Cptnail	$\mathcal{C}$ptnail	*(Def. 11.35)*
Cptpath	$\mathcal{C}$ptpath	*(Def. 11.37)*
Cptpt	$\mathcal{C}$ptpt	*(Def. 11.36)*
Cspring	$\mathcal{C}$spring	*(Def. 11.30)*
Damp	$\mathcal{D}$amp	*(Def. 11.38)*
Gravity	$\mathcal{G}$ravity	*(Def. 11.38)*
PointToNail	$\mathcal{P}$oint$\mathcal{T}o\mathcal{N}$ail	*(Def. 11.38)*
PointToPath	$\mathcal{P}$oint$\mathcal{T}o\mathcal{P}$ath	*(Def. 11.38)*
PointToPoint	$\mathcal{P}$oint$\mathcal{T}o\mathcal{P}$oint	*(Def. 11.38)*
Spring	$\mathcal{S}$pring	*(Def. 11.38)*

Figure 11.7: Math section definitions in the prototype implementation. □

class Lgen *(derived from* ProtoGen*) :*
* constructors:* (int n,k, SysMatIdxField G,H,J)
* members:*   G : SysMatIdxAField
                H : SysMatIdxAField
                J : SysMatIdxAField
* methods:*   eval(MRIG::System Y, double t, ApplicSet S, MMISC::Vec x)
                  : MRIG::ApplMotiveIdx

The class `ProtoGen` is an abstract class that declares a generic `eval` method. The class `Lgen` is derived from `ProtoGen`; it has members for the G, H and J fields and defines `eval` to compute an applied motive index, as per Def. 11.17. The classes `ProtoConstr` and `Lconstr` are defined similarly. These classes all include checks to make sure that n and k are used consistently.

• Constant instances for motive-generator functions: In Section 11.3.8, we defined several specific motive-generator functions, *Garbit*, *Gpair*, and so forth. For each of these functions, we define an instance of class Lgen, with the appropriate values for members G, H, and J. Each instance is defined once, as a global constant, to be used or referenced by any proto-specifier. For example:

```
GpureF = Lgen(n=1, k=3, G=1, H=0, J=0)
```

• Class definitions for explicit constraint functions: In Section 11.3.9, we defined several parametrized families of constraint functions. For each family, we derive a class from `Lconstr`. For example:

> class Cspring *(derived from* Lconstr*)* :
>   *constructors:*   (double l0,k,mu)
>   *members:*   l0 : double   *rest length*
>   k : double   *spring constant*
>   mu : double   *damping coefficient*

The members for Γ, Λ, and K compute their values based on the member variables l_0, k and μ, as per Def. 11.30; for any given triple of parameters, l_0, k, and μ, a specific instance can be created.

• Class definitions for geometric constraint functions (Section 11.3.10): We define a class derived from *Lconstr*.

> class GeomConstr *(derived from* Lconstr*)* :
>   *constructors:*   (int n,k, double tau, SysVecField D,D1,B, SysMatIdxField Ga,La)
>   *members:*   tau : double   *time constant* τ
>   D   : SysVecField
>   D1   : SysVecField
>   Beta : SysVecField

It defines the member for K to compute its value as per Def. 11.34. We derive more specific classes for the various types of constraints. For example:

```
class PointToPoint (derived from GeomConstr) :
  constructors:  (double tau)
```

```
class PointToNail (derived from GeomConstr) :
  constructors:  (double tau, MCO::Location XO)
  members:       XO : MCO::Location
```

For any given time constant τ, along with constraint-specific parameters (such as X_0 above), an instance of a geometric constraint function can be created.

11.5.3 M–N Interface

The scope name for the M–N interface is NFRC. We define a routine that solves the posed problem (Eq. 11.39): Define an applied motive index field that is consistent with given proto-specifier and application set indexes.

```
LsolveProto(LprotoSpecIdx P, ApplicSetIdx S) : MRIG::ApplMotiveIdxField
```

This routine returns an object that can be evaluated for arbitrary values of Y and t. The object is set up internally to follow the solution procedure outlined in Section 11.4:

1. Given values of Y and t,
2. Compute the various terms K, Γ, G, etc.
3. Compute the $\mathcal{M}_{pq}$ matrices.
4. Gather the $\mathcal{M}_{pq}$ and K_p values into **M** and **K**, using NUM::GatScat2 (Section B.4.2).
5. Solve the equation $\mathbf{M\,X} + \mathbf{K} = 0$ to get **X**, using NUM::LinSys (Section B.4.3).
6. Scatter **X** into $\mathcal{X}_q$ values, using NUM::GatScat2.
7. Compute an index of motives A, based on the $\mathcal{X}_q$ values and the precomputed G, H, and J.
8. Return A.

As an optimization, at the time the object is created we partition the matrix into independent blocks, based on the connectivity information in S; then the single large linear system solution becomes a series of smaller ones.

11.5.4　C–M Interface

The C–M interface constructs two indexes $\mathcal{P} \in \{\mathsf{LprotoSpecs}\}_{\mathsf{IDs}}$ and $\mathcal{S} \in \{\mathsf{ApplicSets}\}_{\mathsf{IDs}}$ based on the conceptual force objects. For each force object, the interface must

- Choose a label $i \in \mathsf{IDs}$ for the force object.

- Choose or create the appropriate motive-generator and constraint function instances for P_i.

- Create an application set $s = S_i$. For each $r \in s$, we must

  - Map from each conceptual body name to its mathematical model ID, for $b(r)$.

  - Create a (arbitrary) unique ID for $a(r)$.

  - Set $pt(r)$ to the body coordinates of the application point.

Having done the above, the C–M interface can call `NFRC::LsolveProto` to get an `MRIG::ApplMotiveIdxField`, which can be used as a parameter to `NRIG::SolveForward` of Section 10.5.3, in order to simulate the resulting behavior.

11.6　Derivations

11.6.1　Acceleration of a Body Point

We derive an expression for the acceleration of a body point, for use in Not. 11.5. Given

dynamic body path	$s \in \mathsf{StatePaths}$	*consistent (Def. 10.10) with*
net force, torque functions	$F, T \colon \Re \to \mathsf{Vectors},$	*and*
body point path	$p \colon \Re \to \mathsf{Bodypts}$	*such that*
	$p(t) \equiv Bodypt(s(t), coords)$	
for constant	$coords \in \Re^{3 \times 3}$	

First, we express the derivative of the body's inverse inertia tensor. Since the inertia tensor is fixed in the body frame (Eq. 10.8), Eq. 8.33 gives (after replacing ω^{*T} with the equivalent $-\omega^*$):

$$\frac{d}{dt}\mathbf{I}_s^{-1}(t) = \omega_s^*(t)\mathbf{I}_s^{-1}(t) - \mathbf{I}_s^{-1}(t)\omega_s^*(t)$$

Using the above, we express the derivatives of the body's angular velocity vector (for clarity, we drop the (t) parameters after the first occurrence):

$$\begin{aligned}
\omega_s(t) &= \mathbf{I}_s^{-1}(t)\,L_s(t) \\
\frac{d}{dt}\omega_s &= \left(\frac{d}{dt}\mathbf{I}_s^{-1}\right)L_s + \mathbf{I}_s^{-1}\left(\frac{d}{dt}L_s\right) \\
&= \left(\omega_s^*\mathbf{I}_s^{-1} - \mathbf{I}_s^{-1}\omega_s^*\right)L_s + \mathbf{I}_s^{-1}T(t) \\
&= \omega_s^*\mathbf{I}_s^{-1}L_s - \mathbf{I}_s^{-1}\omega_s^*L_s + \mathbf{I}_s^{-1}T \\
&= \omega_s^*\omega_s - \mathbf{I}_s^{-1}(\omega_s \times L_s) + \mathbf{I}_s^{-1}T \\
&= -\mathbf{I}_s^{-1}(\omega_s \times L_s) + \mathbf{I}_s^{-1}T
\end{aligned}$$

We start with the velocity of a body point, from Eq. 10.13, and differentiate to get the acceleration (again, we drop the (t) parameters):

$$\begin{aligned}
v_p(t) &= vc_s(t) + \omega_s(t) \times arm_p(t) \\
\frac{d}{dt}v_p &= \frac{d}{dt}vc_s + \left(\frac{d}{dt}\omega_s\right) \times arm_p + \omega_s \times \left(\frac{d}{dt}arm_p\right) \\
&= \frac{d}{dt}vc_s - arm_p \times \left(\frac{d}{dt}\omega_s\right) + \omega_s \times \left(\frac{d}{dt}arm_p\right) \\
&= \frac{1}{m_s}F(t) - arm_p^*\left(-\mathbf{I}_s^{-1}(\omega_s \times L_s) + \mathbf{I}_s^{-1}T\right) + \omega_s \times (\omega_s \times arm_p) \\
&= \frac{1}{m_s}F - arm_p^*\mathbf{I}_s^{-1}T + arm_p^*\mathbf{I}_s^{-1}(\omega_s \times L_s) + \omega_s \times (\omega_s \times arm_p)
\end{aligned}$$

The first term above gives acc_F in Not. 11.5, the second term gives acc_T, and the remaining terms give acc_O.

11.6.2   Derivation of the Linear Constraint Equation

We derive Eq. 11.21. Given

$$
\begin{array}{c}
compatible \\
\mathcal{P} \in \{\text{LprotoSpecs}\}_{\text{IDs}} \\
A \in \{\text{AppliedMotives}\}_{\text{IDs}} \\
\mathcal{S} \in \{\text{ApplicSets}\}_{\text{IDs}} \\
\mathcal{X} \in \{\text{Vecs}\}_{\text{IDs}} \\
consistent\ with \\
Y \in \text{Systems} \\
t \in \Re
\end{array}
$$

We plug into the constraint equation, Def. 11.13. For notational clarity, after the first occurrence we leave the (Y, t, p) parameters off K, Γ, Λ, and the (Y, t, q) off G, and H.

$$
0 = Constr_p(Y, t, p, A) \qquad \text{(Def. 11.13)}
$$

If $all_p = 1$, we have

$$
0 = K_p(Y, t, p) + \sum_{j \in Ids(A)} \left(\begin{array}{c} \Gamma_p(Y, t, p)_{body(A_j)} \overset{cab}{} F(A_j) + \\ \Lambda_p(Y, t, p)_{body(A_j)} \overset{cab}{} T(A_j) \end{array} \right) \qquad \text{(Def. 11.18)}
$$

$$
= K_p + \sum_{q \in Elts(\mathcal{S})} \sum_{r \in q} \left(\begin{array}{c} \Gamma_p(Y, t, p)_{b(r)} \overset{cab}{} F(A_{a(r)}) + \\ \Lambda_p(Y, t, p)_{b(r)} \overset{cab}{} T(A_{a(r)}) \end{array} \right) \qquad \text{(Def. 11.11)}
$$

$$
= K_p + \sum_{q \in Elts(\mathcal{S})} \sum_{r \in q} \left(\begin{array}{c} [\Gamma_p]_{b(r)} \overset{cab}{} F(Gen_q(Y, t, q, \mathcal{X}_q)_{a(r)}) + \\ [\Lambda_p]_{b(r)} \overset{cab}{} T(Gen_q(Y, t, q, \mathcal{X}_q)_{a(r)}) \end{array} \right) \qquad \text{(Eq. 11.14)}
$$

$$
= K_p + \sum_{q \in Elts(\mathcal{S})} \sum_{r \in q} \left(\begin{array}{c} [\Gamma_p]_{b(r)} G_q(Y, t, q)_{a(r)} \mathcal{X}_q + \\ [\Lambda_p]_{b(r)} H_q(Y, t, q)_{a(r)} \mathcal{X}_q \end{array} \right) \qquad \text{(Def. 11.17)}
$$

$$
= K_p + \sum_{q \in Elts(\mathcal{S})} \left(\sum_{r \in q} ([\Gamma_p]_{b(r)} [G_q]_{a(r)} + [\Lambda_p]_{b(r)} [H_q]_{a(r)}) \right) \mathcal{X}_q
$$

And if $all_p = 0$, we have

$$0 = K_p(Y, t, p) + \sum_{r \in p} \left(\begin{matrix} \Gamma_p(Y, t, p)_{b(r)} \overset{\mathcal{L}ab}{F}(A_{a(r)}) + \\ \Lambda_p(Y, t, p)_{b(r)} \overset{\mathcal{L}ab}{T}(A_{a(r)}) \end{matrix} \right) \qquad \text{(Def. 11.18)}$$

$$= K_p + \sum_{r \in p} \left(\begin{matrix} \Gamma_p(Y, t, p)_{b(r)} \overset{\mathcal{L}ab}{F}(Gen_s(Y, t, p, \mathcal{X}_p)_{a(r)}) + \\ \Lambda_p(Y, t, p)_{b(r)} \overset{\mathcal{L}ab}{T}(Gen_q(Y, t, p, \mathcal{X}_p)_{a(r)}) \end{matrix} \right) \qquad \text{(Eq. 11.14)}$$

$$= K_p + \sum_{r \in p} \left(\begin{matrix} [\Gamma_p]_{b(r)} G_p(Y, t, r)_{a(r)} \mathcal{X}_p + \\ [\Lambda_p]_{b(r)} H_p(Y, t, r)_{a(r)} \mathcal{X}_p \end{matrix} \right) \qquad \text{(Def. 11.17)}$$

$$= K_p + \sum_{r \in p} \left([\Gamma_p]_{b(r)} [G_p]_{a(r)} + [\Lambda_p]_{b(r)} [H_p]_{a(r)} \right) \mathcal{X}_p$$

$$= K_p + \sum_{q \in Elts(\mathcal{S})} \left(\delta_{p=q} \sum_{r \in q} [\Gamma_p]_{b(r)} [G_q]_{a(r)} + [\Lambda_p]_{b(r)} [H_q]_{a(r)} \right) \mathcal{X}_q$$

This leads directly to Eq. 11.21.

Chapter 12

Swinging Chain Model

This chapter describes a "swinging chain" model: a collection of cylinders linked end-to-end to form a chain. The two ends of the chain are fixed·in space, and the chain dangles between them.

This model demonstrates how we define a top-level physically-based model, illustrating the use of the library of modules defined in Chs. 8–11. In particular, the model makes use of the geometric constraints supported by the "fancy forces" mechanism of Ch. 11.

The functionality for this model is directly supported by the library routines, thus there's little that needs to be defined in this chapter—just a description of the conceptual model, in terms of the conceptual models of Chs. 8–11. However, we illustrate some aspects of the resulting mathematical model.

Swinging Chain Model

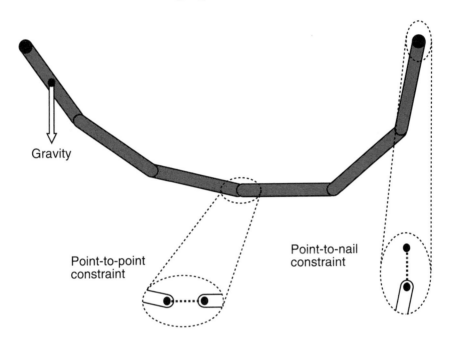

Gravity

Point-to-point
constraint

Point-to-nail
constraint

Figure 12.1: Elements in the "swinging chain" sample model. The chain is formed from a collection of cylindrical links. Each link is acted on by a constant downward gravity force and by a viscous damping force/torque (not illustrated). Each adjacent pair of links is connected with a "point-to-point" constraint, and each end link has its endpoints fixed in space with a "point-to-nail" constraint. After an initial excitation, the chain will swing freely, gradually losing energy due to the damping, until it comes to rest in a catenary shape hanging between the fixed points. □

12.1 Goals

The purpose of this model is to demonstrate how we define a top-level model, and to test the prototype modeling library. In particular, we

- Test and illustrate rigid-body dynamics (Ch. 10)

- Test and illustrate constraints and other "fancy forces" (Ch. 11)

12.2 Conceptual Model

This model has only one high-level conceptual object in it: a linked chain. We fix
the two endpoints in space and let the chain dangle and swing under the influence
of gravity, with some damping so that the chain will come to rest in a catenary
shape (see Fig. 12.1). The chain is made from a collection of six separate links,
each of which is a rigid body as per Ch. 10.

Links. Each link is a cylinder
of length 20 centimeters and radius
2 centimeters with spherical endcaps. The body frame has its origin at the base of the cylinder, and
the cylinder extends along the positive z-axis (see Fig. 12.2). The
mass of the cylinder is 0.5 kilogram,
distributed homogeneously (except
in the endcaps), giving an iner-

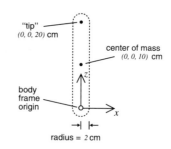

tia tensor of $\begin{bmatrix} 17.2 & 0 & 0 \\ 0 & 17.2 & 0 \\ 0 & 0 & 1 \end{bmatrix}$ kilogram-

Figure 12.2: Detail of a link, in body coordinates
(y-axis goes into the page). □

centimeter^2 in body coordinates,[1]
with the center of mass at $z = 10$ centimeters.

Joints. The joints between each
link are formed using point-to-point
constraints (Section 11.2.3).   We
connect the tip of one link to the origin of the adjacent link. Notice that
the bodies interpenetrate in order to
meet the constraint—but because of
the spherical endcaps, no seams are
formed at the joints (see Fig. 12.3).

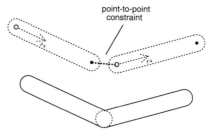

Figure 12.3: Detail of a joint between links. □

Ends. The tip of the "topmost" and origin of the "bottommost" link are held
fixed at locations $(50, 0, 110)$ centimeters and $(-50, 0, 110)$ centimeters in lab
coordinates, via point-to-nail constraints.

---

[1] From Eq. 10.1 we can derive the formula for the inertia tensor of a homogeneous cylinder aligned
with the z axis, having mass m, radius r and length l (or we can just look it up in [Fox67, Table II]):
$$\begin{bmatrix} \frac{1}{12}m(3r^2+l^2) & 0 & 0 \\ 0 & \frac{1}{12}m(3r^2+l^2) & 0 \\ 0 & 0 & \frac{1}{2}mr^2 \end{bmatrix}$$

Other forces. Each body feels a downward gravitational acceleration of 9.8 meters/second^2. We apply a viscous damping force (Section 11.2.2) of 0.1 dyne/(centimeter/second) and torque of 0.1 cendimeter-dyne/(radian/second) to each body.

Initial assembly. We initially place the bodies in an arbitrary configuration, and let the constraint forces assemble the chain and pull it into place. A value of 0.2 seconds for the time constant τ for the constraints (see Section 11.3.10) causes the model to assemble in roughly one second. In their "rush" to assemble, the bodies pick up a fair amount of kinetic energy from the action of the constraint forces. In some circumstances that energy might be an unwanted by-product, but for this model, it serves to start the chain off jangling.

12.3   Mathematical Model

No new mathematical definitions are required for this model, but we illustrate the "proto-specifier ensemble" (Def. 11.11) that describes the various forces. (We are essentially hand-simulating some of the function of the C–M interface of the fancy forces implementation, Section 11.5.4.)

First, we assign IDs to the bodies in the model: Let

$$cyl0,\ cyl1,\ cyl2,\ cyl3,\ cyl4,\ cyl5 \in \mathsf{IDs}$$

correspond with the cylinders in left-to-right order as in Fig. 12.1.

The application of the force objects to the model is described by an index of proto-specifiers and an index of application sets:

$$\mathcal{P} \in \{\mathsf{ProtoSpecs}\}_{\mathsf{IDs}} \quad \textit{(Def. 11.8)}$$
$$\mathcal{S} \in \{\mathsf{ApplicSets}\}_{\mathsf{IDs}} \quad \textit{(Def. 11.2)}$$

We construct the entries in these indexes according to the following table (recall that the two indexes share the same IDs, Def. 11.9):

$i \in$ IDs	$\mathcal{P}_i$			$\mathcal{S}_i$		
	[Constr,	Gen	]	[a ,	b ,	arm]
joint01	[Cptpt ,	Gpair	]	[jnt01a, cyl0, (0, 0, 20)]		
				[jnt01b, cyl1, (0, 0, 0)]		
joint12	[Cptpt ,	Gpair	]	[jnt12a, cyl1, (0, 0, 20)]		
				[jnt12b, cyl2, (0, 0, 0)]		
joint23	[Cptpt ,	Gpair	]	[jnt23a, cyl2, (0, 0, 20)]		
				[jnt23b, cyl3, (0, 0, 0)]		
joint34	[Cptpt ,	Gpair	]	[jnt34a, cyl3, (0, 0, 20)]		
				[jnt34b, cyl4, (0, 0, 0)]		
joint45	[Cptpt ,	Gpair	]	[jnt45a, cyl4, (0, 0, 20)]		
				[jnt45b, cyl5, (0, 0, 0)]		
end0	[Cptnail ,	Gcoupled]		[end0 , cyl0, (0, 0, 0)]		
end5	[Cptnail ,	Gcoupled]		[end5 , cyl5, (0, 0, 20)]		
grav0	[Cgrav ,	Gcoupled]		[grav0 , cyl0, (0, 0, 10)]		
grav1	[Cgrav ,	Gcoupled]		[grav1 , cyl1, (0, 0, 10)]		
grav2	[Cgrav ,	Gcoupled]		[grav2 , cyl2, (0, 0, 10)]		
grav3	[Cgrav ,	Gcoupled]		[grav3 , cyl3, (0, 0, 10)]		
grav4	[Cgrav ,	Gcoupled]		[grav4 , cyl4, (0, 0, 10)]		
grav5	[Cgrav ,	Gcoupled]		[grav5 , cyl5, (0, 0, 10)]		
damp0	[Cdamp ,	Garbit	]	[damp0, cyl0,		]
damp1	[Cdamp ,	Garbit	]	[damp1, cyl1,		]
damp2	[Cdamp ,	Garbit	]	[damp2, cyl2,		]
damp3	[Cdamp ,	Garbit	]	[damp3, cyl3,		]
damp4	[Cdamp ,	Garbit	]	[damp4, cyl4,		]
damp5	[Cdamp ,	Garbit	]	[damp5, cyl5,		]

A few things to notice in the above table:

- Each joint acts on two bodies, thus has two application infos in its application set.

- Each damping object generates an arbitrary force/torque; its generator function doesn't examine the arm aspect value of the application set, so we have left that entry blank.

- The a column lists the IDs of all the motives in the model. Some of these IDs happen to be the same as used in column i, but that's irrelevant.

Chapter 13

"Tennis Ball Cannon"

This chapter describes a "tennis ball cannon" model: A series of balls is shot from a gun; each ball flies in an arc, and bounces when it hits the ground. The model contains discontinuous behaviors—the firing of the gun, the bouncing of the balls, and others.

This model illustrates the *segmented function* formulation: We define the behavior of the model as a function C that encapsulates the discontinuous events; the value of the solution, $C(t)$, includes information such as which balls are part of the model at any time t.

Unlike the "swinging chain" (Ch. 12), this model isn't already directly supported by the library modules in Chs. 8–11. Thus, we build on the library models, but we define extra special-purpose mathematical constructs for this application. (Some of the special-purpose mechanisms that are defined here can be generalized, as discussed in the library extensions, Ch. 14.)

Tennis Ball Cannon
(Sample segmented model)

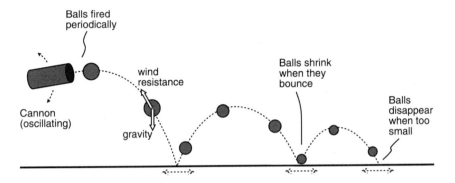

Figure 13.1: Model of a cannon firing a series of balls; illustrates discontinuities in a model. The cannon oscillates up and down, firing a stream of balls. Each ball experiences gravity, and wind resistance based on radius. When a ball hits the ground, it bounces, but also instantaneously shrinks by a fixed factor (thus will experience less wind resistance after the bounce). When a ball shrinks below a minimum size, it is removed from the model. The contact points where the balls bounce shift back and forth due to the oscillation of the cannon. The bounces are completely elastic, but because of the wind resistance energy is lost, so each rebound is lower than the previous. □

13.1   Goals

The purpose of this model is to illustrate the segmented function mechanism described in Section 5.10 and to test the piecewise-continuous ODE solution utilities described in Section B.4.7. In order to fully exercise these tools, we include a few somewhat contrived features in the model (see Fig. 13.1):

- discontinuities regularly in time (cannon fires)
- discontinuities based on state (balls bounce)
- increase of dimensionality (balls created when cannon fires)
- decrease in dimensionality (balls removed when too small)
- change in properties (ball radius changes)
- change in continuous behavior (wind resistance changes)
- discontinuities in motion (balls bounce)

13.2   Conceptual Model

We describe the abstractions of the various elements in the model. Note that we are not trying to accurately model a real thing, but rather have contrived an assortment of features to meet our goals.

Environment. In lab coordinates (Section 8.3), the positive z axis points "up." The ground is an infinite flat surface in the x–y plane at $z = 0$.

Cannon. The cannon is just a barrel: a cylinder, with length 0.8 meters and radius 0.22 meters. The back end is fixed at coordinates $(-5, 0, 5)$ meters in the world; the muzzle points toward the positive x direction, but oscillating ± 0.4 radians from horizontal, with a period of 2 seconds per cycle. (In the body frame, the back end is at the origin, and the muzzle lies on the x-axis.)

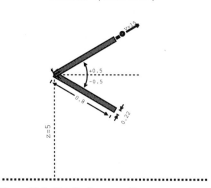

Cannon (not to scale)

Figure 13.2: Detail of cannon. □

Firing. To "fire," the cannon spontaneously creates a ball at the muzzle; the ball has an initial velocity of 15 meters/second outward in the barrel direction. (We create the ball at the muzzle, so it doesn't need to travel down the barrel.) The cannon has an unlimited supply of balls, and fires with a period of 0.2 seconds between shots.

Balls. Each ball is a rigid sphere, with radius 0.2 meters (initially) and mass 1 kilogram.[1] We include no rotation effects—the motion of the ball is that of a point mass (Section 10.2.3) at the center of the sphere.

Bouncing. When a ball hits the ground ($z = 0$), it instantaneously shrinks—the new radius is three-quarters size of the previous. The location of the center of the ball is instantaneously dropped so that the bottom stays on the ground (see Fig. 13.3). The velocity is instantaneously negated in the z direction, but left alone in the x and y directions,[2] i.e., the ball bounces elastically. The mass is not altered.

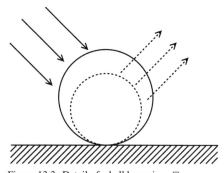

Bounce of a Ball

Figure 13.3: Detail of a ball bouncing. □

Disappearing. If, when hitting the ground, the ball shrinks so that its radius is less than 0.09 meters, the ball is "too small" and is instantaneously removed from the model.[3] With the stated parameters, this happens on the third contact, after two bounces.

---

[1] Perhaps more a bocce ball than a tennis ball!

[2] Actually, because of the configuration of the gun and lack of crosswise forces, the velocity in the y direction is always 0.

[3] Think of it as falling through cracks in the floor?

Forces. Each ball is acted on by two forces: a constant downward gravitational acceleration of 9.8 meters/second^2; and a air resistance (drag) force that is opposite to and quadratic in the velocity, scaled by 0.5 kilogram/meter^3 times the cross sectional area ($\pi\, r^2$). For simplicity, we directly hardwire the net force on each ball to be the sum of the two contributions, rather than using the "fancy forces" mechanism of Ch. 11.

13.3   Mathematical Model

13.3.1   Names and Notation

The scope name for this model is.

TSEG.   ("Test of a SEGmented model")

We use the following terms from other modules:

AppliedMotiveFields	(Def. 10.21)	*Rep*	(Def. 8.5)
IDs	(Def. 5.8)	*Repq*	(Def. 8.8)
IDsets	(Def. 5.9)	RIGID :: States	(Def. 10.4)
FramePaths	(Def. 8.27)	Systems	(Def. 10.14)
Lab	(Def. 8.4)	Vectors	(Def. 8.1)
Locations	(Def. 8.1)		

We use **Systems** to mean RIGID :: **Systems** rather than KINEMATIC :: **Systems**. For convenience, we define the constant parameters for the model:

Definition. (constant parameters)

(13.1)

$$
\begin{array}{lll}
loc_c \in \mathsf{Locations} & {}^{\mathcal{L}ab}loc_c = (-5,0,5) & \textit{cannon position} \\
len_c \in \Re & \theta_c = 0.8 & \textit{cannon length} \\
\tau_c \in \Re & \tau_c = 2 & \textit{cannon oscillation period} \\
\theta_c \in \Re & \theta_c = 0.5 & \textit{cannon oscillation amplitude} \\
\tau_b \in \Re & \tau_b = 0.2 & \textit{cannon firing period} \\
v_b \in \Re & v_b = 15 & \textit{ball initial speed} \\
g \in \Re & g = 9.8 & \textit{gravitational acceleration} \\
w \in \Re & w = .5 & \textit{air resistance coefficient} \\
m_0 \in \Re & m_0 = 1 & \textit{ball mass} \\
r_0 \in \Re & r_0 = 0.2 & \textit{initial ball radius} \\
rmin \in \Re & rmin = 0.09 & \textit{minimum ball radius} \\
\gamma \in \Re & \gamma = 0.75 & \textit{radius shrink factor} \\
\hat{Z} \in \mathsf{Vectors} & {}^{\mathcal{L}ab}\hat{Z} = (0,0,1) & \textit{"up" vector}
\end{array}
$$

Definition 13.1: Constant parameters for the model, as described in Section 13.2. □

13.3.2   Definitions

It is convenient to predefine a sequence of IDs that we will use in the model:

Definition. idq

(13.2)

$$
\textit{We define a nonrepeating sequence of IDs:}
$$

$$
idq \equiv \left\{ idq_0, idq_1, \ldots \,\middle|\, idq_i \in \mathsf{IDs} \textit{ and } idq_i = idq_j \;\Rightarrow\; i = j \right\}
$$

Definition 13.2: A sequences of IDs that we will use to label bodies and motives in the model. □

The motion of the cannon's body frame is described by an explicit function:

Definition. fcannon

(13.3)

$$
\textit{We define a function fcannon} \in \mathsf{FramePaths} \textit{ by:}
$$

$$
P_{\textit{fcannon}}(t) = loc_c
$$

$$
Repq\left(\mathcal{L}ab, R_{\textit{fcannon}}(t)\right) = \begin{bmatrix} \cos(\tfrac{1}{2}\theta_c \, \sin(\tfrac{2\pi t}{\tau_c})) \\ 0 \\ -\sin(\tfrac{1}{2}\theta_c \, \sin(\tfrac{2\pi t}{\tau_c})) \\ 0 \end{bmatrix}
$$

Definition 13.3: Cannon body frame function, *fcannon*. We use a quaternion to describe a rotation of $-\theta_c \, sin(\tfrac{2\pi t}{\tau_c})$ radians about the lab frame's y-axis, so the cannon muzzle's angle from the horizontal oscillates with a period τ_c and amplitude θ_c. □

The instantaneous frame of a ball at the instant it is fired can be described in turn:

Definition. bshot

(13.4)

$$
\textit{We define a function bshot: } \Re \to \mathrm{RIGID} :: \mathsf{States} \textit{ by:}
$$

$$
\begin{aligned}
Rep\left(fcannon(t), x_{\textit{bshot}}(t)\right) &= (len_c, 0, 0) \\
Rep\left(fcannon(t), v_{\textit{bshot}}(t)\right) &= (v_b, 0, 0) \\
\mathbf{R}_{\textit{bshot}}(t) &= R_{\mathcal{L}ab} \\
\omega_{\textit{bshot}}(t) &= 0 \\
m_{\textit{bshot}}(t) &= m_0 \\
\mathbf{I}_{\textit{bshot}}(t) &= 0
\end{aligned}
$$

Definition 13.4: Initial state of a ball. *bshot(t)* describes the instantaneous state of a ball fired at time t. The position and velocity are fixed in the frame of the gun. The orientation, angular velocity, and inertia tensor are 0, since the balls are point masses. Note that *bshot* is *not* a state path as per Def. 10.6—its velocity vectors don't describe its own motion—rather, it is a mapping between a time that a shot might occur and the initial state of the shot ball. □

The model as a whole is described at an instant by the following space:

Definition. States

> ### States
>
> $[$
>
> | | | |
> |---|---|---|
> | ids | $\mapsto$ IDsets | *balls' IDs* |
> | R | $\mapsto \{\Re\}_{\text{IDs}}$ | *radius of each ball* |
> | Y | $\mapsto$ Systems | *state of each ball* |
> | M | $\mapsto \{$AppliedMotiveFields$\}_{\text{IDs}}$ | *motives on each ball* |
> | $tfire$ | $\mapsto \Re$ | *time of most recent shot* |
> | seq | $\mapsto Integers$ | *ball ID sequence number* |
>
> $\quad\overline{}$
>
> $ids = Ids(Y) = Ids(R) = Ids(M)$
> $\forall i \in ids,\ body(M_i) = i$
>
> $]$

(13.5)

Definition 13.5: State of the model. For each ball named $i \in ids$, its radius is given by R_i, its dynamic state is given by Y_i, and M_i is the applied motive that acts on it. *tfire* is the time of the shot most recently fired by the cannon. *seq* is the sequence number of the ID for the ball to be fired next. Since we apply only one motive per ball, we simply label each motive with the ball's ID. □

The motive field that is applied to a ball with a given radius and id is given by:

Definition. netf

> *Define a function netf:* $\Re \times$ IDs $\rightarrow$ AppliedMotiveFields
> *such that, for any* $r \in \Re$ *and* $i \in$ IDs:
>
> $$body(netf(r, i)) = i$$
> $$F([netf(r, i)](Y, t)) = -m(Y_i)\, g\, \hat{Z} - \pi\, r^2 w\, \|v(Y_i)\|\, v(Y_i)$$
> $$T([netf(r, i)](Y, t)) = 0$$

(13.6)

Definition 13.6: Motive applied to a ball. The net force we apply to a ball has two parts: a constant gravitational acceleration times the mass of the ball, pointing downward $(-\hat{Z})$, and a drag force that is quadratic in and opposite to the ball's velocity $(-v(Y_{body(mf)}))$. □

We define a function that returns the post-bounce state of a bouncing ball:

Definition. bbounce

> *We define a function*
> bbounce: States $\times$ IDs $\rightarrow$ RIGID :: States *by:*
>
> $$bbounce(s, i) \equiv \begin{bmatrix} \text{M} \hookleftarrow & \text{M}(Y(s)_i) \\ x \hookleftarrow & x(Y(s)_i) - (1 - \gamma)R(s)_i\hat{Z} \\ v \hookleftarrow & v(Y(s)_i) - 2(\hat{Z} \cdot v(Y(s)_i))\hat{Z} \end{bmatrix}$$

(13.7)

Definition 13.7: Bounce of a ball. Negates the z component of the ball's velocity and lowers the center by the change in radius. Since the ball is a point mass, the mass distribution, position and velocity form an identifying tuple. (Tuple notation is used as per Not. 5.24.) □

Finally, several auxiliary functions that will be convenient later on:

Definition. height, hit, big

(13.8)

$$
\begin{array}{ll}
\multicolumn{2}{c}{\textit{We define several functions:}} \\
\textit{height:} & \text{States} \times \text{IDs} \rightarrow \Re \quad \textit{height of a ball} \\
\textit{hit:} & \text{States} \qquad\qquad\quad \textit{balls hitting the ground} \\
\textit{big:} & \text{States} \qquad\qquad\quad \textit{balls big enough to survive}
\end{array}
$$

$$
\begin{aligned}
height(s, i) &\equiv x(Y(s)_i) \cdot \hat{Z} - R(s)_i \\
hit(s) &\equiv \left\{ i \in ids(s) \;\middle|\; height(s, i) = 0 \right\} \\
big(s) &\equiv \left\{ i \in hit(s) \;\middle|\; \gamma R(s)_i \geq rmin \right\}
\end{aligned}
$$

Definition 13.8: Auxiliary functions. For a model state $s \in$ **States**, the height above the ground of ball $i \in$ **IDs** is given by $height(s, i)$, and the set of balls that are hitting the ground is given by $hit(s)$.[4] Of the balls that hit the ground, $big(s)$ yields those that are large enough to "survive" the bounce—i.e., shrinking them won't reduce them below the minimum radius. □

13.3.3   Behavior of the Model

The behavior of the model over time is that of a segmented function, as per Section 5.10. We describe the behavior using the functional characterization described in Section 5.10.3; but as per Section B.4.9, we have several numerical event functions, each with a corresponding transition function.

For continuous motion, we define a *consistent* path through state space:

*Definition. **consistent***

(13.9)

$$
\begin{aligned}
&\text{A state function } s \colon \Re \rightarrow \text{States} \textit{ is } \textbf{consistent} \textit{ iff:} \\[4pt]
&\qquad ids_s(t) \quad \textit{is constant} \\
&\qquad R_s(t) \quad \textit{is constant} \\
&\qquad M_s(t) \quad \textit{is constant} \\
&\qquad tfire_s(t) \quad \textit{is constant} \\
&\qquad seq_s(t) \quad \textit{is constant} \\
&\qquad Y_s \quad \textit{is consistent with } M_s
\end{aligned}
$$

Definition 13.9: A continuous, consistent path through state space. The set of ball IDs doesn't change, the radius of each ball doesn't change, the motive field that is applied to each ball doesn't change, and the gun never fires. But the balls can move, as long as their motion is consistent (Def. 10.25) with the motive fields. □

---

[4]Because of numerical inaccuracies, in practice we use

$$
hit(s) \equiv \left\{ i \in ids(s) \;\middle|\; height(s, i) < \epsilon \textit{ and } v(Y(s)_i) \cdot \hat{Z} < 0 \right\}
$$

for some small tolerance ϵ. Thus $hit(s)$ is the set of balls that are numerically close to hitting the ground, where we take care not to include balls that have already bounced and are moving away.

To describe the cannon firing, we have an event function that "goes off" when the cannon fires and a transition function that adds a new ball:

Definition. Gfire, Hfire

> *Define event function Gfire:* $\Re \times$ States $\to \Re$ *and*
> *transition function Hfire:* $\Re \times$ States $\to$ States *by:*

(13.10)

$$Gfire(t, s) \equiv tfire_s + \tau_b - t$$

$$Hfire(t, s) \equiv \begin{bmatrix} R & \hookleftarrow & R_s + [idq_{seq(s)}, r_0] \\ Y & \hookleftarrow & Y_s + [idq_{seq(s)}, bshot(t)] \\ M & \hookleftarrow & M_s + [idq_{seq(s)}, netf(r_0, idq_{seq(s)})] \\ tfire & \hookleftarrow & t \\ seq & \hookleftarrow & seq(s) + 1 \end{bmatrix}$$

Definition 13.10: Event and transition functions to fire cannon. For a model in state $s \in$ States, the last time the cannon fired was $tfire_s$; since the period is τ_b (Def. 13.1), the cannon will fire next when $t = tfire_s + \tau_b$. To make a transition to the initial state of the next segment, the function *Hfire* adds an entry for a new ball to the various indexes, sets the time of firing, and increments the sequence number. (The use of $+$ to add elements to an index is as per Not. 5.15, and the use of the tuple notation is as per Not. 5.24.) □

To describe a ball (or balls) bouncing, we have an event function that "goes off" when any ball contacts the ground and a transition function that adjusts the radius, state, and motives of the bouncing balls:

Definition. Gbounce, Hbounce

> *Define event function Gbounce:* $\Re \times$ States $\to \Re$ *and*
> *transition function Hbounce:* $\Re \times$ States $\to$ States *by:*

(13.11)

$$Gbounce(t, s) \equiv \min_{i \in ids(s)} height(s, i)$$

$$Hbounce(t, s) \equiv \begin{bmatrix} R & \hookleftarrow & R_s - hit(s) \bigcup_{i \in big(s)} \{[i, \gamma R(s)_i]\} \\ Y & \hookleftarrow & Y_s - hit(s) \bigcup_{i \in big(s)} \{[i, bbounce(s, i)]\} \\ M & \hookleftarrow & M_s - hit(s) \bigcup_{i \in big(s)} \{[i, netf(\gamma R(s)_i, i)]\} \\ tfire & \hookleftarrow & tfire_s \\ seq & \hookleftarrow & seq_s \end{bmatrix}$$

Definition 13.11: Event and transition functions for balls bouncing. For a model in state $s \in$ States, the value $Gbounce(t, s)$ is the minimum height of any ball, thus is zero when any ball hits the ground. To make the transition to the post-bounce segment, $Hbounce(t, s)$ removes all index entries for balls that are colliding with the ground ($hit(s)$), and adds new entries for all colliding balls large enough to survive the transition ($big(s)$); the cannon-firing aspect values are not altered. Both $Gbounce(t, s)$ and $Hbounce(t, s)$ are independent of t. □

Note that transition functions *Hfire* and *Hbounce* are commutative, so if both types of events happen simultaneously, the two transition functions can be applied sequentially in either order.

13.4   Posed Problems

For this sample model, we have just a single posed problem: determine the behavior of the model over time. If we start with no balls, we just specify the time that the cannon first fires:

(13.12)

$$
\begin{aligned}
\textit{Given:} \quad & \textit{parameters of Def. 13.1} \\
& \textit{initial firing time } t_0 \\
\textit{find:} \quad & \textit{segmented function } C \colon \Re \to \textsf{States} \\
\textit{such that:} \quad & \left\{
\begin{array}{l}
\textit{Continuously, } C \textit{ is consistent, and discon-} \\
\textit{tinuities in } C \textit{ are described by event and} \\
\textit{transition function pairs Gfire, Hfire and} \\
\textit{Gbounce, Hbounce.}
\end{array}
\right.
\end{aligned}
$$

Equation 13.12: Behavior of the tennis ball cannon model. We start with an "empty" model, i.e., no balls. The first ball is shot at time t_0, and the cannon fires regularly from then on. □

The above is an initial-value piecewise-continuous ODE problem, which can be solved as described in Appendix C. The continuous behavior is an ODE as per the rigid-body forward dynamics problem, Section 10.4. The initial state $C_0 \in$ States for the problem can be constructed as:

$$
C_0 = \begin{bmatrix}
ids & \leftarrowtail & \emptyset \\
R & \leftarrowtail & \emptyset \\
Y & \leftarrowtail & \emptyset \\
M & \leftarrowtail & \emptyset \\
tfire & \leftarrowtail & t_0 - \tau_b \\
seq & \leftarrowtail & 0
\end{bmatrix},
$$

which will trigger a "fire" event at $t = t_0$ and add the first ball to the model. (Or, if this gives results in boundary-condition difficulties, we can evaluate $Hfire(t_0, C_0)$ to yield the initial state of the first nonempty segment.)

13.5   Implementation Notes[†]

The implementation of the "tennis ball cannon" follows straightforwardly from this chapter's description of the model.

[†] See Appendix B for discussion of the terminology, notation, and overall approach used here.

Program Definitions in Scope MTSEG:

class name	mathematical object	
State	States	*(Def. 13.5)*
StatePath	$\Re \rightarrow$ States	*(segmented) state function*
Idq	*idq*	*(Def. 13.2)*

routine			function	
fcannon(double)	:	MCO::instFrame	*fcannon*	*(Def. 13.3)*
bshot(double)	:	MRIG::State	*bshot*	*(Def. 13.4)*
netf(double,MM::Id)	:	MRIG::ApplMotiveField	*netf*	*(Def. 13.6)*
bbounce(State,MM::Id)	:	MRIG::State	*bbounce*	*(Def. 13.7)*
height(State,MM::Id)	:	double	*height*	*(Def. 13.8)*
hit(State)	:	MM::IdSet	*hit*	*(Def. 13.8)*
big(State)	:	MM::IdSet	*big*	*(Def. 13.8)*
gfire(double,State)	:	double	*Gfire*	*(Def. 13.10)*
hfire(double,State)	:	State	*Hfire*	*(Def. 13.10)*
gbounce(double,State)	:	double	*Gbounce*	*(Def. 13.11)*
hbounce(double,State)	:	State	*Hbounce*	*(Def. 13.11)*

Figure 13.4: Math section definitions for the sample segmented model. □

13.5.1 Math Section Constructs

The math section for this module has scope name MTSEG ("Math Test of a SEG-mented model"); the definitions are listed in Fig. 13.4.

```
class State :
  constructors:  (MCO::ScalarIdx R, MRIG::System Y,
                  MRIG::ApplMotiveFieldIdx M,
                  double tfire, int seq)
  members:       ids   : MM::IdSet
                 R     : MCO::ScalarIdx
                 Y     : MRIG::System
                 M     : MRIG::ApplMotiveFieldIdx
                 tfire : double
                 seq   : int
```

The class for state space States is defined as per Section B.3.6. The constructor is given the various indexes as parameters; it checks to see that the sets of IDs are mutually consistent and that each motive is labeled with the ID of the body that it is applied to, as per Def. 13.5. The class for state paths, StatePath, is defined in the standard manner as per Section B.3.7.

```
class Idq :
  methods:  seq(int i) : MM::Id
```

The class Idq implements an infinite sequence of IDs, *idq* (Def. 13.2), by a "generator" mechanism: The sequence is maintained as a data structure whose elements are created on demand; when a sequence element is requested that isn't in the data structure, a new, unique ID is defined and added.

The routines listed in Fig. 13.4 are implemented by directly transcribing the corresponding mathematical functions. `netf` constructs an `ApplMotiveField` instance whose force is given by an algebraic combination of `SysVectorField` instances, and whose torque is a constant zero `SysVectorField`, as per Section 10.5.2.

13.5.2 M–N Interface

The M–N interface for this module has scope name `NTSEG`

```
SolveForward(double t0) : StatePath
```

The state path instance returned by this function embodies the solution function $\mathcal{C}$ for the behavior of the model (Section 13.4). In order to evaluate $\mathcal{C}(t)$, the piecewise-continuous ODE solver `NUM::PodeScatExt` (Section B.4.9) is called.

The continuous part of the solution is constructed via `MRIG::SolveForward` (Section 10.5.3). To handle the discontinuities, we set up the numerical solver to invoke the routines `gfire` and `gbounce`—events are signaled when the values they compute cross zero.[5] When an event is found, the solver returns a code telling us which of the two events it is, so that we can invoke `hfire` or `hbounce` as appropriate. The solver may determine that, to within numerical tolerances, *both* events happen simultaneously, in which case it returns both codes; for this model we can safely call both `hfire` and `hbounce` in either order.

13.5.3 Conceptual Section

The conceptual section can use the definitions of the dynamic rigid-body module, Section 10.5.1.

13.5.4 C–M Interface

The state of the solution for any time value includes the set of IDs of balls that are in the model at that time. The C–M interface can dynamically adjust the conceptual section state, adding or removing "`sphere`" objects to conform with the solution for any time value. The various balls can be distinguished by the position of their IDs in the sequence `idq`, if, e.g., we want to cycle through a series of colors for the balls that are created.

For more general models, in which many different types of events may result in the mathematical models generating new IDs, we may want the C–M interface to be able to distinguish between IDs based on the events that caused them. For example, a single model may create a new ball when a cannon is fired and create

---

[5]Notice that both functions are set up to be positive before an event, zero at the event, and negative past the event, as discussed in Section C.2.

new glowing embers when fireworks explode—the C–M interface needs to know whether a given ID in the system belongs to a ball or to an ember. We suggest two methods to achieve this:

- Define separate sequences similar to *idq*. Each event would choose IDs from a separate sequence, and the C–M interface could determine to which sequence any given ID belongs.

- More generally, partition the space IDs into subsets, and require different parts of the model to use IDs from different subsets. This could be implemented as subclasses of the class MM::Id, with run-time tagging to be able to determine which subclass a given instance is a member of.

Chapter 14

Extensions to the Prototype Library

The library and sample models that are presented in Chs. 8–13 serve as a small, prototype example and test case. However, one of our goals for the structured modeling approach is to support extensibility, i.e., the addition of new capabilities that are built on and integrated with an existing library.

This chapter, therefore, discusses how the prototype library could be extended and enhanced to support a handful of new capabilities: collision and contact, finite-state control mechanisms, interchanging kinematic and dynamic motion, and flexible bodies. Note that unlike the models in Chs. 8–13, which have all been implemented as described, the discussion in this chapter is speculative, put forth to suggest ways in which the given library might be extended. Thus we describe some conceptual ideas and informally sketch some mathematical equations, but do not give a formal description of modules or implementation details.

14.1   Rigid-Body Collision

We'd like our rigid bodies to bounce
when they collide with each other.
The rigid-body dynamics module in
Ch. 10 doesn't notice when bodies
collide—it doesn't "know" the ex-
tents of the bodies, and freely lets
them pass through each other. Here,
we'll talk briefly about collisions.

First, we observe that conceptually, the rigid-body abstraction is at
its weakest when addressing collisions between bodies: For continuous free motion, with accelerations
that are small compared to the rigid-

Figure 14.1: Rigid-body collision. When rigid bodies collide, they experience a discontinuous change
in velocity (both linear and angular). □

ity of the material, the rigid-body abstraction works well; but when bodies collide,
there is a sudden extreme change in their velocities—thus there are deformations,
shock waves, and so forth in even the most rigid of materials. Still, it is often useful
to abstract a collision as a discontinuous change in the velocity and momentum of
perfectly rigid bodies (see Fig. 14.1).

Discontinuous changes in momentum are described via *impulsive forces* (or
just *impulses*). The common empirical model for collisions is that the points of
contact emerge from an impulsive collision with some fraction e of the relative
perpendicular velocity that they had going in:

$$\Delta V_\perp^+ = -e\,\Delta V_\perp^-$$

where e is called the *coefficient of restitution* and is determined experimentally
for different pairs of materials. If $e = 1$, the bodies leave with the same relative
velocity that they had going in, whereas if $e = 0$, they will remain in contact.[1] For
more complete discussion of rigid-body collision, see [Fox67, Ch. 10.8], [Baraff89],
or [Moore,Wilhelms88].

Rigid-body collisions can be incorporated into the prototype library by gener-
alizing the method used in the "tennis ball cannon" model in Ch. 13. That is, we
mathematically characterize the behavior as a segmented function by defining two
functions that describe the collisions:

- *An event function* g such that $g(t, Y(t))$ is the minimum separation between
  any bodies, where negative values indicate penetration
- *A transition function* h such that $h(t, Y(t))$ computes the effects of impulses
  on the colliding bodies

---

[1] As discussed in Section 4.6.2, we actually prefer a quasilinear restitution model.

Of course, we need to include the shapes of the bodies into our conceptual and mathematical models, in order to define the event function. In particular, we need algorithms to determine the separation between bodies; see [Baraff90], [Von Herzen *et al.*90], [Moore,Wilhelms88], or [Snyder92].

When several bodies mutually collide, or when collisions involve bodies that are constrained (as per Ch. 11) or in contact (as per Section 14.2), the impulsive collision calculation expands to involve a simultaneous system of equations; see [Baraff89] or [Moore,Wilhelms88].

14.2   Rigid-Body Contact

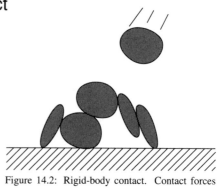

Rigid bodies are often in continuous contact, e.g., a collection of bodies in a pile. In general, we can let rigid bodies touch, or let them move apart, but we don't want them to interpenetrate. Mathematically, this translates into a *nonholonomic* constraint, i.e., an inequality relation: The separation between bodies must be greater than or equal to zero (see Fig. 14.2).

Figure 14.2: Rigid-body contact. Contact forces ensure that bodies do not interpenetrate. □

As long as two bodies maintain contact, they mutually apply *contact forces* to keep from interpenetrating; these forces are essentially the same as those of the geometric constraints described in Ch. 11. The contact forces are "one-way," however, in that they push bodies apart, but don't pull to hold bodies together.

Determining when to introduce and remove contact forces is a complex task, especially in the presence of multiple-body contact, surface friction, impulsive collisions, and so forth. A treatment of the subject is beyond our scope; we refer readers to the series of articles [Baraff89], [Baraff90], and [Baraff91].

For our current discussion, we observe that a description of rigid-body contact can fit into the segmented-model formulation. Extending the functions described in Section 14.1, we have

- *Event function.* Determines when bodies collide, and, for bodies in contact, determines when the contact forces "let go."

- *Transition function.* Computes impulsive behavior, activates contact constraints to keep bodies from interpenetrating, and deactivates contact constraints to let bodies separate.

14.3   Finite-State Control

Often, a model may have several different modes of behavior, which it
switches between based on special
events; control mechanisms to describe these changes of behavior are
often defined as finite-state machines
(FSMs). These are graphs or tables
that have a collection of state *nodes*,
and, for each node, a list of interesting events and the corresponding
transitions (*arcs*) to new nodes.

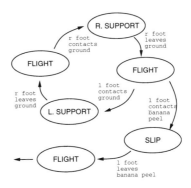

Figure 14.3: Finite-state machine. A finite-state machine can be used as a control mechanism for models. □

   For example, gait control for human or animal locomotion is commonly described as a finite state
machine—when a foot leaves the ground, the model enters a state in which the leg
is brought forward; when the leg contacts the ground, weight is shifted onto it, and
so forth (see Fig. 14.3; see also [Girard,Maciejewski85] or [Raibert,Hodgins91]).
The "tennis ball cannon" model in Ch. 13 can be described via a simple machine
that has one state node: Two event arcs loop back to the node, one followed period-
ically for the "fire" event, and the other followed when a ball bounces. [Brockett90]
discusses a finite-state model for a formal robotics language. [Kalra90] gives a
general formulation for finite-state control over models (from which we take the
notation we use below).

   Mathematically, we can describe a finite-state graph via a collection of triples,
each describing an arc:

$$(B_i, L, B_j),$$

where B_i names a node, L an event, and B_j the node at the terminus of the arc, and
where we use IDs to name events and nodes. The space of all possible finite-state
graphs would then be

$$\textbf{FSMs} \equiv \textit{sets of triples } \{(B_i, L, B_j), \ldots\}.$$

The state of a model controlled by an FSM would include an aspect for the current
state node, as well as an aspect containing the FSM itself.

   ModelStates
   [
   $fsm \mapsto \textbf{FSMs}$ *The controller for the model*
   $B \quad \mapsto \textbf{IDs}$ *The current state node*
   ⋮
   ]

Consider a segmented function through the above space. Since the aspect spaces for B and *fsm* are discrete, they must stay constant within each segment of the function. However, when an event occurs, a transition function can modify B:

$$h(t, s, L) \equiv \begin{bmatrix} B \hookmapsto & B_j \text{ such that } (B_s, L, B_j) \in fsm_s \\ \vdots & \end{bmatrix}$$

Notice that in addition to time t and model state $s \in$ **ModelStates**, the transition function takes a parameter $L \in$ **IDs**, which is the name of the event that occurred, as discussed in Section B.4.9.[2] In addition to updating B, the transition function can adjust the model state appropriately (based on s and L), in the same style as *Hfire* (Def. 13.10) and *Hbounce* (Def. 13.11) of the "tennis ball cannon." We can even modify *fsm*—the model can change its control program!

14.4   Mixed Dynamic and Kinematic Motion

Often, a model has some parts that can most easily be described kinematically, while other parts have dynamic motion. The "tennis ball cannon" model in Ch. 13, for example, has kinematic motion for the cannon barrel, and dynamic motion for the balls. More interestingly, individual bodies may switch between kinematic and dynamic motion, as in Fig. 14.4.

Any desired kinematic motion of a dynamic body can be achieved in principle by introducing appropriate time-varying geometric constraints,

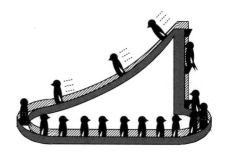

Figure 14.4: Interchanging dynamic and kinematic behavior. Here, the penguins slide down the incline dynamically, but make the return trip via a kinematic conveyor belt. □

such as the point-to-path constraint described in Section 11.2.3—but doing so may be inconvenient and, moreover, requires extra work in the numerical simulation of the dynamics.

Instead, we can directly change the rules of behavior for any given body. For example, we define a model whose state includes both kinematic and dynamic elements:

---

[2]If multiple events can occur simultaneously, and if the transition function can't be evaluated sequentially for each event, the FSM would need to include arcs to follow for each combination of events.

ModelStates

$$
\left[
\begin{array}{lll}
K & \mapsto \text{KINEMATIC}::\textsf{Systems} & \textit{kinematic body states} \\
D & \mapsto \text{RIGID}::\textsf{Systems} & \textit{dynamic body states} \\
M & \mapsto \{\text{RIGID}::\textsf{MassDists}\}_{\textsf{IDs}} & \textit{mass properties of each body} \\
\vdots & & \\
\hline
\multicolumn{2}{l}{\textit{Ids}(K) \cup \textit{Ids}(D) = \textit{Ids}(M)} & M \textit{ records mass of } \text{all} \textit{ the bodies} \\
\multicolumn{2}{l}{\forall i \in \textit{Ids}(D),\ \ \text{M}(D_i) = M_i} & \textit{dynamic bodies agree with } M
\end{array}
\right]
$$

The motion of the bodies in K is governed by some kinematic rule, while the motion of the bodies in D is determined by a set of applied motive fields. For a body named $i \in \textsf{IDs}$ to go from dynamic to kinematic, the transition function would perform

$$
\begin{array}{lll}
D & \leftarrow\!\dashv & D - i \qquad \textit{remove from dynamic index} \\
K & \leftarrow\!\dashv & K + [i, k(D_i)] \qquad \textit{add kinematic state to index}
\end{array}
$$

and for kinematic to dynamic:

$$
\begin{array}{lll}
D & \leftarrow\!\dashv & D + [i, \begin{bmatrix} \text{M} \leftarrow\!\dashv & M_i \\ k \leftarrow\!\dashv & K_i \end{bmatrix}] \qquad \textit{add dynamic state to index} \\
K & \leftarrow\!\dashv & K - i \qquad \textit{remove from kinematic index}
\end{array}
$$

We maintain the body frame (and velocity) across the events, so the transitions appear seamless. The transitions can be controlled via the finite-state mechanism described in Section 14.3.

On a related note, consider a model of 100,000 dominoes arranged on end, ready to be knocked over. To perform a dynamic simulation of all the dominoes would be infeasible. But we notice that there are only a few dominoes moving at any one time—the rest are static (see Fig. 14.5).

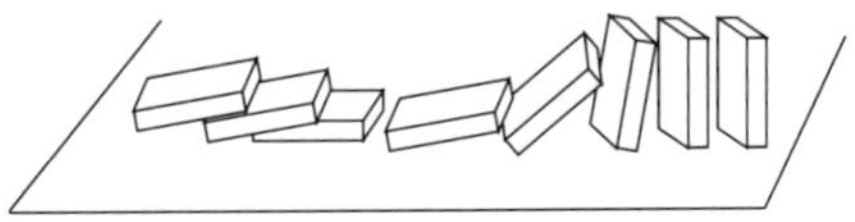

Figure 14.5: Mixed static and dynamic parts. The dominoes are static before and after falling. □

Thus we would design a model with separate "active" and "static" body indexes. When something collides with a static body, we switch it to active, with an initial condition based on the collision impulse (Section 14.1). When an active body is at rest and in contact only with static bodies, we switch it to static. Computationally, we need only compute the behavior of the active bodies and need only test for collisions amongst active bodies and between active bodies and neighboring static bodies.

14.5   Flexible Bodies

We would like to extend our library
to support dynamic modeling of flexible bodies integrated with the rigid
bodies (see Fig. 14.6). It is common
in computer graphics to model flexible bodies as a grid of point masses,
with some some sort of springs linking them together.   This approach
has the advantage that it's easy to
implement, especially given an existing rigid-body modeling system.[3]

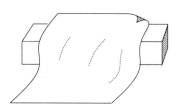

Figure 14.6: A flexible body, interacting with a
rigid body. □

However, we feel that this approach introduces excessive implementation detail
into the conceptual model, as discussed in Section 4.4. Instead, we perform much
the same computation, but with a different outlook (choice A of Fig. 4.8, rather
than the mass-point–spring model, choice C).

Our basic conceptual model of a flexible body is that it is a smooth, continuous surface. For the mathematical model, we follow the development in
[Terzopoulos *et al.*87] and [Platt89]: start with an expression for the strain energy
of the model; taking a variational derivative yields a partial differential equation
(PDE) describing the continuous surface that minimizes the energy. In order to
numerically solve the PDE, it is discretized using a finite element or finite difference approximation. As discussed in [Platt89], a finite difference approximation
can be made that is mathematically equivalent to a system of point masses and
springs.

Programmatically, once we numerically solve the (discretized) equations, we
propagate the result back to the mathematical section, and thence to the conceptual
section—this means reconstructing a continuous function from the discretized
results by an interpolation appropriate to the discretization method.

There are several advantages to creating a smooth surface at the mathematical
and conceptual levels, rather than using the mass-point–spring model:

- The body can be rendered without regard to the numerical discretization.
  Many rendering methods will resample the smooth surface (adaptively) to
  create high-quality graphics; this resampling is not restricted to the numerical discretization grid points.

- The interaction with the other objects in the model is not restricted to grid
  points. Penetration tests, e.g., can be performed on the smooth surface,
  without having to worry if small objects will "slip between the cracks."

---

[3]In fact, we've done so: We've succesfully simulated models of flexible 3D bodies as roughly 1,000
point masses on sparse grids, with roughly 10,000 springs between them, using our implementation of
the prototype library modules of Chs. 8–10.

- The grid density can be chosen automatically by the numerical solver, based on problem-specific data, or can vary adaptively over time or across the body. The user doesn't need to guess a grid density in advance which will suffice throughout the simulation.
- The solution method is independent of the higher levels. The numerics section doesn't always have to use the finite-difference method if in some configurations, e.g., a modal analysis (see [Pentland,Williams89]) or deforming-rigid-body method is appropriate. The various methods can be swapped in without affecting the higher level of the program.[4]

It might seem expensive to make and use the interpolated solution, rather than directly using the numerical data. However, we feel that it will buy us much in the way of cleanliness, robustness, and applicability. Moreover, the eventual use of "smart" or adaptive solvers will allow us to simulate systems that require fine sampling for only a few extreme configurations; if we were to have only a pre-assigned sampling density, we would need to choose the finest sampling globally, thus making the overall computation too slow to be feasible. Thus, ultimately, this approach may be faster.

In order to integrate rigid-body and flexible-body dynamics, we must have a compatible mathematical formalism. For rigid bodies, in Ch. 10 we chose a force-based, Newtonian formalism; but flexible bodies are typically expressed using an energy-based, Lagrangian formalism. We may need to extend Ch. 10 to include the energy formulation, or, conversely, we may wish to express flexible bodies using a force-based formulation. Or both.

14.6 Summary

This chapter has speculated on how several techniques and features could fit into the prototype library of Chs. 7–11. In doing so, we have doubtlessly glossed over many difficulties, incompatabilities, and so forth. Our intent is to try to convey a feeling of where the modeling methodology might lead, and also to illustrate how we use the methodology in thinking about as-yet-unsolved issues.

Our choice of topics in this chapter has deliberately emphasized models involving discontinuous events and changes of state. We feel that a primary benefit of the structured approach toward modeling will ultimately be in the ability to create models that are heterogeneous—i.e., that incorporate various different behaviors mixed together—both across time and across the elements of the model.

---

[4]This is analogous to the linear system solver NUM::linsys, discussed in Section B.4.3, that chooses between a sparse method or singular-value decomposition.

PART IV

CONCLUSION AND APPENDICES

- Ch. 15. Concluding Remarks
  A summary of "structured modeling"; an evaluation of its various aspects; and some thoughts on where it might lead.

- Appendix A. Miscellaneous Mathematical Constructs
  A few mathematical definitions that are used by modules in Part III.

- Appendix B. Prototype Implementation
  A discussion of our implementation of the prototype library in Part III.

- Appendix C. Solving Piecewise-Continuous ODEs
  An algorithm for solving ordinary differential equations (ODEs) that have occasional discontinuities.

Chapter 15

Concluding Remarks

This chapter offers retrospective evaluation and comments on aspects of the design strategy. We will elaborate on a small assortment of issues, based in particular on our experience with the prototype modeling library of Chs. 7–14, and conclude with thoughts about where the ideas we have presented may lead.

15.1   Notes on the Design Strategy

The reader may recall that the strategy was presented as a progression: We started with a general discussion of modeling (Ch. 3), focused next on physically-based modeling (Ch. 4), then addressed mathematical modeling (Ch. 5), and finally discussed computer implementations (Ch. 6).

The strategy was developed, however, through a gradual process of experimentation and modification over a period of several years, until reaching its current form.[1] In all, we are happy with the result, and feel that its various elements fit together well.

This section gives notes for the various steps of the progressive presentation and follows with an overall commentary.

15.1.1   Analysis of Modeling

Of the abstraction–representation–implementation (ARI) structure and subsequent discussion in Ch. 3, we feel that the fundamental idea is that of the abstraction:

- The abstraction is the set of features of the thing being modeled which are included in a model; these serve as the "axioms" for the model.

Less basic, but still useful, is the paradigm of progressive decomposition in model design and in computer support for modeling.

15.1.2   Physically-Based Models

As per the discussion of applied mathematics in Ch. 4, we think that a primary part of physically-based modeling is

- Identification of a well-defined mathematical model that has no "conceptual" or numerical solution influences mixed into it.

The separation of equations from problems (as per Section 4.4.3) is perhaps less basic: For given goals, there are often specific problems to be posed, and we may be best off posing them directly. But when we are interested in reusable general-purpose models, in which different problems may be posed for different applications, the separation becomes significant.

---

[1] Applying our model-design terminology, we would say that the strategy was not developed "top-down," but rather through an "annealing" process.

15.1.3   Mathematical Models

We have found the mathematical techniques in Ch. 5 to be convenient and helpful in designing complete mathematical models. But can these techniques (or future ones) keep a rein on mathematical models that can grow arbitrarily complex? It would be nice if mathematical models were always tractable by hand via the use of modularity, structuring techniques, and so forth. In our experience with the "fancy forces" mathematical model in Ch. 11, however, we have found that we construct a long chain of definitions that can be tricky to use correctly.

If our goal of having well-defined mathematical models *written on paper* proves to be unattainable or impractical, we may need to modify it: We'd rather not give up well-defined mathematical models, but we may give up writing them on paper—that is, we may turn to computer-aided mathematical modeling, as discussed in Section 15.4.

15.1.4   Program Framework

Our experience using the program framework that we defined in Ch. 6, with its conceptual–math–numerics separation, has been favorable. In particular, we are happy with our choice to use different programming styles—object-oriented, functional, and procedural—to best meet the needs of different parts of the program, rather than adopting a single style overall. Nevertheless, given the volatile nature of computer program technology, we're skeptical about *any* specific program structure passing the test of time.

We have found that the approach of identifying and supporting changes of representation, as discussed in Section 6.6, has been particularly valuable in defining a high-level, structured numerics library. The numerics library described in Section B.4 has proven useful not just for our own prototype physically-based modeling library, but for other projects as well.

In defining "math section" objects and classes for the modules of Chs. 8–11, we essentially implemented a limited, special-purpose symbolic mathematics mechanism directly in the C++ programming language. This was a straightforward task, given well-defined "blackboard" mathematical models. Nevertheless, it would perhaps be more elegant to define these in a mathematical modeling language; see Section 15.4.

15.1.5   On the Progression of the Design Strategy

As the focus of the design strategy progressively narrows from general principles down to the programming details, the breadth and importance of the ideas narrow correspondingly. Our intent in this work was to begin with the idea that a structured approach toward modeling is worthwhile, and "go with it": From that starting point we carried the idea all the way through until reaching a concrete implementation. The specific destination that we reached is less important than the fact that it is possible to make the journey.

The ultimate "message" of this work is not in the particular mathematical or programming details, but in the overall emphasis on structure, clarity, and organization of models at all stages in their design. We could perhaps have stated these ideas and stopped there, rather than continuing with the elaborate design strategy—but had we not taken the ideas to completion, any claims that we might have made about their applicability and effectiveness would have been specious.

15.2 Did We Meet Our Goals?

Section 1.4 lists several goals for the design strategy. We list the goals again here accompanied by discussion of how well the strategy meets those goals, based on our experience developing and implementing the prototype library of Chs. 7–14.

- **To facilitate the understanding and communication of models.** We have found that the ARI and CMP structures (Chs. 3 and 4) helps us to understand models by providing a powerful and convenient partitioning of the major parts of a model. Having a common framework and terminology has proven helpful for discussing models that are under development and for presenting written versions of models (as in Chs. 8–11).

- **To facilitate the creation of models with high degrees of complexity.** The use of modularity in the design of models (Section 4.5) helps manage complexity. The use of structured mathematical modeling techniques (Ch. 5) helps us to isolate and write well-defined mathematical equations for complex models. In particular, the ability to defined the behavior of a complex model as a segmented function (Sections 5.10 and 6.7) lends itself to a clean organization for models and programs.

- **To facilitate the reuse of models, techniques, and ideas.** Modular design as per Section 4.5 is helpful in the reuse of models at the blackboard level. The toolbox-oriented program framework lets us reuse models and program code at the implementation level.

- **To facilitate the extension of models.** The "fancy forces" module (Ch. 11) in our prototype library was successfully designed and implemented as an extension to the earlier rigid-body modeling modules; it did of course engender some minor alterations to the earlier models, but the modular design and implementation framework kept those changes localized. Similarly, as per our discussion in Ch. 14, future extensions to the library seem relatively straightforward.

- **To facilitate the creation of models that are "correct."** The annealing design strategy (Section 3.5.3) and the emphasis on explicit statement of the conceptual properties of a model (Ch. 4) helps make sure that we are on track as we design models. The emphasis on standalone mathematical models (Section 4.4 and Ch. 5) helps us to verify mathematical consistency. The overall framework helps us to debug a model by identifying and localizing various types of bugs, as discussed in Sections 4.6.4 and 6.9.

- **To facilitate the translation of models into programs.** Since the program framework follows the blackboard structure closely (Ch. 6), it has proven to be straightforward to implement models. In particular, our final version of the "fancy forces" module was implemented without much difficulty by following the written description in Ch. 11.

15.3   Have We Made Modeling Easy?

We can't claim that we've "magically" made modeling easy. It can be a lot of work to completely specify a model in the "structured modeling" manner we have described—for example, if nothing else, the prototype modules in Part III have a lot of bulk. In fact, for a small, one-time-use model, it would probably be easier just to express and implement the model from scratch.

So what have we done? Our goal has been to maximize correctness, modularity, and reusability so that we can build models more intricate than we could otherwise. Thus we

- invest more effort in the small—i.e., carefully describe the details of individual modules,

to yield

- better results in the large—i.e., complex models that are robust and flexible.

Even our simple prototype library has provided us with models and modeling programs that are more flexible than were previously available to us. For example, we now construct programs that support the calculation of work done by each force object—this is achieved "for free" given the pre-existing modular library.

But what about models that are *very* large? If we look at programming, we see that modularity and structure are crucial elements for the design of large programs, but as projects get increasingly large, structured programming is in itself insufficient: High-level languages are used, and for large enough projects, we enter the realm of software engineering (which addresses issues such as revision control, metrics, management techniques, and so forth). Similarly, we feel that our "structured modeling" approach includes some fundamental elements for the design of large models, but for large models, higher-level mechanisms than we have described will need to be created, and for sufficiently large projects, an approach to "model engineering" will be needed; this need is discussed by [Brooks91].

15.4   Computer-Assisted Mathematical Modeling

Computer tools can potentially aid us to define and use mathematical models. We identify three areas in which computer tools can be of use; there is of course some overlap between them.

CAD for mathematical models. Remember that for our purposes, a mathematical model is a collection of definitions and equations, as opposed to a posed problem. Thus we want computer-aided design (CAD) tools that help us to *construct* equations and definitions, rather than tools to solve equations. A mathematical modeling CAD tool would include such features as:[2]

- Declarative definitions (rather than procedural)
- Modularity, including support for libraries, name scoping, etc.
- Data abstraction, i.e., definition of new abstract spaces
- Extensible notation
- Type-checking of operators and domains
- Interface with programming languages and problem-solution tools
- Ability to arrange and annotate models for clarity of presentation

Note that the emphasis is not on automated generation of equations and definitions, but rather on a utility that helps us to generate manually the equations and definitions that we're interested in.

---

[2]Our hypothetical CAD tool is similar in many respects to a "Smart Paper" proposal of [Barr86].

Solving posed problems. Symbolic mathematics programs, such as Maple ([Char *et al.*91]) and Mathematica ([Wolfram91]), are powerful tools for problem-solving.[3] These programs incorporate the ability to manipulate expressions symbolically with built-in numerical evaluation and solution capability. On a different slant, [Abelson *et al.*89] describes techniques for automated construction, execution, and analysis of numerical problems from high-level models.

Program construction. Numerical problem-solving subroutines often require that the user provide "callback" subroutines; e.g., a subroutine that computes a derivative for an ODE solver, or an objective function for an optimizer. These subroutines are derived from mathematical model constructs, and thus can potentially be created automatically by symbolic manipulation. The subroutines can be constructed at run-time, based on end-user specified model configurations, resulting in special-purpose routines that efficiently evaluate the necessary components for a given problem; this approach was used in [Witkin,Kass88].

15.5   Future Directions

We hope that we have provided a stepping stone upon which others may build to create new generations of modeling methodologies. We can imagine the existence of rich modeling environments, full of building blocks and modules (rigid bodies, constraints, flexible bodies, fluids, walking and running, quantum mechanics, weather, aerodynamics, molecular modeling, etc.) that can all be interconnected and expanded, so that users and researchers can easily build highly complex models. Future work for such environments might entail:

- Specification languages for physically-based models
- Standards for exchanging physically-based models
- Automated techniques to link together different model components
- Interactive modeling-and-simulation workstations
- Specialized hardware to support key aspects of the modeling and simulation processes

---

[3]Note that these programs are not quite suited to our idea of CAD for mathematical modeling. They have procedural approaches; they emphasize automation in order to minimize the user's work; and finally, they don't emphasize modularity or data abstraction, both of which are fundamental to our mathematical modeling strategy.

Clearly, the ideas that we have presented don't directly provide the above capabilities—but we have tried to identify and examine some of the concepts that may underlie them.

Appendix A

Miscellaneous Mathematical Constructs

This appendix contains a few mathematical constructs that are used by some of the models in Part III. Notice that these are purely mathematical utilities, rather than physically-based models. Thus they do not include conceptual models, goal statements, and so forth, just some mathematical definitions.

The mathematical constructs defined here are not as fundamental as the various constructs of Ch. 5 (such as IDs and state spaces); thus we have chosen not to include them in that chapter. On the other hand, these constructs seem too general-purpose to be defined as auxiliary constructs of some specific physically-based model.

Therefore, to give such constructs a home, we have defined here a small library of miscellaneous mathematical definitions. This library includes program implementations of the constructs, in the math section, numerics section, and M–N interface parts of the program framework (Ch. 6).

A.1 Trees

The index mechanism of Section 5.8.2 provides a basic structuring capability for mathematical models: The ability to manipulate groups
of elements by name. Here, we define an additional structuring capability familiar from computer science: hierarchical "tree" relationships between mathematical IDs.

We define a state space, such that
each element of the space is a forest:

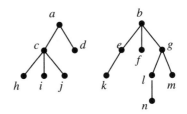

Figure A.1:   A sample forest. c's *parent*
is a, h's parent is c, and so forth. a's *children* are $\{c, d\}$, and so forth. $\{a, b\}$ are the
roots. $\{d, f, h, i, j, k, m, n\}$ are the *leaves*. c's
descendants are $\{h, i, j\}$, a's descendants are
$\{c, d, h, i, j\}$, and so forth. □

Definition. IDforests

(A.1)

IDforests
[
ids	$\mapsto$ IDsets	*All IDs in the forest*
roots	$\mapsto$ IDsets	*The IDs at the roots*
nonroots	$\mapsto$ IDsets	*The IDs not at the roots*
leaves	$\mapsto$ IDsets	*The IDs at the leaves*
parent	$\mapsto \{$IDs$\}_{\text{IDs}}$	*Parent of an ID*
children	$\mapsto \{$IDsets$\}_{\text{IDs}}$	*Set of children of each ID*
descendants	$\mapsto \{$IDsets$\}_{\text{IDs}}$	*Set of descendants of each ID*

—

1. $\text{Ids}(parent) \subseteq ids$
2. $\text{Ids}(children) = \text{Ids}(descendants) = ids$
3. $roots \cup nonroots = ids, \ roots \cap nonroots = \emptyset$
4. $nonroots = \text{Ids}(parent)$
5. $leaves = \left\{ i \in ids \ \middle| \ children_i = \emptyset \right\}$
6. $\forall i \in$ IDs, $\quad j \in children_i \ \Leftrightarrow \ parent_j = i$
7. $\forall i \in$ IDs, $\quad descendants_i = children_i \bigcup_{j \in children_i} descendants_j$
8. $\forall i \in$ IDs, $\quad i \notin descendants_i$

]

Definition A.1: The space of forests of trees of IDs. Each element of IDforests is a forest,
which may have several trees. (1) Not all IDs need have parents. (2) All IDs have a set of
children and a set of descendants. (3) Every ID is a root or a nonroot. (4) The nonroots are
those IDs that have parents. (5) The leaves are those IDs that have no children. (6) Every ID
is the parent of its children. (7) The descendants of an ID are its children and its children's
descendants. (8) No ID is its own descendant. □

This space is used for the kinematic hierarchical configurations in Ch. 9.

A.2 Arrays

It is convenient to define some constructs for arrays. We define a *vec* to be an arbitrary-size, 1D array of real numbers, and a *mat* to be an arbitrary-size, 2D array of real numbers:[1]

Definition. Vecs, Mats

(A.2)
$$
\begin{aligned}
\mathsf{Vecs} &\equiv \left\{ x \in \Re^k \;\middle|\; \text{positive integer } k \right\} \\
\mathsf{Mats} &\equiv \left\{ x \in \Re^{j \times k} \;\middle|\; \text{positive integers } j, k \right\}
\end{aligned}
$$

Definition A.2: Vecs is the set of all 1D arrays of real numbers, no matter what their size; for example, if $a \in$ Vecs and $b \in$ Vecs are two vecs, it may be true that $a \in \Re^2$ while $b \in \Re^3$. Similarly, Mats is the set of all 2D arrays of reals. Thus, Vecs and Mats are disparate unions as per Section 5.7.3; two vecs or two mats are *agnates* if they have the same sizes. □

In order to tell us the size of a mat or vec, we define operators:

Definition. lsz, Rsz, Sz

(A.3)
$$
\begin{aligned}
&\textit{For } m \in \mathsf{Mats}, \; v \in \mathsf{Vecs} \\[4pt]
&lsz(m) \equiv j, \text{ where } m \in \Re^{j \times k} \\
&rsz(m) \equiv k, \text{ where } m \in \Re^{j \times k} \\
&sz(v) \equiv k, \text{ where } m \in \Re^{k}
\end{aligned}
$$

Definition A.3: Operators for the "left size" (*lsz*) and "right size" (*rsz*) of a mat and for the size (*sz*) of a vec. □

It is convenient to give ourselves shorthand notation for arrays of known sizes:

Notation. Vecs and Mats

(A.4)
$$
\begin{aligned}
\mathsf{Mats}[j, k] &\equiv \left\{ m \in \mathsf{Mats} \;\middle|\; lsz(m) = j, \; rsz(m) = k \right\} \\
\mathsf{Mats}[j, *] &\equiv \left\{ m \in \mathsf{Mats} \;\middle|\; lsz(m) = j \right\} \\
\mathsf{Mats}[*, k] &\equiv \left\{ m \in \mathsf{Mats} \;\middle|\; rsz(m) = k \right\} \\
\mathsf{Vecs}[k] &\equiv \left\{ v \in \mathsf{Vecs} \;\middle|\; sz(m) = k \right\}
\end{aligned}
$$

Notation A.4: Arrays of known sizes. We use the bracket notation on the left as shorthand for the subsets on the right. For example, Mats[4, 3] is the space of 4×3 arrays of reals; Vecs[3] is the space of all arrays of 3 reals. Mats[2, *] has its size partially specified—the space includes, e.g., 2×2 as well as 2×3 arrays. □

We use standard matrix arithmetic for mats and vecs.

---

[1] We chose the names "vec" and "mat" to be reminiscent of "vector" and "matrix"; we chose not to use the latter names directly, so as to avoid potential confusion with the geometric objects in Ch. 8.

Program Definitions in Scope MMISC:		
class name	*abstract space*	
Forest	IDforests	*(Def. A.1)*
Mat	Mats	*(Def. A.2)*
MatIdx	$\{\text{Mats}\}_{\text{IDs}}$	*index of mats*
MatIdx0	$\{\text{Mats}\}^{\circ}_{\text{IDs}}$	*index of mats, with 0*
Vec	Vecs	*(Def. A.2)*
VecIdx	$\{\text{Vecs}\}_{\text{IDs}}$	*index of vecs*

Figure A.2: Math section definitions for the miscellaneous mathematical constructs. □

A.3 Implementation Notes[†]

A.3.1 Implementation of Trees

The class MMISC::IdForest that implements the space of forests could in principle be implemented in our standard manner for state spaces (Section B.3.6), i.e., explicitly store all the aspect values. However, that can quickly grow unwieldy, especially for the *descendants* aspect. Instead, a more compact mechanism is used, and routines are defined to compute the various aspect values on demand.

For numerical computations involving trees, one often needs to perform an operation on each ID in a tree. The routines NMISC::IdForestPreorder(...) and NMISC::IdForestPostorder(...) call a user-provided subroutine once for each ID in a forest, the former visiting a parent before visiting its children, and the latter, after.

A.3.2 Implementation of Arrays

The classes MMISC::Vec and MMISC::Mat are straightforward interfaces to a standard array package.

[†]See Appendix B for discussion of the terminology, notation, and overall approach used here.

Appendix B

Prototype Implementation

This appendix discusses a prototype implementation of a structured modeling environment as per Ch. 6 and used by the modules in Part III. We discuss here the fundamental support routines and structure for the conceptual–math–numerics framework discussed in Ch. 6; this structure is not specific to the rigid-body modeling library in Part III.

The appendix is in four parts. First, we give an overview of the presentation style that we use to describe the implementation, both here and in the models in Part III. This is followed by a brief discussion of the conceptual section. Next, we describe the math section—focusing in particular on how to implement a mathematical model such as in Part III, using the support that is provided by the environment. Finally, we discuss the numerics section, which contains a modular interface between low-level numerical subroutines and the higher levels of the programming environment.

The discussion is at the level of functional specification, intending to provide a starting point for the design of future implementations, rather than a prescription of syntactic details of the prototype. Note, however, that the specification is taken from existing, working code—it is not speculation.

B.1   Overview of the Presentation Style

In describing the prototype implementation, both here and in the modules in Part III, we have tried to convey the essentials of the structure and methodology, so that readers interested in designing and implementing their own modeling environments would be able to draw on our experience.

We have chosen not to include listings (or even snippets) of our working C++ source code or class definitions—we feel that the syntactic intricacies of the C++ language ([Stroustrup91]), compounded by the programming idiosyncrasies of the author, would obfuscate the mostly simple mechanisms that are at work. Instead, we give functional specifications of modules and classes. But we try to sprinkle in enough "grit" to keep the description anchored to the implementation, rather than drifting off into hyperbole.

Object-oriented programming today does not have a widely accepted uniform terminology. We list the terms that we use, and refer the reader to [Booch91] for further discussion:

- *Class.* An abstract data type, in an object-oriented language.

- *Instance.* An object that belongs to some class.

- *Data Member* (or, just *member*). A named data element that contains part of the state of an instance.

- *Method.* A named operation on an instance.

- *Operator.* A method invoked via special syntax.

- *Constructor.* A method that is invoked to initialize a new object.

We will describe a class using the following form:

```
class Classname :
    constructors:  (...parameters...)     a constructor for the class
                   (...other parms...)    we may have several constructors
    members:       gamma : double    data member named "gamma" of type double
                   width : integer   we may have several data members
    methods:       eval(...parms...) : integer   method "eval" returns an integer
                   rep(...parms...)  : double[3]  returns an array of 3 doubles
```

We will leave various details out of our descriptions: implementation details such as private or hidden data members (any interesting implementation issues will be discussed in the accompanying text); optimization details such as pass-by-reference or inline definitions; class-mechanism administratrivia such as destructors or assignment operators; debugging tools such as instance names and tracing methods; numerical details such as tolerance parameters.

Our program descriptions will follow the LISP-like namespace style that is discussed in Section 5.6.2, in which we specify a "current scope" for a module; all nonprimitive terms are presumed to be in that scope unless explicitly prefixed with a scope name. Since C++ scoping doesn't work in that way, the actual implementation explicitly prefixes all symbols with their scope names. To keep the program definitions from being too unwieldy, we use abbreviated scope names:

Scope name	Defined	Program section	Description
MCO	Sec. 8.6	Math	COordinate frames
MKIN	Sec. 9.5.2	Math	KINematic rigid bodies
NKIN	Sec. 9.5.3	m–N interface	KINematic rigid bodies
MRIG	Sec. 10.5.2	Math	dynamic RIGid bodies
NRIG	Sec. 10.5.3	m–N interface	dynamic RIGid bodies
MFRC	Sec. 11.5.2	Math	fancy FoRCes
NFRC	Sec. 11.5.3	m–N interface	fancy FoRCes
MTSEG	Sec. 13.5.1	Math	Test SEGmented model
NTSEG	Sec. 13.5.1	m–N interface	Test SEGmented model
MMISC	Sec. A.3	Math	MISCellaneous mathematics
NMISC	Sec. A.3	Numerics	MISCellaneous mathematics
MM	Sec. B.3	Math	support Modules
NUM	Sec. B.4	Numerics	structured nUMerics library

B.2   The Conceptual Section

The conceptual section maintains a data structure containing objects that correspond to things in the model. The data structure objects are updated based on user interaction, simulation results, and so forth.

As discussed in Section 6.2.1, the conceptual section of the program performs many of the same tasks as a traditional (kinematic) modeling program, except that the behavioral computation is offloaded to a mathematical/numerical computation "engine," via the C–M interface. We have focused on the construction of that engine as the most novel part of the program framework and have given short shrift to the conceptual section. Our prototype implementation provides some basic support interfaces:

- to [Snyder92] for shape models and their mass-distribution properties,

- to rendering software and hardware,

- to animation/control and recording software and hardware.

There is still much room for work at the conceptual level. In particular, there is a need for high-level physically-based modeling description languages and data formats.

B.3 The Math Section

The math section of a program, as discussed in Sections 6.2 and 6.4, is primarily a collection of definitions of data types—i.e., classes—that support the various entities in the blackboard mathematical models. Here, we discuss how these definitions and support are implemented. Although the math section is functional in style (see Section 6.2.3) we implement it using object-oriented technology.

B.3.1 Overview: Classes and Abstract Spaces

Our mathematical models are based on abstract spaces, as discussed in Section 5.7 (and evidenced in the models of Chs. 8–11). This maps well into object-oriented programming—our basic procedure to implement a given model is

- *For each abstract space of interest in the mathematical model, we define a corresponding class in the program.*

For example, some classes that we define, and their corresponding spaces, are:

Class name	Abstract space	Defined
MM::Id	IDs	(Def. 5.8)
MM::IdSet	IDsets	(Def. 5.9)
MCO::Vector	Vectors	(Def. 8.1)
MCO::VectorPath	VectorPaths	(Def. 8.19)
MRIG::ApplMotive	AppliedMotives	(Def. 10.20)
MRIG::ApplMotiveIdx	$\{\text{AppliedMotives}\}_{\text{IDs}}$	*(an index, Not. 5.11)*

Notice that we use singular names for the classes, in keeping with the programming style that the name is that of the data type. Notice also that we often explicitly create classes, such as ApplMotiveIdx, for commonly used abstract spaces that are mathematically defined implicitly or indirectly, such as the space of all indexes of applied motives, $\{\text{AppliedMotives}\}_{\text{IDs}}$; we discuss indexes in Section B.3.5. Finally, notice that we create classes even for abstract spaces whose elements are functions, such as VectorPaths whose elements are functions from reals to vectors; we discuss functions in Section B.3.7.

Each class defines various methods that support mathematical operators and functions defined over the abstract space. For example, as discussed in Section 8.6, the MCO::Vector class has a method rep(Frame) that supports the mathematical operator *Rep* (Def. 8.5), returning the representation of a vector in a given coordinate frame.

B.3.2 Immutable Objects

In Section 5.5.1 we pointed out that mathematical model entities have no changeable "internal state"—as opposed to program objects, which typically do. However, we would like to follow closely the mathematical model in our implementation. Thus we adopt a restricted style for the math section objects:

- *The state of a math section object may not be changed after the object is constructed.*

This can be supported in object-oriented programming by defining no "modifier" methods—only "accessors"—and by declaring all the member data to be constant or read-only. The constructor method for the class must correctly initialize the contents of the object, since it will not be changed later on; thus the arguments to the constructor must be sufficient to specify an instance completely.[1]

We think of an instance of a math section object as a being a primitive abstract value, rather than a storage area whose contents can be modified.[2] We will use math section objects as if they were primitive data types like integers or floating-point numbers. If we have two instances that represent the same value, they can be used interchangeably.

In addition to being close to the mathematical model, this approach lends a certain ease of use to the math section: An instance of a math object is always correct, by construction. We manipulate and copy entire instances rather than pointers, so that pointer corruption and data aliasing are not major issues. We write functions or operators that take math object instances as arguments and construct new instances for the result. (To minimize the run-time cost of copying arguments and return values, the arguments can be passed by reference, and the user can specify the destination into which the return value should be constructed; see Section 6.8.)

The strict adherence to immutability works well for primitive, fixed-size objects—even rather large ones, such as MRIG::State (Section 10.5.2). But for compound, variable-size objects such as sets and indexes, it can be impractical as the objects grow large: We often perform operations such as $x \leftarrow x \cup y$ in which we replace the value of variable x with a new value; but constructing a new value from scratch, only to immediately throw away the old value can be prohibitively expensive. But since we know that the old value will no longer be needed, we can provide an "increment" operator, $\leftarrow\cup$, so that $x \leftarrow\cup y$ efficiently updates variable x to have the new value. Thus we relax our immutability requirement, to support arithmetic increment operators for variable-size objects.

---

[1] If it is too cumbersome to require all necessary construction parameters to be available at once, we can take a more procedural approach: Define a class to have a flag that indicates "under construction," to have modifier methods that may only be used if the flag is set, to have accessor methods that may *not* be used if the flag is set, and to have a special "wrap" method that resets the flag.

[2] Note the contrast with conceptual section objects: Each instance of a conceptual object corresponds with a thing in the model—it is a storage location that holds various parameters that describe the configuration of the thing and that are updated and modified as we manipulate or simulate the thing—and it may not be destroyed during the lifetime of the thing.

B.3.3   IDs

We define a class `Id` to implement the abstract space IDs (Def. 5.8). The only operations that the class supports are constructing a new unique ID and testing to see if two instances are equal. Internally, an ID is simply represented as a 32-bit integer code; to create a new ID, a global counter is incremented.

B.3.4   ID sets

We define a class `IdSet` to implement IDsets, the space of sets of IDs (Def. 5.9). The class is implemented using a standard "container" mechanism, including support for iterating through all elements of a set and testing to see if a given ID is an element of the set.

B.3.5   Indexes

We provide templates for defining indexes (Def. 5.10) and indexes with zero (Not. 5.12). The template for indexes provides:

```
class Indexed<Thing> :
    members:   ids : IdSet      the set of IDs used as labels in the index
    operators: [i] : Thing      the element labeled by ID i
```

The subscripting operator `x[i]` for an index `x` generates a run-time error if `i` is not in `ids`. The template additionally provides set and arithmetic operators (Not. 5.15), both normally and in "increment" form as discussed in Section B.3.2. Internally, the class is implemented using a standard "container" mechanism that keys on the IDs internal integer code. The template for indexes with zero is the same except that it requires an argument indicating the zero element for the class that is indexed; that element is returned by `x[i]` if `i` is not in `ids`.

B.3.6   State Spaces

State spaces are implemented by using the object-oriented mechanism directly. Consider the example space **Rectangles** of Not. 5.25:

$$
\begin{array}{l}
\textbf{Rectangles} \\
[\\
\quad length \ \mapsto \Re \\
\quad width \ \mapsto \Re \\
\quad area \quad \mapsto \Re \\
\quad \rule{2cm}{0.4pt} \\
\quad length \geq 0 \\
\quad width \geq 0 \\
\quad area = length \times width \\
]
\end{array}
$$

We support each aspect directly as a data member—thus we are representing an element of the state space by the full tuple of aspect values:

```
class Rectangle :
    constructors:  (double length,width)           minimal identifying tuple
                   (double length,area)            minimal identifying tuple
                   (double width,area)             minimal identifying tuple
                   (double length,width,area)      full tuple
    members:       length : double
                   width  : double
                   area   : double
```

All the data members are declared to be constant, as per Section B.3.2. As discussed in Section 5.9.2, for this space any pair of the aspect values is sufficient to identify an element; we define three constructors accordingly, each of which computes the third aspect value from the given two. We also define a constructor that accepts a full tuple. All the constructors verify that the arguments are nonnegative and that the area property holds; a run-time error is generated if this is not the case.

In general, we don't implement constructors for all possible identifying tuples—merely for those that we find to be useful. But all constructors must be careful to construct an instance that satisfies all the internal properties of the space (or else to generate a run-time error). As discussed in Section B.3.2, we want to guarantee that all math object instances are valid, by construction.

We do generally implement state spaces by providing members for all aspect values, as described above, because of its simplicity. However, if memory space is a concern, or if we don't want to spend the time computing all aspect values at construction time, we can use a more compact representation. For example, Rectangle could store just the length and width as members and could provide an accessor method to compute the area.

Nested state spaces (Section 5.9.4) are implemented as ordinary data members. Inherited aspects can simply duplicate the data of the nested space, or can be references to the nested space's aspect values.

B.3.7   Paths and Other Functions

The mathematical models often define abstract spaces whose elements are paths (functions from the reals) or more general functions. For example, we have KINEMATIC :: StatePaths (Def. 9.2), SysVectorFields (Def. 10.16), and ProtoGens (Def. 11.6).

Like state spaces, we don't provide any direct support for function spaces, but they are implemented readily using the object-oriented mechanism. Consider the space of Rectangles (Section B.3.6) as a function of time:

$$\text{RectanglePaths} \equiv \textit{the set of functions } \{\Re \to \text{Rectangles}\}.$$

It is implemented simply as:

```
class RectanglePath :
    methods:  eval(double t) : Rectangle    evaluate the function at time t
```

The class doesn't provide an implementation of the eval method. Instead, it is a base class, and we use the object-oriented mechanism to define subclasses that implement various specific functions, based on their constructor arguments. For example, one subclass might define eval to return a given constant value. Another might define eval to compute a rectangle that moves as some explicit function of time.

Most importantly, we can define a subclass that invokes a numerical routine to solve a posed mathematical problem—this is the primary "hook" through which we access the numerics section of the program. For example, Section 10.5.3 describes a subclass of MRIG::SysPath that invokes a differential equation solver, and Section 11.5.3 describes a subclass of MRIG::ApplMotiveIdxField that sets ups and solves a linear system of equations.

For paths into state spaces, we can often compose paths for each aspect operator. For example:

```
class RectanglePath :
    members:   length : doublePath
               width  : doublePath
               area   : doublePath
    methods:   eval(double t) : Rectangle
```

Each aspect path is set to a subclass that implements its eval by calling RectanglePath's eval, and returns the proper aspect value of the result.

Every index of functions has an implied function that returns an index by simply evaluating all the element functions and making an index of the results (Def. 5.17). Correspondingly, we may have a class ThingFuncIdx, being indexes of functions, and another class ThingIdxFunc, being functions that return indexes. The latter could support a subclass that is constructed from a specific index of functions instance, and whose eval method simply evaluates all the element functions and constructs an index to hold the results.

B.3.8 Discussion

We have used the methods that we have outlined, to implement the mathematical models of the modules in Part III. We have found that the mathematical modeling method fits well with an object-oriented implementation. Implementing a mathematical model from a given blackboard specification is not hard—simply a matter of typing in the appropriate class definitions and so forth. There is a great deal of rote in the task, especially in the minutiae of the object-oriented class specifications. We can imagine embedded or special-purpose mathematical modeling languages that more directly support our mathematical modeling constructs. See discussion in Sections 15.1.4 and 15.4.

B.4   The Numerics Section

The numerics section of a program, as discussed in Ch. 6, is responsible for computing numerical solutions to the posed problems. There is a large body of knowledge and software for numerical computation, which we can take advantage of for physically-based modeling; see, e.g., [Press *et al.*86], [Ralston, Rabinowitz78], [Golub,Van Loan85], and [NAG].

We can assume that we have a rich library of numerical subroutines readily available to us. So what more needs to be done? The answer is that we need to join the "back-end" numerical subroutines with the higher levels of abstraction in a modeling program. This section discusses the structure and mechanism that we build on top of an existing numerical library.

B.4.1   Overview of the "Structured Numerics" Library

The numerics section bridges between the numerical subroutines and the mechanisms that are used by the math section and M–N interface of a program (Section 6.2.4), in order to overcome some basic design differences (see Fig. B.1). In bridging between them, we perform changes of representation as discussed in Section 6.6.

Thus we build a *structured numerics* library: a modular, object-oriented collection of interfaces to numerical techniques. The library is designed to provide access to numerical techniques in a form convenient for the high-level abstraction and goals, rather than driven by the low-level design and implementation goals.

Figure B.2 illustrates the hierarchy of modules in our prototype structured numerics library. As per Sections 6.1 and 3.7.3, we provide a collection of tools at various levels of representation so that for any particular application, the programmer may choose the most convenient form. We are not attempting to provide a single interface or paradigm to span all problems.[3]

Despite our high-flown talk of "abstraction," "changes of representation," and so forth, the structured numerics library is very mundane: It deals with programming details such as data format and subroutine interfaces, and the bulk of its implementation is involved with housekeeping issues such as storage allocation, cacheing intermediate results, and so forth. Note in particular that little or no

---

[3]In general, numerical computation today is a job for "hobbyists": To get meaningful results most effectively, one must have an understanding of issues such as accuracy and tolerance, a feel for the character of the particular problem being solved, a familiarity with the strengths and weaknesses of various known solution techniques, and so forth. This limits our ability to provide "universal" high-level interfaces that allow the user to ignore implementation and solution details. Still, well-packaged interfaces can be designed that apply to a reasonably broad range of problems. And, by designing our library as a collection of tools at various levels, we allow users to "reach down" and access lower-level routines as necessary without breaking the spirit or function of the library.

Numerical subroutine design *versus*	Program requirements
Data formats:	
• *Arrays of numbers.* Numerical subroutines most commonly operate on arrays of numbers.	• *Conceptually separate objects.* We may group together separate objects for the purpose of solving a particular problem; e.g., an index of dynamic body states is grouped into an array for Eq. 10.35.
Access methods:	
• *Procedural, arcane.* Special-purpose routines or sequences must often be followed to provide data or access solutions; e.g., ODE solvers typically require repeated calls to a subroutine to advance the solution by steps; a different routine can interpolate within the most recent step.	• *Uniform interface.* For any given problem, we would like to specify the problem conveniently and access the solution freely; e.g., we want to evaluate a solution function $Y(t)$ for arbitrary values of time t, as discussed in Section 6.7.
Choice of algorithm:	
• *One algorithm per subroutine.* Each subroutine and algorithm is typically suitable to a specific regime of the problem; e.g., a routine may solve a sparse linear least-squares problem using a Lanczos algorithm.	• *One interface for various algorithms.* A problem may need to be solved in different regimes; e.g., a linear system of equations may be sparse or dense, or ill or well conditioned.
Programming paradigm:	
• *Subroutine paradigm.* Numerical routines often assume or are geared toward use by a program that solves a single problem; they are often not re-entrant.[4]	• *Object-oriented paradigm.* Many separate objects can coexist, each of which solves a particular problem; solution evaluations may be intermingled.

Figure B.1: This table lists various differences in design between numerical "back-end" subroutines and higher levels of the program. The design of numerical routines is low-level, driven by algorithm and implementation issues, whereas for the higher level of the program we have explicitly tried to be driven by abstraction and high-level goals. The *structured numerics* library is designed to bridge between the low and high levels. □

numerical computation takes places within our modules—ultimately, they are merely interfaces to existing numerical subroutine libraries.

The next several sections discuss various modules in our prototype library

---

[4]A *re-entrant* technique is one that can be used simultaneously or in an interleaved manner by different applications. For example, we might want to advance one ODE solution, then solve a

"Structured Numerics" Library

Module Hierarchies

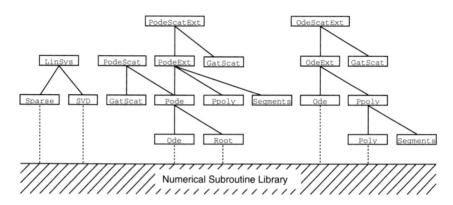

Figure B.2: Schematic diagram of some module hierarchies in our prototype "structured numerics" library, built on top of a standard numerical subroutine library. The library is intended to be used as a toolbox, with modules at various levels of representation available for different applications. For example, Ode, OdeExt, and OdeScatExt provide different interfaces to ordinary differential equation initial-value problems; the "best" one to use depends on the application. Sections B.4.2–B.4.11 describe the modules. □

(those that are used by the models in Part III). We simply outline the structure and interface to the modules to "give a feel" for the library—complete implementation specifications are beyond the scope of this book. For the underlying solution techniques, we refer readers to [Press *et al.*86].

B.4.2   GatScat: Array Gather/Scatter

This is a utility class that does the housekeeping to map between a collection of separate elements, each having local data, and a single linear array of data. The following methods are supported:

add(...)   Add an element to the collection—an element is specified via subroutines to read and write its local data, or simply by the memory location of the local data. Each element can be a different size.

gather(array)   Gather each element's local data into an array.

scatter(array)   Scatter an array of data into each element's local data.

---

different ODE, then continue advancing the original. FORTRAN numerical libraries often store information about a problem in shared "common blocks," so that starting a second problem solution precludes the ability to continue the first.

After adding each element once, the gather and scatter methods can be used repeatedly with different data sets. Other methods map between elements and their array indexes, return the total size of the array, and so forth. GatScat is used by OdeScatExt (Section B.4.6) and PodeScatExt (Section B.4.9).

The class GatScat2 is similar, but maps between separate elements and a 2D block matrix of data. Each element specifies its row and column in the matrix; not all entries in the matrix need to be specified. The gather and scatter methods support both sparse and full arrays. Additionally, GatScat2 can partition the matrix into independent blocks, based on which entries have elements associated with them. GatScat2 is used by the "fancy forces" model, NFRC::LsolveProto (Section 11.5.3), and is compatible with LinSys (Section B.4.3).

B.4.3   LinSys: Linear Systems of Equations

This is a class that solves matrix equations of the form $MX + B = 0$, computing values of matrix X given values of M and B. If the matrix M is singular or ill conditioned, the least-squares solution is computed.

For our applications, M is commonly sparse, though not always, and M may sometimes be ill conditioned or singular. We can't always tell in advance—for example, a system may generally be well conditioned, but may occasionally pass through an ill-conditioned "zone" during the course of a simulation.

LinSys is a "black box" that lets the user specify the system using ordinary 2D array data format and that runs as fast as possible in the general case, yet is guaranteed to work (albeit more slowly) in the special cases. Its features are

- It partitions M into independent blocks, and solves each one separately.
- Within each block, if the matrix is sparse, it constructs the appropriate sparse representation, and uses Sparse (an interface to a Lanczos method) to solve the system. Sparse may report failure if the matrix is too ill conditioned.
- If the matrix is not sparse, or if the sparse solution fails, singular-value decomposition is used instead, which is slow but essentially has guaranteed success.

LinSys is compatible with GatScat2 (Section B.4.2), which can be used to pre-compute the partition and sparsity of the matrix.

B.4.4   Ode: Ordinary Differential Equation

This is a class that solves ordinary differential equation (ODE) initial-value problems: It computes $y(t)$ where $\frac{d}{dt}y = f(y, t)$, given a value $y_0 = y(t_0)$.

Ode provides an object-oriented interface to various techniques in the numerical library; that is, an abstract base class is defined, and assorted derived classes implement Runge–Kutta, Adams, and other techniques. Ode performs no changes of representation, supporting array data format and sequential access methods:

step()   Advance the solution to some larger value of t.
interp(t)   Interpolate the solution within the last step.
solve(t)   Advance until and return the solution at time t.

Unlike LinSys (Section B.4.3), our current implementation of Ode does not choose solution techniques automatically.

B.4.5 OdeExt: Extruded ODE

This is a class that solves ordinary differential equation (ODE) initial-value problems, as does Ode (Section B.4.4). Unlike Ode, however, this class doesn't require sequential access to the solution $y(t)$. Instead, the solution is "extruded," allowing the user to evaluate $y(t)$ for any values of t, in any order. Its primary interface method is thus:

eval(t)   Evaluate the solution for any time $t > t_0$.

OdeExt uses array data format, the same as Ode.

Internally, OdeExt works by maintaining the solution as a piecewise-polynomial function, using Ppoly (Section B.4.10). If evaluation is requested at a time beyond the bounds of the stored solution, Ode is used to advance the solution as needed; the result of each step along the way is added to the stored solution.[5]

For many problems, we only need to evaluate $y(t)$ for monotonically or almost-monotonically increasing values of t. Thus, to save memory, OdeExt can maintain a "sliding window" that moves forward automatically as the solution is advanced—solution values prior to the start of the window are thrown away.

B.4.6 OdeScatExt: Scattered, Extruded ODE

This class combines the extruded ODE-solving functionality of OdeExt (Section B.4.5) with the array gather/scatter functionality of GatScat (Section B.4.2). This is used, for example, by the rigid-body dynamics model routine NRIG::SolveForward (Section 10.5.3) to construct an object that computes an index of rigid body states, for any value of time t.

---

[5]Most ODE-solving techniques internally compute a polynomial to describe the value of the function in the most recent step. Often, the polynomial itself is not made directly available—but its order k is known, thus we can accurately resample the solution to construct an explicit polynomial function.

B.4.7 Pode: Piecewise-Continuous ODE

This class is analogous to Ode (Section B.4.4), but supports piecewise-continuous ODEs, using the solution technique discussed in Appendix C.

B.4.8 PodeExt: Extruded PODE

This class is analogous to OdeExt (Section B.4.5), but supports piecewise-continuous ODEs. The solution $y(t)$ is a segmented function, as described in Section 5.10, whose size may change at the discontinuous events. PodeExt allows the transition function that starts a segment (see Appendix C) to specify arbitrary data for the solver to associate with that segment. The eval(t) method returns the associated data for the segment that spans time t, and the size of the solution within that segment, as well as the array containing the solution at time t.

The Segments utility (Section B.4.11) is used to keep track of the separate segments of the solution; within each segment the solution is accumulated as a piecewise-polynomial function in the same manner as OdeExt.

B.4.9 PodeScatExt: Scattered, Extruded PODE

Analogous to OdeScatExt (Section B.4.6), this class combines the functionality of PodeExt (Section B.4.8) with the array gather/scatter functionality of GatScat (Section B.4.2). It is used by the "tennis ball cannon" model (Section 13.5.2).

In addition to gathering and scattering the solution values, PodeScatExt allows the user to specify separate event functions (see Appendix C), and will gather their values into an array for PodeExt. When an event is detected, i.e., a root of an event function is discovered, the user's transition function is passed a code indicating which of the events was found (see Section 13.5.2).

We also provide a class PodeScat that supports scattered data, but only provides sequential access to the solution. Functionally it is equivalent to using PodeScatExt with a "sliding window" of zero width, so that no prior values are saved—but the interface is simpler.

B.4.10 Ppoly: Piecewise-Polynomial Functions

This class supports piecewise-polynomial functions. It uses the Poly class (which implements Chebychev polynomials) for each piece and keeps track of them via the Segments utility (segments). It supports the following methods:

addl(...)	Add a polynomial segment on the left end.
addr(...)	Add a polynomial segment on the right end.
eval(t)	Evaluate the solution for any time t within the endpoints of the stored function. This method uses Segments to determine which polynomial spans time t, then evaluates that polynomial.

The class also provides miscellaneous support, such as methods to "trim" the function throwing away polynomials outside a given range.

Ppoly is used by OdeExt (Section B.4.5) and PodeExt (Section B.4.8).

B.4.11 Segments: Partition of the Real Number Line

This is a utility class that does the housekeeping to maintain a collection of adjacent segments of the real number line, maintaining arbitrary data for each segment. Starting with an initial endpoint for the structure, it supports the following methods:

addl(t, data)	Add a segment on the left end, and store the provided data.
addr(t, data)	Add a segment on the right end, and store the provided data.
data(t)	Look up and return the data of the segment containing t.

The class also provides miscellaneous support, such as methods to iterate through all the segments.

Segments is used by PodeExt (Section B.4.8) and Ppoly (Section B.4.10).

B.4.12 Discussion

We have presented the "structured numerics" library as part of the overall program framework for physically-based modeling that we described in Ch. 6. However, it is not specific to that framework.

Our prototype structured numerics library has been used (and extended) by colleagues for applications other than physically-based modeling: a modular, object-oriented numerics library that supports high-level representations is useful even for projects that don't include the rest of the "structured modeling" mechanism.

Currently, numerical subroutine libraries are as we have described—low-level, array-oriented, and so forth—typically written in FORTRAN. However, with the advent and popularity of object-oriented programming, it is likely that in the near future, the bottom-level numerical routines available from vendors will be object-oriented and modular and will support high-level representations such as we described. If so, our comment at the start of Section B.4:

> We can assume that we have a rich library of numerical subroutines readily available. ... So what more needs to be done?

will need to be updated:

> We can assume that we have a rich library of object-oriented numerical modules readily available. ... Nothing more needs to be done.

Appendix C

Solving
Piecewise-Continuous ODEs

This appendix describes an algorithm to solve initial-value problems for piecewise-continuous ordinary differential equations (PODEs). The solution to a PODE is a "segmented function," as discussed in Section 5.10; we use the mechanism developed there to specify a PODE to be solved.

The solution technique makes use of common ODE-solving and root-finding techniques as "black boxes," allowing easy tailoring of the solution mechanism to specific problems, by appropriate choice of "boxes" and their parameters. Solution techniques such as we describe, which locate events in continuous ODEs, are recent additions to the field of numerical computation; we refer readers to [Shampine *et al.*91] for further discussion.

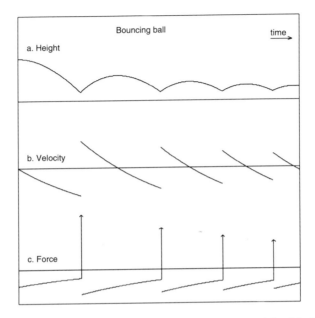

Figure C.1: Example of a PODE: a bouncing ball, with damping. (a) The height of the ball. (b) The velocity of the ball. (c) The force on the ball; at each bounce, an infinite force is required to change the velocity instantaneously. □

C.1 Formalism for Piecewise-Continuous ODEs (PODEs)

C.1.1 Definition

We define a *piecewise-continuous ordinary differential equation* (PODE) to be an ordinary differential equation[1]

$$(C.1) \qquad \frac{d}{dt} y = \mathcal{F}(y, t)$$

for which the function $\mathcal{F}(y, t)$ is piecewise-continuous in y and t; that is, $\mathcal{F}(y(t), t)$ is continuous and has a bounded derivative, except at isolated values of t. The solution to a PODE is a *segmented function*, as per Section 5.10, i.e., is piecewise-continuous. Note that in general we are interested in solving for functions

---

[1] The PODE method described in this chapter will work in exactly the same manner with piecewise-continuous differential–algebraic equations (DAEs), e.g., of the form $\mathcal{F}(y, dy/dt, t) = 0$ (see [Petzold82]). However, because of their greater familiarity, we present the discussion in terms of ODEs.

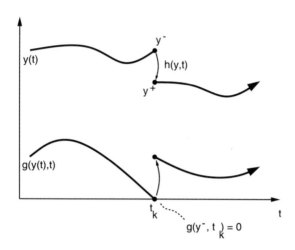

Figure C.2: A PODE. $y(t)$ is the continuous solution of $\frac{d}{dt}y = f(y,t)$ [not shown], until $g(y(t),t) = 0$. Then $y(t)$ is changed discontinuously by adding $h(y,t)$, and the solution progresses continuously again. □

$$y: t \rightarrow \bigcup_{i=1,2,\dots} \Re^i,$$

but for the present discussion we will assume that the solution stays in $\Re^n$ for constant n; Section C.2 reintroduces arbitrary dimensionality in the solution.

We use a "functional characterization" to describe a PODE, as discussed in Section 5.10.3. That is, we define three functions:

(C.2)
$$
\begin{array}{lll}
\textit{"body function"} & f: \Re^n \times \Re \rightarrow \Re^n \\
\textit{"event function"} & g: \Re^n \times \Re \rightarrow \Re \\
\textit{"transition function"} & h: \Re^n \times \Re \rightarrow \Re^n
\end{array}
$$

Note that unlike Section 5.10.3, here we define the functions numerically rather than in predicate form.

$f(y,t)$: $f(y,t) \equiv \mathcal{F}(y,t)$ wherever $\mathcal{F}(y,t)$ is continuous and has a bounded derivative. $f(y,t)$ need not be defined where $\mathcal{F}(y,t)$ is discontinuous or singular.

$g(y,t)$: An "event" function, which locates discontinuities by defining legal states: As long as the solution $y(t)$ is in a legal state, $f(y,t)$ must be continuous and well behaved; if the solution attempts to enter an illegal state, a discontinuity occurs at the boundary. Thus we define

(C.3) $g(y, t)$
$$\begin{cases} > 0\text{:} & y \text{ is a legal state at } t \\ < 0\text{:} & y \text{ is an illegal state at } t \\ = 0\text{:} & \text{Boundary state:} \quad \mathcal{F}(y, t) \\ & \text{may be discontinuous or} \\ & \text{singular; } y(t) \text{ may be dis-} \\ & \text{continuous} \end{cases}$$

$g(y, t) = 0$ occurs only at the discontinuities or singularities in $\mathcal{F}(y, t)$.[2] The solution $y(t)$ always has the property that $g(y(t), t) \geq 0$. $g(y, t)$ itself must be continuous where it is nonzero.[3],[4]

$h(y, t)$: A "transition" function, which bridges discontinuities by describing the change in the solution $y(t)$: At each discontinuity, $y(t)$ is offset by adding $h(y, t)$ (see Fig. C.2). That is, given a t_k such that $y^- = y(t_k)$ and $g(y^-, t_k) = 0$, we have

(C.4) $$y^+ = y^- + h(y^-, t_k).$$

In effect $h(y, t)$ integrates $f(y, t)$ across the discontinuity; thus if $f(y, t)$ contains a delta function, then $h(y, t)$ is nonzero. i.e.,

(C.5)
$$\textit{if}$$
$$\mathcal{F}(y, t) = \mathcal{H}(y, t)\, \delta(t - t_k) + \left\{ \begin{array}{c} \textit{terms w/o} \\ \delta \textit{ functions} \end{array} \right\},$$
$$\textit{then}$$
$$h(y, t) = \int_{t_k^-}^{t_k^+} \mathcal{F}(y, t)\, dt$$
$$= \mathcal{H}(y(t_k), t_k).$$

---

[2]For some applications there may be several conditions, any of which might signal a discontinuity. Thus $g(y, t)$ may be an array, and the comparisons $g(y, t) > 0$, < 0, and $= 0$ refer to its minimum element. The implementation can support arrys; this allows us to support multiple independent events, as discussed in Section B.4.9.

[3]That is, we may have: $g(y(t), t)$ continuous for $t \neq t_k$, with $\lim\limits_{t \to t_k^-} g(y(t), t) = 0$ and $\lim\limits_{t \to t_k^+} g(y(t), t) \neq 0$, as in Fig. C.2.

[4]We could also just have $g \neq 0$ is the continuous state, and $g = 0$ signals a discontinuity. But having legal versus illegal states is convenient for debugging and is typically not a hardship for the designer of the event function (just negate it if you want it to be legal but it's negative).

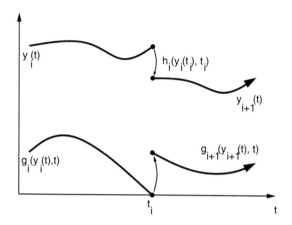

Figure C.3: A PODE considered as a sequence of continuous ODE segments. $y_i(t)$ is the continuous solution of the ith segment $\frac{d}{dt}y_i = f_i(y,t)$, until $g_i(y_i(t),t) = 0$ at $t = t_i$. $h_i(y_i(t_i),t_i)$ yields the initial conditions for segment $i+1$. The sequence $\{\ldots, < t_i, y_i >, < t_{i+1}, y_{i+1} >, \ldots\}$ is the sequential representation (Def. 5.37) of the solution to the PODE. □

C.1.2 Continuous ODE Segments

As an alternative to Eq. C.2, a PODE can be conveniently specified by a sequence of continuous ODE segments, whose solutions form a sequential representation (Section 5.10.2) of the segmented function that solves the PODE (see Fig. C.3):

(C.6)
$$\frac{d}{dt}y_1 = f_1(y_1, t) \ while \ g_1(y_1(t), t) > 0$$
$$\frac{d}{dt}y_2 = f_2(y_2, t) \ while \ g_2(y_2(t), t) > 0$$
$$\vdots$$
$$\frac{d}{dt}y_i = f_i(y_i, t) \ \ while \ g_i(y_i(t), t) > 0$$
$$\vdots$$

where each of the f_i's and g_i's are continuous. t_i is the time of the end of the ith segment; that is, we define t_i to be the earliest $t \geq t_{i-1}$ such that:

(C.7)
$$g_i(y_i(t_i), t_i) = 0.$$

Notice that we may have $t_i = t_{i-1}$; in such a case, we refer to segment i as having *zero-length*.

At t_i, we switch from the ith to the $(i+1)$th ODE. The initial conditions for the new ODE are given by:

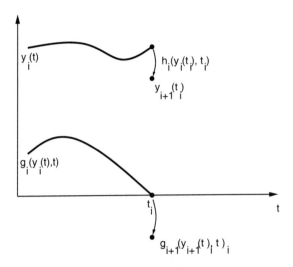

Figure C.4: Unsolvable PODE: The initial conditions of segment $i + 1$ are such that $g_{i+1}(y, t)$ is negative at the start of the segment. $\square$

(C.8)
$$y_{i+1}(t_i) = y_i(t_i) + h_i(y_i(t_i), t_i).$$

The functions of Eq. C.2 are produced by:

(C.9)
$$f(y, t) = f_i(y, t), \text{ where } t_{i-1} < t < t_i$$
$$g(y, t) = g_i(y, t), \text{ where } t_{i-1} < t \leq t_i$$
$$h(y, t) = h_i(y, t), \text{ where } t = t_i,$$

and the solution is[5]

(C.10)
$$y(t) = y_i(y, t), \text{ where } t_{i-1} \leq t \leq t_i.$$

C.1.3 Errors

There are two errors that are endemic to PODEs defined as per the previous section:

---

[5]Notice that at each t_i the solution $y(t_i)$ has two values: the value before and that after the discontinuity (see discussion in Section 5.10.2). The solution technique described in Section C.2 finds and returns both these values.

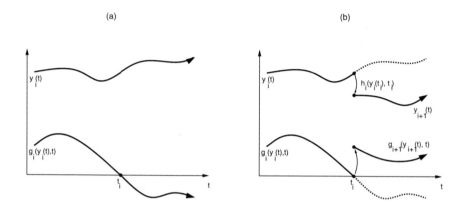

Figure C.5: Solving a PODE: (a) $y_i(t)$ is determined using a standard ODE-solver. An ODE solution step might extend past the end of the segment; $g_i(y_i(t), t)$ is sampled to see if it goes below zero; if it does, the root t_i is found by using a standard root-finder with the interpolation of $y_i(t)$ over the last ODE step. (b) Once the end of segment i has been determined, at $t = t_i$, then $h_i(y_i(t_i), t_i)$ is added to $y_i(t_i)$ to yield the initial conditions for segment $i + 1$. The solution of segment i for $t > t_i$ is discarded. $\square$

- If $g_{i+1}(y_{i+1}(t_i), t_i) < 0$, the initial conditions for segment $i + 1$ specify an illegal state; the PODE cannot be solved (see Fig. C.4).

- If $t_i = t_{i-1}$ for all i after some i_0, i.e., if all segments after segment i_0 have zero-length, the PODE cannot progress beyond t_{i_0}. Such an occurrence is often an indication of an attempt to simulate a continuous process by repeated application of the transition function $h(y, t)$.

The solution technique described in Section C.2 can detect both these errors.

C.2   Solving a PODE

Note: For notational convenience, we define the following three functions:

$$
\begin{aligned}
F_i(t) &\equiv f_i(y_i(t), t) \\
G_i(t) &\equiv g_i(y_i(t), t) \\
H_i(t) &\equiv h_i(y_i(t), t).
\end{aligned}
$$

(C.11)

Overview

A PODE described as a series of continuous ODEs (as per Eq. C.6) can be solved easily: Each segment can be solved in turn using a standard initial-value ODE-solver; the end of a segment is marked by a root of the composite function $G_i(t)$.

Thus the algorithm for solving a PODE, illustrated in Fig. C.5, is

1. **Solve segment** i. Use a standard ODE-solver to determine the function $y_i(t)$.

2. **Monitor** $G_i(t)$. Watch to see if the value crosses below zero.

3. **Find root** t_i. If a zero-crossing is encountered, use a standard root-finder to find the time t_i, as per Eq. C.7. This marks the end of segment i.

4. **Switch to segment** $i + 1$. $H_i(t_i)$ is added to $y_i(t_i)$ to yield the initial conditions of segment $i + 1$ (Eq. C.8).

Note that the algorithm works by solving $y_i(t)$ some distance past t_i, and by observing a negative value of $G_i(t)$. Thus there are extra restrictions on the f_i's and g_i's:

- $f_i(y, t)$ and $g_i(y, t)$ must extend continuously some amount past t_i.

- The algorithm finds zero-crossings, rather than zeros, of $G_i(t)$; the composite function must be negative for some $t > t_i$.

To minimize the amount that $y_i(t)$ is solved past the end of its segment, we alternate (1) and (2) above. That is, we have the ODE-solver solve $y_i(t)$ for one step; then we verify that $G_i(t)$ remains positive; then we take another ODE step, and repeat.

We discuss the four parts of the algorithm in greater detail in the following sections.

C.2.1   Solving Continuous Segment i

The standard ODE-solving technique may be used as a "black box" to produce the continuous function $y_i(t)$ that is the solution to $\frac{d}{dt}y_i = f_i(y_i, t)$. The initial conditions are determined from the final state of the previous segment (for the first segment, the initial conditions are provided by the user). We assume that the ODE-solver takes steps, and reports back a local solution function after each step.[6]

Note that, at each step, we are interested in a continuous local solution function $y_i(t)$, rather than just the value of y_i at the end of the step. Thus our choice of ODE-solver is restricted to techniques that support interpolation of the solution in

---

[6]The ODE-solver is free to use whatever step size it determines to be appropriate; the step size does not have to be constant.

the last step; Adams-based methods work well. Extrapolation-based techniques (e.g., Bulirsch–Stoer) are not well suited to our PODE method. (See, e.g., [Ralston,Rabinowitz78] or [Press *et al.*86] for discussion of Adams and extrapolation methods.)

C.2.2   Sampling $G_i(t)$

Given the result of an ODE step, i.e., given a continuous function $y_i(t)$ over some interval, we want to determine whether $G_i(t)$ is always positive. We attempt to do so by sampling $G_i(t)$ at several values of t.

We can't guarantee to find all zero-crossings of $G_i(t)$ without extra information, such as a Lipschitz bound on $G_i(t)$.[7] Rather than require the user to provide explicit Lipschitz information, or perhaps the partial derivatives of $g_i(y, t)$ with respect to y and t, the implementation described here takes the following approach:

- Sample at the end of every ODE step.

- Sample at least every τ_g, where τ_g is a user-adjustable sampling interval.

To allow adaptive control over the sampling interval, the user may adjust τ_g "on the fly," e.g., as a side effect of evaluating $g_i(y, t)$.

Again, we emphasize that this approach is chosen for programming convenience, and does not guarantee correctness unless the user adjusts τ_g based on the Lipschitz bounds of $G_i(t)$.

For some PODEs, it is sufficient to sample $G_i(t)$ only at each ODE step (e.g., because $G_i(t)$ changes slowly compared to $y_i(t)$, or because $G_i(t) < 0$ for all $t > t_i$). The implementation supports "turning off" the minimum sampling interval.

C.2.3   Finding t_i, the Root of $G_i(t)$

If a sample of $G_i(t)$ is negative, we have detected a zero-crossing. The previous (positive) sample and the new (negative) sample bracket a root of the composite function $G_i(t)$. A standard root-finder can be used to determine the root value t_i at which $G_i(t_i) = 0$. (Since $G_i(t)$ is continuous, and since we start with a bracketing interval, techniques such as Regula Falsi are guaranteed to find the root. See, e.g., [Press *et al.*86].)

Because $G_i(t)$ is sampled at the end of every ODE step, we know that the root bracket lies entirely within the current step. Thus the ODE-solver's local solution function $y_i(t)$ can be used; no new ODE-solving steps need to be taken during the root-finding process.

---

[7]A Lipschitz bound is a value L such that $|G_i(t_2) - G_i(t_1)| \leq L|t_2 - t_1|$ for all t_1, t_2 in a region of interest. See [Kalra,Barr89].

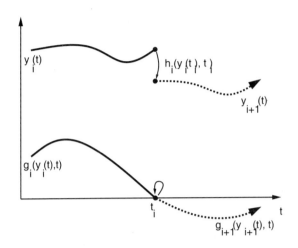

Figure C.6: Zero-length segments: $g_{i+1}(y, t) = 0$ at the start of segment $i + 1$ at $t = t_i$, and $g_{i+1}(y_{i+1}(t), t) < 0$ for $t > t_i$. Thus the end of the segment is the same as the start: $t_{i+1} = t_i$. □

C.2.4 Switching to Segment $i + 1$

Given that we have found a discontinuity at $t = t_i$, the following occurs:

- We compute the initial conditions for the next segment: $y_{i+1}(t_i) = y_i(t_i) + H_i(t_i)$.

- i is (implicitly) incremented; i.e., the user switches to the next set of functions, f_{i+1}, g_{i+1}, and h_{i+1}. For solutions that are segmented functions which switch between disparate components of the solution space (see Section 5.10), y_{i+1}, f_{i+1}, g_{i+1}, and h_{i+1} can be given different dimensionality than the previous segment.

- We reset the ODE-solver to have it discard history and start integrating the new segment from the new initial conditions.

$G_{i+1}(t_i)$ should be evaluated to ensure that the initial conditions of the new segment describe a legal state. If $G_{i+1}(t_i) < 0$, the PODE is unsolvable (see Fig. C.4).

C.2.5 Zero-Length Segments

A zero-length segment occurs if two conditions hold (see Fig. C.6):

- $G_i(t_{i-1}) = 0$; i.e., the initial conditions of the segment are on a boundary of the legal state, and

- $G_i(t) < 0$ for $t > t_{i-1}$; i.e., the solution immediately attempts to enter an illegal state.

No special care need be taken to detect zero-length segments; we can merely check if $t_i = t_{i-1}$.

C.2.6   Numerical Issues

There are several numerical issues that arise in the implementation of the PODE solution algorithm:

- As discussed earlier, without Lipschitz bounds on $g(y_i(t), t)$, it is possible to sample too sparsely and thus miss zero-crossings.

- The test of $g > 0$ should be tolerant to within some bounds; proper error-analysis should be done to determine the tolerance. A simplifying approach is to put the burden on the user to add the appropriate absolute tolerance terms in the calculation of $g(y, t)$, so that comparison against zero is valid.

- The root-finder typically doesn't find the exact zero, but instead brackets the root with a t^{pos} and a t^{neg}, such that $G_i(t^{\mathrm{pos}}) > 0$ and $G_i(t^{\mathrm{neg}}) < 0$, where t^{pos} and t^{neg} differ by some small tolerance. A handy trick is to choose t^{pos} as the root, thus ensuring that $G_i(t)$ is never negative.

- If $G_i(t) = 0$ over a finite region before becoming negative, the root-finder is likely to choose an arbitrary point within the region as the root. If $G_i(t) = 0$ and then becomes positive, no zero-crossing will be detected, and hence no root will be looked for.

- As discussed in Section C.2.3, the initial root bracket lies within a single ODE step. The positive g-value at the left side of the bracket, however, may have been determined by the value of $y_i(t)$ at the end of the previous step. Because of numerical imprecision, interpolating the current step back to the end of the previous step yields a different value for $y_i(t)$; thus the composite function $G_i(t)$ may have a discontinuity at the left endpoint of the bracket. Occasionally, the discontinuity is such that we have a positive value at the left endpoint, and negative values in the rest of the region; in such a case, we take the left endpoint to be the root.

- In adaptively adjusting τ_g, the user must avoid continually decreasing τ_g in a converging series, or the solver will not be able to make any forward progress. (This might happen, e.g., if at each sample of $g(t)$, the user estimates that the next discontinuity will occur at some t_0, and conservatively sets $\tau_g = \frac{1}{2}(t_0 - t)$.)

C.3 Computational Costs

The PODE algorithm doesn't directly do any numerical computation; rather it serves mainly to control the execution of the underlying ODE-solver and root-finder. The computational cost thus depends heavily on the choice of those routines.

We break down the costs into three major parts:

- "Startup overhead" for the ODE-solver at each discontinuity

- Cost of solving and testing the continuous segments

- Cost of determining t_i for each discontinuity

C.3.1 Startup Overhead

The ODE "startup overhead," if any, at a discontinuity depends on the solution method. For example, adaptive step-size methods may start with very small steps; multistep methods may use slower methods to generate initial samples; and implicit methods may need to determine the initial Jacobian matrix numerically.

For equations with a large number of discontinuities, the startup overhead may be a significant factor to be considered when choosing the ODE-solver.

C.3.2 Continuous Segments

To solve each continuous ODE-segment, the only cost added by the PODE method over the underlying ODE-solver is the cost of sampling $g_i(y_i(t), t)$ to ensure that the end of the segment hasn't been reached.

For globally continuous equations, the PODE method may be used by providing a constant positive function, e.g., $g(y, t) = 1$, with τ_g large. The cost of using PODE over using the underlying ODE-solver is then minimal. (But, of course, for this case PODE provides no advantage over using the underlying ODE-solver directly.)

C.3.3 Determining t_i

It is important to note that once a discontinuity has been detected, no ODE-solving is performed to determine t_i. Rather, $y_i(t)$ is interpolated in the last ODE step.

Thus, the cost of determining t_i is the cost of doing the root-finding. This depends on the root-finding technique, which will require evaluation of $g_i(y_i(t), t)$ some number of times.

Each evaluation of the composite function incurs the cost of doing the interpolation to evaluate $y_i(t)$; this depends on the ODE-solver, but is typically a relatively fast operation.

References

[Abelson *et al.*89] Harold Abelson, Michael Eisenberg, Matthew Halfant, Jacob Katzenelson, Elisha Sacks, Gerald J. Sussman, Jack Wisdom, and Kenneth Yip, "Intelligence in Scientific Computing," *Communications of the ACM,* Vol. 32, No. 5, May 1989, pp. 546–562.

[Badler *et al.*91] Norman I. Badler, Brian A. Barsky, David Zeltzer, eds., **Making Them Move: Mechanics, Control, and Animation of Articulated Figures,** Morgan Kaufmann, San Mateo, CA, 1991.

[Baraff89] David Baraff, "Analytical Methods for Dynamic Simulation of Non-penetrating Rigid Bodies," *Computer Graphics,* Vol. 23, No. 3 (Proc. SIGGRAPH), July 1989, pp. 223–232.

[Baraff90] David Baraff, "Curved Surfaces and Coherence for Non-penetrating Rigid Body Simulation," *Computer Graphics,* Vol. 24, No. 4 (Proc. SIGGRAPH), August 1990, pp. 19–28.

[Baraff91] David Baraff, "Coping with Friction for Non-penetrating Rigid Body Simulation," *Computer Graphics,* Vol. 25, No. 4 (Proc. SIGGRAPH), July 1991, pp. 31–40.

[Barr86] Alan H. Barr, *personal communication,* 1986.

[Barr87] Alan H. Barr, chair, "Topics in Physically-Based Modeling," *Course Notes,* Vol. 16, ACM SIGGRAPH, 1987.

[Barr91] Alan H. Barr, "Teleological Modeling," in [Badler *et al.*91].

[Barzel88] Ronen Barzel, *Controlling Rigid Bodies with Dynamic Constraints,* Master's Thesis, California Institute of Technology, Pasadena, CA, 1988.

[Barzel,Barr88] Ronen Barzel, and Alan H. Barr, "A Modeling System Based on Dynamic Constraints," *Computer Graphics,* Vol. 22, No. 4 (Proc. SIGGRAPH), August 1988, pp. 179–188.

[Bishop,Bridges85] E. Bishop, and D. Bridges, **Constructive Analysis,** Springer-Verlag, Berlin, 1985.

[Blaauw,Brooks93] G. A. Blaauw, and F. P. Brooks, Jr., **Computer Architecture,** Addison-Wesley, Reading, MA, in press.

[Blinn92] James F. Blinn, "Uppers and Downers," *IEEE Computer Graphics and Applications,* Vol. 12, No. 2, March, 1992, pp. 85–91.

[Boehm88] Barry W. Boehm, "A Spiral Model of Software Development and Enhancement," *Computer,* Vol. 21, No. 5, 1988, pp. 61–72.

[Booch91] Grady Booch, **Object-Oriented Design with Applications,** Benjamin/Cummings Publishing Company, Redwood City, CA, 1991.

[Boyce81] W. E. Boyce, **Case Studies in Mathematical Modeling,** Pitman Advanced Publishing Program, Boston, MA, 1981.

[Boyce,DePrima77] William E. Boyce, and Richard C. DePrima, **Elementary Differential Equations and Boundary Value Problems,** John Wiley & Sons, New York, 1977.

[Brockett90] R.W. Brockett, "Formal Languages for Motion Description and Map Making," in **Robotics** (Proc. Symposia in Applied Mathematics, Vol. 41), R. W. Brockett, ed., American Mathematical Society, Providence, RI, 1990.

[Brooks91] F. P. Brooks, Jr., speaker, *Panel Proceedings,* ACM SIGGRAPH, 1991.

[Bruderlin,Calvert89] Armin Bruderlin, and Thomas W. Calvert, "Goal-Directed, Dynamic Animation of Human Walking," *Computer Graphics,* Vol. 23, No. 3 (Proc. SIGGRAPH), July 1989, pp. 233–242.

[Caltech87] Caltech Computer Graphics Group, "Caltech Studies in Modeling And motion," *ACM SIGGRAPH Video Review,* Issue 28, 1987.

[Carroll60] Lewis Carroll, **The Annotated Alice** *with an introduction and notes by Martin Gardner,* New American Library, New York, 1960.

[Chadwick *et al.*89] John E. Chadwick, David R. Haumann, and Richard E. Parent, "Layerd Construction for Defomable Animated Characters," *Computer Graphics,* Vol. 23, No. 3 (Proc. SIGGRAPH), July 1989, pp. 243–252.

[Chandy,Taylor92] K. Mani Chandy, and Stephen Taylor, **An Introduction to Parallel Programming,** Jones and Bartlett, Boston, MA, 1992.

[Char *et al.*91] Bruce W. Char, Keith O. Geddes, Gaston H. Gonnet, Benton L. Leong, Michale B. Monagan, and Stephen M. Watt, **Maple V Language Reference Manual,** Springer-Verlag, New York, 1991.

[Cleaveland86] J. Craig Ceaveland, **An Introduction to Data Types,** Addison-Wesley, Reading, MA, 1986.

[Cook *et al.*84] Robert L. Cook, Thomas Porter, and Loren Carpenter, "Distributed Ray Tracing," *Computer Graphics,* Vol. 18, No. 3 (Proc. SIGGRAPH), July 1983, pp. 137–145.

[Craig89] John J. Craig, **Introduction to Robotics: Mechanics and Control,** 2nd edition, Addison-Wesley, Reading, MA, 1989.

[Crow87] Frank Crow, "The Origins of the Teapot," *IEEE Computer Graphics and Applications,* Vol. 7, No. 1, January 1987, pp. 8–19.

[Dahl *et al.*72] O.-J. Dahl, E. W. Dijkstra, and C. A. R. Hoare, **Structured Programming,** Academic Press, London, 1972.

[Dijkstra72] Edsger W. Dijkstra, "Notes on Structured Programming," in [Dahl *et al.*72].

[Dijkstra76] Edsger W. Dijkstra, **A Discipline of Programming,** Prentice Hall, Englewood Cliffs, NJ, 1976.

[Edwards,Hamson90] Dilwyn Edwards, and Mike Hamson, **Guide to Mathematical Modeling,** CRC Press, Boca Raton, FL, 1990.

[Foley *et al.*90] James D. Foley, Andries van Dam, Steven K. Feiner, and John F. Hughes, **Computer Graphics: Principles and Practice,** Addison-Wesley, Reading, MA, 1990.

[Fournier,Reeves86] Alain Fournier, and William T. Reeves, "A Simple Model of Ocean Waves," *Computer Graphics,* Vol. 20, No. 4 (Proc. SIGGRAPH), August 1986, pp. 75–84.

[Fox67] E.A. Fox, **Mechanics,** Harper and Row, New York, 1967.

[Frailey91] Dennis J. Frailey, **Managing Complexity and Modeling Reality: Strategic Issues and Action Agenda from the 1990 ACM Conference on Critical Issues,** The Association for Computing Machinery, New York, 1991.

[French85] M. J. French, **Conceptual Design for Engineers,** Springer-Verlag, London, 1985.

[Girard,Maciejewski85] Michael Girard, and A. A. Maciejewski, "Computational Modeling for the Computer Animation of Legged Figures," *Computer Graphics,* Vol. 19, No. 3 (Proc. SIGGRAPH), July 1985, pp. 263–270.

[Goldberg,Robson89] Adele Goldberge, and David Robson, **Smalltalk-80,** Addison-Wesley, Reading, MA, 1989.

[Goldstein80] Herbert Goldstein, **Classical Mechanics,** 2nd edition, Addison-Wesley, Reading, MA, 1980.

[Golub,Van Loan85] Gene H. Golub, and Charles F. Van Loan, **Matrix Computations,** Johns Hopkins University Press, Baltimore, MD, 1985.

[Henson87] Martin C. Henson, **Elements of Functional Languages,** Blackwell Scientific Publications, Oxford, 1987.

[Horebeek,Lewi89] Ivo Van Horebeek, and Johan Lewi, **Algebraic Specifications in Software Engineering: An Introduction,** Springer-Verlag, Berlin, 1989.

[Horn,Johnson85] Roger A. Horn, and Charles A. Johnson, **Matrix Analysis,** Cambridge University Press, Cambridge, 1985.

[Hughes92] John F. Hughes, *personal communication,* March 1992.

[Isaacs,Cohen87] Paul Isaacs, and Michael Cohen, "Controlling Dynamic Simulation with Kinematic Constraints, Behavior Functions and Inverse Dynamics," *Computer Graphics,* Vol. 21, No. 4 (Proc. SIGGRAPH), July 1987, pp. 215–224.

[Jain,Binford91] Ramesh C. Jain, and Thomas O. Binford, "Ignorance, Myopia, and Naiveté in Computer Vision Systems," *CVGIP: Image Understanding,* Vol. 53, No. 1, January 1991, pp. 112–117.

[James,James76] G. James, and R. S. James, **Mathematics Dictionary,** Van Nostrand Reinhold Company, New York, 1976.

[Kalra90] Devendra Kalra, *A Unified Framework for Constraint-based Modeling,* Ph.D. Dissertation, California Institute of Technology, Pasadena, CA, 1990.

[Kalra,Barr89] Devendra Kalra, and Alan H. Barr, "Guaranteed Ray Intersections with Implicit Surfaces," *Computer Graphics,* Vol. 23, No. 3 (Proc. SIGGRAPH), July 1989, pp. 297–306.

[Kernighan,Plauger78] Brian W. Kernighan, and P.J. Plauger, **The Elements of Programming Style,** 2nd edition, McGraw-Hill, New York, 1978.

[Kernighan,Ritchie88] Brian W. Kernighan, and Dennis M. Ritchie, **The C Programming Language,** 2nd edition, Prentice Hall, Englewood Cliffs, NJ, 1988.

[Lakatos76] Imre Lakatos, **Proofs and Refutations,** Cambridge University Press, Cambridge, MA, 1976.

[Landau,Lifshitz75] L. D. Landau, and E. M. Lifshitz, **The Classical Theory of Fields** (Course of theoretical physics, Vol. 2), 4th edition, Pergamon Press, Oxford, 1975 (1983 printing).

[Lewis,Papadimitriou81] Harry R. Lewis, and Christos H. Papadimitriou, **Elements of the Theory of Computation,** Prentice Hall, Englewood Cliffs, NJ, 1981.

[Lien,Kajiya84] Sheue-ling Lien, and James T. Kajiya, "A Symbolic Method for Calculating the Integral Properties of Arbitrary Nonconvex Polyhedra," *IEEE Computer Graphics and Applications,* Vol. 4, No. 10, October 1984, pp. 35–41.

[Lin,Segel74] C. C. Lin, and L. A. Segel, **Mathematics Applied to Deterministic Problems in the Natural Sciences,** Macmillan Publishing Co., New York, 1974.

[Liskov,Guttag86] Barbara Liskov, and John Guttag, **Abstraction and Specification in Program Development,** MIT Press, Cambridge, MA, 1986.

[Lucasfilm84] Lucasfilm Ltd. Computer Graphics Division, *The Adventures of Andre and Wally B.* (film), 1984.

[Magnenat-Thalmann,Thalmann85] Nadia Magnenat-Thalmann, and Daniel Thalmann, **Computer Animation,** Springer-Verlag, Tokyo, 1985.

[Marion70] Jerry B. Marion, **Classical Dynamics of Particles and Systems,** 2nd edition, Academic Press, New York, 1970.

[Millman,Parker77] Richard S. Millman, and George D. Parker, **Elements of Differential Geometry,** Prentice Hall, Englewood Cliffs, NJ, 1977.

[Misner *et al.*73] Charles W. Misner, Kip S. Thorne, and John A. Wheeler, **Gravitation,** W. H. Freeman and Co., San Francisco, 1973.

[Moore,Wilhelms88] M. Moore, and J. Wilhelms, "Collision Detection and Response for Computer Animation," *Computer Graphics,* Vol. 22, No. 4 (Proc. SIGGRAPH), August 1988, pp. 289–298.

[NAG]   *NAG Fortran Library*, Numerical Algorithms Group, 1400 Opus Place, Suite 200, Downers Grove, IL 60515.

[Nihon Sugakkai77] Nihon Sugakkai (Mathematical Society of Japan), **Encyclopedic Dictionary of Mathematics,** MIT Press, Cambridge, MA, 1977.

[OOPSLA91] "Can Structured Methods Be Objectified?" Panel, Conference on Object-Oriented Programming Systems, Languages, and Applications, ACM Sigplan Notices, Vol. 26, No. 11, November 1991.

[Pahl,Beitz88] Gerhard Pahl, and Wolfgang Beitz, **Engineering design: a systematic approach,** Springer-Verlag, Berlin, 1988.

[Pentland,Williams89] Alex Pentland, and John Williams, "Good Vibrations: Modal Dynamics for Graphics and Animation," *Computer Graphics,* Vol. 23, No. 3 (Proc. SIGGRAPH), July 1989, pp. 215–222.

[Petzold82] L. R. Petzold, *A Description of DASSL: A Differential/Algebraic System Solver,* SAND82-8637, Sandia National Laboratories, 1982.

[Platt87] John Platt, *personal communication,* 1987.

[Platt89] John Platt, *Constraint Methods for Neural Networks and Computer Graphics,* Ph.D. Dissertation, California Institute of Technology, Pasadena, CA, 1989.

[Platt,Barr88] John C. Platt, and Alan H. Barr, "Constraint Methods for Flexible Bodies," *Computer Graphics,* Vol. 22, No. 4 (Proc. SIGGRAPH), August 1988, pp. 279–288.

[Press *et al.*86] William H. Press, Brian P. Flannery, Saul A. Teukolsky, and William T. Vetterling, **Numerical Recipes/The Art of Scientific Computing,** Cambridge University Press, Cambridge, U. K., 1986.

[Raibert,Hodgins91] Marc H. Raibert, and Jessica K. Hodgins, "Animation of Dynamic Legged Locomotion," *Computer Graphics,* Vol. 25, No. 4 (Proc. SIGGRAPH), July 1991, pp. 349–358.

[Ralston,Rabinowitz78] Anthony Ralston, and Philip Rabinowitz, **A First Course in Numerical Analysis,** McGraw-Hill, New York, 1978.

[Reynolds87] Craig W. Reynolds, "Flocks, Herds, and Schools: A Distributed Behavioral Model," *Computer Graphics,* Vol. 21, No. 4 (Proc. SIGGRAPH), July 1987, pp. 25–34.

[Schröder,Zeltzer90] Peter Schröder, and David Zeltzer, "The Virtual Erector Set: Dynamic Simulation with Linear Recursive Constraint Propagation," *Computer Graphics,* Vol. 24, No. 2 (Symposium on Interactive 3D Graphics), March 1990, pp. 23–31.

[Shampine *et al.*91] L. Shampine, I. Gladwell, R. Brankin, "Reliable Solution of Special Event Location Problems for ODEs," *ACM Transactions on Mathematical Software,* Vol. 17, No. 1, March 1991, pp. 11–25.

[Shoemake85] Ken Shoemake, "Animating Rotation with Quaternion Curves," *Computer Graphics,* Vol. 19, No. 3 (Proc. SIGGRAPH), July 1985, pp. 245–254.

[Snyder92] John M. Snyder, **Generative Modeling for Computer Graphics and CAD: Symbolic Shape Design Using Interval Analysis,** Academic Press, Cambridge, MA, 1992.

[Spanier66] Edwin H. Spanier, **Algebraic Topology,** McGraw-Hill, New York, 1966.

[Steele90] Guy L. Steele, Jr., **COMMON LISP: The Language,** 2nd edition, Digital Press, Bedford, MA, 1984.

[Strauss85] Paul. S. Strauss, "Software Standards for the Brown University Computer Science Department," Brown University Computer Graphics Group, Technical Memorandum, June 1985.

[Stroustrup91] Bjarne Stroustrup, **The C++ Programming Language,** 2nd edition, Addison-Wesley, Reading, MA, 1991.

[Terzopoulos *et al.*87] Demetri Terzopoulos, John Platt, Alan Barr, and Kurt Fleischer, "Elastically Deformable Models," *Computer Graphics,* Vol. 21, No. 4 (Proc. SIGGRAPH), July 1987, pp. 205–214.

[Terzopoulos,Fleischer88] Demetri Terzopoulos, and Kurt Fleischer, "Modeling Inelastic Deformation: Viscoelasticity, Plasticity, Fracture," *Computer Graphics,* Vol. 22, No. 4 (Proc. SIGGRAPH), August 1988, pp. 269–278.

[Traub *et al.*88] J. F. Traub, G. W. Wasilkowski, H. Woźniakowski, **Information-Based Complexity,** Academic Press, Cambridge, MA, 1988.

[Traub,Woźniakowski91] J. F. Traub, and H. Woźniakowski, "Theory and Applications of Information-Based Complexity," in **1990 Lectures in Complex Systems: The Proceedings of the 1990 Complex Systems Summer School, Santa Fe, New Mexico, June 1990,** Lynn Nadel, and Daniel L. Stein eds., Addison-Wesley, Redwood City, CA.

[Truesdell91] C. A. Truesdell, **A First Course in Rational Continuum Mechanics,** 2nd edition, Academic Press, Cambridge, MA, 1991.

[Upstill90] Steve Upstill, **The RenderMan Companion: A Programmer's Guide to Realistic Computer Graphics,** Addison-Wesley, Reading, MA, 1990.

[Von Herzen *et al.*90] Brian Von Herzen, Alan H. Barr, and Harold R. Zatz, "Geometric Collisions for Time-Dependent Parametric Surfaces," *Computer Graphics,* Vol. 24, No. 4 (Proc. SIGGRAPH), August 1990, pp. 39–48.

[Wedge87] Chris Wedge, "Balloon Guy," *ACM SIGGRAPH Video Review,* Issue 36, 1987.

[Wexelblat81] Richard L. Wexelblat, ed., **History of Programming Languages,** Academic Press, New York, 1981.

[Williams,Abrashkin58] Jay Williams, and Raymond Abrashkin, **Danny Dunn and the Homework Machine,** Scholastic Book Services, New York, 1958 (1969 printing).

[Witkin *et al.*90] Andrew Witkin, Michael Gleicher, and William Welch, "Interactive Dynamics," *Computer Graphics,* Vol. 24, No. 2 (Symposium on Interactive 3D Graphics), March 1990, pp. 11–21.

[Witkin,Kass88] Andrew Witkin, and Michael Kass, "Spacetime Constraints," *Computer Graphics,* Vol. 22, No. 4 (Proc. SIGGRAPH), August 1988, pp. 159–168.

[Wolfram91] Stephen Wolfram, **Mathematica: A System for Doing Mathematics by Computer,** 2nd edition, Addison-Wesley, Redwood City, CA, 1991.

[Zeidler88] Eberhard Zeidler, **Nonlinear Functional Analysis and its Applications IV: Applications to Mathematical Physics,** Springer-Verlag, New York, 1988.

[Zeleznik *et al.*91] Robert C. Zeleznik, D. Brookshire Conner, Matthias M. Wloka, Daniel G. Aliaga, Nathan T. Huang, Philip M. Hubbard, Brian Knep, Henry Kaufman, John F. Hughes, and Andries van Dam, "An Object-Oriented Framework for the Integration of Interactive Animation Techniques," *Computer Graphics,* Vol. 25, No. 4 (Proc. SIGGRAPH), July 1991, pp. 105–112.

[Zwillinger89] Daniel Zwillinger, **Handbook of Differential Equations,** Academic Press, Cambridge, MA, 1989.

Index

N

[NAG], 57, 60, 126, 296
names in mathematical models, 81, 86ff, 116, 145
    full-word names, 86–87
    overloading, 88–90
    see also namespaces
names of bodies, 174, 177, 179, 181, 187, 196–197, 199, 217–218, 240
namespaces, **87–88**, 289
    see also scope name
nested state spaces, *see* state spaces
net force and torque, *see* forces and torques
Newtonian mechanics, 64, 141–142, 186, 189, 194, 214, 273
[Nihon Sugakkai77], 57, 92, 100
notation, mathematical, 22, 78, 85
numerical computation techniques, 6, 12, 21, 24, 42, 59–60, 62, 71, 118, 122, 126, 129–130, 134–135, 188, 206, 239, 272, 296–303, 304ff
see also simulation
numerical representation, *see* representation of geometric objects
numerics section of a program, 124, **126**, 296–303
    see also program structure

O

object-oriented programming, 4–5, 13, 47, 49, 73, 79, 81, 84, 95, 102, 126, 128–129, 138, 278, 289ff
    terminology, 289
ODEs, *see* ordinary differential equations
ordinary differential equations, 60–61, 126, 129, 133, 136, 308ff
    for rigid-body motion, 205–206, 262
    solvers, 8, 210, 282, 297, 299–300, 311ff
[OOPSLA91], 4
operators, *see* aspect operators
optimization, *see* efficiency
orientations, **149**, 151–152, 154–156, 159, 162, 165, 167, 169, 216

origin of a coordinate frame, **150**, 152, 156, 160, 165
origin of body coordinates, 174, 176, 186, 189, 191–192
    different from center of mass, 186, 189–191
overloaded functions, **88–90**, 94, 101, 104, 153, 164

P

[Pahl,Beitz88], 27
paradox, moving frame/body, 165, 176, 194
parameters, explicit, 77, 79, 85, 119
parentheses, 85, 87, 89, 101, 107
partial differential equations, 62, 272
paths, 111–115, 118, 144, 260
    geometric objects, 161–167
    implementation, 294–295
    power motives, 202–204, 210
    rigid bodies, 176–177, 189, 193–194, 197–198, 201ff
    see also point-to-path constraint
PDEs, *see* partial differential equations
penalty method, 5, 8, 38
pendulum model, 34, 42–44
penguins, 270
[Pentland,Williams89], 273
[Petzold82], 305
phase space, 144
physical interpretation, **53**, 57, 59, 61, 71, 75, 116, 128, 216
physically-based modeling, 3ff, **17ff**
    computer programming, 122ff
    language, 18, 282, 290
    prototype library, 140ff
    structured, 50ff
piecewise-continuous functions, *see* segmented functions
piecewise-continuous ODEs, 115, 135, 211, 255, 304ff
    for rigid-body motion, 207, 262
    solvers, 264, 301, **304ff**
pipeline for modeling, 133, 136
pipeline for rendering, 133